WITHIN WHICKER'S WORLD

'Whicker is one of television's great men, and this book goes some way to explaining why . . . The book is the equivalent to a good evening's TV viewing'

Sunday Times

'Whicker at his dry, entertaining best . . .'

Sunday Mirror

'Alan Whicker's book will delight his fans and convert sceptics . . . His book is bound to be a bestseller – and deservedly so'

Sunday Standard

'Full of the most thrilling episodes and lovely wry humour'

Michael Aspel, Capital Radio

'WITHIN WHICKER'S WORLD saves all the hassle and expense of travel, and nearly as much fun as the real thing . . .'

Daily Mail

'The joy and excitement and the sense of adventure and wonder comes through triumphantly in the book WITHIN WHICKER'S WORLD. It's a marvellous adventure – read . . .'

Michael Parkinson

WITHIN WHICKER'S WORLD

'It is obvious from WITHIN WHICKER'S
WORLD that its author is a remarkable man . . . A
highly revealing book in which Whicker covers the
world with inter-city speed never missing the
opportunity of a caustic comment or a witty
one-liner . . .'

The Bookseller

'WITHIN WHICKER'S WORLD is the
distillation of an odyssey – the globe's most
distinguished trotter . . .'

Jersey Evening Post

'Nobody will be disappointed when they pick up
WITHIN WHICKER'S WORLD, a brilliantly
written insight into a life in journalism which has
brought pleasure to so many.'

Grimsby Evening Telegraph

'A devastatingly subtle reporter . . . his zest for
travel is legendary . . .'

Over 21

'His absorbing book . . . fascinating
behind-the-scenes stuff and immensely enjoyable
. . .'

Dorset Evening Echo

WITHIN
WHICKER'S
WORLD

'A series of well-told anecdotes from far-flung places. Whicker has had a wonderful globe-trotting life . . .'

Cosmopolitan

'Behind the scenes of a remarkable career, this is the autobiography of a roving journalist. Alan Whicker writes as well as he broadcasts . . .'

Yorkshire Post

'Racily readable . . . and entertaining . . .'

Daily Express

'Highly diverting . . .'

New Statesman

'Once away from the camera and behind the typewriter, the urbane Mr Whicker becomes a veritable tiger . . .'

Punch

'The anecdotes are well told, the behind-the-scenes reportage always interesting . . .'

Hampstead and Highgate Express

'Some very funny stories of his own adventures'

Daily Telegraph

ALAN WHICKER celebrates 26 years in television in 1983. During this time he has received almost every award the Industry has to offer including the Screen Writer's Guild Award for the Best Television Documentary Script, the Royal Television Society's Silver Medal for Outstanding Artistic Achievement, the University of California Dumont Award for Excellence in Television Journalism, and the British Academy of Film and Television Arts Richard Dimbleby Award for the year's most important contribution to factual television.

He is currently preparing the next Whicker's World series.

WITHIN WHICKER'S WORLD

Alan Whicker

CORONET BOOKS
Hodder and Stoughton

Copyright © 1982 by Qail International Ltd

First published in Great Britain 1982
by Elm Tree Books/Hamish Hamilton Ltd

Coronet edition 1983

British Library C.I.P.

Whicker, Alan
　Within Whicker's world.—(Coronet books)
　1. Whicker, Alan　　2. Television personalities—
Great Britain—Biography
I. Title
791.45'092'4　　　PN1992.4.W5/

ISBN 0-340-32811-8

Printed and bound in Great Britain for
Hodder and Stoughton Paperbacks, a
division of Hodder and Stoughton Ltd.,
Mill Road, Dunton Green, Sevenoaks,
Kent (Editorial Office: 47 Bedford
Square, London, WC1 3DP) by
Cox & Wyman Ltd., Reading,
Berks. Photoset by
Rowland Phototypesetting Ltd.,
Bury St Edmunds, Suffolk.

For Valerie . . .

who was always ready to help with my research –
unless there was something more amusing to do,
like going to the dentist or cleaning the dovecot or
washing an unsanitised longhaired Afghan or . . .

ACKNOWLEDGMENTS

My publishers and I are grateful to Yorkshire Television for permission to reproduce photographs taken with patience and skill by Nigel Turner. We similarly acknowledge pictures from the BBC, *Radio Times*, *TV Times*, Keystone, Syndication International, Rolls Royce, the War Office and the US Army. President Stroessner and President Duvalier were photographed with my camera by Terry Ricketts, while recording, and Papa Doc's shopping expedition by Frank Pocklington, while not filming. A couple of our pictures were taken by Olga Deterding, and others by Valerie Kleeman while the remainder came from the Whicker archive – which means that old suitcase under the stairs.

Judy Burnley, author and widow of my old friend Fred – who directed twenty Whicker's Worlds – applied the initial stimulation. Laureen Fraser then typed tirelessly – without her I'd still be only half way through.

Before leaving I should also acknowledge the tolerant friendship of all those who have provided this kaleidoscope of Whickerwork through the years; it just wouldn't have been the same without you . . .

To those who obviously should have been within these pages but somehow ended on the cutting-room floor at the very last moment, when I ran out of space . . . all I can say is: Don't think you've escaped – you're *bound* to be in the next one!

CONTENTS

PART ONE – ACTION!

PART TWO – FLASHBACK!

PART THREE – CURTAIN RAISER!

PART FOUR – CUE WHICKER!

PART FIVE – TURN OVER, CAMERA!

PART SIX – CLOSE-UP!

PART SEVEN – MONTAGE!

PART EIGHT – WIND HIM UP!

WITHIN
WHICKER'S
WORLD

PART ONE

ACTION!

INDIA

Camel Post Office, with Sash . . .

WHICKER'S Second Law holds that since you can tell who your real friends are when you're Down, you can also tell your Unfriends when you're Up. I once had a brief period of Up, and duly suffered for it.

It was, I suppose, typical of my peripatetic television life that the first hint of a major Award should arrive as I sailed away from the isle of Bali, bound for Surabaya – camera crew in tow, of course. We were filming on the *Prinsendam* – which afterwards sank. Yorkshire Television came crackling through on the ship's radio, via satellite: 'Look, yours is the only Award we're collecting this year, so we'd like you to pop back and pick it up. It's being transmitted Network, with Princess Anne, so you're booked on BA889 out of Singapore.'

'Popping back' sounded like calling a cab, but upon reflection meant some 16 hours and 8,000 miles in a Jumbo – with the prospect of turning round and flying right *back* again, to rejoin my crew and carry on filming. I had just left LA, crossed the Pacific to Tahiti, Fiji and Auckland, spent a month flying round New Zealand, headed north to Hong Kong, zig-zagged south to Penang, sailed round Sumatra and was about to fly from Java to India and spend three months making Whicker's Worlds. I was not exactly *looking* for more flight time.

However, there is nothing like the prospect of a little overpraise to help the jetlag go down, so I entrusted all my possessions to Cecil and flew home.

Cecil had been hovering around my professional life for years: a prim, angular youngish man given to cerise T-shirts, skimpy suits with shoulders sloping up like epaulettes, and a beehive-bouffant hairstyle. He had joined my team as a researcher and grown into a sort of unit-manager, precisely efficient with airline timetables and seeing off PROs. My camera crews distrusted his self-acknowledged infallibility and vanity, but I appreciated his prep-master's competence – though his self-praise was so instant that when he did something well, which was often, it was hard to get in first with the congratulations.

He also earnestly reported back all compliments, real or imagined: 'The manager said it was a *delight* to deal with a real English gentleman . . . The telephonist told me I looked *exactly* like Roger Moore . . .' I always hoped he was joking, but he never was.

As he moved towards middle-age, the beehive thinned and his name dropped back towards the more important credits, my team found him harder to take. In a fairly emphatic statement of antipathy, one director tried to push him out of a high-rise window in New York. Another, in Salt Lake City, stared bleakly and silently through him during weeks of filming, refusing any contact at all. A third, appalled by his fiercely insensitive driving – particularly at night, behind thick dark glasses – refused to travel with him, and hired his own car. Cecil – whose passions were shopping, sightseeing and never being left out – got a second car and tore around Florida right behind him, night and day, as though On Tow.

On the *Prinsendam* that night my crew were being most generous about the BAFTA Award, and champagne flowed: 'I think we're more pleased than he is,' the Sparks told shipboard friends. Cecil, on reflection, was less enthusiastic – even sniffy: 'I think it's *outrageous* YTV haven't asked me back too.' My crew pointed out, reasonably, that the Richard Dimbleby Award was a personal recognition by the Craft after 21-years-hard on The Box, during much of which he had been at college, or a desk; that although the Whicker's World on Palm Beach *was* in the final four of the Documentary prize (it did not win) it was a programme with which he had had little to do. Unmollified, he flounced off towards the airport and Delhi, growing even huffier when temporarily entrusted with a caseful of my books, files and belongings, to take with him to India.

Unaware of the gathering disapproval and pursed lips, and full of camera-crew champagne and euphoria, I also broke off the tour, flew to Wembley and sat, greatly gratified though gaga with jetlag, indulging in our Craft's annual orgy. It was revealing to move so quickly from the sharp end of television to its massed cigar-smokers.

After an interesting evening I dozed in the taxi back to the hotel, clutching my one-eyed Award, packed, flew to Bombay and caught the early Indian Airlines 737 north to Jaipur, bumping alarmingly through the rising hot air.

'We've had a lot of trouble with your case,' said Cecil defensively as I arrived, pale and perspiring. 'It disappeared – the label must have come off in Bangkok.' He was quite brave about my fearful loss: 'Just one of those things. Should turn up.'

The prospect of spending three searing, stifling Indian summer months filming in my winterweight blazer and heavy flannels dawned, as did the suspicion that only limited concern had been lavished upon a case which was my entire office and wardrobe. 'If it went missing seven days ago,' I said, aghast, 'why didn't you cable me in London? I've just flown out from home with two *empty* suitcases. I could have brought a second shirt. A razor, even.'

He had been sending self-congratulatory telexes to London announcing victories over Indian customs and urging my immediate return from those much-resented celebrations: 'Imperative repeat imperative Alan returns immediately before Maharajahs depart for cooler climes . . .' In fact we shot nothing but desultory mute for a further five days, most of which I passed begging unwanted toothpaste from the Maharajah's polo players, and trying to shop for clothes.

You can love India or loathe it, but what you can *not* do in the bazaars of Jaipur, where salesmen will not release your arm, is to kit yourself out from zero for a three-month television expedition. Ideal perhaps for picking up Rajasthani brasswear and blue-and-white pottery, Kashmiri boxes and somewhat suspect emeralds, but short on electric razors, malaria pills and shoes that do not curl up in the front. Even in the stately Rambagh Palace the toilet soap was grey and gruesome and too harsh for washing socks.

Directed by the hopeless shrugs of local shopkeepers to the Rajputana Cloth Store on the Tholia Circle ('Dedicated to Better Dressed') I urged them to create a cool and televisual safari suit within 12 hours, so Whicker's World would have some sartorial continuity and I should not collapse from heat stroke. Shaking their heads sideways in that encouraging way, they went ahead with quiet Indian confidence.

The fitting that night by the blue light of fly-infested fluorescents was emotional. Cut along generous 1930s lines, the limp jacket dangled below my fingertips, the trousers hung in sad folds like the legs of an elderly elephant. The whole ensemble had the dash and style of one of Khruschev's older suits, after he had stopped caring.

Growing desperate, I bought a brilliant orange mango-patterned see-through voile shirt which fluttered under the fans like Barbara Cartland chiffon, a pair of camel-skin slippers – pointed, scooped and Alibaba – and little card-board socks, dung-coloured. The effect was, well, different.

My opening conversation on film was with the Maharajah of Jaipur, a crisp ex-commando Colonel educated at Harrow and known as Bubbles. He had just changed after polo into an elegant dark suit, stiff white collar and regimental tie. He tried to keep his eyebrows down as I wafted into view in my voile. 'Have you, er, been out long?' he said.

At Bikaner we stayed at another Maharajah's palace, and if that sounds grand you have not kept up with the condition of the Princes. He had sold his furniture and turned the crumbling Indo-Saracenic red sandstone folly into a dusty, desolate hotel where Cecil's high heels clattered eerily along marble corridors. The Manager was an amiable ex-Camel Corps officer with skin cancer of the face. We ate in gloom, in what seemed like the waiting-room of an abandoned railway terminus: smoky yellow walls dotted with motheaten stags-heads. As we entered, dark figures would emerge from their slumbers beneath tables upon which we were about to eat.

Butter and sugar dishes stood, black with flies, on cloths encrusted with droppings. The meals, cooked in a sooty hallway outside and carried in by men continually coughing, were dark congealed platefuls of anonymous *something*. Diets normally begin tomorrow; mine got off to a jump-start.

Watched by cringing scrofulous dogs, we sat dispirited at table and listened to the sound of spitting, outside. As we asked for hard-boiled eggs and tried to keep our thoughts above it all, Cecil received each ominous fly-blown mound with gasps and moues of wonderment, the same delighted appreciation he had shown in my home when greeting fresh crab, beef Wellington and strawberries from the garden. I made a mental note: on any future visit – *tins*, from the back of the emergency reserve.

Escaping from such depression into the wholesome desert, we spent 11 searing hours of arid discomfort travelling to film – wait for it – a mobile Camel Post Office. The organisation of this project had been Cecil's main creative effort. Our hired coach set off towards Jaisalmer, led by Post Office staff in two jeeps we had provided. We paused to buy them petrol, repair their punctures, and stock up with sticky drinks. Several stifling hours later our bus left the road in the middle of nowhere and sank exhausted into the sand, heaving quietly, while we transferred to the jeeps and struck off across the dunes.

After a long hot haul we reached the collection of wattle huts where the camel was being groomed for stardom. Outside the village I talked to-camera about India's problems of communication, while behind me (I could tell, from the crew's bemusement) the mobile Post Office was slowly approaching. Then I turned and saw, simpering towards us across the empty sands, a camel wearing a sash, like a parading bathing beauty.

The sash said, not Miss Bikaner, but Camel Post Office. This improbable announcement was in English, which could hardly have illuminated the Rajasthani tribesmen or drummed up much local business. In its small red official tin, Cecil posted cards to everybody he knew.

Feeling well-conned by so supercilious an apparition, we

jeeped on towards the camel's destination: another village which, it transpired, we could have reached by bus in a few minutes along a perfectly good road. Our Camel Post Office, covering six kilometres of nothing, began to seem only an astute PR exercise; certainly what the expedition cost us in hire of transport, men and travel – apart from the crew overtime – will now support that lumbering Post Office for years, spare sashes included. We never used the film.

In such devious ways, trying to make programmes in poverty-stricken India can prove costly. It is the only demo-cracy where television teams must be escorted and control-led, so our crew of seven was joined by an Indian official from Delhi, who also had to be fed and transported. Though sent by the Government to check up on us, our handler usually stayed in his room: the sun was too hot, and the food upset his stomach. Those curries, no doubt.

Our cheerful crew coped far better; the munificent TV company paid for their accommodation, one meal and laun-dry, and gave them a further £27.50 each to spend on their other two meals. That is not easy in India, where living is cheap and you can eat for one rupee – sevenpence. Our coach-driver had to keep his whole family for a month on less than one of their two-meal daily allowances. After many shopping expeditions they found, as I had when so abruptly cut off from all my worldly goods, that apart from the trinkets there was little to buy – though on occasion one of them would show me some emerald ring he had selected for the wife.

Then in the desert one day, still dressed like a gone-to-seed flower child, I suddenly remembered with a yelp of delight that on my Indian recce a few weeks before I had left a cache of inessentials in Delhi, with Cecil: stationery, toothpaste, aftershave, books – all the trivial necessities which local bazaars ignored, now elevated to unimaginable luxuries.

No, no, said Cecil dismissively, lips pursed, he had not bothered to bring the box from Delhi. 'But what about my Duty-Frees,' I cried in anguish, as it all came flooding back. Brandy and Scotch bought at Bangkok Airport for friends and contacts, and hoarded; and now, as India moved to-

wards Prohibition again, overseas gifts that would over-
whelm, absolutely unavailable and without price. 'I gave
them away,' he said, with a small sniff, 'to the customs men.'

So it's all right to win an Award occasionally but remember, it may not go unpunished . . .

PART TWO

FLASHBACK!

CAIRO

All Bachelors are Expendable . . .

THE good fortune of others can be hard to take, and so can a good turn. I once had a friend for whom I was able to do an enormous favour and manoeuvre towards a position which made him rich and powerful within our Craft. He found this hard to forgive. From his new and commanding role he repaid me, obliquely, with considerable harm. He was fighting against an obligation and, in a way, I understood. I did not reproach him, nor stop regarding him as a friend. After a few years he came to my side again. That good turn had finally been exorcised.

So – are you ready for this? I have had the happiest and luckiest of lives. There – I've said it. Gratitude slips so easily into defiance, or penitence. I often find myself apologising to stroppy interviewers who come to do me over. Their brief is: nobody in your position is entitled to be content, so what's *wrong* with you? There has to be plenty, and I try to dredge up a few moans but, with the best will in the world, make a poor job of it; they go away as dissatisfied as they darkly suspect I ought to be.

Good luck can sometimes be acceptable in others if seen to be appreciated and relished. In this way I may just get by, for I have always been truly thankful. Without planning or forethought, my whole life seems to have been aimed purposefully towards Whicker's World. Everything down the years has slipped into place: all that training and travel, all those riots and revolutions, even the Second World War . . .

Such good fortune helped me towards the kind of life that can seem like a dream of escape. The cheerful reaction I get in the street is always: 'Your life's one big holiday – where are you off to next?' The giant advertising agency J. Walter Thompson once conducted a poll into the lives of people known to the public, which revealed I was the most envied man in Britain. Whicker's World was seen as a good place to be. What appealed, researchers discovered, was all that carefree, irresponsible, no-strings wandering – and most of all, the excitement of it all. I seemed to spend my life doing things everyone longed to do.

When they told me, I was quite unnerved; had I owned a gold ring, it would have gone straight into the sea. Recovering from the shock of seeing my cover blown in public, I had to agree. Everyone has been most kind and generous – both down here and Up There. I can only believe one of my ancestors Did Something Right.

As a child I yearned to travel the world and to write – and have never stopped doing both. As a schoolboy I sent off for those glossy travel brochures with piercing royal-blue skies, white beaches and turquoise seas and, when they landed on the doorstep by the pound, pored over them – planning, planning. An admired cousin, Colonel Reginald Lester, was an author and President of the Institute of Journalists. He fired my ambitions, so one of my early presents was a nine-guinea portable typewriter. By 14 I was knocking out articles and short stories and gathering the regulation pile of rejection slips without which no would-be writer can properly approach life.

In the war, by luck and persistence, I found myself a brand-new Second Lieutenant directing Army cameramen in battle, taking pictures and writing covering articles. Afterwards I was a foreign correspondent and war correspondent in Fleet Street, travelling the world for a news agency as their 'fireman' – the ever-ready bachelor who could take over the newsdesk on Christmas Day, or be sent to Korea because nobody would care much if he were killed – not even the insurance company. Just as freelances live on plankton, so bachelors are known to be expendable.

No agency correspondent gets a by-line; his copy is included in the newspaper's general report or under a staff man's name, for newspapers like their readers to believe they have men everywhere. I would always read my stories from the Far East and Egypt and South Africa, from America and Kenya under some other by-line. Agency reporters – who do more work and get less pay than the by-liners – carry no sense of injustice. That is just the way life is, in Fleet Street.

After ten years in total news agency anonymity, I moved across to television, heading the first wave of escapees from EC4, and found myself travelling and working in much the same way – but with total publicity. I was in the living-rooms of the land and being interviewed, asked for my autograph, roughed-up by the critics, answering fan-mail. The pendulum had swung and, I'm happy to say, stayed swung!

In those days the BBC's Tonight programme demanded total devotion; I worked seven days a week for years and relished every minute of it, for I was doing what seemed absolutely right. It was, as I said, as though all that had gone before had been merely a practice, a rehearsal for Whicker's World.

I am no fatalist; I believe Destiny needs helping along – a little shove here, a backtrack there, some ducking and dodging. We make most of our own luck by spotting opportunities and reacting, and I go along with the author who explained, 'I can only write when I'm inspired – and I arrange to be inspired at nine o'clock every morning.'

When I was in Korea in 1950 the *New York Herald Tribune* had two correspondents at the front: the very experienced Homer Bigart and a young woman new to the Big Time, Marguerite Higgins. Though supposedly working together, they were fiercely competitive. She told me she only kept pace with the better and more experienced writer by getting up several hours earlier, running faster and further during the day, taking more risks and working later into the night. So in the ultra-male society of a war front she made it – with just a leetle help from her femininity – by going at it that much harder. It seemed a reasonable recipe for success in any field, and I took it to heart.

People sometimes wonder why I was born in Cairo; they

find it unreasonable and out of character. I explain that I wanted to be near my mother, at the time. Indeed photographs show her to be most stylish and my father properly dashing. Unfortunately I remember nothing of Egypt – though upon my return there many years later it made an immediate and tragic impact.

My father had been a captain in the Denbighshire Hussars during the Great War, eventually serving with General Allenby in Palestine. He was drawn to the colonial lifestyle, the climate suited him well – so he chose to stay on in Cairo after the war. I am told we had a happy home, a cook who for one of my mother's dinner parties stuffed a chicken with the tail of his shirt, and a houseboat on the Nile.

My father became gravely ill with heart trouble, and the first long journey of my life was when we sailed home through the Mediterranean so that he could undergo hospital treatment. It was perhaps aboard the TSS *Mashobra* that I absorbed my lifelong wandermania, by osmosis.

He was soon to die. Sadly I have no memory of him – only those pictures of what now looks like a younger brother upon a horse in Palestine, on a camel by the Pyramids . . . It seems he bequeathed his enthusiasm for photography, along with a mass of pictures taken during his war and some fairly caustic captions. So *that's* where I got it from . . .

A woman walks through Ismailia in 1919 and with her fan coyly hides her face from his candid camera. 'The young lady apparently objected,' he notes on the back of his picture, stung by her reaction. 'Perhaps it was just as well – for my camera's sake.' Steady on, Dad – *I'll* do the jokes . . .

I also have his pictures of my Coptic Godfather, a distinguished *homme d'affaires* in a white suit and boater, like some slim Farouk. The silver christening mug he gave me still holds my toothbrushes. He had once been gravely offended when my mother was goaded to remonstrate at his habit of picking his teeth. Years afterwards I gave up smoking and copied him – sacrificing 50 a day, yet satisfying my atavistic instinct while agonising before a typewriter by grinding up wooden toothpicks. Such inelegant behaviour is not much criticised today, but in those more correct times he had been desperately wounded by her comment (we pickers can be hurt too) and she could only redeem herself by perpetuating the foible and presenting him with a more permanent gold and ivory toothpick.

Years later during the troubles in Egypt, when the mobs put a match to Shepheard's Hotel and threw distinguished members of the Turf Club out of its windows before disembowelling them in the streets, I was a correspondent moving cautiously about Cairo, and had considered trying to find him. By then he *had* to be a Pasha – some leading politician or tycoon and good for a story, at least. I even looked forward to ?5 lavish birthday and Christmas presents, all in one lovely lump. However those were desperate days and I never found the time to begin my quest for my spiritual father. By now I am sure he has gone to his reward, toothpick and all, untapped by his expectant Godson and escaping his worldly obligations. I still like his mug, though.

I went to Haberdashers' Aske's, one of the Public Schools of the City Guilds. I was then, and remain, unenthusiastic – though I suppose it was a reasonable place with reasonable standards of scholarship and sport. I Captained a 2nd XI; won the statutory lifesaving medal for Schafer resuscitation and the tiniest silver cup I have ever seen for Under Sixteens freestroke; it was no scintillating record. I did fairly well in subjects taught by masters I liked, and poorly in others. When I said Goodbye to Mr Chips there was relief on both sides and I do not look back upon those years with any great affection. Schoolboys who are told they are going through the happiest days of their lives are in for a pleasant surprise, I have always believed, when life goes on getting better and better.

I was startled, years afterwards, by the perception of an unworldly child: I had returned to school after the war as an Old Boy and noted instantly that the masters I remembered as kind, skilled and agreeable were indeed pleasant men with vocations. Those I had disliked or feared as shallow and sarcastic bullies were, to my adult eye, still as objectionable. The windbags, the lazy, the neurotic and dissatisfied – each was exactly the master I recalled. The boy had weighed every one of them and, years later, found no cause to change a single judgment.

A child also accepts without question what he is told by those he loves; this appealing trait disappears as soon as we grow wary of life. I remember once at an early age wondering why I had no brothers or sisters. My mother explained: 'You did – you had an older sister, but we lost her.'

That seemed perfectly reasonable: Cairo was a busy city where it was all too easy to get lost. Presumably she had wandered out one day and been unable to find her way home through those milling streets. I never thought to question further, and indeed it was not until years later when I was in the Army and had to fill in a form asking questions about next of kin, that opposite 'Relatives' I started to write: 'One older sister, lost in the streets of Cairo.' Then I thought, Hey – *wait* a minute . . . It had taken me a lifetime to dredge up and question that matter-of-fact remark and realise that Miss Whicker, silly girl, was not still milling around absent-mindedly somewhere in Cairo trying to get home . . .

Mother came from a Suffolk family called Cross. They were modest farmers – except one who in the Twenties decided to move nearer London and bought a spread in Middlesex. Soon afterwards he found the Underground wanted to end the Edgware Line in his paddock. This was almost as good as striking oil. He took his millions to an estate in Wiltshire and stopped writing.

She was an unusually wise woman; as a child and young man I did not, of course, appreciate her sufficiently. When my father died she brought me up thoughtfully and without visible effort or doting, and in due course sent me forth upon the world as an independent and, it seemed, reasonably balanced only-son who, thank goodness, liked girls. Her love may have been deep but it was lightly and unpossessively offered. Much later I learned that when during the Blitz she had to go down to the shelter, the only valuables she took with her were my letters from the Front.

She was happy and attractive, with numerous admirers. Her constant companion – or whatever the going phrase was – ran a vast cathedral to banking in Lombard Street:

Glyn, Mills. George Cruttenden, a kind, shy and very gentle man was part of our lives for 30 years. Though she was widowed and he a bachelor, they did not marry. She enjoyed and guarded her independence – a family trait, it seems.

'We might get together when you're settled down,' she once told me, doubtless casting around for some excuse; but by then I was starting out upon a wandering life, and her bluff was never called.

One Sunday night in the summer of 1948 I returned from the country to Richmond Green and found her already in bed. 'I had such bad indigestion today I thought I should *die*,' she said, mildly. Before I left, she asked for a glass of brandy – an unusual request. 'Are you all right?' 'Yes of course.' I was about to leave. 'Are you *sure* you're all right?' She was, and settled down to sleep. I slipped out quietly.

Next day, rushing by cab from Fleet Street upon some Olympic Games story, I broke a taxi journey to call the news desk from a pub in Whitcomb Street. Uncharacteristically disinterested in my query, they transferred me to the editor: she had been found dead in bed – a massive coronary.

It was just as poor George Cruttenden was due to retire, and she was due to stop messing him about. We were bereft. 'What have I been living and working for, all these years?' he wondered as he went into retirement to the New Forest – alone.

They say that the most important thing in life is to select healthy parents. I was fortunate in every way but that: my father died of valvular disease of the heart in his forties, my mother of a coronary in her sixties – so for years now I have been living on borrowed time and playing with Fate's money, not my own. It has been a terrific game and so far, I'm ahead . . .

WALES

The Saturday Night Punch connected . . .

THE war was getting noisier every day so I decided to
volunteer early, when one had some slight control over dear
old Destiny, rather than wait for conscription and direction.
The Institute of Journalists had decided the best path for
would-be writers was through the Royal Army Ordnance
Corps – something to do with shorthand and typing, no
doubt. For better or worse I stepped forward and instantly
found myself in the ranks at Chilwell, an enormous Ordnance Depot outside Nottingham. I could tell at once the
Institute had got it very wrong.

The RAOC was not about to make a man of me. It might
have tucked me away safely and securely for the Duration,
left me filling forms or issuing tank tracks in that secure
provincial cul de sac, but it was not going to demand much,
or broaden my horizon. The place was full of storemen in
uniform and morose clerical officers determined to outlive
the war. A monstrous Depot out of Kafka, it would have gone
on strike had it been permitted, just to make the daily grind a
little interesting. For someone earning ten bob a week and
not-much-found, there was horrible fascination in that early
taste of penniless factory-life. Ever since then I have appreciated how the mindless monotony of a vast establishment can
dull the human spirit and make bloody-mindedness and
strikes a welcome distraction.

On the strength of my Certificate A from the school
Officers Training Corps, where we had played at soldiering
one night a week and gone to a summer camp, I was brushed
by glory and instant-power and created a Local Acting

Unpaid Lance-Corporal. Sewing on that one stripe was a significant moment, rather like the ecstatic sight of one's first bicycle. (I can still see mine, all chrome and gleam: compared with such utter bliss the sight of my first Bentley was as of dust.)

I was also selected for a commission in the Infantry, which promised adequate excitement, building up to almost instant death.

I drove north with another would-be journalist, Harry Hamilton, a friend who had joined up with me. He had a Ford Anglia and a carefully-conserved petrol ration. Along almost deserted wartime roads we headed north for Carlisle Castle and a pre-Officer Cadet Training Unit course with the Border Regiment. A hundred of us passed an icy January in two vast Crimean barrackrooms, sleeping on iron bedsteads and using a couple of cold taps, when not frozen. My battery razor became the envy of the unit as the wind whistled through cracked windows and miserable queues broke the ice and shaved with regulation blades. It was a scene Florence Nightingale could have drifted through, looking concerned about the poor boys . . .

Ham struck a considerable blow for comfort and the conservation of life by chatting-up to some effect a girl who owned a snack bar. There, behind gloriously steamy windows, we repaired for warmth and consolation from an Army life which seemed exactly the way it was in those rugged boys' books: horrible.

We were standing shivering on parade one day when the Sergeant's arm came down between Ham and myself – and his half of the squad turned left and marched towards some OCTU in Scotland. The rest of us turned right and headed for 164 OCTU at Barmouth, in North Wales. We did not meet again until after the war, when he was married ('I thought I was going to be killed and I wanted someone to be sorry') and I was Godfather to his son. From then on our lives diverged even more as he kept marrying, and I kept not.

In the months of training which followed, the natural splendour of Merioneth never got through to me; a mountain was to wade through, a sun-dappled rocky chasm a place to cross while balancing on a rope, white with fear. It was not until I returned to Dolgelly and Cader Idris after the war that I realised I had lived, head down and fists clenched, amid scenic magnificence.

Among Army skills which, once taught, remained for life . . . was how to ride a motorcycle. I tried to manoeuvre my powerful beast up a one-in-two cliff path at Harlech while my instructor insisted I stall the monster at the steepest point and then re-start without losing equilibrium. That heart-bursting morning wrestling with vicious, obstinate machinery on a Welsh hillside put me off motorbikes for life. I have never ridden again, thus saving myself countless broken collarbones and torn ligaments. No experience is all bad.

As officer-cadets, we were lorded-over on parade by the regulation Coldstream Guards Regimental Sergeant-Major, straight from Central Casting: enormous, bristling, ramrod, foghorn voice. He daily spread terror and doubled platoons smartly into the sea and out again, sodden. He put me on several charges for being lazy, unsoldierlike and dreaming on parade; all these heinous offences were justified though none was pursued or I might have suffered the ultimate disgrace of being RTU'd (Returned to Unit – who said the BBC invented initials?).

I relished one small and unexpected moment of glory: I had foolishly allowed myself to be badgered into volunteering to represent my company at boxing – a lunatic decision deeply regretted at leisure. I remember climbing reluctantly into the floodlit ring in the packed town hall one miserable Saturday night and glumly noting in the opposite corner a glowering opponent the size of a gorilla.

The only way to avoid total disgrace before the massed ranks watching from the surrounding darkness, I decided, was to forget all that stylish gentlemanly dancing around, that Queensberry finesse and keeping-your-guard-up we had been taught, and to tear into him regardless and go down swinging. At least he would finish me off quickly – and I might even get one in first.

At the bell I leapt from my corner and hurled myself upon

him in a frenzy of hopeless determination, arms going like windmills. It was the least scientific approach in boxing history. Within ten seconds of our violent clash in the centre of that brilliant ring, the enormous gorilla was lying unconscious at my feet. Never again was I to feel such surprise, or receive such applause.

When I recovered from my amazement I was suitably modest, as though that sort of thing happened all the time. The gorilla was brought round with difficulty and carried away through the ropes with great disdain.

You can achieve a lot in ten seconds, and my reputation as the killer with fists of iron instantly spread through the unit. The Commanding Officer called me in to take a thoughtful look at this unexpected whirlwind in his midst. The ATS girls in the messhall giggled at their mean streetfighter and gave me larger portions. Even the sergeants spoke kindly – and that's unnatural. The rest of the company backed away politely as I approached the tea urn.

However, Retribution was not to be escaped: the next Saturday night my aggressive bluff would be called at the final bouts. I was about to blow my reputation. I briefly considered desertion, but finally and with growing alarm went reluctantly to the town hall, wondering which ferocious Man Mountain would emerge to wreak terrible revenge.

My seconds bravely urged their champion to Go In and Kill Him, whoever he was; they only had me to lose. Once again I climbed glumly through the ropes and into the brilliance. There was a price to pay for all that limelight, and I was anxious to sell my life as dearly as possible and step out of it. Fortunately Barmouth had an excellent hospital.

The stool opposite was empty. We waited. It stayed empty. It slowly dawned on me that I had underestimated my own publicity. My opponent, evidently a man who believed what he heard, had Gone Sick. His strategic withdrawal on medical grounds gave me a walkover.

I received another ovation, even more undeserved than the first, and instantly retired from boxing for ever, undefeated. Quit fast, is my theory, while you're ahead and uninjured.

I remain convinced the reason I walked through OCTU

with top marks was due, not to conscientious study, not to all
that sweat and effort – but to one lucky Saturday night
punch that connected.

Since my father's family came from Devon, I was commissioned into the Devonshire Regiment, the 'Bloody Eleventh'
of the Line. Feeling chipper and frightfully dashing with that
single hard-won Pip up, I reported for duty to the Adjutant at
Plymouth's Crownhill Barracks. To my disappointment he
was not a Regular Ramrod with rows of ribbons, but a
burbling beery ex-Territorial from Fleet Street. I felt he was
playing in the wrong game.

When I returned from his office to quarters, my batman
had unpacked my kit, layed out the service dress, polished
buttons and Sam Browne, and run my bath. I had become,
overnight, an Officer and a Gentleman. The war was never
as good as that again, *ever*.

I savoured the moment. It seemed that running up all
those mountains had been time well spent – despite the
prospect, as an infantry platoon commander, of the Army's
shortest lifespan.

Soon after that Little Moment I prepared to pay the piper:
I was ordered to report to another regiment in training at
Alloa. This had a lilting hula-hula ring about it, like a
magical posting to some Hawaiian island in the South Seas.
Could Whicker's Luck be holding? No, it could not. Alloa
turned out to be a grey and mournful town in Scotland where
the battalion was billeted in empty houses and route-
marched through the rain around Stirling. The mess was a
damp pub, the senior officers were Regular wafflers, the
NCOs morose, the men despairing. As one of the newer
Crusaders, I found the atmosphere unjolly.

Depression grew until there came the next decisive redirection. On leave after being commissioned and gleefully
putting my Pip about, I had lunched in Lombard Street with
George Cruttenden and one of his clients, a Whitehall
Warrior who, it emerged, was looking for some young officer
with news-sense to join a unit filming at the war front. Could
I, he wondered over the Stilton, direct sergeant cameramen
in battle? You bet I could – *Sir!*

The War Office now offered me the posting – an escape I leapt at, eagerly. If I had to go and fight an enemy I did at least want to get along with my own side . . .

TUNISIA

Our Brothel Bed lost its Appeal . . .

AT the start of the war in the autumn of 1939, a solitary cameraman was sent out to cover the British Expeditionary Force in France. The War Office had still not learned the powerful propaganda lessons of Dr Goebbels and Leni Riefenstahl, so few pictures and no films emerged from that first, unhappy battlefront; neither the Guards' stand at Calais nor the epic of Dunkirk was covered pictorially. The Government had not awoken to the power of a picture – of a truth that could be seen to be true – and the Treasury refused to find money to equip a film unit. Two years later the power of Nazi propaganda began to permeate and, after questions in Parliament, the War Office was finally permitted to provide pictorial coverage for newspapers and newsreels and, perhaps more important, for History. It was a grudging concession; the Treasury refused to pay for the recording equipment – so we shall never hear the true sounds of Montgomery leading the Eighth Army into battle or Churchill addressing the victorious First at Carthage.

The first Section, 146 strong, went to Cairo to cover the Middle East – then regarded as extending from Malta to Persia. It had 60 cameramen, half always to be on duty in the Western Desert. Their pictures of the Eighth Army in battle remain classic, as does the first war film, 'Desert Victory' – a copy of which Churchill was proud to present to President

Roosevelt. In this respect at least, the Treasury had edged
reluctantly into the 20th century.

War, we now know, is the most difficult event in the world
to photograph – even with today's technology and marvellous miniaturised optical equipment, as used in Vietnam.
Audiences have grown accustomed to John Wayne capturing
a plaster Guadalcanal in close up and artificial sweat while
smokebursts go off over his shoulder and are dubbed afterwards in death-defying stereo. They are not impressed by a
couple of soldiers hugging the dirt in foreground and a tank
in middle distance, even though real men may at that
moment be shedding real blood. Reality can be dull, unreality cannot afford to be; yet should a cameraman get close
enough to war to make his pictures look real he is soon, more
often than not, a dead cameraman.

The second unit, which I was to join, covered the new
southern warfront in Sicily and Italy. To provide Britain and
the world with pictures of our armies in battle the No 2 Army
Film and Photo Unit took 200,000 still pictures and well over
half a million feet of film. To get those pictures, eight of the
little band of 40 officer and sergeant cameramen were killed
and 13 badly wounded; they earned a Military Cross, an
MBE, three Military Medals, 11 Mentions in Despatches.
Today, any picture you see of the Eighth, Fifth or First
Armies in action was certainly taken by these men.

I caught up with them, improbably, at the Hotel Great
Central at Marylebone Station, then the London District
Transit Camp. At the reception desk I asked, 'Where do I
find AFPU?' The corporal clerk looked at his list: 'Army
Field Punishment Unit, Sir?'

'No,' I said. 'At least – I hope not.'

One of my early duties seemed quite close: I was instructed
to give the whole unit an illustrated lecture on venereal
disease and the dangers of illicit sex, a subject on which I was
not then fully informed. The order that someone had to lay
an Awful Warning on them had come from Headquarters
and been passed down the line to be side-stepped by every
available officer . . . before stopping at the least significant. I
was a fuzzy-cheeked youth but, as I faced that mass of

world-weary 35-year-olds, aging fast. They were family men who seemed like elderly and experienced uncles, plus a few grizzled Regulars who at various postings around the world had obviously looked into the whole subject quite closely. It was not an easy moment. However, I gave them the benefit of my inexperience and they were most tolerant, listening as though I was telling them something new.

We were all commanded by Major Hugh St Clair Stewart, a large gawky and humorous man who after the war returned, quite suitably, to Pinewood to direct Norman Wisdom and Morecambe and Wise film comedies. Some of our sergeants had been professional cameramen, others bus drivers and insurance clerks, salesmen and theatrical agents. All had been through Army basic training. 'I'd rather have soldiers being cameramen,' said Major Stewart, 'than cameramen trying to be soldiers, because they may have to put down their cameras and pick up rifles.' So they did.

By today's standards their equipment was pathetic; any weekend camera enthusiast would be scornful. Each stills photographer was issued with a Super Ikonta – a Zeiss Ikon with 2.8 lens, yellow filter and lens hood; no telephoto lens. To get a picture of a shell exploding he needed to will one to land nearby, then wait for smoke and dust to rise before shooting – otherwise the explosion which could have killed him was invisible on film. A German tank had to be close and centre-frame before he could take a reasonable shot – by which time the tank might well take one too, more forcibly. It was no recipe for a long life.

Ciné men covering for newsreels, films and television-to-be had American De Vry 35mm cameras with 35mm, 2″ and 6″ lens. There was no sound equipment; effects were always dubbed in afterwards. Cameramen travelled the war zone in pairs, with a truck and driver.

The AFPU billet at Sedjenane was in the local brothel, by then out of action. Its remaining attraction was a fine double bed. As the Germans advanced and the cameramen made a strategic withdrawal they were anxious to retain this new-found luxury, which had a comforting peacetime feel about it, but their only transport was a motorcycle. The local Arab population was impressed, and a slow procession carried the double bed down the only street to a safer billet – which next day was destroyed by a bomb. This however was a hardy bed which had obviously seen a lot of action; it survived and was moved yet again into the safest place around: a deep mine. When the German advance continued, the bed finally had to be sacrificed as a spoil of war. Later, when Sedjenane was recaptured, there stood the long-suffering AFPU double bed, none the worse for recent German occupation – apart from a slight green mould; but somehow, it had lost its appeal.

Tunis was the first major city to be liberated by the Allies during the war, the first with streets full of deliriously happy people, when men proffered hoarded champagne and pretty girls their all – a scene to be repeated many times in the freed cities of Europe. The crowd around us in the Avenue Jules Ferry was so jammed and ecstatic we could not move. I was standing on the bonnet of my car looking down at laughing faces and toasting *'Vive la France'* when I saw Sidney Bernstein, even then a cinema mogul. He had arrived from the Ministry of Information bringing films like 'In Which We Serve' to show the lucky liberated people. 'Can't get into my car,' he grumbled. 'It's full of French.' One of my cameramen apologised in his dope sheet for the quality of his pictures: 'I have been kissed so many times by both women and *men* that it really is difficult to concentrate . . .'

As the enemy armies surrendered and 250,415 Germans and Italians laid down their arms in Cap Bon, we took pictures of thousands of Afrika Korpsmen driving themselves happily into captivity, of General von Arnim surrendering to a Lieutenant-Colonel of the Gurkhas and explaining that his officers were 'most anxious' to surrender only to the British, of one of their oompapa brass bands playing 'Roll Out The Barrel' inside a crowded prison cage.

For a Victory celebration, at a time when the British Army was noticeably short of victories, Prime Minister Winston Churchill flew into El Aouina airport and drove straight out to the Roman amphitheatre at Carthage to congratulate his First Army. To cover this historic celebration we had cameramen all over the amphitheatre. Captain Harry Rig-

nold was up on the top tier with our Newman Sinclair and the
unit's one and only 17-inch telephoto lens. We also needed
close-ups of Churchill, so I was sitting on the large rocks just
in front of the stage – in the orchestra stalls – feeling rather
exposed before that military mass. Indeed the task proved
more difficult than expected.

In the brilliant African sun Churchill climbed on stage and
with hands dug into pockets in best bulldog style, faced 3,000
of his troops. Next to him stood Anthony Eden and the
ultimate red-tabs: the victorious Army Commander, Lieutenant-General Kenneth Anderson, and General Sir Alan
Brooke, Chief of the Imperial General Staff. Their only
prop was a wooden table covered by a Union Jack. It
was not Riefenstahl's Nuremburg, but was naturally
splendid.

The troops roared their welcome. Churchill seemed staggered and delighted by a reception made even more acute by
perfect Roman accoustics. 'Get a picture of that', he said,
spotting me before him, busily focusing. He waved towards
the amphitheatre. 'Don't take me – take *that*.'

I wanted to explain that several of our cameramen were at
that moment filming the cheering mass as he stood at its
heart, that he was the star and a picture of a lot of soldiers
without him was not significant . . . when once more he
ordered, 'Get a picture of that.' He was clearly not used to
saying things twice – certainly not to young lieutenants. For
a moment I wavered. General Anderson, breathing heavily,
took a step forward, and my court martial flashed before me.
'Take a picture of that!' he snapped.

I took a picture of that.

I had to wait until Churchill was well into his panegyric
before I could turn and sneak my picture. Afterwards he
walked out to his car, took off his pith helmet and waved it
from the top of his stick, gave the V sign, and drove away
with the Generals. *That* bit of our war had been won.

There was a brief pause while the armies digested their
victory and prepared for the next step, and our life became
almost social. It was spring and, what's more, we were still
alive. I requisitioned a villa at Sidi Bou Saïd, near Carthage.

It overlooked the Bay of Tunis and had indoor sanitation, to which the Army had grown unaccustomed.

I had liberated a spendid staff car, an Opel Kapitan in Wehrmacht camouflage, for my little Austin utility was still bent from the weight of liberated Tunisiennes. We were not supposed to use unauthorised transport, so along the German bonnet we craftily painted some imaginary but official-looking War Department numbers. I thought I had got away with it until my guilty car was admired at embarrassing length – by King George VI. As I stood to attention before His Majesty, it seemed cruel that the first finger of suspicion should be Regal . . .

The King had just arrived in Tunis at the start of his Mediterranean tour with Sir James Grigg and Sir Archibald Sinclair. In his cortège at the airport he spotted my unusual Afrika Korps convertible, and pointed it out to General Alexander: 'That's a fine car,' said His Majesty. 'Very fine.' The General studied it for what seemed a long time. All I could see, following his eyeline, were our phoney numbers, growing larger and larger under Royal inspection.

'Yes,' he said, finally. 'A German staff car captured near here by this young officer, I should imagine.' He gave me a thoughtful look – then they drove away in a flurry of flags. I went in the opposite direction, quite fast.

The car transported me in splendour for some happy weeks until, parked one afternoon outside the office of the Army newspaper in Tunis, it was stolen by – I discovered years later – a brother officer from the Royal Engineers. Some people have no innate sense of honesty.

SICILY

Could be a Sticky Landing, chaps ...

THE Royal entourage sailed in the cruiser *Aurora* to Malta. By
the time the King arrived in Libya I had driven down from
Tunisia to cover his reception. The city was a cheerless
contrast to Bizerte and Tunis, where they loved us. Streets
had to be cleared of sullen Tripolitanians who evidently
preferred Italian occupation. I waited for the arrival ceremony in an open air café and for the first time heard the song
the Desert Rats had captured from the Germans: 'Lili Mar-
lene', played for British officers by a bad-tempered band. It
felt strange to be unwelcome.

The King was greeted by General Montgomery, who as
usual dressed down for the occasion: black beret, shirt and
slacks, long horsehair fly whisk. Later the General invited
into the Royal caravan Major Geoffrey Keating, our new
Commanding Officer who was to become my lifelong friend
until his death in 1981. Keating had been a considerable
figure in the desert. His photographs and those of his cameramen made Montgomery a popular national hero at home,
when in truth he was a man with little charm and no
charisma, unable to relate to his troops privately or publicly.

However such is the power of publicity that he was
becoming the Army's first father-figure, loved by one and
all – or so it said in the captions of those photographs
showing Monty standing stiffly in his open Humber handing
out cigarettes to baffled soldiers by the roadside. The happy
fact that he was a brilliant tactician who never started a
battle until sure he could win also helped his popularity; until
Bernard Montgomery Britain had suffered a procession of
losing Generals.

Keating had been to London with Montgomery and returned with the news that we were about to attack Churchill's 'soft underbelly of the Axis'. The Eighth Army, combined with the First, was to attack Sicily, that hinge on the
door to Europe, and then Italy. Invasion forces were already
gathering at Mediterranean ports from Alexandria to
Sousse, so I left dreary Tripoli with a convoy of new jeeps just
off the ship from America and headed back to Sousse, from
where we should sail. At the Libyan border we slipped off
Mussolini's splendid tarmac road on to the sandy track
through Tunisia; this had been deliberately left in bad
condition by the French to slow down the Duce's armoured
columns – or that was their excuse. Through Medenine and
the Mareth line the hot desert which so recently had been a
bloody battlefield stood quiet and empty, dotted with the
rusting hulks of tanks and the occasional rough wooden
cross – a few sad square feet of England, or America, or
Germany.

Sousse was bustling with 30 Corps, under its Commander,
Lieutenant-General Sir Oliver Leese. We placed our cameraman with battalions which were to lead the invasion; I
was to land with the famous 51st Highland Division, and was
promised a noisy time.

Just before the armada sailed I drove back to Sidi Bou Saïd
with secret film of the preparations. Coated with sand and
exhausted, I arrived at the villa I had requisitioned to find a
scene of enviable tranquillity: on the terrace overlooking the
Bay our Adjutant was giving a dinner party. At a long table
under the trees sat John Gunther, the *Inside Europe* man
then representing the Blue Radio network of America, Ted
Gilling of the Exchange Telegraph news agency who was later
to become my first Fleet Street editor, and other correspondents.

After a bath I joined them and sat in the dusk while the sun
slipped behind the mountains, drinking the red wine of
Carthage and listening to crickets in the olive groves. In a few
days I was to land on a most hostile shore, somewhere.
Would life ever be as peaceful and contented and *normal* as
this again?

Back in Sousse I boarded my LST: the Landing Ship
Tank, the star of every invasion, was a strange monster with
huge jaws in its bows that opened wide and a tongue that
came down slowly to make a drawbridge. With shallow
draught, it could ride right up to the beaches, unload, and
go astern. The fleet sailed for Sicily at dusk, starting off in
a single line and then coming up into six rows. The senior
officer on each paraded the troops and briefed them on the
coming landing. We were to go in at Pachino, on the bottom
right-hand corner of the great rock island. Back in the wardroom our General took a pink gin and said, 'Could be a
thoroughly sticky landing, chaps.'

I have often wondered whether novelists and scriptwriters
imitate life, or whether we all go around deliberately copying
them, even when there is no one to shout Cut!

The armada sailed on through the night, blacked-out and
silent but for the softly swishing sea. We tried to sleep,
sweating and fully dressed with lifebelts handy, until the
troops came cursing and coughing out of the thick air below
decks into the grey dawn, buckling equipment and queuing
for the rum issue. Some took a last glance through the Army
pamphlet 'A Soldier's Guide to Italy'. If we had not been
preparing to die, it could have been a cut-price package
cruise.

At first light on 10 July we watched British troops go
ashore near Pachino. To our left along the coast Canadians
and Americans landed. North towards Syracuse more British divisions were beaching. In this first wave 750 ships put
16,000 men ashore, followed by 600 tanks and 14,000 vehicles and supported by 4,000 aircraft. It was the first great
invasion.

Our LST had come to anchor just off shore. A few enemy
miss-and-run spotter planes came over, too high to make
pictures, so Sgt Radford and I thumbed a lift on a smaller
Landing Craft Infantry and from it waded ashore armpit-
deep, lifting our cameras up out of the Mediterranean. The
LCI Captain, a young Australian Lieutenant, waded behind
me holding the film-filled pack on my back out of the waves.
We were on the Continent of Europe.

Troops formed up and started to dry out in the early sun; then they pressed on inland, through the fields. Beach-masters were already in control. RAF liaison officers were talking into their radios. The Navy was flagging craft into landing positions. One LST was stuck, and another was towing it off a sandbank. Soldiers began clearing mines and laying wire-netting road strips. Tank Landing Craft disgorged enormous self-propelled guns, armoured bulldozers, Sherman tanks. DUWKS – three-ton amphibians – purred purposefully between ships and shore. The first prisoners arrived on the beach, and wounded went into Aid Posts. Military police came ashore and began to direct the traffic. Bofors crews took up positions and dug in. Fresh drinking water was pumped from LST tanks into canvas reservoirs. Petrol, ammunition, and food dumps were started. A de-waterproofing area for trucks was marked out. Pioneers started to build and improve roads. The Eighth Army was getting set to go places – and so far, to our relief and amazement, not one shot had been fired in anger.

More of our cameramen landed and, converging, we celebrated with our first brew-up; on went the tea, and the bacon sizzled. From the fields around us we selected our first trophies of war: big ripe tomatoes. The day was spent taking pictures on the beaches; at dusk, finding our blankets still somewhere at sea, we settled down miserably on the damp rocky soil of a tomato grove and, exhausted, were soon asleep.

The fearful thud of bombs shook us to life. The nightscape was bright as day. As we jumped up in alarm, our shadows stretched out before us. The Germans had finally reacted and their aircraft were dropping flares and hunting for targets. They had sufficient: we were hard to miss, even at night.

Attempting to strike back, thousands of bright Bofors shells moved slowly through the air, up into the darkness above the flares. The invasion fleet and beaches were bombed all night. The Luftwaffe did some damage and had one awful success it would not have sought: a hospital ship full of nurses and wounded was sunk by a direct hit.

There may be no justice in life, but in battle the percentages go even more astray. My batman, Driver Fred Talbot, was a regulation cheery Cockney sparrer and a peacetime London busdriver. After the war when we met one night on the Underground he told me he was, improbably, working as a ladies hairdresser in Norwich. Before that assault-landing in Sicily he had been relieved to learn that, while I was going in with the first wave of the infantry when I could reasonably be expected to get my head knocked off, he was to stay with our jeep and all our kit in the relative comfort of a larger, safer transport ship which would land with some dignity a few days later.

On Invasion Day my first wave went in to a total silence, without hearing a shot fired in anger; the worst we got was wet. His ship, proceeding south at a leisurely pace through the night from Sousse to Sfax, before following the fleet to Sicily . . . hit a mine and sank immediately.

Driver Talbot spent some hours in the dark sea before being picked up – and then another ten hours in a lifeboat. He was one of the few survivors. He was rather rueful about the injustice of it all when we met and I passed a few unkind remarks about life being safer at the sharp end.

My appreciation of the situation was dulled by the knowledge that our jeep had been loaded with everything we possessed. My greatest loss, apart from that service dress and Sam Browne I had worked so hard to achieve and only worn a few times, was a diary religiously kept. Had those notes not been sent to the bottom of the Mediterranean, you could have suffered this book *years* ago . . .

Next day, curiously carefree after losing everything but my life, I watched General Montgomery and Lord Mountbatten land from their Command ship, and set off inland after them. The first place of size we entered was Noto, attractive and undamaged by war. A Carabiniere brought out a copy of Churchill's 1940 speech to the Italians and read it from the steps of the Casa del Fascio; our Prime Minister had been promoted from monster to hero overnight.

Near the Primesole Bridge the 7th Battalion Green Howards captured a large Italian coastal defence position of

12-inch gun-howitzers, each able to throw a 610-pound shell 20 miles. We noted with some bitterness towards international Arms Kings, wherever they may be, that they had been manufactured by British Vickers-Armstrong. Our 74th Field Regiment got the guns firing on German positions near Catania. They were the biggest guns the Eighth Army had ever operated – so I suppose it worked out all right in the end. Nearby another capture was equally welcome: Sergeant S. A. Gladstone got some expressive pictures of sweating British troops liberating a cellar containing 7,000 gallons of good red wine . . .

Sergeant Radford and I then drove across the island to be in at the capture of Palermo by General Patton's Americans. In many untouched mountain villages we were the first Allied soldiers to arrive: wine was pressed upon us, and haircuts were a couple of cigarettes. In Palermo people peeped timidly from their windows, wondering anxiously whether our dust-covered khaki was field grey. The wide harbour was littered with sunken Italian gunboats, each surrounded by huge shoals of fish. We caught several by hitting them with stones: Izaak Walton must have been spinning.

The rest of the town was little damaged – even the blue trams were still running. Posters showed the monster John Bull with the world as his swollen stomach reaching out to swallow more lands, and a grinning skeleton in a British steel helmet. I took some pictures, while passers-by hurried on, fearful lest I turn and blame them.

We crossed Sicily again, returning to our camp on the malarial Lentini Plain, and during the night felt huge shuddering explosions and watched sheets of flame light the sky: the Germans were blowing their Catania ammunition dumps. A new officer had come to join us: Lieutenant A. O. McLaren who, when captured by the Afrika Korps in the desert while using two cameras, had refused to hand over one of them because it was his personal property, and demanded a receipt for the War Office Ikonta. He later escaped, still carrying the receipt.

An operational message came in that Catania was about to fall, so we scrambled off to get the pictures. McLaren was standing up in the cab of his truck watching, as we all had to, for enemy aircraft. We went in column around a diversion at reeking Dead Horse Corner. In the dust yards ahead lay a German mine. His warning scream came too late. He had been in Sicily one day.

It took the population of Catania some while to realise the Germans had gone. Then they rushed into the streets to cheer, carrying flowers, fruit and wine. It was hard to see them as enemies. Our pictures showed Italian nurses tending wounded of the Durham Light Infantry. At this point Sergeants Herbert and Travis unintentionally captured the city's entire police force.

They had lost their transport and were filming the advance upon the town on foot, when a civilian car came along. Surprised by such an apparition in a warzone, they commandeered it and ordered the driver to take them into Catania. Speeding ahead of the army, he whizzed excitedly along endless back streets and finally through two huge gates into a palace courtyard full of armed Carabinieri. The gates slammed behind them. The suspicion dawned that *they* might be the prisoners . . .

Then a dressy Commandant snapped to attention, saluted, and asked for their orders. They ventured that they were two lonely photographers and did not really want a police force, not just then. However, they *did* want a car. At that they were ushered into a large garage crammed with every type of vehicle, their choice was filled with petrol and the ignition key presented with an Italianate flourish. They drove out through the massive gates, at speed. Honour had been satisfied on all sides.

After 39 days' fighting, during which we suffered 31,158 casualties and the Germans and Italians lost 167,000 – mostly prisoners – the enemy evacuated 60,000 men across the Straits of Messina to Italy, to fight another day. At the end of August, when the only Germans left in Sicily were the 7,000 ruminating behind barbed wire, General Montgomery's headquarters at Taormina prepared for the first visit of the Commander of the Mediterranean Theatre, Dwight D. Eisenhower. An American General with all those stars, he was something new to us, and was to be accorded full peacetime pageantry as only the British Army knows how.

He flew in to Catania with American Generals Bradley, Patton, Keyes, Truscott and Gay. A fighter escort roared overhead as the multi-starred party processed north to Taormina. The Highland Division – the men with whom I had invaded Sicily – turned out their most impressive Guard of Honour: pipers, swirling kilts, white blanco and stamping feet. They put on loads of swank, then crashed to attention and Presented Arms. We waited for General Eisenhower's soldierly appraisal. 'Say!' he said at last. 'Some swell outfit!'

It seemed a fair comment.

ITALY

Sir Gerald was Allergic to Lead . . .

Our last picture from the Sicilian campaign showed Generals Eisenhower and Montgomery staring symbolically through fieldglasses out across the Straits of Messina at the toe of Italy – the next step towards the end of the war. Behind them in Sicily, a military government was being established – though in fact the island was falling back through the years into the hands of the Mafia, which had been successfully held down by Mussolini. *Mafiosi* from New York were attached to the American Army and, through threats and graft, soon became the government. Fortunately for our lively sense of mission, we in our shining armour had no time to occupy ourselves with the crime and corruption that was to inherit our victory, and pressed on with the war.

Major Keating and the war artist, Captain Edward Ardiz-

zone, had requisitioned for our mess a beautiful villa on the
Taormina hillside which belonged to an English painter. Its
garden was heady with the exotic scent of orange blossom, its
library equally heady with pornography. Between the two
distractions we prepared for the coming battle, and each
evening drank Sicilian white and watched the sun go down
behind Mount Etna.

In one of those serene sessions at dusk it had to be decided
whether Captain Harry Rignold or I should lead the cameramen across the Straits to cover the Eighth Army's opening
attack on Italy. The other would return to Africa and join
Operation Buttress – a landing by the new and mainly
American Fifth Army to be made later up the coast near
Salerno, 35 miles south of Naples.

Rignold, my senior, had the choice. He had caught the
excitement of landings at Narvik, so selected Salerno – and
was killed on the beach. I went across the Straits with the 2nd
Inniskilling Fusiliers – the ferocious Skins – and landed
safely. I had drawn another lucky card.

As my sergeants and I boarded the LCI in Catania docks,
the invasion fleet was attacked by German fighter-bombers.
So much, we thought, for surprise. We sailed that night,
another silent armada approaching the dark mountains and
narrow beaches of Reggio Calabria. As we went in, the
massed artillery behind us used the RA's Sicilian reserves,
supporting our rocket-firing Devil-ships. Some shells
crashed around us into the sea; they were ours, falling short,
but even so were not welcome. There was still no answer from
the enemy coast.

At 5.30 am we hit the beach and ran inland to escape any
enemy fire. It did not arrive. The Luftwaffe flew in to strafe
and bomb, but otherwise the Eighth Army once again
walked ashore unopposed.

Encouraged, Driver Talbot and I set off inland, past huge
Italian coastal guns near Pellaro – made by Vickers in 1930
but fortunately unmanned. Rounding a bend in the mountain road we were confronted by a column of at least 200
Italian soldiers, all heavily armed. As Talbot froze in horror,
it dawned upon me that my .38 Smith and Wesson was still at

the bottom of my new kitbag . . . I had been thinking too much about pictures, when war was for fighting.

In a film unit and preoccupied with observation, it was all too easy to fall into the role of sympathetic spectator. It began to seem as though all those chaps were using artificial blood.

At OCTU I had learned that Attack was the best form of Defence, so I leapt from the jeep, brandishing my camera. It was, at that moment, all I had to brandish.

To my surprise it was most effective. The Italian troops were delighted. Guns were put down, combs appeared, and they gathered around flashing hold-it smiles. They were all going home, they told me inaccurately, for peace had been declared between our countries. I was not about to argue. I warmly commended to them our nearest fighting unit a few miles down the road, regretting I was at that moment too busy to accept prisoners, however willing. We parted with mutual expressions of relief and goodwill.

Their eager surrender to the following infantry was, unfortunately, premature; Italy did not capitulate for another five days. They all went, not home, but to a POW camp in Africa, without even getting their prints. I still feel rather guilty about that.

With the three Allied divisions landing at Salerno, Captain Rignold's party of four officers and 11 sergeant cameramen covered another sort of war: a bitterly opposed assault landing. This was not the Italians' musical-comedy war of bellicose *bella figura* they had undertaken without the equipment or the will to fight. This was fierce and determined resistance by crack German units which had been expecting – even rehearsing for – our invasion fleet. The Salerno beaches were at the very limit of our fighter cover. The Fifth Army was exposed and vulnerable and seemed about to be destroyed before gaining even a toe-hold on enemy territory.

As they sailed in, the LST on which some of our men were travelling was hit 20 times by enemy shells. In the hold of one landing craft our smallest cameraman, Sgt R. P. Lambert, sat in the gloom next to a very tall soldier of the Queen's Regiment. They headed towards the beach and the tense silence was broken when one infantryman looked down at

him and whispered, 'If that chap in front of you steps into the
sea and disappears, Sarge – *you* ain't half gonna get wet!'

With a cheerful Cockney straight out of some Ealing
thriller, life exactly followed those war movies. From officers
came equally suitable stiff-upper-lip remarks about seeing
Naples and dying. These soon proved to be very bad jokes
indeed.

Rignold had landed and was driving across the beach
when a shell burst in front of his jeep. His right hand was
blown off; Sergeant Penman and the driver were also injured.
He walked calmly to the sea wall, carrying his camera in his
remaining hand. Putting it down carefully he said, 'I'm going
to that RAP to get my arm fixed.'

He was lying on a stretcher at the Regimental Aid Post
when a mortar shell fell amid the wounded and killed that
gentle and excellent man. He died without knowing he had
been awarded the Military Cross.

A little way up the beach Sgt J. Huggett had just come
ashore when he learned some commandos were holding a
small promontory against heavy German attack. He started
up the hill to get pictures of the action. Near the top a voice
ordered: 'This way, this way!' It was a commando officer.
'You're late, Sergeant,' he shouted, 'but never mind. Where
are your men?' Huggett admitted that he had come alone,
just to get pictures. '*What!*' cried the officer, deeply emotional. 'I asked for a relief party, not a fucking photographer!'
One understood exactly how he felt.

In the south, the Eighth Army had occupied the town of
Bari and weary but victorious British troops sat in pavement
cafés trying to look as smart as the vanquished Italian officers
peacocking around, as untouched by war as their town. The
shops were stuffed with goods, all cheap for the first few days.
The fee at the top local brothel was seven lire – then worth
less then 2p and, I was told, worth every penny.

Disregarding, in the main, such inexpensive distractions
the Eighth pushed forward up the toe of Italy in an attempt to
relieve the beleaguered Fifth. I went by sea with General
Montgomery for his first meeting with the Fifth Army Commander, General Mark W. Clark. We made the voyage in a

big arc around enemy-held coast in a torpedo boat. After four hours at sea, there was General Clark and his staff waiting on the beach. 'Mighty pleased to see you, General,' he said, and as his army seemed about to be thrown back into the sea, we could believe he meant it. We drove to his Headquarters through hastily-built airstrips where fighters were continually taking off and landing. Roadside notices said: 'Aircraft have right of way.'

The assault was going so badly General Clark had begun to draw up plans for withdrawal; he had been deterred only by the protests of the British Admiral.

Then German resistance weakened. Commandos and paratroops stormed the mountains of the north-west of Vietri which commanded the defile through to Naples. The enemy withdrew – the beaches were saved. Soon afterwards Italy capitulated, and Naples fell amid a clamour of urchins shouting at our first armoured cars for food, and women giving themselves for a packet of biscuits. Once again the dope sheets apologised: 'We were fêted and hugged so much we were unable to get many pictures . . .' So effusive was the welcome that notices went up saying, 'Dangerous type of VD in this area.' We never discovered where the safe type was.

Reaching the River Sangro, General Montgomery issued one of those calls to action which always sounded like an invitation to cricket: 'We will now deal the enemy a colossal whack . . .' Some Russian officers under General Vasiliev were visiting the Front. Old hands greeted Major-General Solodovnic with surprise, for he had last been seen in Africa as a war correspondent with the First Army, apparently representing TASS. He was not bemused by Monty's sporting appeals – indeed he had a habit of putting haughty brigade majors on the defensive: 'I suppose you're one of the Upper Classes?'

In that bleak winter the Eighth Army was decimated by infective hepatitis, a jaundice which first made you feel like death, while looking fine – then turn yellow and feel fine, while looking like death. Suffering the first stage, I was carried some hundreds of miles by ambulance

from the snowy central mountains of Italy back to Bari,
and then experienced my maiden flight – while flat on
my back.

That first of the hundreds of thousands of airborne jour-
neys that were to follow down the years was in a Red Cross
plane – a Dakota with stretchers – which carried me back to
Catania, and then on in another aircraft to Tunis. There I
was put in an ambulance train to Constantine. By the time I
had come to rest in Algeria and treatment was about to start,
I was well again. I started to work my way back to the Front,
and arrived just in time for the unit Christmas party. This
was as cheerful as it could be in out billet – the Vasto
Theological College.

The irony of life on a warfront was underlined for us all by
a popular silver-haired Public Relations Officer, Captain Sir
Gerald Boles. Our brother war correspondents were civilians
in uniform and moved around only with Conductors – usually junior officers who had been wounded, or were regarded
as useless by their parent units. Sir Gerald was, to put a fine
point upon it, allergic to lead. He was very deeply anxious
not to be killed – injured, even – and in a charming and
patrician manner would shy away from the most distant
explosion.

While escorting correspondents around the Front in
search of their stories, he refused to go anywhere near the
action. 'Might get the jeep damaged,' he would explain,
apologetically. 'War Department property, you know.' Some
correspondents were quite content to go along with such
timidity and to fight-the-furious-fight only upon their portable typewriters. The more gung-ho reporters would not be
fobbed-off by the gentility of 'Sir Gerald and Lady Boles', as
Ted Gilling called him scornfully. They were missing all the
action. After indignant protests it was decided that Sir
Gerald had to go.

He was too sweet a man to humiliate by RTUing, so his
superiors cast around for an acceptably safe job away from
the Front where Sir Gerald could pursue his gentle life
undisturbed. They finally decided on Bari; it was then miles
behind the Front, but a sufficient number of correspondents

were passing through on their way to Yugoslavia and the Balkans to justify the posting.

With obvious and touching relief he turned his back on the war, leaving his brother officers to continue their dangerous role – without, as it transpired, further casualty. Sir Gerald drove south and settled into a comfortable harbourside hotel in that tranquil, unscathed city to sit the war out, peacefully.

A few nights after his arrival an ammunition ship anchored just outside his hotel exploded. The blast was felt for 20 miles. Sir Gerald was blown through several walls, and into eternity.

ANZIO

Buck Rogers was on Their side . . .

THE Anzio Experience has always remained with me; mainly, I suppose, because I never expected to live through it. One retains a proprietorial attitude towards any hazardous expedition experienced totally, from planning to victory. Also, the unique Beachhead Spirit which permeated everywhere was unforgettable.

An urgent message from Major Keating had sent me jeeping through the mountains of Italy to Naples, where I learned I was to command cameramen covering the landing of 50,000 British and Americans on enemy coastline south of Rome. The intention was to cut off the enemy and liberate the Eternal City. We sailed on 21 January 1944, the British 1st Division to land north of Anzio, the American 3rd Division to the south. Knowing Field Marshal Kesselring was expecting an attack behind his lines and that the German radio often spoke of it, we prepared for another Salerno.

On our ship troops wrapped themselves in blankets and kipped-down on deck. In the wardroom officers played poker for ludicrously high stakes, trying to get rid of cash. Just when there was no need for money I won big, of course, and landed lumbered with useless lire which took me many months to spend. It was the first (and last) time I faced such a problem. That night we headed our preparatory dope sheets 'The Invasion of Rome', and I told my cameramen to hoard scarce filmstock for the Liberation. I did not foresee the next 18 desperate weeks.

Resistance to the landing was at first lighter than expected: a few 88mm shells, and air raids. Most casualties were caused by wooden box mines on the beaches, to which the RE's detectors did not react. I learnt afterwards from Prince Stefano Borghese, whose Palace overlooked Anzio harbour, that the ominous approaching rumble of hundreds of ships' engines out at sea had been heard long before our devastating supporting barrage began, but the German Harbourmaster thought his supply boats were returning from Leghorn.

The huge armada anchored in Anzio Bay. LSTs had their barrage balloons up. Guns on every ship were manned. Destroyers cut protectively through the fleet, laying a thick black smokescreen. Further out, cruisers moved ponderously around in a semi-circle, rocking as their thunderous broadsides supported the troops ashore. Red air raid warning flags flew almost permanently. Sometimes protecting Spitfires held off the Luftwaffe, but more often their fighter-bombers got through to drop bombs and hurtle away, low over the water.

After an hour on the beaches our couriers left to carry the early film back to Naples. The first mishap came when a bomb blew Sgt Lambert off the quayside. He landed in the water, still conscientiously clutching his bag of film.

I started up the coast road from the beach dump area, heading for Rome – which was after all, the object of the exercise. The countryside was deserted. After some time it seemed as though the capital must be just around the corner, but at a road junction before the river Moletta Sherman

tanks were hull-down on a hill, firing over it. The 1st
Battalion of the Loyals had been held up and, as snipers'
bullets hissed by, we watched the shelling they had called
down hit a German-held house; and that, for many fearful
weeks, was the limit of our advance upon Rome. I returned to
the port, frustrated.

The timid old American General Walter Lucas, commanding the Beachhead, had ordered everyone to dig in and
consolidate. With such co-operation, the Germans had little
difficulty in containing us. Their reaction to the invasion had
been swift and almost overwhelming. Two more Allied
divisions were landed, but by that time seven German
divisions had been rushed in, including Panzers with the
fearful Tiger tanks.

In the evening I went down to Red beach to look for some
of my sergeants; as I arrived another hit-and-run raid came
in. Flaming Bofors shells spewed up into the night. Suddenly
out at sea the air shuddered and a sheet of orange flame
spread across the horizon against the blackening sky. A
bomb had hit the destroyer *Janus*, which exploded. The flame
died down quickly, leaving only a glow against the night. All
hands were lost.

As one of the attacking aircraft screamed away shells hit its
tail. The fanned flames grew. Every man on the beach was
cheering as it crashed to earth and exploded – but it was a
poor exchange for a destroyer and so many lives.

I had taken a large house overlooking the harbour for
quarters, and to get pictures as our shipping was shelled and
bombed. We slept in its cellars, until deciding that bombs
were preferable to rats and moving up to the ground floor.
Keating and I considered the best drill should the Germans
break through. There were some tattered clothes in a garden
shed; we decided to wear these and make for Rome, rather
than attempting to get back to our army through the German
lines to the south.

The few remaining civilians were evacuated, leaving
Anzio a small and desperate military state, shelled all day
and bombed all night. Huge German guns had been brought
up; directed from observation posts in the surrounding

mountains, their shelling was incessant and accurate. Our supplies arrived in LSTs already loaded into fleets of six-wheeled lorries. These would roar down the ramps and off the quayside, while empty lorries drove onboard, fast. Nobody hung around that harbour. We all developed 'Anzio twitch'.

War correspondents took over the villa next to us. One American photographer tumbled over as he ran downstairs during a bombing, and was instantly awarded a Purple Heart medal for injury in action against the enemy. He then wore the medal – and that *did* call for bravery.

The BBC's cheery Wynford Vaughan-Thomas, attempting to record an artillery barrage, left his mike open one night and instead picked up the nightingale of Anzio; this happy bird won him more fame than any other wartime assignment.

The Germans began to fire propaganda leaflets as well as high explosives at us. They proclaimed what was then the truth: that Anzio was the biggest and best prison camp in the world, because the prisoners were self-supporting. Some demanded, 'Where will Russia stop?' Others showed a soldier's wife back in England preparing for bed while in the background an American Master Sergeant was taking his tie off, purposefully: 'What English girl could refuse these handsome men from the wide open spaces?' The troops' reaction was to collect the leaflets, tear off the text and use the girl as a pinup.

The Germans also unleashed upon our shipping the first secret weapon to lift the curtain on robot warfare: the glider bomb, controlled from the plane which fired it. From our balcony we saw these earliest V-bombs sink ship after ship. The great crimson glare across the night sky as a Liberty ship carrying ammunition and petrol exploded was the most beautiful and awful sight I have yet seen. They also introduced the Goliath, a tiny remote-controlled tank carrying 800lbs of explosives, and their tiny one-man submarine. We began to feel Buck Rogers was on *their* side; also Flash Gordon.

At the end of May the main army in the south began to

advance towards the Beachhead. The commanding American 6th Corps had its headquarters in the catacombs under
Netunno and at each evening briefing in the Map Room we
watched the two lines converge.

After 17 weeks in that small cratered bridgehead, Lieutenant Peter Hopkinson and I ventured out one morning
across the Mussolini Canal and down into the Pontine
marshes. There with fear and then with ecstasy, we met
troops of the Fifth Army, advancing north. It had been a long
time.

As we took the traditional join-up pictures, General Mark
Clark arrived to get in on the publicity, shaking hands with
men of the relieving 85th Dvision. To get our pictures to the
outside world we pressed on south, the way they had come,
heading for Naples 100 miles away. We were not sure
whether the enemy had withdrawn, and wondered whether
we might find ourselves *behind* some German rearguard that
was not looking both ways.

Certainly the road had not been cleared for mines or booby
traps – but we were too happy to worry. With relief we found
ourselves surprising and alarming advancing American
troops by appearing in front of them – where the Goddam
Krauts should have been.

At one river we had to wait on the north bank while they
built their Bailey bridge across to us. Then with Relief of
Anzio pictures the world was waiting for we pushed on, every
mile flat-out and singing, towards Naples. Driving weary but
triumphant down the Via Roma towards our darkrooms, a
white-helmeted American military policeman in a shining
jeep waved us down – and handed me a ticket for speeding.

Our pictures were radioed around the world. The BBC
announced that the first men to get through had made
history – so when it was unkindly suggested that we had only
returned to relish a night in the Naples Officers' Club, we
were able to reply with nonchalant modesty: 'Just made
history, old boy – that's all . . .'

VICTORY

A mysterious Millionaire, very nearly . . .

It was eerie, driving from Naples back to Anzio through the old German lines as we positioned ourselves to cover the break-out north, towards Rome. Back at our poor battered villa, I detected that the beleaguered men of the Beachhead regarded the relieving troops with slight resentment; they seemed not rescuers but trespassers, intruders. Like its predecessor Tobruk, Anzio had become the most exclusive club in the world – membership restricted to those who for months had endured the fighting, bombing and ceaseless shelling. With everyone in the same dangerous hole, there had even grown up new and solid comradeship between British and Americans.

Then suddenly, strange men with different battledress flashes had appeared, driving vehicles with another kind of camouflage. The clean staff cars of Base Wallahs from Naples and Caserta stood out amid our dusty jeeps with their sun-reflecting shell-attracting windscreens laid flat. The Beachhead we had fought for was being taken over – by *our* side!

The main break-out attack under General Lucien Truscott was to go through Cisterna. Two British divisions would be in at the kill, for the 1st Division had moved to the coast. I hurriedly placed teams with the Reconnaissance Regiments likely to enter Rome first. Then came the unexpected news that General Frederick's Special Service Corps of American and Canadian shocktroops had been diverted to Route 6, the main road into Rome.

What we did not know was that General Mark Clark was

so obsessed with the idea of getting to Rome ahead of his allies that he disregarded General Alexander's orders and drove his army north, thus failing to cut the German lines of communication from the Cassino front and permitting Kesselring's army to escape. He put Publicity ahead of Victory – and lengthened our war.

The American belief that public relations are paramount has today spread around the world; then it was new. At the height of some of the most desperate fighting I received by despatch rider a signal from the Fifth Army Commander. I assumed it was some operational order, but it began: 'My calendar tells me today is your birthday . . .'

A Greetings telegram from General Mark Clark, delivered amid shot and shell; I couldn't believe it. Speechless, I showed it to an American friend, who said, 'He's running for President.'

He did not, for when I met the General 32 years later, the handsome old man was living unhappily in retirement with an unsympathetic second wife at Charleston, South Carolina. He still defended that fatal determination to be first in Rome which cost him his political career.

So before dawn on 3 June 1944 I was driving along the Appian Way, passing slow-moving columns of tanks and troopcarriers. Five miles from the Rome boundary we were stopped by sniperfire and shells: to delay our advance, a German 88mm was making a last stand around the corner. As we waited for our tanks to deal with the gun, a dozen Italians in their Sunday-best came along behind us, strolling towards the German position. It was a wedding procession – the bride too determined to get to church on time to worry about the war going on around her. The group waved their flowers and, sedate and smiling, sauntered around the corner towards the 88mm.

We waited, breathless, for the bang. Silence. An hour later they all returned, with everything apparently signed and sealed. We were still pinned down. Every movement towards the city still brought a shell, so we regarded with admiration that ex-signorina with an acute sense of priorities.

By first light next morning the Germans had withdrawn

and we were able to drive into Rome, past the Colosseum and into the Piazza Venezia. I went up into the Palace to stand on that balcony from which Mussolini had addressed his empire: his viewpoint seemed to symbolise our victory.

After drab, demolished Anzio we marvelled at the peacetime cleanliness of the Open City, the excitement and joy of another Liberation, the bright and lovely women. Italian partisans were emerging – as they usually did when the fighting had moved on – to beat up Fascists or settle old grudges. Stern girl Communists were already parading homemade red flags. The first barber shops were lifting their shutters. British prisoners who had escaped and been hidden by Italians came out on the streets to cheer – in English. General Mark Clark and his commanders arrived at the Capital to take over the city. More modestly, we took over the Hotel de la Ville, above the Spanish Steps in the Via Sistina, and celebrated victory with a bath. Then we went out to a barber's for the full treatment. As Peter Hopkinson said: 'You don't shave yourself when you've just liberated Rome.'

The Pope received the war correspondents in audience, and blessed us. There was a great flurry among gum-chewing New York photographers who all seemed to be called Bernie Goldstein. With great half-plate cameras and determined ambulance-chasing approach, they were a breath of peacetime air and noticeably unawed by the grandeur of the Vatican. It restored equilibrium to hear those urgent cries in Brooklynese: 'Hold it, Pope!'

That evening, having held it many times, His Holiness appeared on the balcony before a crowd of 200,000 Italians, most of them weeping with joy and emotion. He thanked God and the warring nations for sparing Rome and, as he raised his hand to bless the people, I planned to stand and take that great dramatic picture. The multitude around me sank to its knees with bowed heads, and I attempted to remain on my feet – but could not. Against my will I was drawn down with them, camera dangling ineffectually around my neck. I remained upon my knees during this Blessing. It was the end of Rome's first day of freedom.

Next morning on the infantryman's wireless receiver in my

jeep we heard it was D-Day: the Second Front had been opened in France. We had won an Axis capital but lost our limelight and our picturespace.

Winston Churchill flew to the Mediterranean to observe the Eighth Army struggling up Italy. At a Royal Artillery battery in action on the Front he scribbled: 'To Hitler, from Churchill' on a shell, which was then fired at the enemy. 'It's like writing a rude letter,' he said, 'and being there when it arrives!'

I put two cameramen with a special commando unit as it raced for Florence to capture the German SS Headquarters at Villa Spellman; they found it locked and empty. Other cameramen went with the first South Africans into the glorious city. The Germans had blown every one of the graceful bridges across the Arno except the Ponte Vecchio, so in that summer sunshine Florence resembled a beautiful woman with her teeth knocked out.

The Eighth Army occupied the city up to the river and, not wanting to cause further damage, waited while partisans dealt with the enemy on the opposite bank. With little idea of street fighting, they conducted a vigorous but unscientific war. I watched a group of them attempting to throw hand-grenades 100 yards across the river. It was a war game – amateurs versus professionals – which they fought with spirit; scores were killed and wounded by skilled German marksmen.

Driver H. H. Wood chatted with an Italian doctor and nurses while his sergeants took pictures of a hospital full of such casualties. In stumbling army-Italian, with gestures, he explained he was from Sheffield, the city where they made the steel for surgical instruments. He was then surprised to find himself enthusiastically wafted around the wards and asked incomprehensible questions. Wishing to be polite he shook his head where it seemed suitable, or nodded. They reached the operating theatre. A partisan with his chest blown open lay upon the table. The surgeon asked advice as to how he should operate.

Driver Wood was a nice obliging lad, ready to turn his hand to anything. Fortunately I arrived at that moment and

snatched the scalpel away as he examined the unconsci
man in a businesslike manner, as though approaching a
stalled jeep.

Florence captured, the Allied armies now faced the Gothic
Line – a chain of mountains and rivers stretching across the
land from Pisa to Rimini. Italy provided some of the hardest
fighting of that World War, and this was the most formidable
of all its natural obstacles. As winter closed in and the rains
came, our blitzkrieg slowed, halted – and became trench
warfare. Food and ammunition had to be carried by mule up
to mountain positions. Our pictures showed grim shell-
shattered frontline villages looking like the Somme or Ypres.
The object now was merely to hold the 25 German divisions, to deny them to Hitler's other armies in Russia and
France.

Despite the icy, numbing wretchedness of a winter war in
the mountains of Sunny Italy, we were a surprisingly contented unit. As Director of the cameramen covering Fifth
Army, I had quickly requisitioned an enchanting mansion
upon a hill overlooking the Arno, the Villa Paradisino. As the
front stabilised I retained it as headquarters during that long
winter. Our Christmas party was memorable: I still have
pictures showing us having as good a time as is possible,
without girls.

My two lieutenants would be out in the field, along with
our 20 teams. Every day I joined them in the mountains
or – far more popular – some would return from the Front
for a wash-and-brush-up at HQ and a night in *Fascisissimo
Firenze*, as the Duce called it. I remember Lieutenant George
Groom coming in triumphantly with a splendid pair of suede
desert boots he had somehow obtained from Cairo. He was
planning to wear them on important occasions, to show he
had been a Desert Rat. My young Welsh batman took a lot of
trouble polishing them into a distinctive hairy-shine. This
was not appreciated, and George went sourly back to regulation army issue.

The stalemate lasted until the spring, when the Fifth and
Eighth Armies launched their final attack and the partisans
rose in the northern cities. We captured Bologna in mid-

April and a week later I crossed the Po and reached Verona. Everywhere German resistance was collapsing.

In a large and liberated Fiat limousine – so much cosier than those chilly jeeps – I headed for Milan. The armies were engaged elsewhere, and the autostrada was deserted. With a few diversions for blown bridges, we reached the enormous industrial city without being shot at, and drove through empty streets into its heart – the Cathedral Square. There some heavily-armed partisans raced up to tell me that the SS Headquarters of the Wehrmacht in a nearby hotel was stubbornly refusing to capitulate. The German General had announced they would surrender to no one but an Allied officer – and so far, I was the only one in town . . .

I was looking for pictures, not prisoners, but allowed myself to be led towards the enemy stronghold. High barricades surrounded the hotel and Germans with guns stood at every window. They were, it seemed, quite prepared to go down fighting, and to take part of the population with them. I made a quick appreciation of the situation, and concluded that this was a silly stage of the war at which to get killed . . .

Pushing aside my sense of survival, I strode past the German guardposts and into the lobby. A punctilious SS General, politely concealing his disappointment at my insignificant rank, clicked his heels, saluted and handed me his Walther revolver. Through an English-speaking Adjutant he announced: 'My men are at your disposal. We could not surrender' – with a scornful gesture towards the Italian clamour outside – 'to that rabble.'

I had a sneaking sympathy for his appraisal; his men would surely have been massacred. His Adjutant in turn handed me a key and indicated a large tin trunk which he appeared to regard as important. Later, when taken aside and requested to open it, I could see why.

It was their Paymaster's safe, jammed to the brim with every type of currency: lire, marks, sterling, dollars, Swiss francs. I had never before seen so much money in one place – and never have since. Suddenly, I felt like Aladdin.

I have sometimes wondered, idly, how my life would have developed had I accepted my remarkable luck and quietly told them to carry that unaccountable spoil-of-war out to my unmarked car. I could have driven south to Florence and entrusted it to some Italian friends for a year or two until the dust settled – and then gone back and, like Ali Baba, opened the trunk . . . In the turmoil and confusion of the war's twilight, it would have been too easy and was hardly robbery – more like an enormous Pools win. Those untraceable millions would have dissolved into nothingness, like the gold in Lake Toplitz.

The only effect of that unexpected trophy would have been my transmogrification from a potentially penniless post-war ex-officer into a young and mysterious millionaire, facing a life of luxury. An interesting prospect, and one of those Moments of Decision.

After several hours of confusion within the hotel, during which I held the partisans at bay and untruthfully reassured the increasingly nervous German Command that I had their whole capitulation well under control, an American tank regiment arrived to liberate Milan – and I handed over my tin trunk of great good fortune. I also gave them my General and all my SS men, making a clean break with that moment of Victory. It was the end of my war – and at quite a high note. From then on, it was downhill all the way.

As the Germans formed up and prepared to march out under the protective guns of the tanks, a 'planeload of correspondents escorted by Major Pat Henderson arrived from Public Relations in Rome, with notebooks out and high excitement. It seemed the war was returning to everyday abnormality, so I went back to the Cathedral Square again to start taking the pictures which had been so neglected during my small role amid the ashes of Hitler's crumbling Reich.

While I had been resisting temptation in Milan, the other end of Hitler's Axis had been escaping. Mussolini had joined a German column retreating through the alpine passes towards Switzerland, taking his mistress, Clara Petacci, and a fortune in gold and valuables. At Dongo on Lake Como they ran into a partisan road-block and were locked in a farmhouse while it was decided what to do with them. Next day, as the valiant Clara tried to shield her podgy lover, partisan Lieutenant-Colonel Valerio shot both of them. The gold disappeared for ever. Some Italian had faced my two choices – and made the other one!

Their bodies were carried back to Milan. One of my last pictures of the 600-day war in Italy shows Mussolini, his mistress and four of his *capo Fascisti* hanging upside down outside a garage in the Piazza Loreto while an hysterical Milanese mob bays and spits and screams and hits out at the lifeless faces. It was not, at that moment, a very splendid victory.

There was one other man to be caught: the Italians' Lord Haw Haw – John Amery, son of Leopold Amery, then Secretary of State for India, and brother of Julian. During the war he had been the traitorous English voice of Rome Radio.

I went to the Milan radio station and told them to broadcast an announcement calling for his whereabouts. Within minutes a message arrived to say he was being held in one of the city jails. I drove over with Sgt Huggett and ordered the Governor to produce him.

'Thank God you're here,' said a very pale Amery when led into the Governor's office with his girlfriend, an appealing brunette in a dark trouser-suit. 'I thought they were going to shoot me.'

Amery, small, dark-haired and unshaven, was still wearing a black shirt proclaiming his Fascist sympathies: 'I've never been anti-British,' he told me. 'You can read the scripts of my broadcasts through the years and you'll never find anything against Britain. I've just been very anti-Communist, and if at the moment I'm proved wrong, well – one of these days you'll find out that I was right. . .'

He seemed a pleasant, reasonable man. I took him from the partisans, to his relief, and handed him over to our military police. He was later repatriated to Britain and at the Old Bailey stood trial for Treason. To save his family further humiliation Amery pleaded Guilty, was convicted – and hanged.

BUDAPEST

Overtaken in a Revolving Door . . .

THE war was over. After a spell covering mopping-up operations around Bolzano and among the gorgeously blushing
Dolomites at Cortina D'Ampezzo in Northern Italy, learning
not to be surprised when everything was so clean and
undamaged, I drove on through the Alps into Austria. That
occupied enemy nation was being divided by already-
squabbling victors into four zones. We passed among the
British in Klagenfurt, Carinthia, between storybook castles
and lakes, and kept carefully to the road through the Russian
Zone until the gaunt, stricken skeleton of St Stephen's
Cathedral stood above Vienna's ruined skyline.

The waltztime capital was shattered and starving. It had
just found itself on the wrong side in a world war, for the
second time running. After German occupation and fire-
bombing, two nations had fought through its streets. The
Russians had captured the city three weeks before the end of
the war and had not yet withdrawn the victorious assault
units of the Third Ukranian Army and replaced them with
better-disciplined garrison troops, as they were later to do.
Traditional pillage and rape continued. The population was
depleted and scattered, but within a month of liberation the
Austrian health authorities reported 70,144 new cases of
gonorrhoea, 6,402 of syphilis.

At the Public Relations mess off the Landstrasse-
Haupstrasse I met a pretty actress called Gretel Glogau who
had worked with Hedy Lamarr at the famous Femina. Her
family lived in what became one of the Russian districts.
Soldiers had burst into the next door apartment and, in front

of the family, raped the daughter of the house. She had torn
herself away and jumped out of their sixth-floor window. The
mother went to look at her daughter lying on the pavement
below – and jumped after her.

The arrival of British, American and French troops later
that summer was a civilising influence: military police
patrols of four spick-and-span nationalities in one jeep were
symbolic and reassuring – each nation on its best public
behaviour.

I moved in to Sacher, the old red-plush hotel in the shadow
of the burnt-out Opera House which the British Army had
requisitioned. The silver-haired concierge, Herr Schmidt,
looked and behaved so much like a Viennese actor that the
professional who later impersonated him in the film 'The
Third Man' seemed insufficiently theatrical.

The Americans had taken the flashier Hotel Bristol, the
Russians retained the grander Imperial on the Ringstrasse
where, in the scintillating ballroom, their soldiers slaught-
ered oxen and tore up the floor to make fires on which to cook
their rations. They were not familiar with kitchens – nor
indeed with indoor sanitation. Even today I cannot pass that
hotel without a frisson.

At Christmastime the ever-generous Americans brought
in masses of food to be given to Viennese children at street
parties. From Schönbrunn Palace the British – a poorer
relation – asked all units if they would be prepared to under-
draw their rations so the remainder could go to those parties.
Every unit agreed.

City reconstruction began; a workman's salary was then
around 210 schillings a month – and one cigarette in the
black market cost 20 schillings, or three days' pay. Along
with the anxiety of those savage days was a weary relief that
the war was over, overlaid by the frenetic gaiety that comes
with the end of an ordeal and the certainty of a new day
tomorrow. Soon the endearing Viennese blend of nostalgia
and gentle hopelessness reasserted itself.

The charming rustic village of Grinzing was undamaged
and safely in the British zone, so *heurige* parties broke out as
new wine arrived from vineyards around Vienna first

planted by Roman soldiers. We sat over the bully beef I had smuggled from the mess, drank pale raw wine and listened to a tearful violin.

At the first peacetime ball, Congress danced again: the officers of four nations at their most splendid, the prettiest women of Vienna in whatever they could create or salvage. Gretel wore her surviving piece of jewellery, a string of pearls. The whole event was in waltztime, and you felt such a fool if you could not click your heels. While I went in search of wine a Russian officer, clicking like anything, asked her to dance. Fearing to anger him she said she would, but later. 'Then I shall make sure you return,' he said, pulling the pearls from her neck. I returned and searched the ballroom in a fury. He had gone, with his trophy.

One night I boarded a train bound for Prague at the gloomy Nordwestbahnhof. A thin night fog swirled through the shattered roof and around the few weak yellow lights. On the cratered platform another young correspondent was also saying goodbye to a *Fräulein*. Some Russian soldiers already aboard had small candles in their compartments, the flames flickering behind sooty windows. At the end of the platform, next to the huge grimy engine hissing thoughtfully to itself, was one shining blue Voiture Lits coach. Inside, an unreal oasis of warmth and light, hot water and mirrors and crinkly white sheets amid the desolation of the ruined capital.

As the train pulled away, the correspondent came in and introduced himself as John Peet, of Reuters. It took 11 hours for the so-called Prague Express to move haltingly through dark pinewoods and push aside the Iron Curtain; we reminisced through the night. He was later to throw his agency and indeed the West into some confusion when he defected to the Russians in Berlin, amid a blaze of publicity. He was the first man to go across.

When I heard of his decision I was amazed that one who had lived through a Russian occupation in raw and primitive reality could have retained enthusiasm for their political system. Anyone who experiences what a Communist regime actually brings – who does not merely read a version from a safe distance, and join a club – usually becomes a Conservative for life. Just as there are no atheists in foxholes, so there are few eager theoretical Marxists in cities occupied by the Red Army.

At the border a Czech customs officer wanted to charge duty on my regulation 200 cigarettes. Knowing the ways of that world, I silently broke open the carton and handed him three packs. Expressionless, he took them, warning me stiffly that this was in no way to be considered a precedent. 'Yes, yes,' I said, wearily. As he left, in a baffling gesture of honest dishonesty he handed me back one pack. There was, it seemed, a going rate.

Prague, the first capital to go down before the Nazis, had been the last to be liberated – four days after the end of the war. Coming from Vienna's distress, it already seemed a warm, well-fed and well-lit room in the bleak, hungry house that was Middle Europe.

I flew on to what has become a contradiction in terms: an East European democracy with more than one Party. The Russian Army had withdrawn from Hungary and in its first free elections the Communists polled 800,000 out of 2½ million votes. A King's Messenger and I were the only passengers in a RAF Dakota from Schwechat. We landed on a snow-covered field outside Budapest and moved into the apartment block occupied by the British Mission. Our mess was the aristocrats' Park Club, splendidly catered by the only organisation then equal to the job: Wagons-Lits. The service was brisk.

My flatmate, a grey-haired linguist from the Intelligence Corps, was Captain Edgar Sanders. Soon afterwards he went back to England to be demobbed – and returned to Hungary as a businessman. With that sensitive and knowledgeable background he was – not surprisingly – arrested in 1949 for spying. He suffered a major show trial and was imprisoned for 13 years.

Transport in the Vaci Utca, the Bond Street of Budapest, was mainly horsedrawn, but this agricultural country was already starting to live well: 'We didn't realise how rich we were,' a Hungarian told me, 'until we had nothing.' They had begun to relish once again their rueful maxim: 'If *only* we could afford to live – as we live. . .'

Hungarians may have retained their international reputation as charming con men who overtake you in a revolving door, but in those hard post-war years their economists handled brilliantly the world's greatest monetary landslide, which outpaced even the Weimar Republic's classic inflation. In the middle of 1946 one Hungarian friend of mine drew his salary and found that he had earned the magnificent sum of 50 billion pengos. Before the war a pengo had been worth about 5p – so by that reckoning he had earned £2,500 million, which seemed unlikely. He knew the purchasing power of his paper fortune was fast decreasing so, pondering how best to use it, called at a market on his way home intending to spend, spend, spend. At a pastry shop he first bought himself a cake – and found his money problems solved: the cake cost 45 billion pengos.

Even with ten thousand million pengo notes, workers carried their wages home in sacks. It was the worst inflation the world had ever seen. Then on 1 August 1946, directly after the harvest when peasants had perishable goods to sell, pengos were withdrawn and exchanged for forints. The exchange rate was interesting: 400,000,000,000,000,000,000,000,000,000,000 pengos to one forint. On that summer day four hundred thousand quadrillions of pengos suddenly equalled – about 2½p.

Made Sterling seem downright balanced . . .

Such economic sleight-of-hand at least filled the Budapest shops with goods few could afford and gave the impression of plenty. Vienna was still the most battered of capitals, yet when I asked Gretel what she wanted brought back from those luxuriant shopping-streets she chose, of all things, one of Hungary's famous fish: I flew with an enormous ice-cold carp on my lap. It was cooked with difficulty and eaten with diminishing delight for days and days.

I spent the following months travelling Central Europe, with occasional forays south to Rome. The Press corps had been reinforced by peacetime volunteers curious to see what remained of Europe – even the American millionairess Doris

Duke was on a magazine assignment. One rather appealing girl reporter had something of a scoop, which she shared with me. She had discovered that the widow of Heinrich Himmler, Hitler's odious SS chief, was in the prison cage at Cine Citta, outside Rome. I went with her and took the pictures as she interviewed the elderly woman with tight bun of hair and hard screwed-up face. The Himmlers appeared perfectly designed to run the Nazi SS and must have made an unusual household.

By now the Fifth and Eighth Armies were beginning to pack up and go home, and with them our film unit was disintegrating as first-in were first-out. I had left England as a rosy-cheeked youth (I seemed to remember) and after years of war returned home to the Motherland I had been fighting for with a totally improbable group: not a romantic bunch of bemedalled warriors – but the cricket team of the Central Mediterranean Forces, with whom it was not easy to cut a battle-scarred dash.

They were playing the Services' Home XI at Lords and included Captain Norman Yardley, later to lead England, and other Test cricketers. We flew from Rome in a DC3. At the time it seemed total luxury to travel for eight hours in a bucket-seat at 140 mph or so, coming down now and again in France to refuel. We all congratulated ourselves upon our great good fortune. I can imagine the indignation of the most humble package-tourist today if asked to put up with such basic transport.

It was disorientating to be back in the grey austerity of victorious Britain after the bright luxury of vanquished Italy, and my interest in the Test Match was limited; I went only once to Lords. After the match we collected our American crew from the Cumberland Hotel for the return flight from Stansted. I offered the Lieutenant slumped beside me my paper. He tried to read, but gave up. 'On the town last night,' he muttered, 'can't see a thing.' Perhaps he could sleep in the plane? 'No – I'm the navigator.'

Somehow we reached Rome, and it seemed more like home: lots of friends, and the living was easier. By then the film unit was fading away, its efforts entombed in files and storerooms – to emerge in later years in war histories and Do-You-Remember documentaries.

I moved to the *Eighth Army News* as its putative editor. Lieutenant-Colonel Hugh Cudlipp had been demobilised, though Captain William Connor was still on duty: he was 'Cassandra', the *Daily Mirror's* trenchant columnist. Other members of the unit were journalists of varying distinction. The paper transferred to the premises of *Il Gazettino* in Venice and became the *Union Jack*. As editor I had a grand office and not much work, which seemed about right.

Living in Venice was like belonging to an exclusive club: the Piazza San Marco had reverted to its role as an elegant medieval museum where one socialised over a negroni at the Florian or the Quadri, nodding to other members, while all Venetian life drifted around the tables. I never lost my joy and wonder at the sea city – and never have. Each time I passed down the Grand Canal in a *vaporetto* it was as though I was seeing all that timeless beauty for the first time. I doubt whether Venice has ever been so lovely or as happy as in that summer of '46 when we were all enchanted to be alive.

I was ready to become a permanent Venetian, despite the sorry fact that our chief sub-editor, a competent Company Sergeant-Major, had been demobilised and I had been compelled to combine his role with mine. This cruel blow meant working very hard indeed. Even so, the fête continued.

Then came a letter from Ted Gilling, home from war corresponding to become news editor of Exchange Telegraph: the agency was reorganising and if I wanted to join I should get back to the reality of Fleet Street. The call-back seemed worse than the call-up. Reluctantly I left my Venetian friends in their palaces within that sunny self-obsessed cul-de-sac and caught a slow train away from the sweet life, towards cold rationed England.

They sent my medals through the post – a small box containing concentrated apprehension. At some Army depot in Surrey I received my demob suit; it was everything I had been warned about. I gave it to the porter in our block of flats, took the Underground to Mansion House and joined ExTel.

I was no longer an Officer and a Gentleman – just another utility civvy.

On reflection, the Army had not been a squandering of young years but a forced-feeding of what one expected out of life – only more so. It had managed to be at once boring and exciting, frightening and uplifting, misery and fun. It had shown me something of the world and how people behaved under pressure. I had seen a lot of violence – yet managed to stay alive. I knew how to have a good time – and put up with a bad time. I could take photographs and write clearly, at least. Despite itself, the Army had given me another shove towards Whicker's World.

As I prepared for the new demands of a civilian life I braced myself by recalling Dr Johnson's judgment: 'Every man thinks meanly of himself . . . for not having been a Soldier.'

PART THREE

CURTAIN RAISER!

FLEET STREET

The Lady Wrestler was Not Amused . . .

THE Exchange Telegraph then covered the world, as Britain's smaller news agency. The Press Association was the massive co-operative providing Home news, while Reuters handled Foreign; we were the private-enterprise No 2 in both fields. The agency originally had exclusive right to transmit Stock Exchange prices – hence its name – and to cover the proceedings from the Press galleries of Parliament. Such extraordinary monopolies should have made it one of the world's major agencies, but a timid managing director saw the organisation growing beyond his control and invited the Press Association in to share the spoils. Such commercial idiocy meant that by the time I joined the news-gathering role was already less profitable than the Sports department 'Blower' which carried prices-runners-winners from meetings to bookmakers.

There was also the column printer which chattered away in hotels and clubs, offering a tidied-up version of the service which went to every newspaper office and the BBC. ExTel was proud to have its teleprinters in the King's study at Buckingham Palace, at No 10 Downing Street, the Foreign Office and Embassies – in every significant official location. From the reporter's point of view such distinguished outlets meant only that reaction to any inaccuracy or unexpected honesty was swift – and often from a very great height.

I spent ten crowded years with this agency, covering everything from wars in the Far East to Royal tours of Africa, from Egyptians rioting in Alexandria to Conservative ladies applauding in Eastbourne. I avoided Parliament whenever possible – my shorthand could not stand the pace. The pay was not overwhelming, but the news editor had intimated that expenses could be heavy and unqueried. As the smallest agency we were outnumbered and outspent on every story, so had to run harder just to keep up. We were justly proud of our maxim: we may not be first, but we're *always* wrong . . .

Upon joining I was put on the sub-editors' desk, to knock out of me any of that Officer-and-Gentleman nonsense; four shifts, talking to reporters in Berlin or Brighton, handling and rewriting copy from around the world. After entering the tatty office in Cannon Street and settling down at a type-writer in the newsroom, it was head-down-and-flat-out for eight hours. Subs, receiving all the kicks and few of the ha'pence, are the drones of the newspaper hive; reporters its warriors and players who do the leg work, take the risks and, on occasion, have the fun. As fast as I could, I became a reporter.

ExTel had a few bureaux around the world: Paris, Bonn, Rome and some other capitals. From the US we took the United Press service, as they took ours. Elsewhere we had only Stringers. Being thin on the ground meant that wher-ever an important story broke, we had to send. I became ExTel's fireman, flying off at a moment's notice. As a bachelor I had the drop on most of the young marrieds in the office: they needed to consider the children's holidays and a grumbling wife, back in Croydon. I would volunteer to work on Christmas Day – so they could be home with the turkey – and to cover stories in faraway places that might prove rough.

When the news editor marked the diary he doubtless appreciated that if I got shot up in some war, crashed in some aircraft or sunk without trace, there was no one waiting at home who cared much, and no widow to support. In so casual a way is a lifestyle formed.

The joy of Fleet Street life – of my whole life, come to that – is that every day is different. It could bring a busride to Chelsea for the Flower Show or a flight to Paris to join our team of five at the Palais de Chaillot, covering the first European Assembly of the United Nations.

It meant interviewing anyone in the news: the handsome Lady Norah Docker was a formidable social figure around town at that time. Her final millionaire husband, the long-suffering Sir Bernard, was head of the BSA Company, and her public appearances seemed to centre upon the preparation of ever more stunning Daimlers for each Motor Show. I went to talk with her at Earl's Court before an enormous pale blue monster impossibly loaded with crafted luxury. In those days she brandished their wealth on the assumption that all publicity helped the Company. This was later disproved, when Sir Bernard was fired.

She was detailing the lavish expenditure on her new Daimler with many a flourish when I asked with some irony, 'Why not have it upholstered in mink?' Lady D, quick as a flash: 'Mink's too hot to sit on.' There was our Motor Show sidebar story, in one throwaway phrase.

Years later, after Lady Docker's flag-tearing banishment from Monaco and social decline, I was looking for a house in Jersey and was offered their home at Rozel. They were moving to Majorca. Its position overlooking the harbour was lovely, but all furnishings had been Dockered: everything was mirrored, curlicued, be-ribboned, flouncy or gilded. The agent was asking £100,000, or £150,000 furnished. I felt sure he had it wrong way round: it was £150,000, but they would let it go for £100,000 to anyone prepared to take the furniture . . .

An early Fleet Street assignment was to return to Plymouth aboard HMS *Amethyst*, the warship which escaped from the Chinese after being damaged by their shore batteries. She had been pinned down for more than 100 days in the Yangtse River, in the twilight of Gunboat Diplomacy. Lieutenant-Commander Kerans, Naval Attaché in Peking, smuggled himself on board to command that dash for freedom under the guns.

From Gibraltar Frank Gillard covered the homecoming for the BBC, and with us was a Fleet Street photographer who titillated the Navy – and particularly Simon, the ship's cat – by bringing on board a cage of carrier pigeons. He planned they should fly his negatives off the ship before we landed, thus giving him a useful lead over the competition. This was Fleet Street enterprise of the Old School. The Navy recovered fast and one night in the wardroom set before us a most tasty dish; the poor chap only noticed the menu and 'Pigeon Pie' when he was half way through masticating his scoop.

When we sailed into Plymouth the Hoe was black with cheering crowds. As at Dunkirk, the whole nation had turned this retreat under gunfire into a Victory, and was deep in Amethysteria – fuelled no doubt by my daily reports from on board. The Admiral signalled: 'Well done Tiddy Oggy', and Kerans mustered all ranks and warned them, 'Put on your drinking caps.' It was a rapturous Devon welcome – and those pigeons were all right after all. Simon received the animals' VC, the Dickin Medal, and was Mentioned in Despatches for rat-killing.

Reporting for ExTel meant going to cover our highest human Tribunal – the first peacetime case before the International Court of Justice at the Hague. Sir Hartley Shawcross spoke for Britain in the dispute with Albania over the mining of an RN warship in the Corfu Channel. After the increasing tension and rude words at all world conferences, this gentle judiciary seemed to offer a soothing promise of worldly moderation.

The 16 venerable judges in their black gowns and lace collars had names almost fictionally exact: Justice Green Haywood Hackworth could have been nothing but American; Sir Arnold Duncan McNair was not to be confused; Milovan Zoricic had to be Yugoslavian. Judge Sergei Borisovitch Krylov was approached at a reception by some silly woman: 'Russian – how interesting' she gushed. 'Are you a Red or a White Russian?' 'Madame,' he told her, judicially, 'I am from the North.'

One Sunday afternoon I was deep in the papers at home when the news desk called to say the worst floods of the century were hitting the East coast. I set off at once for Norfolk to cover what was evidently a considerable disaster. The story ran for days and most of the Press on our sector of 'the front' stayed at a King's Lynn hotel. On the night of the dreaded high Spring Tide I went with a friendly girl reporter to examine the state of the river, before calling in our stories. In the gloom of a sodden and starless night, we groped our way across the Magdalen railway bridge above the swollen, raging Ouse. I was leading the way, moving carefully along some muddy planking 30 feet above the torrent, when I slipped – and dropped into the darkness.

My fall was broken, violently but luckily, by an iron girder under the railway line. I was lying across it, winded and disorientated while the girl above twittered in distress, when there flashed before me a remark by the local Police Chief, Superintendent Calvert: 'With those undercurrents no one would stand a chance in that river.'

I could not see the threatening water rushing beneath me, but I could hear its fury. Then, as I lay there, my sustaining iron bar began to vibrate. It was weird. In the distance we heard a whistling and rumbling: one of the few trains of the night was about to cross the bridge. Pauline's Perils were upon us.

With the girl's help I managed to clamber up, gasping and croaking, and we stumbled across in the darkness. We reached the bank just ahead of the engine. I checked at the General Hospital in the early hours and they strapped-up a couple of cracked ribs. It was painful – but it sure beat drowning.

More sedately, I covered the first meeting of the Council (then Congress) of Europe in the Hague. Reporting for a Socialist magazine was a lean, earnest chap in a green sportscoat called Denis Healey. Julian Amery, the MP whose brother I had saved from the Milan partisans only to see executed by our side, was there with Randolph Churchill – whose father stood in triumph in the Assembly to support his dream of a United Europe.

This voluntary coming-together of nations was of course poorly organised; in the medieval conference hall politicians talked into the night. When they took a vote on Adjournment we spectators of the Press, sitting wearily among the delegates, always enthusiastically voted with the Ayes.

One afternoon Churchill made a rare extempory speech;

afterwards anxious British reporters repaired to the Central Hotel bedroom of Geoffrey Cox, the *News Chronicle* man who afterwards ran ITN, to check their notes. Few foreign correspondents have good shorthand, unlike the Americans – who have none at all. Dan Schorr, later to be drummed out of the CBS for leaking Nixon's secrets, was even more hopeless than the rest of us. Together we contrived a collated version of that rolling prose.

The Congress led to the formation of the Council of Europe at Strasbourg, where we went to eavesdrop Churchill again – this time in its corridors having heated words with Herbert Morrison. We listened to a young and self-satisfied Anthony Crosland, and were joined over drinks at our hotel – the Maison Rouge in the Place Kleber – by those little-known backbenchers Harold Macmillan and David Maxwell-Fyfe.

In the Fifties I really believed Europe might become United, until one of our Labour delegates put it succinctly: 'Could you expect me to ask miners in my constituency to vote tax money to build another casino in the South of France?' There has never been an answer to that. Today European parliamentarians enjoy an annual budget of £125 million, yet still wander like rich nomads between Strasbourg, Brussels and Luxembourg.

As they have found, Strasbourg was a most acceptable assignment, for Alsation food was superb and Sylvaner and Traminer flowed freely. I remember unwinding one night with a few correspondents, including John Beavan, London editor of the *Guardian*. In some club we chatted-up a cheerful tableful of girls to such effect, it transpired, as to raise their expectations above the level of our intentions.

Their leader had been proudly introduced as a lady-wrestler, and boasted the rippling physique to prove it. We politely admired all her flexings and when we left, a jolly group, I found to my distress that I was closeted in the lift with this muscle-bound madame. We emerged into the street, and I called uneasily for support. All I could hear was the sound of distant running feet . . . as my distinguished colleagues, editor and all, disappeared into the night.

They had left me, their friend, alone upon the dawn

pavements with a tight-lipped lady wrestler growing more convinced by the minute that her investment in communication was not about to show a dividend . . .

It is not a scene one lightly forgets. By the time I could take up the matter of this shameful desertion in the face of duty with John Beavan, he had become Lord Ardwick. From the security of the Upper House he treated the whole inglorious episode, I thought, in a rather lofty manner.

KOREA

My God, he said – You're dead . . .

WHEN the North Koreans attacked across the 39th Parallel in June 1950 and President Truman called for United Nations 'Police Action', I was instantly accredited as war correspondent – or police reporter – and flew east. The everready overnight bag had to be reinforced for this one, which looked like a long hard slog.

In these days of one-hops to Bangkok it is surprising to recall that such a little while ago, a BOAC Argonaut took four days to reach Tokyo. That deafeningly noisy airliner, converted from a wartime bomber, left London on Tuesdays and Fridays and put down at Rome, Cairo, Basra, Karachi, Calcutta, Rangoon, Bangkok, Hong Kong and Okinawa; Tokyo was the tenth stop. We flew at 15,000 feet, at a steady respectable 250 mph. The journey was like a long voyage at sea: romances and enmities began and flourished. We would meet at intervals in the lounge at the back of the aircraft which suffered a discouraging sort of whiplash – a tendency to quiver. This increased the sale of hard and reassuring liquor.

We went ashore to pass a sultry night at the Great Eastern Hotel in Calcutta, and another in greater comfort at the Peninsula in Hong Kong. The goodbyes at each airport were most touching, the new arrivals considered critically. On the last day at Haneda Airport we founder-members dispersed sadly – we had been through a whole lot of turbulence together.

I checked into Radio Tokyo, General MacArthur's Press Headquarters, and then at the Commonwealth Officers' Hotel, the Marunouchi. In those days the Japanese were a very small race indeed and the little woodlined bedrooms were like tiny third-class cabins: the bed was a child's bunk, and I had to bow low to use the washbasin.

The first person I saw in the bar was Christopher Buckley, wartime friend and a *Daily Telegraph* senior man – tall, stooping, professorial and in line for the Chair of the History of War at Oxford. He had made his journalistic name with Alan Moorehead and Alex Clifford in the Western Desert and had just married for the first time, relatively late in life. He was predictably enamoured with the new wife who sat by his side. When we went to dinner they held hands under the table. I was touched.

Since we were on our way back to war, the three of us talked about Destiny, and the prospect that some imminent cataclysm might destroy all that made life worth living. In 1950 the world seemed to have only a loose grasp upon peace. We both felt strange to be back in uniform again so soon – as though somehow destined to soldier the years away while the world lurched from war to war. Ian Morrison of *The Times* had just been killed in Korea, and in Hong Kong Han Suyin was to become wealthy from her version of their love affair, *A Many Splendoured Thing*. Once again, violent death was becoming unremarked and everyday.

After all his recent battle experience, Christopher was fatalistic: 'I wish I could do a deal with the Devil', he reflected, in an echo of that other Chrisopher's Dr Faustus as we sat in chill air-conditioning eating hearty Australian rations made delicate by Japanese chefs. 'If I could be guaranteed ten years without a war, ten years of happiness so that my wife and I could go back to Italy and buy a villa and settle down to write in peace – well, I'd willingly give up what was left of my life after that.'

Being young and eager and believing there were answers to all questions, I protested against such a despairing view of the future. He should not be ready to accept such a rotten deal. 'I'm shooting for 80,' I said, thinking of a number, 'and so should you – which means you've got a good 40 years to come, at least.' They were both quietly adamant that a sure guarantee of ten years undisturbed tranquillity would be a reasonable bargain, so I shut up.

Next morning Christopher said goodbye to his wife, who was to wait in Tokyo, and we boarded a C54 and flew together to Korea at the start of a new adventure. At Taegu airstrip we separated to set out upon our first stories. I hitched a lift with some officers of the First Cavalry Division towards their front, while he got into a jeep with an Indian Colonel of the United Nations bound for another area. An hour later they hit a mine. Christopher was killed instantly.

Had he been able to do that deal with the Devil, he and his wife would have been exactly ten years in credit, minus one day. He was buried on a hillside above Taegu, near Ian Morrison.

After the well-regimented, almost gentlemanly war we had known in Sicily and Italy, I saw at once Korea was going to be something else: dirtier, more confusing, more uncomfortable, more frightening. There was no front line: every Divisional HQ was in as much danger as its forward company. As the American Army was to rediscover later in Vietnam, all an enemy soldier had to do to become a peaceful and invisible civilian was to hide his weapon, take off his jacket and walk through the lines.

Most of the first American troops hopelessly attempting to stem the invasion were 'Ginza cowboys' – young GIs from the occupation force in Japan, with little training and less discipline, unhappy and unready to fight. By the time I arrived the North Koreans had cut through them and almost reached the southern port of Pusan.

I went there to see the first British reinforcements arrive

from Hong Kong: two battalions, from the Middlesex Regiment – the Diehards – and the Argyll and Sutherland Highlanders. As the light cruiser *Jamaica* sailed into Pusan harbour, pipers of the Argylls stood playing on the gun turret aft. It was an emotional moment for those of us who had become used to being a part of a retreating rabble, to American officers and non-coms shouting orders – and seeing their men considering whether to obey or not. Now we heard regimental sergeant-majors bellowing at soldiers who stood to attention, quivering, before leaping into action. To beleaguered correspondents it was not only reassuring, but moving. One felt these two hard and professional battalions, their men lean and brown and cheerful after Hong Kong training, could see off the whole North Korean Army on their own.

We needed all the encouragement we could get, for the UN Police Action was proving a miserably dangerous assignment. There was no censorship, which paradoxically made the job even more difficult. In the well-organised world war we had just lived through, correspondents had the honorary rank of captain – with the US Army, colonel – and were fully briefed in advance. They knew what was happening and where, for their copy was censored before transmission – sometimes stupidly, but at least securely.

In Korea the Americans were operating a curious peacetime system: it was indeed as though we were crime reporters, checking at the Stationhouse to see what was on the blotter. Find out what's happening, if you can, and maybe we'll issue a handout. Some of the releases, written Madison Avenue style, had to be read to be disbelieved. It was like Ben Hecht's Chicago newspaper thriller 'Front Page'. We scurried around, checking facts, chasing scoops, running after leads, following tips, tricking each other. American papers printing news agency copy handed down from GHQ in Tokyo often captured places days before the troops, or held them long after they had been evacuated.

In a major amphibious landing behind the enemy lines, when thousands of American lives were in danger – and come to that, mine too – two of the three American news agencies discovered details of our battleplans and raced to get the news on the streets around the world *before* the invasion had gone in! The enemy had only to listen to the radio for advance information of the coming assault. Sitting in landingcraft we learned, along with the North Koreans, where we were going ashore. The Press was not popular.

The third agency, the International News Service, was for once more responsible and, though it had the story, also had the grace and wisdom to hold it until our troops had landed. Howard Handleman, their Bureau chief, almost lost his job for thinking of lives before leads. He received a furious service message from his New York office demanding, 'Are you working for the US Army or INS?' The war often seemed an unreal public relations exercise, by Errol Flynn out of Betty Grable.

After some weeks at the Front I had to return to Tokyo with an important story, for as a loner I had no base office to pass on my cables, and transmission was always haphazard. I set off at dawn from Divisional HQ, bumming a ride with some artillery officers. Of all the hardships correspondents suffered in Korea, that was one of the worst: no transport.

To write a story the event had to be covered, it had to be written and despatched – and it had to arrive. Lack of transport and reliable communication turned us into a scattered group of lone wolves wandering nervously, scrounging food, dossing-down where we could, and for ever begging lifts. Once we flagged down a six-wheeler as it hurtled towards us through the dust and when it stopped, clambered into the back – to find it full of corpses . . . Then we understood why the obliging driver had smiled like that.

There were three ways of getting a story away: we could use army signals which were slow and erratic and, not unreasonably, gave Press messages low priority. We could hand the copy to anyone returning to Japan who could be trusted to act as courier or – the only reliable method which I was that day adopting – we could fly back ourselves to cablehead. This entailed, with luck, a flight of some four hours in a desperately overloaded cargo aircraft, and a number of jump take-offs. Each flight used up too much nervous energy and too many of our rapidly-diminishing Nine Lives. The story needed to be a good one.

On our way to the airstrip that morning my Gunner friends called in at a section of their regiment which was operating two Piper Cubs as spotters, as aerial observation posts. They had an exciting short-lived role, for the enemy knew all too well what the little aircraft were up to, and they always attracted heavy counterfire.

I was offered a flight, and was too cowardly to refuse. We flew low along a ridge of hills where the pilot believed the enemy might be, looking for positions or artillery flashes. I was working out the map references of what we saw, being useful for once, while he radioed the locations. We waved at the second plane as it passed us to plot another valley. After an hour we turned south and my pilot put me down at the bigger airstrip, where I hoped to find a C119 of Combat Cargo Command to take me back to Japan. We were drinking canteens of coffee in the Operations hut when a radio message came in to say that our second plane had been shot down in flames.

'That's the fifth we've lost,' said my pilot, badly shaken. After a while he took off to fly back to camp, wondering I suppose whether he was to be the sixth.

I had to wait until the next day for a flight to Ashiya, where I filed my story, caught a train to Tokyo, checked in at the Marunouchi and slept for 18 hours in my tiny wooden bunk. Then, by popular demand, I relished the bath prepared by the cute little room girls. They all took great exception to the beard I was growing, crying 'Dirty! Dirty!' between giggles. Defiant, I just let it grow and swept down to the basement to experience one of those over-active Japanese shampoos which finish with you clinging to the chair while the barber pounds your spine with clenched fists. You walk out feeling cool, not to mention relieved.

When I strolled into the Press Room at Radio Tokyo I was spick-and-span and glowing as never before. The burly pinkish figure of Richard Hughes, Rabelaisian Australian who worked for *The Times*, looked up and stared at me with open mouth. 'My God,' he whispered at last, 'you're dead.'

In fact I was in unusually good shape. To disprove that feeling of wellbeing he showed me his story of my death, and supported it by the front page of the latest *Daily Mail*, which also reported my loss in action.

I was a statistic – and so young.

Apparently Divisional HQ had been informed that I was in the crashed plane. An eerie feeling, reading such a head-line above (I noticed with some irritation) a rather short piece.

The Tokyo Press corps took a deal of convincing I was still around; 'But we saw the signal,' they kept repeating with exasperation, 'and it was in the paper.'

In an attempt to dispel such widespread doubt, Dick and I went along to the Reuters cubicle where they were delighted to file a disclaimer saying Whicker believed, along with Mark Twain, that reports of his death had been Greatly Exagger-ated. We read it on the tape just in time: I was beginning to get that unworldly feeling.

To save ExTel despatching a replacement I filed my own Service which, since cables cost an exorbitant 1s. 1½d a word, said only: UNKILLED UNINJURED ONPRESSING.

SEOUL

Top of the Hit Parade on the Wild East show . . .

IT was war, all right. An old creaking Dakota with flapping wingtips, heavy overloading, bucket seats, parachutes and prayer. The pilot, I had just learned with a wild laugh, was the Catering Officer at Haneda Airport putting in the flying time required for his air pay. The navigator had been hurried out of some Quartermaster section for the emergency. Unskilled hands were guiding me back to Korea again, and Happy wasn't the word.

The Dak bounced and lurched its way across the Japan Sea like a Model T tackling a ploughed field, while I sat gingerly on a tin box of hand grenades. I was not feeling at home. I did not know how they were managing up in the cockpit, and I cared terribly.

By my side a colleague, a large Australian, was also quietly emotional. The day before, in stiff competition, he had craftily achieved the last place in a twin-tailed, bulbous-bellied C119 and, half way to Taegu, one of its two engines had expired. The Flying Boxcar, desperately overloaded, swung round and began to limp back to Ashiya, tilting suicidally. He passed the next hours struggling to push 500lb bombs out of its great backdoor, down into the drink. The whole expedition had made a deep impression on him.

In Korea every flight was an adventure, every safe landing a triumph. At that time war correspondents, always flying everywhere urgently, had the highest casualty rate in the UN Army. We did not care to be Top of their Hit Parade.

Our Dak teetered about over Pusan for a while and then thumped down on the landing strip, lurching clumsily through the dust. I descended on to Korea once again and patted the ground, thankful to have made it, and lugged my bursting valpack across to the Operations hut. Over it someone had written 'Pusan, airfield of Beauty and Hospitality.' A shimmering heat-haze hung over baked white dust. A pair of Shooting Star jets whistled furiously along the runway, wing-tips almost touching, and screamed up and away.

In the shade of an olive green tent hung a lister bag, bloated canvas full of warm and odorous chlorinated water. I half-filled my canteen, but spat out the first gulp and stayed thirsty. A jeep scurried by, churning up thick dust-clouds. I shouted after it, and tumbled into the back.

There were mud-hut villages every few miles along the sun-baked track, and skinny brown children with cropped black heads rushed out after us, flashing fine white teeth and

screaming for food. Women of indeterminate age padded
along the roadsides wearing the long-sleeved shoulder-
covering white garment which allowed pendulous breasts to
hang clear. Babies were bound to most backs, arms outflung
as if in despair, heads lolling sideways in sleep.

The yellow, arid fields were fertilised only by nightsoil, a
word then new to me. I should have stayed ignorant. The foul
malodorous stomach-turning reek recalled the Rome road
outside Naples during the war, when one small stretch
suffered an unbearably vile odour that reached out half a
mile. Drivers would take a deep breath and hold it, foot well
down, until the singing fields were in the past. In Korea, I
discovered, most cultivated fields were like that, or worse,
and breathing had become a hard habit to break. The stench
came from the droppings of each village, carefully collected
and stored over the months, when watered and spread out
under a blazing sun.

It was great to be back, I kept telling myself. I'm not
always very convincing.

The United Nations force which had gone in to support the
South Koreans had been beaten back so far it seemed it
would be thrown into the South China Sea. To restore the
position General MacArthur mounted a major combined
operation behind the enemy lines, landing 75,000 men of the
10th Corps on the coast at Inchon, near Seoul, the South
Korean capital, thus hoping to encourage the Eighth Army
in the south to fight north and join-up. For me it was Anzio,
all over again.

A marine and an infantry division went in first and their
landings were not hotly opposed, for the firepower the
Americans called down was formidable – even the heavy
guns of cruisers out at sea supported us. I was with the 1st
Marine Division, and they were splendid. Our first triumph,
after mere survival, was to capture Kimpo airfield south of
the Han River with its 6,000-foot runway almost undamaged. Then the buildup started: every few minutes during
daylight cargo planes landed and disgorged trucks, food and
ammunition on to the beachhead – and occasionally, wary
correspondents.

With typewriter on an ammo box, I knocked out my story of our slow advance from the beaches and into the mountains. The young pilot of a C119 who had promised to take it back to Ashiya stood reading over my shoulder, and making comments. Then it was his turn to perform, so I watched his Boxcar lumber uncertainly into the sky and head for southern Japan, where with any luck he would hand my deathless into the cable office.

It was only seven o'clock but already almost dark. Lights attracted enemy fire, so no nightwork was possible. I prepared for sleep.

American troops, knowing War is Hell, seemed determined to prove it. It had become effete to wash or shave, except heads, and their uniforms did little to help: in scruffy green fatigues they all looked like convicts or, at best, mechanics. So did the officers. It was a long way from our endless spit-and-polish. The scruffier you were, the worse you must have suffered so, by implication, the braver you had been.

A sort of inverse glamour grew up around discomfort. It went with the current in-phrase: 'We were shot to Hell.' This covered everything from one sniper's bullet to a barrage. We were *always* being Shot to Hell – and sometimes Pinned Down, with it.

After all those OCTU weeks spent stamping around the esplanade at Barmouth and being shouted at by military martinets if my creases were dented, I found it more natural to keep as clean and presentable as sleeping in ditches would permit. I even carried a pair of Italian red silk pyjamas, originally for sensuous comfort but later for defiance. There would be a stunned silence from the American Army when, weather and enemy action permitting, I climbed with some dignity into these and settled down luxuriously to earn my reputation as an eccentric English nut or 'some sorta Limey Lord'.

My only concession to War-is-Hell had been to grow the beard which so displeased those Tokyo room girls. This is something that every man has to do once, and its slow daily progress seemed to make my deprived life at the Front richer

and more meaningful. It also saved shaving in the chill dawn
out of a can of icy water.

However there's more to the romantic life of a war correspondent than cutting a dash. It was chow time, and I went
rummaging hopefully through the airfield desolation. In a
stray C-ration box, a can of frankfurters with beans and –
major triumph – a small tin of peaches. A delicate dinner
had been arranged.

Four rows of huts stood near the tangled skeletons that had
been hangars and terminals. One, relatively whole and
wholesome, had been allocated to the Press and evidence of
Communist habitation brushed out by chattering Korean
boys. These orphaned children picked up here and there by
friendly GIs became Americanised so speedily that within
days they were calling the Koreans 'gooks'.

After a swift dusting of DDT the place was practically a
honeymoon cottage. No windows or beds, of course, but a
good supply of sandbags. I spread some of these on the floor
and laid my sleeping-bag on top. Last clean handkerchief on
folded field-jacket for a pillow – and who could ask for more?
Not cosy, not even one-star, but above par for the war and a
great improvement on a damp ditch. I had just spent 18 days
without taking my clothes off, and was not expecting luxury.

While I ate my cold frankfurters, half a dozen other
correspondents in varying degrees of disarray and despair
converged upon the hut, and we began to settle down for
another night. Four United Nations men came in from
Tokyo, all pressed pants, shiny equipment and brand new
everything, and we made room. They were unpacking by
candlelight, doubtfully, when an Air Force Lieutenant
rushed in, breathless, and confirmed their worst suspicions.
He was shouting, 'Bad news, men!'

Resigned sighs from correspondents weary at being
pushed out of undesirable billets by noisy enemy action.
Silent terror from new arrivals.

'Last daylight air patrol reported 700 gooks heading this
way down the Kumpo peninsula!' He paused for effect. No
reaction. 'We got nothing to stop them – cooks and ground-
crews are on airfield defence right now. They're after the

Field. Anyone got weapons, have 'em ready. Don't show flashlights, don't smoke outside. We'll try to hold 'em off.' He went bravely out into the night.

It kept happening, and it was less amusing each time. Usually they were crying wolf, but now and then – and very bloodily indeed – they were not. Communists by-passed in our advance would move down from the mountains at night, put a match to a few trucks or planes, bayonet anyone in sight – and disappear like ghosts. Our sentries were, one could say, jumpy.

Life was even more worrying for British correspondents because we did not have the right outline. Trigger-happy American guards fired instantly at any shape approaching that was not wearing a GI helmet. Though that globular shiny silhouette could make the difference between life and a hail of bullets, most of us clung stubbornly to our various identities: I wore my old service dress cap with the gold and green 'C' badge. It had seen me through one war and was comfortable – though in the wrong company, highly dangerous.

Under the Geneva Convention it was also quite improper for correspondents, as neutral observers, to be armed; but having seen what happened to Pressmen in units overrun by North Koreans, most of us abandoned the Convention and opted to go down shooting. No point in being legally right *and* disembowelled.

I undressed, Korean style – that's to say, I took off my death-defying cap, and boots. With 700 gooks about to join us I could see this was not going to be a red pyjama night. I squeezed into my long narrow sleeping-bag. It fitted so tightly I often dreamed of pyramids, but it was cosy, and I zipped it up to the neck. A terrible scream shattered the night.

It was me. My virgin beard was caught in the zip. The silence was electric; they all lay wondering who had been bayoneted, this time. Slowly, I unzipped, wrenching out a useful strip. The pain has to be experienced. 'Relax, men,' I said lamely, eyes full of tears. They relaxed, muttering unkindly.

Concealed in my valpack was a guilty secret: a quart of Scotch, more rare in Korea than diamonds. I had been lugging that priceless liquid around for weeks, for use in some suitable emergency, and it was probably the only hard liquor on the entire Front. Now, with the enemy bearing down and a straight white furrow up the centre of my chin, seemed to be The Time.

In the sheltering darkness I wriggled my arms out of the bag and took a warm stealthy swallow. At that moment the door burst open and a large Master-Sergeant clumped in, flashing his torch. 'Someone shout?' he bellowed, waking everybody. 'Yawl all right?' The beam wandered questioningly around until it fell on me, rising out of sandbags and sleeping-bag with the whisky bottle clutched protectively to my breast. I felt like a Sabine woman.

The beam locked onto me and he came over: 'Got enough blankets, sir?' he asked, wistfully. 'Anything you need?'

'Yes,' I said firmly. 'No.' He hung around hopefully for a while, but this was war. I lay back and shut my eyes: the subject was closed. In Korea you don't even give whisky to your *friends*.

After he had slammed the door, muttering, the muffled breathing in the hut grew heavier. Opposite me one of the newer fellers, a UN Colonel, was thrashing about restlessly on the concrete floor. Before lying down he had grimly shoved one round up the spout of his carbine, remembering Custer, and propped the loaded gun against the wall, at the ready. Each uneasy movement clattered the magazine as he brushed against it. I could see what was going to happen: one of those turns would knock the thing over and I should receive the full discharge right up my sleeping-bag. I had a small sustaining swig of Scotch.

Abruptly, crashing through the night, came the imperative stutter of a machine gun, just outside. Rifles joined in. Our outposts had spotted something. The Colonel, remembering some old military maxim, struggled out of his blanket and began to pull up his trousers. Everyone else was very still. 'Good job we're lying down,' said a voice, unhappily. 'Smaller targets.' The Colonel lay down again.

The door was kicked open and a small figure stumbled in from the night, jabbering fiercely in a strange language. I was nearest, and reached for my .45 Colt. Safety-catches clicked off all round the hut. The figure stood in front of me, framed against weak moonlight. Weapons of every calibre were trained upon it and I knew that, even if they missed him, they would certainly not miss me . . .

Gradually it came to us – to me perhaps rather later than to my American colleagues – that the menacing figure was mouthing, not North Korean, but Bronxian expletives. Nothing was being deleted. It was a New York photographer and someone, it seemed, had taken his bedspace: he'd spread his roll, gone out to the can and now some sonofabitch, some mother was in his goddamned sack . . .

The firing outside dropped away along with the squabble and we relaxed, squirming for hipholes in the ungiving floor. Again and again during the night an uproar of firing left us lying tense and expectant while bullets hissed through the night, swishing away over the rice paddies. At each alarm I had to resist the inclination to leap up, and cower. There was nothing to be done, nowhere to hide. If the enemy reached the airfield all they had to do was chuck a grenade into each hut: no survivor would have lived through the panicky crossfire. I returned now and then to the Scotch, remembering my duty to leave nothing for the Reds.

Towards morning we were sleeping fitfully when the quiet was shattered by a long, awful gurgle: someone had screamed 'Oh, my God.' I braced and lay motionless, waiting for explosion or knife-blow. 'Oh, my God!'

I moved my eyes slowly, so as not to make a noise. By moonlight I could just make out a convulsed figure at the other end of the hut. Then, 'For crissakes, get to sleep.' It was not a prudent place to have a nightmare.

When morning dragged round at the end of the long noisy night I peered hesitantly out into the chill dawn. I was sure the ground would be piled high with enemy corpses. There had obviously been a nightlong pitched battle, for the US Air Force and GIs on perimeter defence had laid down enough fire to wipe out a regiment.

Not one body – not even a walking-wounded. It was like Brigadoon: everything had returned to normal. The only dead thing around was my whisky bottle.

PYONGYANG

Caviar and Champagne in the Russian Embassy . . .

NEXT afternoon I was lying on a hillcrest near Yongdung-Po, in the regimental command post of 'Chesty' Puller, a little fighting-cock of a Colonel who afterwards became No 1 Marine in Washington. We were watching his dive-bombers go over Seoul, street by street. Radio-controlled by forward troops, the Marine's own air force picked out with precision buildings just across the road from their own men. It was a Wild East show that restored confidence.

In the face of such overwhelming fire power the enemy was in retreat and their Command had pulled out of the Chosen Hotel, biggest in the capital. It was empty and relatively undamaged, so I wandered through the terraces and pagodas of its Eastern Gardens, looking for a place to write in comfort. Inside its dusty, deserted dining-room I sat alone amid the plush and through wide windows watched the street-fighting. It was Cinemascope, not war.

I told the few terrified servants who remained to warm my inevitable tin of frankfurters in beans, chop chop. They brought back the little red sausages on a delicate china dish, served with a deferential flourish. Encouraged by the potential of the place, I demanded a drink. Up came – of all things in that shattered Oriental capital – a Guinness. The situation required investigation, so I went down to the cellars.

There behind a heavy door was Aladdin's cave, bursting with priceless liquid.

There were hundreds of thousands of thirsty men in Korea and at that time, not a hard drink among them. Here the Communists had fled and left behind a cellarful of liquor, a remarkable stock built up over the years by this luxury hotel. In the midst of the desolate capital of a war-torn country – where six bottles of Scotch would buy a jeep, at least – stood shelf upon shelf of spirits and liqueurs, champagnes and fine wines . . . The custodian watched expressionless as I stood on tiptoe, wondering whether to have a bath in the glorious stuff or just get them to pour magnums of vintage champagne over my dusty head.

Then I appreciated the irony of it. There was enough drink within arm's reach to fill ten removal vans and this stupendous spoil of war was mine, all mine – but I had no transport. I had hitched ten miles from Kimpo to get the story, crossing the Naktong in an amphibious Alligator, and would have to get back that way too if I wanted to file and spend another nightmare night in that hut. My field jacket had only two bottle-sized pockets. Tomorrow the Head-quarters staff would arrive in the newly-liberated capital, taking over every useful building and posting sentries. It was now or never.

In anguish I roamed the well-ordered racks, searching for a selection I should not regret the rest of my life. There was every type of whisky and gin, rum, port, sherry, madeira, marsala, the whole range of aperitifs and beers in well-regimented lines. From Bordeaux a Château d'Yquem and a '28 Château Latour; a '48 Nackenheimer Engelsberg Riesling Auslee; the red Burgundy was Grands Echezeaux, the white Corton Blanc, both '37. All the best champagne years were there and the brandy was 50-year-old Magnier Grande Fine Champagne and Martell Cordon Bleu. There was Armagnac, green Chartreuse, anis, Kummel, Strega, vodka, Tia Maria, Maraschino, Vieille Cure, Benedictine, Kirchwasser, Barack, Grand Marnier, Van der Hum, Cointreau, Cseresnye – I could go on. I still wonder whether I selected the right two . . .

The HQ commandos arrived next day, on cue, and my Aladdin's cave of booze disappeared like a mirage. In exchange we got a number of new shiny generals, right up to the Ultimate Mikado and godhead, Douglas MacArthur. He flew from Tokyo for a triumphant entry and one of his ringing 'I have returned' declarations, aimed at the home market. His multi-starred descent upon the battle zone had been the ultimate Top Secret, Eat Before Reading.

It was of course as hush-hush as Coronation Day. Anxious senior officers with pigskin suitcases had already appeared, wondering how best to time the Press release for the Stateside editions. Hordes of Public Information officers materialised out of nowhere and I ingratiated myself by demanding, 'Where the hell were you when we needed you?'

They urged us towards a waiting line of 60 polished jeeps, with drivers. That did it. After months of hitchhiking around a war, correspondents mutinied. This agitated the PR regiment: they feared He would detect disinterest. 'He's got to be covered,' they kept saying, using the capital H. They had even – turning the knife – organised special transmission of our stories about the General. Not the war, mind you: the Declaration.

MacArthur's assumption of divinity had always infuriated the Press, as had his attempt to control news by funnelling it through preferred sources at headquarters and his attempt to expel from Japan 17 critical journalists, including Frank Hawley, Japanese-speaking orientalist and *Times* man.

His route from Kimpo to the shattered National Capitol building was being sprayed with disinfectant by six water-trucks. Guards stood at 25-yard intervals. Military police flown in to control the First Coming wore shining white steel helmets, like inverted chamberpots. Printed copies of the speech he was about to make were distributed: it dealt mainly with Almighty God and gave us the Lord's Prayer in full, which some tame correspondents later cabled home at 1s. 1½d a word.

After a suitable delay the General arrived, leading the awful Syngman Rhee, head of the venal South Korean government for which we were fighting. They looked like two crafty old men – which was not at all the way they saw themselves. As the celebration continued, spears of glass from panels of the ruined barrel roof of Rhee's parliament building fell on both well-dressed and weary-unwashed in the congregation below, like a malediction. The curious show bizzy ceremony with its flashbulbs and cheer-leading colonels ended in a final shower of glass. The Great returned to Tokyo and the bright lights, leaving us to our real life – and our war.

The enemy was still retreating north, so we shook ourselves and hitched a ride after them. The jeeps and PROs had vanished; they already seemed a highly-polished mirage . . .

With its remarkable logistical ability the US Army had pushed in overwhelming supplies and support, and the United Nations forces soon crossed the 39th parallel in pursuit of a defeated enemy. We had taken 120,000 prisoners, and put their casualties at 320,000. The imminent capture of the North Korean capital of Pyongyang seemed to signal total Victory.

All this was good news, but there was even better: I had transport! It was like winning the pools. I had liberated a jeep which the North Koreans had earlier captured from the Americans, who had probably junked it. We called her Alice. She was battered and war-worn and could not quite make top gear, but was good for 15 mph in second, and I always felt there might be low-ratio to fall back on in desperation. She went downhill beautifully. In Korea, Alice was a Rolls.

I found I had lots of new friends, and from the likely lads invited aboard Tommy Thompson who, with Randolph Churchill, had come out to replace Christopher Buckley, and Steve Barber of the *News Chronicle*. The three of us became quite celebrated among the troops as Alice lurched, wheezed and exploded her way around the Front, frequently breaking down but always recovering with the help of some amiable American, British or Australian mechanic who would emerge to get us going again, with tolerant disdain. We usually got shoved up hills, if only to keep the war moving, and once had a hair-raising tow from a press-on Brigadier who just did not know when to stop. There was another narrow shave when I had to fast-talk an impatient American tank commander who was about to push poor stalled Alice off the road and into a paddyfield. Upon my appeal he relented and gave her a sort of a nudge with his tank – and a nudge to Alice was as good as a rebore. Off we shot, waving hysterically.

Once while we were up in an OP watching the war, a wandering photographer actually tried to steal Alice. She would not perform for him, of course. It had taken me weeks of coaxing and affection to learn how to handle her funny little ways. We easily caught the swine before he'd gone 100 yards. What infuriated me was that he then asked for a lift . . .

One of the correspondents who was always welcome aboard was Homer Bigart of the *New York Herald Tribune*. He had a round innocent face, mild blue eyes behind glasses and a considerable stutter; but once he started to say something he would always finish, come what might – even if he lost his audience. His urgent warnings during mortar bombing and shelling always cheered me considerably, from my position facedown in the ditch. 'WWWW-w-w-w-watch . . .' Homer would begin earnestly, hearing the swish of an approaching mortar bomb. Then came the terrible crump. '. . . *out!*' said Homer finally, as we prepared to stand up again. He never managed to beat a bomb – but he always gave it a jolly good go.

At 10.45 on the morning of 20 October 1950, on the roadside nine miles south of Pyongyang, Alice finally gave up the ghost. A squadron of self-propelled guns in a hurry had edged her off the road, quite politely, but Alice was incapable of getting herself back. She had served us well, and it was not a bad end: with victory in sight, Alice died with her tyres on. RIP.

The first jeep to come by in a swirl of dust as we stood on the roadside, mourning, was driven by Colonel Holmes of the 1st Cavalry Division, so leaving poor Alice without a backward glance we set off for Pyongyang, to be in at the kill. With Gordon Walker, a good friend from the *Christian Science*

Monitor who was soon to die of cancer at 43, we went on foot through tanks hull-down on the river bank, crossed in a native boat and walked into the city suburbs.

There was some sniping, and anti-aircraft guns were firing on low elevation, but soon the streets grew quiet. The enemy was withdrawing. Armed Koreans wearing armbands ran out to shake our hands, indicating they were the Resistance, and guiding us cheerfully to the Russian Embassy.

Inside that mansion the first thing I noted (everyone's entitled to *one* weakness) was a crate of cans of caviar. The garden, we found, was littered with open tins flung away half-eaten by North Koreans. Then it dawned on me the kind of men I was fighting; damn foreign fellers with *no* taste at all.

To go with our trophy we located – you see what I mean about Whicker's Luck – some bottles of Hungarian champagne. A trifle sweet, but quite acceptable at that hour in the morning. Korean elevenses had never been so good.

Everything in the Embassy indicated a rapid departure; it was as though the Russians had just knocked off for a samovar of tea and were about to return. An hour later American Intelligence arrived and, attempting to blow open the Ambassador's safe, brought down most of the villa. By then the champagne was safely hidden and I was in the garden, munching caviar. The safe was empty.

We moved on to the Presidium and the office of Dictator Kim Il Sung, with its bust of Stalin. Our war had begun behind its heavy crimson-lined black silk curtains. Later we located a wandering group of American prisoners, just escaped from a train taking them north. Gaunt men with spectral eyes, they gulped army tomato juice, still shocked.

I passed my last night in Korea on the floor of that Russian Embassy, along with Dwight Martin of *Time*. We finished the caviar and champagne. It seemed a good note on which to end an awful campaign.

Next day I got a flight back to Kimpo and there scrambled on a dreaded C46 bound by stages for Japan.

The enemy armies had, it seemed, been destroyed or captured, and United Nations forces were advancing into the heart of the north. On 7 November General MacArthur declared the war had been 'brought to a practical conclusion'. He knew it, we were doubtful, the Chinese did *not* know it . . .

Three weeks earlier, on 16 October – a week before our tiny celebration in the Pyongyang Embassy – three of their armies had begun to move south across the frontier. The Chinese were not prepared to tolerate an American army – not even a United Nations police force – along their Manchurian border, so 200,000 men crossed the Yalu.

In Tokyo we knew none of this; even at GHQ it was impossible to discover what was happening. MacArthur's staff officers were baffled or uncommunicative. After his Victory communiqué they had airily dismissed reports of Chinese intervention: 'Just North Korean farmers returning home.' As it became apparent that these farmers were remarkably well-armed and organised, they admitted they could be 'aliens', and complained that the enemy had been 'surreptitious'. We allowed, it was certainly ungentlemanly behaviour.

In a typical Press release, the Commander of the Eighth United States Army, Lieutenant-General Walton H. Walker, complained: 'We naturally had hoped to find at least some semblance of truth in the public assurances of the Chinese Communist authorities that no formal military intervention had been perpetrated.' The indignation of this little roly-poly General who looked like a Michelin man in his GI winter-wear was soon silenced by a South Korean truck, which killed him when his jeep skidded. His place was taken by a more convincing figure, Lieutenant-General Matthew Ridgway, but in Tokyo tension continued to fray nerves.

Defensively, Public Information officers began to exaggerate the numbers of Chinese involved in the advance and it seemed to us that GHQ briefings were growing ever more imaginative. Michael Davidson, a waspish *Observer* man, administered the final blow by asking a Colonel at his arrow-covered map: 'How many Chinese battalions make a horde – or vice versa?' After that, briefings were cancelled.

Many feared we could be approaching the start of a wider conflict – even World War Three, when President Truman would unleash The Bomb. As we stood on the verge of the holocaust, when cool and considered statesmanship was imperative, we read that Truman had sent a furious letter to some obscure Washington critic called Hume, calling him son-of-a-bitch for criticising the piano-playing of his daughter Margaret. This was the man with his finger on the Button. We were aghast. An American news magazine's reaction was headlined: 'Let us pray . . .'

The flood of service messages calling us home had been increased by the abysmal state of US Army communications. To file my round-up I went to Eastern Telegraph; it was the only place where I knew for sure the cable would be in London within a couple of hours. In return they handed me a pile of anguished messages from ExTel: in past weeks few of my stories had got through. US Signals were so chaotic that despite the assurances of PIOs, most messages had been delayed, by operations or incompetence, until long after they were dead – then sent at full rate.

Behind our backs in icy Korea, which we had left so triumphantly and happily, the enemy had recaptured Pyongyang and Seoul and that busiest, dreariest airport in the western world, Kimpo. The UN Army was back where it began.

Despite all this, or perhaps because of it, the Tokyo Press corps continued to fly away. It was not a big story, any more. The world was as weary of Korea as we were. My recall was followed by Louis Heren of *The Times* and Tommy Thompson. Others were moving back to their normal stations or going south to look at the increasingly troubled situation in French Indo-China, which seemed favourite for the next upheaval. Gordon Walker drove me to Haneda with Randolph Churchill and gave us, Japanese-style, our farewell presentos; then we flew towards Mount Fuji and home.

Randolph, easily diverted by conviviality, had not been a spectacular success as a correspondent. Unlike his father he had little experience of the nuts-and-bolts of legwork in the field, of cabling and deadlines. I had on occasion stepped in at the last moment when he was overtired-or-emotional to write and file some *Daily Telegraph* piece for him; that may

have been why this choleric character was usually consider-
ate towards me. He was also something of a celebrity,
particularly among Americans, which could prove a hind-
rance for a working Pressman – though he rarely objected to
holding the stage.

'I can never win,' he once confided. 'If I achieve anything,
they all say it's only because of Father; and when I do
something badly they say "*What* a tragedy for the Old
Man . . ." '

We stopped in Hong Kong, where I bought an export
Humber for delivery at home, to avoid a waiting list of
several years on the UK market. Such were the idiocies of
Control. In Bangkok we saw some blue movies in a palatial
house of pleasure – appreciating the photography of the
Thais which was somehow delicate even in gross situations.

Socially, I relished Randolph on the rampage. He was
excellent and amusing company but always in a state of
suspended explosion. One thing you *could* say for him was
that he was as rude to Ambassadors as he was to waiters; he
made no nice distinctions.

After a brief spell in Delhi with Fred Sparks of the *Chicago
Tribune* – who had known poor Alice – I stopped off in Istan-
bul and was surprised to be fêted as a hero, once-removed.
The Turkish Brigade was fighting in Korea and I was the
first eye-witness to return with an account of Johnny Turk in
action. I told them what I thought was going on, back in the
icy mountains south of the Yalu, and then boarded the Pan
Am airliner that was carrying me to Frankfurt and home,
away from the cold and dirt, the discomfort and sudden
death of Korea.

I had warned my office the fighting was not over, though
did not appreciate that it had hardly begun – indeed the
Armistice was not to be signed until July 1953. Four years
later Kimpo Airport, that scene of our nightmares, was
opened for civilian traffic and air hostesses, as though it had
all never happened.

It was not the war we had won, it was only the Rehearsal;
but I had to abide by that editorial direction, so settled back
and accepted another glass of airline champagne, bravely.

EGYPT

Death from the Bougainvillaea . . .

NEXT year I returned to my birthplace, feeling rather sentimental after so many years away, and within minutes was sitting in a locked taxi besieged by a furious Cairo mob intent upon disembowelling me, at least.

They rocked and bounced the old Fiat while I sat inside behind locked doors, alone and thoughtful. Finally some ingenious chap hit on the idea of dropping a lighted match into the petrol tank. It was not exactly the homecoming I had expected.

In 1951 the Wafd party had been struggling for a year to drive the British out of the Kingdom of Egypt, and I had arrived to cover the situation growing daily more violent. The British Army had withdrawn its 80,000 men behind the garrison defences of the Canal Zone base, where terrorism and baying for blood continued. At Farouk Airport I had hired a taxi to carry me the 100 miles to Army headquarters at Ismailia, on the Canal, for a quick briefing. A cab was the only way to get there. We were passing through the Cairo suburbs when my taxi driver knocked down a child and, as always in those teeming streets, a mob gathered within seconds. When they saw I was British, all their worst suspicions were confirmed.

The driver, no doubt experienced at this sort of thing, instantly slipped out of the cab and disappeared. I, not totally inexperienced, locked all doors and sat looking casual in the dusty steamheat while they screamed, hammered on the roof and pressed furious faces against the glass, trying to get at the English murderer. None appeared to appreciate I had been born in Cairo.

When they wrenched off the petrol tank cap and began to strike matches, I could see this was going to be a hot story and, it appeared, my last. An Australian colleague, Ronnie Monson, had recently been killed in just such a situation. Egyptians do not go much for individual conflict, but they're very strong on mobs.

After a while I noticed the screamers and spitters were growing distracted, and saw two policemen with long staves beating their way through the crowd to find out what all the uproar was about. Their arrival led to a brief lull in the excitement. I lowered a window and, through the slit, gave them what encouragement I could; no one else was even faintly on my side.

This passing riot appeared to be routine, and the Law moved about cracking a few heads casually and without malice until the first fine frenzy of bloodlust had dissipated and the mob calmed to a rabble. It stopped hammering and rocking, but did not disperse.

The dead child, Exhibit A in the evidence, dusted itself down and limped away, abashed. My craven driver – who had doubtless been screaming and spitting with the best of them crept back, bowing and talking fast. At the end of our journey he got a *very* small tip, I can tell you.

Life spared, we set off more sedately towards the Canal Zone. This stretched from the Gulf of Suez north to Port Said, on the Mediterranean. The headquarters of British Troops in Egypt was at Moascar, a tree-lined camp outside Ismailia founded in the First World War, where my father had served. It had grown into a brave attempt at civilisation street lighting and chip shops amid the sand dunes.

The world's Press was converging upon Cairo for the Egyptian angle and the political story, and Moascar for the British and the action. An unknown Major called Nasser had told the *New York Herald Tribune* how Egypt intended to behave: 'Not formal war – that would be suicidal. It will be a guerrilla war. Grenades will be thrown in the night. British soldiers will be stabbed stealthily. There will be much terror.' It was not the welcome Mother had told me about.

The road from Moascar into Ismailia ran alongside a foul

turgid moat called, as you might expect, the Sweet Water Canal. It contained dead dogs and old bicycles, and was used for drinking and bathing; its banks were the local lavatory. Snipers within the Casbah would fire across at military transport using the road which in despatches we called, as you also might expect, Murder Mile. Another might-expect phrase at the time, I remember, was 'Death from the bougainvillaea'.

When the terrorism became insupportable the Army reacted, and we followed Centurion tanks into Ismailia. Their 20-pounders blew chunks off the Egyptian Police Headquarters, where the action was being organised, killing 46 and wounding 60. It was a noisy morning and revolutionary ardour cooled quickly. For a short while afterwards, fewer British soldiers were ambushed and murdered.

The position of the Press in the Zone was unusual: we were not accredited war correspondents because there was no war, so could not be offered WD accommodation or transport. However since we were patently not Egyptian and seemed to be more or less on their side, the Army were at least prepared to defend us, during normal working hours.

As Christmas approached they decided to move us out of sight and mind into the local United Services Club, which stood outside the camp perimeter. Some 20 members of the international Press – British and American, with a leavening of French, Belgians and Swiss – were formally escorted there by armoured cars. This may have been for our protection and to make sure they did not have innocent blood on their hands – or because they did not want us to escape into the desert. Having assured themselves the club's storeroom contained an adequate supply of tinned NAAFI sausages, the Army retreated with many expressions of seasonal goodwill to enjoy its holiday behind barricades, leaving us to face whatever the terrorists might have in mind.

We locked the doors behind them and, without much festive joy, got ready to repel boarders. It was a holiday that had no significance at all for the Egyptians lurking outside and, under those particular circumstances, not much for us. We had no transport and no communications so, no work, and resigned ourselves to the recreational facility available: a dartboard. Fortunately the bar shelves were weighed down with Star beer and some spirits, so the first game began with ascending merriment.

Then from the silent night outside a fusillade of rifle fire shattered all the windows – and much of our stock of good cheer. It seemed a poor start to the festivities. Some correspondents were cut by flying glass, but no one was hit. We lay on the floor in the dark, reflecting upon Goodwill to All Men.

When the shouting died down and Jacques Marcuse, from Agence France Presse, had spread cups around to collect dripping cognac, we put out the remaining lights and made a careful inspection. It seemed our floodlit dartboard was in a direct line of fire from the top of the minaret above the Ismailia mosque, and our unfriendly neighbourhood snipers across the canal had it firmly in their telescopic sights.

They evidently assumed we were some new military outpost, and were taking steps. It was only by the grace of Allah and an inborn and God-given lack of marksmanship that they failed to double-top us. This was *Christmas*?

Dismissing the idea of a white flag as asking for trouble, we gave them First Fall, deserted our bullet-ridden dartboard and retreated to the lounge at the back. There we embarked upon the longest poker game I have yet experienced: it went on for three days and nights. If Father Christmas had come down the air-conditioning we would not have noticed – unless he had the cash ready to ante-up and take a hand.

Players would drop out, literally, and climb back in again when they woke. I cannot recall who was the big winner, except that it had to be Tom Stone. He worked for Associated Press and had been a dealer at Las Vegas before deciding journalism might be an easier life. With an earful of glass, he now knew he had been wrong.

He once practised dealing cards in front of a mirror for ten hours a day, he told me, until there was nothing he could not do with a deck. To illustrate the double-shuffle he would warn us he was about to cheat, riffle while we watched, hawklike, let someone cut – and then not only deal himself the best hand but make sure there was a good second-best hand: no point in holding four aces if no one wants to play. He was the perfect illustration of Auntie's awful warning about Playing Cards with Strange Men.

Because of that fatal fluence he always passed the deal – such a formidable player was going to win anyway, but with fewer suspicious looks if he had not handled the cards. I just made sure I was sitting on his left.

As life turned out that marathon was the last poker I ever played; but it surely took care of Christmas by the Sweet Water Canal.

Afterwards the Army relented and decided in view of the attacks we could move within the security of the camp. They put some iron beds into a dusty schoolroom, and I moved in with David Walker of the *Daily Mirror*. The third man was James Morris of *The Times* – an attractive, rather prim young man who on assignment had already climbed most of Everest. He wrote beautifully: his first book on Venice is incandescent. He was later to go to Casablanca for a sex-change operation and became Jan Morris – still writing well but, curiously enough, not *quite* as beautifully.

During the months we covered the Troubles we assorted three lived without a cross word, though the strain began to show when we had to do our own laundry, for the Egyptians had withdrawn their labour. David Walker would write home to his mother for advice about getting shirts white in sun-warmed water with Army soap. After a lot of correspondence our dorm became so expert we decided to start a laundry when we got home and call it Mum Inc.

It seemed strange in so warlike an atmosphere to be able to peel-off and go into Ismailia for a drink at the Suez Canal Club, or to get a visa extended. The Egyptians were fighting the Army, they said, not British civilians, so the rules of the game were that we should not be attacked. We could not always rely on this.

Certainly their Consular office always gave us a hard time, but that comes naturally to Egyptian officials. Once, goaded beyond endurance by bureaucratic idiocy, I played my ace and reminded them triumphantly that I had been *born* in Cairo, so there. They did not wish to know that.

My life was even more complicated by the fact that within that British base I suffered the only major robbery experienced in a lifetime of travel. I have negotiated Mexico and India, Rio and Beirut without losing as much as a pack of cigarettes, but in a tight British security zone someone went through my possessions and lifted everything, including my passport – which was then a distinctive bound bundle of three. This made renewing my visa even more of a headache, for the Egyptians were convinced I had been dropped by parachute, at night.

Our military police and field security reacted with considerable calm, for the theft was perpetrated on a Saturday afternoon – you appreciate the fiendish cunning? Any afternoon would have been bad enough – but at the weekend! The British Army, which appreciates a well-ordered life, always shut tight from lunchtime to breakfast, emergency or not, on the principle that in the Egyptian afternoon it was far too hot to work in shady offices under electric fans – so everybody went out into the sunshine and played tennis or cricket.

Any constructive action on Saturday afternoon was, of course, unthinkable. The rare MP on duty was drifting about making sure no off-duty soldier had brown shoes without toecaps or was doing 22 mph within the Camp area.

Whenever correspondents went into Ismailia in those unamusing days it had become traditional to buy one piece of Egyptian porn from the eager vendors outside the French Club. This was Victorian, hilariously bad – even better when read aloud after dinner in the Mess. When I complained to the General that his police had been totally disinterested in my robbery, I suggested the thief was surely not foreign since he had taken the almost-English porn from our dorm. 'We are sorry you lost such important possessions,' he replied, ever so acid. Neither porn nor passport was ever seen again.

Our day-to-day coverage of the terrorism was also broken by one-off stories, like the court-martial of a corporal who had killed his wife's lover, who was also his sergeant. It seemed he was affected by the khamsin, the feverish Middle-

Eastern wind, and had become schizophrenic. We offered our escorting officers a new recruiting slogan: 'The Army makes a Manic of you.' They were highly unamused.

Outside Ismailia our main story was hotting up. In an anti-Christian frenzy, a Suez mob set fire to a Coptic church and beat up its caretaker. When that seemed inadequately hateful and violent, they stuck a meathook up through his chin and dragged him around town behind a jeep. Wearying of this, they found to their surprise he was still alive, just – and a Moslem . . .

In the streets of Cairo other mobs were coming out, so for a Correspondent that seemed the place to be. Ralph Izzard of the *Daily Mail* had arrived in Moascar to file an early story about the coming storm, and was glad of company on the return journey, for roads were dangerous and snipers active. His totally unsuitable car was a large green Packard convertible – hard to miss, even with Egyptian rifles that fired round corners.

We decided to cut across from the Canal Zone to the main Alexandria road – busier and safer than the little-used direct desert route. It was usually all right, we kept saying, going fast along an open road.

What we had not bargained for was that the Wafd Prime Minister, Nahas Pasha, had a large estate on that route. To discourage passing bomb-throwers, his police were directing all traffic into a wide detour which led us, with sinking hearts, directly through the centre of one of those teeming Delta towns where anti-British feelings were most intense. Its streets were so jammed we could only nudge our way along at walking pace. There had been no chance to put up the hood, so we sat bolt upright in the open convertible, unsmiling and staring straight ahead – and appreciating what was meant by Sitting Targets.

As we edged our way through the massed ghalabiehs I urged him, out of the corner of my mouth, not to knock down too many children . . . I've done that bit already, I said.

We reached Cairo's best hotel, the Semiramis, unharmed. It stood near the sanctuary of the British Embassy, but was located too far from any likely action. Shepheard's was full.

This upset me at the time – though I was soon to be grateful enough. I moved in to the elderly Metropolitan, in the city's noisy heart. It was convenient for the Middle East News Agency office and Tommy's Bar, a hole-in-the-wall owned by a tiny Englishman, a retired senior officer of the Cairo police called Hudson Bey and known, naturally, as the Fur Trappers Arms.

Cairo then had a curious atmosphere – a sort of polite hostility. In the street any European was watched silently; Marilyn Monroe was never followed by so many intense masculine eyes. It was hard to tell whether one was about to receive a salute, an *effendi* and an open palm – or a knife between the shoulderblades. There was generally some rude shouting. The braver sometimes spat. Villainous children merely wanted to polish your suede shoes, but if refused might spray them with goo.

Yobbos who normally respected females, at least, adopted the custom of standing before any European woman who ventured on to the streets and lifting their long ghalabiehs in an Arabian flash. After a defensive huddle the women found a useful phrase – a scornful Arabic 'Is that *all*!' delivered with a derisive jeer. The offensive habit was then dropped, along with the ghalabiehs.

Despite flies and dust, heat and aggro, the city could still be agreeable. In bars they continued to dip your glass into an icebucket before pouring the beer. At big Groppi's the chilled mango juice was the most glorious nectar I have tasted, before or since. The Semiramis roof, open to the moonlit African night like some filmset above the Nile, waited only for Astaire and Rodgers to come dancing down its stairs.

The Gezireh Club, about which I had learned at my mother's knee, remained an elegant oasis where disdainful Egyptian princesses sat on the poolside slab watching their uncles play chess, and sipping iced Stella. Once a British-only club, the Pashas' sons had come roaming around after the Army's withdrawal tearing down all notices in English – even flower names; but Egyptians cannot keep anger going any longer than we can, so the rich kids now shared the polo grounds and cricket fields with tolerant older members.

During this time the Wafd party was trying to get rid of the British – and the Cairo Free Officers Committee and Muslim Brotherhood were trying to get rid of the Wafd, along with King Farouk. A lot was happening and for an Englishman, it was all hostile. On the night of 22 July 1952 the officers, led by Major Gamel Abdul Nasser but fronted by an avuncular Major-General called Muhammad Neguib, took over Cairo. Only two soldiers were killed in that coup d'état, but it signalled the kind of noisy, murderous rampage Egyptian mobs so enjoy.

Seeing the Army and its guns safely back in barracks, the mob took over the streets, which became full of screaming fury. They put a match to Shepheard's and burned it to the ground. Then they turned on the Turf Club, bursting in to kill any available Briton. A number of elderly members were flung from balconies and disembowelled in the street below. The Club was then put to the torch. One English gentleman of 84 with a lifetime of service to the Egyptian Government stood to attention on a blazing balcony and died with dignity before a suddenly-silenced crowd.

I observed what I could of this, then fought my way back to the Metropolitan to try to phone the sickening story. While I was upstairs, struggling with operators, the mobs turned their attention to our hotel. At its entrance, four of the hotel's large Sudanese porters stood side by side at the top of the flight of steps leading from the street up to the lobby. They had 'Metropolitan' in white curved across their dark blue jerseys. The mob leaders rushed screaming up the stairway – and were promptly thrown down to the bottom.

The porters, large, fearsomely moustachioed and Army-trained, stood shoulder to shoulder, exhibiting that utter Sudanese scorn for Egyptians. The outraged mob sorted themselves out, gathered strength and ran angrily back up the steps again. The Sudanese threw them down again. This simple but emphatic action and reaction was repeated several times, until the mob decided they did not want to play that game any more, and moved off towards some easier target.

The lives of scores of us within the hotel had been saved by four porters who disapproved of unruly non-residents. The mob went on to do £40 million of damage to their own city.

Three days later King Farouk jeeped through the main streets of Alexandria with tears streaming down his face. He had already transferred most of his funds to Switzerland, so was not crying about *that*, but about his enforced abdication in favour of his son Ahmed Fuad. He wisely took that infant with him when he left for Naples aboard the royal yacht *Mahroussa*. He also took Queen Narriman and 204 pieces of baggage. He was not seen again, except in European night-spots.

I went to call on Neguib, President of the Free Officers Committee which ruled the land. He received me in his suburban home, ill at ease at being interviewed. He was not politically aware nor indeed particularly intelligent, but he smoked a pipe – so he could not be all bad. He also smiled like everyone's uncle and his eyes crinkled at the sides; he was patently a very nice man. His mother was Sudanese, which soothed Egypt's Southern border, and the sturdy reliable image of this career soldier was what the country then needed. However he was 50, while the average age of the Revolutionary Command Council which had organised Farouk's dismissal was only 33. In less than two years this father-figure was replaced by Nasser and under house arrest. That pipe had not been enough.

In Cairo a tubby Egyptian army captain broke the red door seals on the entrance to the Koubbeh Palace, the ex-King's winter home, and in triumph showed me round the Committee's prize capture. In its Treasury, protected by four-inch steel doors and invisible rays, I saw a collection of priceless jewels and tasteless junk. In the King's suite, puerile pornography – and cherished childish letters from his daughters. In the leather-bound library massive tomes – and by his bedside, Western pulps. I ran my hands through drawerfuls of jewels, medals and gold coins – and on my way out, hurrying back to my slightly-scorched hotel before curfew, was carefully searched.

I decided that on reflection, whatever life had been like in my father's day, it was no place for *my* retirement – a decision I have had no cause to regret.

The day after my return from the chaos of Cairo, my first assignment was the funeral of the matinée-idol, Ivor Novello. This time the mobs I was braving were made up of stricken middle-aged women mourning the loss of that charming theatrical homosexual, the soulful King of Drury Lane's Ruritania.

I caught the tube to Golders Green, fearing my descriptive powers might be unequal to the emotion of the occasion, and stood among a vast and tearful crowd at the Crematorium. Over loudspeakers flowed 'We'll gather lilacs in the spring again'. I could not see anyone who was *not* crying and, recalling his friend Noel Coward's potent phrase, surrendered to a surreptitious gulp or two myself.

Fleet Street offers a rich and varied life . . .

ROYAL TOURS

Why don't we try that chap Whicker . . .

As news agencies, ExTel and PA had Court correspondents – Louis Nicholls and Louis Wolff – who travelled with the Queen's entourage. The Two Louis grew more Royal than the Royals: black suits, bowlers, brollies and lots of regal 'we'. Fortunately *our* Louis disliked foreign travel, so I covered many Royal tours.

Nigeria had not achieved Independence in 1956 when the Queen and Prince Philip flew out in the Royal Argonaut. At Ikeja Airport they were greeted by the Governor-General and dignitaries, but stayed longest with a giant figure who set the mood of the tour: Chief Festus Okotie-Eboy, Federal

Minister of Labour. He wore a jaunty straw boater with two-foot red and white plumes rampant and a 30-foot train of purple and yellow silk. He had absolutely no competition.

Nigerian crowds relished the occasion and called her 'Mrs Queen'. When my stories were printed with that happy title in the headline the Authorities were indignant, seeing in the colloquialism a reflection on their dignity. It was an early experience of the sensitivity of new nations. She was in fact their *Oba Obirin* or King-Woman – but that would have been harder to shout.

That autumn I travelled with Princess Margaret on her five-week tour of East Africa and Mauritius. She flew in an aircraft of the Queen's Flight, while we followed in a chartered DC3 of East African Airways. I was working against Reuters' Sandy Gall, now the ITN newsreader; with Sylvia Lamond, an enchanting girl from the *Sunday Express*, and a dozen others. We were a jolly planeload. The *Daily Express* man, David Wynne-Morgan, was running the William Hickey gossip column – which suggested Fleet Street was not taking the tour too seriously.

Two years before the Princess had lived in and out of the Peter Townsend affair; a lonely little figure, she was already brandishing that conflicting blend of regal impatience and chummy amiability that made it hard to know how to react to her approaches. Only the Governor-General of Tanganyika, Sir Edward Twining, had the secret. A natural comedian with handlebar moustaches, he was amusing and amused, and for once the solitary Princess could enjoy those long official banquets.

The tour finished in Kenya. We called the capital 'an equatorial Ealing' and it was there I first heard the question 'Are you married – or do you live in Nairobi?' Princess Margaret, an emphatic double-negative, joined 8,000 people at a Government House garden party without much enthusiasm, then retired to bed with tummy trouble.

On the way home from Australia at the end of their long 1954 Commonwealth world tour, the Queen and Prince Philip were joined in Gibraltar by Prince Charles and Princess Anne, who had sailed out aboard *Britannia* on their first foreign jaunt. I remember going up The Rock with the Royal children to take a look at those scrofulous apes upon which British occupation is still believed to depend. They had the unnerving habit of leaping down upon visitors and grabbing anything that seemed interesting or could be eaten. In his sailor suit Prince Charles, who was five-and-a-half, hid behind his Nannie, plainly terrified. Princess Anne, not quite four, was totally unperturbed and scampered with delight among the loathsome monkeys, most of them bigger than she was. It was the first display of her appreciation of animals which in later years was so to pique the British Press.

Such Royal tours were for me an enjoyable wind-down in Fleet Street. For years the agency had been drawing in its financial horns, and foreign assignments were becoming rare – though I was fortunate enough to go on a 5,000-mile tour of the United States. It was my first large bite at that marvellous country, and concluded in the Waldorf Towers with ex-President Harry Truman.

After the Emmett-Dunne murder trial in Dusseldorf, I covered the usual run of home assignments, which included Holloway Prison the morning they hanged poor Ruth Ellis. ExTel now began to cut its losses. First it closed all foreign bureaux, then dropped its whole overseas service, cutting off in one cruel blow all my overseas travel – and changing my life. The home news service continued temporarily – but a few years later ExTel was to kill its entire news department, and later still grow prosperous as a multi-million-pound information services group.

In 1956 I became its Diplomatic Correspondent, which sounded splendid but really meant catching a No 11 bus to the Foreign Office every day, sitting-in at 'the circus' – an untidy briefing – and going to a number of stunningly dull cocktail parties on National Days.

Late one afternoon the news desk called : 'Go to Westminster – Kim Philby's got something to say.' In Parliament the master spy had just been officially cleared of accusations that he was the Third Man in the Burgess and Maclean triumvirate. He was triumphant, as well he might have been – having deceived the incompetent machine of Government yet again. As he gazes sincerely and honestly at the cameras, I sit amid a maelstrom of photographers. It is happening long ago – for I am smoking; in such trivial ways are significant events recalled.

To occupy unaccustomed free time I took on more free-lance work for magazines and radio, and wrote a number of short stories. I even produced a novel based on post-war Venice and Vienna; it was published with a well-deserved display of disinterest. The title, though, seemed rather good: *Some Rise By Sin*. It was lifted from Shakespeare, as are all good titles – a relevant passage from *Measure for Measure.*

I had for years written for *Men Only* – not the soft-porn disgrace it became, but then the British *Esquire*. This splendid little monthly had been founded in 1935 and incorporated Sherlock Holmes' own magazine *The Strand*, and later, *London Opinion*. It was edited by the brilliant Reginald Arkell, who wrote *1066 and All That*. Among other regular contributors: Negley Farson, Lord Hailsham, S. P. B. Mais, Alec Waugh, A. P. Herbert . . . Excellent value for 1s 6d, and to be found in every mess and wardroom. Going aboard some warship in Eastern waters I was always nonplussed to be asked: 'Does *Men Only* often send you abroad?' In fact I was working 18 tumultuous hours a day as an anonymous agency correspondent and spending one half-day a month on a light-hearted piece of nonsense for that magazine – but it had disproportionate impact. Even today, after 25 years of total exposure on television, I still run into people who puzzle over my name, wrinkle their brows and ask, 'Er – weren't you the chap who wrote those funny bits in *Men Only*?' I am always greatly flattered that such ephemeras should be remembered; none of my more serious work is . . .

So as ExTel wasted-away I took on more radio commissions, writing and broadcasting for At Home and Abroad, Woman's Hour, Town and Country.

Then during a newspaper strike a bright young BBC producer, Ronnie Gibson, asked if I could handle a nightly radio programme he planned to call Going Places, Meeting People. He was engaging various presenters to use the relatively small EMI L2 recorders and assemble a fast-paced chatty taped programme. Today it would be commonplace; then it was revolutionary. For interviews away from the studios the BBC had been accustomed to despatching great Humber limousines filled with mountains of gear, and recording on to discs.

Regular broadcasters like Wilfred Thomas were to be used, supported by a couple of outsiders: Tom Driberg, the brilliantly original William Hickey, future MP and, it was said, homosexual spy; and me – heterosexual correspondent of no fixed abode. Gibson later found to his surprise that the newcomers won by far the highest rating from the listeners' Reaction Index.

Unfortunately for his career, this clever and inventive producer was a few years ahead of his time. He had ginger hair, a loud voice, loved opera and football and was the only person I have met who laughed the way they do in the cartoons: Ha-ha-ha-ha . . . The BBC was fast approaching the end of its stodgy Reithian Civil-Service era, but Gibson was new-style and too impatient and tactless with the departing Old Guard. He peaked too early and, as in everything else in life, timing is All.

The Head of Talks, an academic who lived at Maidenhead and each day travelled first-class to Paddington with his *Times* and took a cab on to Broadcasting House, fired his wrath by declaring, 'The trouble with you, Gibson, is that you don't understand the working class.' After many rows this product of the terraces at Craven Cottage and the Scala at Milan was manoeuvred out, and went off in a huff to New York. A few years later he would have headed the young lions bringing new vitality to the Corporation.

To help us on Going Places there arrived a young trainee just down from Oxford, dark and intense. He loafed around thoughtfully in his camelhair coat, noting everything. Somehow he seemed promising – and so he proved: today Alasdair Milne runs the whole shebang as Director-General of the BBC. When he left our little programme he went over to television to help Donald Baverstock start an early-evening interview series called Highlight.

In those days it was seriously believed parents would never get their children to bed if television remained on tap, so both BBC and ITV went off the air between six and seven for the Toddlers' Truce. Commercial television, then struggling for financial survival, soon realised how much income it was losing by abandoning that fertile hour and agitated for continuous transmission. When it was granted, ITV could produce no new programming but fell back upon fillers and old cartoons. The BBC, however, had a very definite idea: it was going to expand Highlight into a 45-minute magazine programme and call it Tonight.

Baverstock had Cliff Michelmore, Geoffrey Johnson Smith and Derek Hart ready for the studio, but needed new faces on-camera. Milne remembered the radio programme on which he had cut his teeth a year before and suggested: 'Why don't we try that chap Whicker . . .'

PART FOUR

CUE WHICKER!

TONIGHT

Why not do it in Flames, like Everyone else . . . ?

My very first television programme involved travel. I went to the near-East: Ramsgate.

I still have the *East Kent Times* photograph of my talk with one of the seaside landladies who featured in that early investigation into their seasonal livelihood: Mrs Evelyn Stone, from 45 Grove Road. Her pet poodle Candy had a new red and blue coat for the occasion. Behind us in Nelson Crescent, overlooking the sea, a sight that surely dates the picture: a bombed building.

Next to the bulky old Mitchell camera that took two men to position, a saturnine Antony Jay is directing. I had to finish the report with my first piece to-camera, talking confidentially to no one. 'It's either the easiest thing in the world to do,' said Tony, 'or the most difficult. Depends on you.' I was paid 15 guineas for the interviews, plus ten guineas for research, and did not appreciate that 19 March 1957 was for me the start of Something Big; yet somehow that report did not set the world on fire – not even Ramsgate.

I could not evaluate its impact, since I never saw it. I was working when that first of thousands of my programmes was transmitted – indeed in those days was always too busy to watch. I appeared on television for another five years before I gave in, bought a set – and got hooked, along with everyone else.

So in Ramsgate I dipped my toe into television; the experiment had gone reasonably well and led to further assignments. I was delighted, for this new direction felt exactly right. Here was something I believed I could do, given the chance, and relish doing. Though aware of my limitations, I was an experienced reporter who could recognise a story and write fast. I had travelled the world, knew about directing and cameras and, though certainly not good looking, was at least neat and not noticeably shy. Most important of all, I enjoyed people – indeed I remain the only person I have ever met who truly delights in other people's holiday snaps.

During the following spring months I worked on in tandem, reporting as usual for ExTel and, when it could be managed, freelancing for Tonight. Something had to give, and it was obviously going to be the newspaper business – though after ten good years I hesitated before the final break. My agency's contraction had been an early warning of the woe that was to descend upon Fleet Street – while across town in Lime Grove, television could be seen preparing to take off. Our 'Street of Adventure' was running West, from EC4 to W12. I decided I should go that way, too.

My final move across was caused, curiously enough, by the very programme I was about to join. Tonight had asked me to go to Hastings where, at a summer conference, the Shipbuilding and Engineering unions were agitating for a 40-hour-week. Disentangling traditional jargon, I filmed conversations with chairmen and general secretaries on a windy pier. It was an interesting day, and went well; but while I was returning to London, Tonight with its usual enterprise was interviewing a murder suspect. His dramatic story of a killing was heard with fascination by the watching millions. Had I been back in Fleet Street in time I should have been one of them, observing professionally and writing the story, for Tonight was already an important news source. I had made complicated arrangements to be covered during my absence, but unfortunately the only unpleasant man I met during ten years in Fleet Street was that evening on the news desk. He complained noisily about my late arrival. There was a small uproar. Philip Burn, the editor, was piqued: ExTel had already suffered one bad experience with television, he said. A promising sports sub – Peter West – had been lured away by those same bright lights, and he did not want to experi-

ence such fickle behaviour again. I was deeply in the dog-
house.

Afterwards the two sub-editors handling that story came
up and told me they knew the true situation and if 'that little
creep' was intent upon creating mischief, they would resign.
I was touched. Fleet Street was a jungle in which jobs were
not easy to obtain, and they were in no way beholden to me. I
told them on no account to quit on my behalf for I was
considering packing my notebook and heading West to try
my luck on the new-fangled frontier of television.

So Tonight projected me towards Lime Grove rather faster
than I had planned – and it was the best thing that ever
happened to me. I had been nudged over the brink by the
little creep – who later also left Fleet Street for the PR office
of some Civil Service department. I did not wish him ill but I
did wish those two subs well, and indeed they soon went to
their just reward.

One of them, Leslie Thomas, then wrote *Virgin Soldiers* and
other best sellers; Ted Duggan got a splendid job running
BOAC's Far Eastern Public Relations in Hong Kong and
married a lot of Chinese girls. Years later I was able to thank
both of them publicly when This Is Your Life devoted a
programme to Leslie. It is always a joy when good blokes
succeed and good deeds are found out.

Tonight became the first successful magazine on television, and wrote the grammar for all such programmes that
were to follow. Originally transmitted at 6.05 every evening,
its 40 crowded minutes changed the eating habits of the
nation. Furniture manufacturers told me the sales of coffee-
tables suddenly increased astronomically, for upon coming
home from work everyone wanted to settle down to an
evening meal in front of that cheery gang on Tonight, where
something was always happening. The programme soon had
seven, then ten million viewers – enormous figures in those
early days. ITV had gone on the air 18 months earlier to
200,000 viewers in London, but still did not cover the nation;
it offered The Flintstones and pallid Tonight copies
only to London, Birmingham, Manchester and Yorkshire.

Donald Baverstock and Alasdair Milne ran Tonight – a telling partnership. Donald was the catalytic agent: a wiry little Welsh terrier, permanently excited and overflowing with ideas and opinions, an outpouring of well-rounded conviction. He was rude, he ranted and raged and frightened everyone, but inside – marshmallow. Alasdair was his opposite: quiet, charming and concerned, but inside – granite. Grace Wyndham Goldie sat upstairs with the Brass, protecting the venture of her young tigers. Tony Essex was a skilled editor and the only one of us who then knew much about film. Other originals included Tony Jay, a writer of some brilliance, Cynthia Judah, a distrait and dissatisfied girl, and the ebullient Gordon Watkins from *Picture Post*.

Cy Grant got us on the air every night with a topical calypso, often written by Bernard Levin. Cliff Michelmore proved the ideal frontman – everyone's jolly bumbling uncle. He had a happy homelife down in Reigate with Family Favourites presenter Jean Metcalfe and their two children, and the nation worried when he caught a cold. There was Geoffrey Johnson Smith, a clean-cut tennis-anybody blond in a blazer who later went into Parliament and became a junior Minister; Derek Hart, tiny and puckish and – far more significant – Mrs Dale's nephew Bob. There was Fyfe Robertson, beard bristling magnificently, an avenging John the Baptist brandishing a stick-mike at recalcitrant officials. Gilbert Harding called him the Saint of Sauchiehall Street. Along with Fyfe, I was mainly on film in the early days as a sort of jaunty, inquiring man-about-the-world. Slim Hewitt came in as a cameraman, but went on-screen to deliver lugubrious Cockney-sparrer pieces written by Tony Jay. Macdonald Hastings, Trevor Philpott and John Morgan joined the team, then Polly Elwes, Kenneth Allsop, Christopher Brasher and after five years, Julian Pettifer. All were freelances.

I remember once answering the phone in some office and noticing upon the desk an internal memorandum from Leonard Miall, then Head of Television Talks. It had been decided not to offer those who appeared on-camera Staff jobs, he wrote, since when their usefulness was over 'they can easily be dispensed with'. I clutched the desk. It seemed only a matter of time before we were all put down.

The object of the producers of this regular programme was not only to provide attractions to encourage viewers to switch on but, even more important, to remove irritations. People who come into your home every night should not antagonise, should not have any maddening on-screen habits, however trivial. Many reporters came and went, usually finding the work far more difficult and intensive than it appeared, and the fierce internal criticism too hot to take. A not very pleasant man from the *Daily Herald* did a couple of so-so film reports and was outraged when Baverstock told him he would no longer be used: 'To tell the truth, boy, you just don't have the humility.'

The infuriated reporter grabbed Baverstock by the lapels: 'What!' he roared, shaking him. 'Humility's one of my *best* points!'

We all worked, the rough with the smooth, in a rabbit-warren created by the BBC out of the artisans' terraces stretching along Lime Grove from the vast Gainsborough film studio of the Thirties, like dinghies tethered to a mothership. Walls had been knocked down and the houses interlocked. Baverstock and Milne, as producers, had the Front Room of one of the houses; my office was the Scullery. It was quite cosy and I did not take my below-stairs position to heart. I was later promoted to a First Storey Back. If you wanted anyone you went into the hallway and shouted – except with Mike Tuchner, a particularly nice but noisy director: for him you would go into the hall and *listen*.

So we ploughed along from night to night, learning by doing and creating the rules of the game. There was no one to copy. The fast-paced blend of film and studio was revolutionary – though by present standards as rudimentary as the equipment. We had no Autocue, without which none of today's fluent Stars would dare approach a camera. If we needed such a crib it was typed out in jumbo print on a piece of cardboard and clipped under the lens – which often meant talking to-camera but looking to-floor. For film reports the BBC was still using its double-camera, a homemade monster the size of a refrigerator which two or three cursing men would struggle to heave up on to a tripod. The Corporation was still working on magnification, not miniaturisation. On my first world tour we had no zoom – the basic lens without which no cameraman would today leave home.

Where we were fortunate was that to the viewer, as to us, everything was new – a blank canvas upon which we could draw. When I strolled along Change Alley in Singapore, beating off persistent stallholders while trying to talk to-camera and reach the open street without buying anything, it was an unexpected look at a new world. So was eavesdropping Fyfe haranguing some self-important dignitary on our behalf. Even our short studio conversations had unusual point, because for the first time the television interview was being studied, considered and up-graded. Before Tonight, BBC reporters would approach any Brief Authority with a deferential and thoughtless, 'Is there anything you'd care to say, Sir?' With no BBC tradition behind us, we set out to be pertinent, informed, polite – and not easily put off. In a four-minute situation we had so little time it was imperative each question carried the interview along and produced a revealing answer.

Every afternoon, as soon as we knew who was in the studio that night, the interviewer and a programme assistant would settle down for four hours to read about the subject and work on those few questions. It was the first time such consideration had gone into what came over, hopefully, as casual conversation. The interview had once been a filler not thought to require preparation. An interviewer might scribble a few notes on his palm as he went into the studio – and doubtless produce from his subject desultory waffle which short-changed the viewer.

We liked questions to stimulate, to have bite; they did not need to be aggressive, complicated or even profound to penetrate. A light-hearted reaction could also be telling. I remember once talking to a circus performer who had achieved some stunning and unique feat – probably diving backwards, bound and blindfolded, from a very great height down into a small bath of water. He was prepared for much-deserved congratulations, but since what he was doing was patently impossible I merely wondered, 'Why don't you do it in flames – like everyone else?' *That* got him going.

Even the best-considered questions could be deflected by skill or bloody-mindedness. In an early interview on High-light the saturnine Indian Foreign Minister, Krishna Menon, had replied to every one of Cliff's queries with a monotonous, 'That question is not couched within the framework of my thinking.' When I came to interview him we struggled to ensure he would not escape into such haughty dismissal. His performance under polite pressure was fascinating and revealing. As we went downstairs afterwards in the rickety old Lime Grove lift he studied me thoughtfully and said, 'English television is getting like American.' I was not flattered but I saw what he meant – that politicians seeking publicity on the screen were no longer being given the easy ride to which they had become accustomed.

At some time most people of passing interest from this country and abroad appeared on one of our 2,000-odd programmes. We once thought of creating a Tonight tie or handkerchief for our many thousands of Old Boys and Girls. They were a remarkable group: Prime Ministers and prosti-tutes, bishops and bandits, the known and the unknown coping with a little brief fame, and usually enjoying the experience before a total weekly audience of some 40 million who watched our four hours of live television.

Tonight came on the air as a makeshift without much money or support; it grew into a television triumph. For some reason its pioneering, irreverent chemistry worked: the hu-man formula seemed to provide the right blend of stimula-tion and amusement. It had a strong but informal style that is hard to define; without it the programme would have been a mere jumble of bits and pieces. Each night something for everyone – and should you not be interested, wait a minute.

Two or three people in the studio or down the line, a couple of film reports from home or abroad, an outside broadcast, a little music, some significant film – a kaleidoscope and, a quarter of a century ago, totally new and a lot of fun.

All of us who jointed in the Tonight experience look back

upon those eight years with enormous affection as, I hope, do the regular viewers we would greet nightly. They may remember Cliff's familiar sign-off: 'Goodnight – and the next Tonight is . . . tomorrow night.'

BRITAIN

Cosmic messages by Moustache . . .

So Tonight, and my television life, set off at full speed. Every day I was out filming somewhere in Britain or, if at Lime Grove, writing and recording commentary over mute film in the afternoon and interviewing live in the studio during transmission. After the programme and the fierce post-mortem in the BBC club, I would get home to my Richmond Green apartment – and crash; yet as part of a winning team, every day was an invigorating experience, not work.

We began in those exploratory days by attempting film reports on the kind of people who had then not been seen on television. I spent days with the Bunko boys flogging plastic rubbish from suitcases in Oxford Street, watching them build up the crowd with ricks, do some fast and dubious transactions – and scarper at sight of the Law. I went with them to buy their kitch rubbish at East End warehouses, lent them money after a bad day, resisted playing cards with them, heard their view of the punters in the Straight world upon whom they preyed, mildly.

We covered a conference of Private Eyes held off Chancery Lane – but still a long way from Raymond Chandler. We looked at sharp kerbside car dealers in Warren Street, down-and-outs under Brighton Pier, all-in wrestlers, cross-channel swimmers, pawnbrokers, bodybuilders, hop-pickers, science fiction writers; all came over as interesting people – the object of that nightly investigation.

We introduced vox pops – vox populi, the voice of the people – by stopping passers-by at random and getting their views on some relevant topic, usually light-hearted. It could be influenza cures – or the Budget. New Year resolutions – or how to spend a £1 million note. We would set up the camera on Shepherd's Bush Green or in the City – Royal Avenue in the King's Road was a favourite of mine – and PAs would ferret out likely subjects with anything amusing or surprising to say. In those days television was new and exciting, and almost everyone was flattered to be asked. Advertising agencies soon picked up and over-used this pithy and easily-edited form of comment, and nearly a quarter of a century later the BBC's That's Life reintroduced it as an innovation (Care to taste bat stew?) and got pinched, not for plagiarism but for obstructing the pavements in Fulham.

I sat in St James's Square with Heather Jenner considering the first marriage bureau and meeting a number of her supplicants; the mating game, then quill pens and five guineas a go, was a far cry from the slick computer-dating we considered later – though the same sad lottery. We looked at London's very first parking meters, an ominous line marching down Spanish Place in Marylebone. It was September 1957 and passers-by stopped and wondered what were those strange things along the kerb? I went to an elocution class in Birmingham where they were learning to neutralise that accent, to Maestag to sample the inner-warmth of life in the valleys, and the less-warm Welsh Sunday; BBC overnight subsistence, two guineas.

We reported on the winemakers of Whitchurch in Hampshire – enthusiasts who brought their finest vintages into Andover, spread them around us, and enthused. A young mad scientist aged about 16 showed me how to age wine instantly in some fiendish way I have fortunately forgotten. Normally when we finished filming and said 'Wrap!' our crew would be heading for home within minutes; that night, as merry winemakers urged us to finish everything in sight, they settled back bravely to do their best. The wine, which we learned could be made out of anything including old boots, was insidious. We heard of one vicar who, after obliging politely at a lengthy tasting, had been found at four in the morning with a silly smile on his face – asleep in his own graveyard.

The nightly parade continued: big game hunters, finishing schools, dogs' beauty parlours, butlers . . . We unearthed one marvellous Cockney whose task in life was to clean the Albert Memorial. I passed a strenuous Saturday with some long-distance walkers, pounding along beside them with a stick-mike as they went heel-and-toeing through Middlesex, swinging their elbows and panting. In each breathless interview we both looked pretty damn ridiculous. In the kitchens of the Dorchester Hotel we watched the orderly chaos of Christmas preparation, sitting in the Master Chef's glassed cubicle; I noted the discipline was army-strict, the Chef living high on the hog and terrorising the Other Ranks. I went down to Porchester to investigate a tannery stench that was stunning the neighbourhood and discovered it was called the Wicor. Endless fun out of *that* one. 'When the wind's in the East,' they said, 'you can smell Wicor for miles . . .'

In Fulham we considered a slum clearance off Lillie Walk: rows of tiny terraced cottages, pitifully primitive and without indoor sanitation or adequate running water. After we had filmed in those Dickensian surroundings the residents were moved from their archaic hovels to spanking new Council flats – and hated them. Lillie Walk had been a warm and totally enclosed community: 'We was all one.' Now they were in high-rises with enormous windows which required too much curtaining, the kids were out of sight and off the leash, the neighbours toffee-nosed and no one dropped in or cared.

Children of course provide marvellously natural television. At a school in South London we filmed a group of juvenile gardeners. One young expert aged about five told me at length how he was preparing and planting some delphiniums. His enthusiasm was enchanting, so our director, Elizabeth Cowley, set up the camera and asked him to tell the nice gentleman what he had just said, all over again. We prepared to film the conversation and I approached the young horticulturist again, squatted down and asked, 'What are you doing?'

'I'm having my picture taken,' he said, accurately.

At Haslemere Museum we watched the unwrapping and postmortem of its oldest inhabitant: Pa-Er-Abu, a 2,300 year old Egyptian mummy who had been resting in Surrey and exposing his embalmed toes since 1912. The X-Ray revealed a most unfortunate death: a broken jaw, damaged teeth, injured ribs. It seemed probable that 26-year-old Pa had been a priest, killed defending his temple. The crew made all the usual jokes about Tutankhamun and the curse of the Pharaohs, but half way through filming the cameraman was taken ill and had to be driven home. Later the director and a driver became faint and went to sit in their cars, pale and prepared for the worst. I kept telling the mummy I had not meant those things I'd said about Egypt. After all, we were both *born* there . . . At the end of 11 hours' filming I gabbled the payoff and drove home fast, before the protective spirit could reach out and do for me too.

While not a news programme, Tonight relied upon topicality. Production went on right up to transmission – often during transmission. Many times I was still recording commentary in the dubbing theatre when the programme went on the air, and neither Ned Sherrin, then studio director, nor Cliff in the hotseat in front of camera, knew whether the film would arrive in time.

In those days dubbing theatres had no rock-and-roll – the system by which one can stop recording after a mistake or wrong emphasis, wipe by winding the film back a few feet, and quickly re-start. Then if you fluffed you had to stop, rewind back to the beginning – and start the whole roll again. Should you bungle your delivery under stress, you were not at all popular. It was useful training to get the damn thing right first time for Pete's sake. It was also the reason I gave up smoking: we just could not afford my occasional frogs!

After dubbing, the cutter would grab the film and race down to Telecine to get it laced-up for transmission. Tearing down the Lime Grove stairs one night Mike Tuchner fell, dropped the film – and pied it. He lay there winded, while hundreds of yards of our good work rolled on down the stairs in a scrambled ball of graunched film. It was a scene too emotional for words. I had to jump over him to get to my chair in the studio to do a calm, thoughtful interview.

Even on screen Tonight could be an undignified romp, for always we took ourselves down, along with everyone else. We once appeared in wheelchairs as toothless ancients doing Tonight's 50th anniversary programme. Today we should need considerably less make-up – if any at all.

We did a cod programme on the Billy Cotton Show actually *singing* Tonight's bouncy signature tune : 'Michelmore . . . Hart . . . Whicker-and-Johnson-Smith . . .' Horrendous it may have been, but we enjoyed it.

In another of our not-too-serious film vox pops I stopped a number of people along the banks of Loch Lomond and asked which was the High Road, and which the Low Road? As you may know, the Low Road was the route supposedly taken by the spirits of departed Highlanders returning to their native land. 'The Bonnie Banks', the song from which it came, concerned the '45 Rebellion: in the retreat from Derby some Highlanders left behind to garrison Carlisle were captured and sentenced to death. One condemned man told his sweetheart: 'Ye'll tak' the High Road and I'll tak' the Low Road.' His spirit would reach Scotland before her.

As we had hoped, the Scots I approached had no idea of their traditional story and started giving me directions: 'Go right here, past the garage, turn left at the lights . . .' Most thought the Helensburgh Road was the Low, the Balloch Road the High. At a garage overlooking the Loch a young Scots pump attendant was as uninformed as the rest; years later when I interviewed him on quite another matter he reminded me of his ignorance. He was Jackie Stewart, then World Champion racing driver.

Walter Skilbeck, a 76-year-old farmer from Easingwold, Yorkshire, also had a winner: he had turned down a lot of good offers for his goat, Minnie. Childless couples were queuing to pay pounds for a pint of her milk, for every woman who tested it became pregnant. Just patting Minnie was enough to spread conception. Walter's son Frank refused to touch her: 'I've got four already.'

After we had filmed Farmer Skilbeck and his potent goat, he was interviewed by the Press. 'I didn't want Whicker to stroke her,' he told the reporters with alarm, 'but he said it didn't matter because he was a bachelor. Someone should warn him – that doesn't mean a *thing* to Minnie . . .'

Despite the different requirements of television I could not lose my old Fleet Street instinct to get the story out first. I went to cover a West Middlesbrough by-election, interviewing candidates while the crowd howled around us, and gave the result live into the Panorama programme ten minutes before the Returning Officer announced it to the world and ITN. There followed a cross reaction by officials unamused at being scooped on their own story. Counting procedures were afterwards changed.

In 1958 the programme was spreading its wings and my foreign travels for television began. I went first to New York with Baverstock; we flew in a Britannia, a brand new airliner christened the Whispering Giant. I reported it as the world's most deafening whisper, and the company was wounded. Sound, they said, was relative. We filmed a number of stories, including a light-hearted one about New York taxi drivers. That shows just how far back we go: to a time when Manhattan cabbies were new – and *funny*.

During a Eurovision interview from Paris, Salvador Dali told me he believed himself to be 'an angelic genius' who received messages out of the cosmos through his moustache. He mentioned in passing that he was immortal and that the psychiatrist he had been attending had gone mad. The *Birmingham Mail* was unimpressed: 'Whicker discovers another Goon.'

In Monaco we used the Radio Monte Carlo balcony overlooking the massed white yachts in the harbour and transmitted that splendid scene live to dismal Shepherd's Bush. One of our interviewees was the splendidly wicked Sir Thomas Beecham, making, I believe, his last public appearance.

It was hard to find a new approach to the basic filmed

interview, but I thought it might be fun to try a conversation in which I was rapt and intent upon the interviewee – but the *camera* was bored. On a beach near Cannes an estate agent and I settled down in deckchairs to consider Côte d'Azur property. While we were talking director Jack Gold pushed in a succession of very pretty girls in bikinis, who strolled between us and the camera. Each time the lens would notice the wandering girl in the foreground, get distracted, forget the conversation, follow the jiggling figure along the beach – then switch back guiltily to us, still droning away. The pictures were fine and the programme fun – but my poor interviewee was somewhat baffled by that daydreaming camera.

I went to Kuwait for the opening of a new ocean terminal by the Ruler, over to New York for more filming, home in time for the first anti-nuclear march to Aldermaston, and into the Cotswolds to look at Prinknash Benedictine Monastery, where the monks had started to build a new Abbey. To Venice with Slim Hewitt and to the Sudan and Aden for a major BBC programme on an early crisis in the Middle East . . . Television was gathering pace.

In July 1958, nothing loath, I set off upon my first world tour, and did not return until the end of October. In that time we travelled 30,000 miles and completed more than 50 reports from eight different countries. Each was transmitted at between seven and 20 minutes; say ten or 11 hours of cut film, in all. My contract was for £400 – so for screen-time the BBC came quite well out of that first expedition.

THE WORLD

Please leave your Guns outside . . .

THAT first international tour transformed me into Tonight's man-around-the-world and set the foundation for all Whicker's Worlds to follow during the next quarter of a century. Cyril Moorhead was the cameraman, Freddie Downton the sound recordist; we three made up the full crew. Today 13 or more people may travel on such a project, doing exactly the same job – and the only difference is that modern equipment is smaller and lighter!

We flew in a KLM Constellation along the route I had taken to Korea years before, landing in the steamheat of Singapore on my birthday, 2 August. At every touch-down from then on until the tour wound up in Mexico and Louisiana three months later, we hit the ground running . . .

In Singapore I talked to the Chief Minister Lim Yew Hok and looked at the Death Houses in Sago Lane. The Chinese believe death in a home brings bad luck down upon it, so the elderly were sent, resigned and uncomplaining, to die in Waiting Rooms above the funeral parlours amid the explosion of firecrackers and the wailing of paid professional mourners.

We considered the workings of Chinese Secret Societies, which make *Mafiosi* look friendly. Men who incurred their displeasure usually had a little finger chopped off, as an early warning. After that the official Executioner would remove an ear or, if very cross, two ears. From then on, they got rough.

I examined their armament for gang warfare which included dockers' grappling hooks and, less conventionally, the snouts of swordfish. One weapon had a horrible simplicity: electric light bulbs filled with sulphuric acid. It took a couple of violent decades for that refinement to reach the West.

In the Philippines we shot, in both ways, the 14 Hapsanhan rapids and went, damp but undaunted, to interview the Mayor of Manila, Arsenio Lacson, an outspoken former prize-fighter with a splendidly broken nose. The Wild-East was underlined by a disarming notice outside his parlour: 'Please leave your guns here.' Inside, closely attended by his bodyguard, he airily dismissed the polite sign: 'We lost a damn good City Treasurer before we put that up.'

It was no empty message, for kidnapping was a major industry. A few days earlier, in a fairly forthright vote of no-confidence, a Colonel had burst in, kidnapped the Mayor and carried him off in an Army car to be executed. Just before the end of the journey, said His Worship, 'I stick a leetle gun in his ribs. What happens? He gets religion.'

We flew north to film around Thailand, and afterwards in Hong Kong were installed luxuriously in the penthouse atop the splendid monolith of the Hongkong and Shanghai Bank. From our balcony we looked down upon all surrounding buildings. Today, seen from a ferry or from Kowloon that building is a squat bungalow amid towering highrises – such has been the outburst of prosperity within the Colony. To re-establish dominance, they are pulling the Bank down and starting again, building much, much higher: 600 feet and 41 floors this time – which should take a few years to look down upon . . .

We were then enjoying the hospitality of its Managing Director, Michael Turner. Returning sweaty and weary from filming in squatters' camps, impeccable Chinese servants would greet us with an unaccustomed 'Sherry wine, sir?' With the Governor-General and Jardine Matheson, the Bank was the third arm of the trident which ruled the Colony – though some say the Jockey Club is in there too. Turner, a leading member of the Legislative Council, was a great Taipan. Years later I once stopped for petrol in Surrey and the attendant, noting my Colony-bought Humber, told me a chap called Turner lived around the corner: 'Used to be a bank clerk in Hong Kong,' he said. We are all demoted by retirement.

We filmed a police launch patrolling the night seas and intercepting illegal immigrants; today, more than 20 years afterwards, they have still not been able to stem that wretched human flood.

One of the decrepit old junks we were about to stop and inspect suddenly went into overdrive and disappeared into the darkness like a speedboat. Many smugglers' junks had 350hp diesels installed for just such an occasion.

After a long chase through the night, we closed in. Its crew leapt overboard into the dark seas, leaving the boat steaming ahead at full speed with tiller lashed. It was like chasing a frenzied ghost ship – the Flying Chinaman.

When finally we stopped and boarded the junk, 50 illegal and terrified paying-passengers squatted below battened-down hatches. Afterwards we went-about and picked up some of the crew, without much tenderness. The others preferred to take their chances with the sharks on the five-mile swim to shore – or drown.

Another of my reports seemed about to start World War Three: it was the first of several occasions when I became an International Incident, and it's never fun. To get aerial shots of the magnificent Colony – one of the sights of the world – I had arranged a flight in an RAF Auster of the Auxiliary Airforce. The enthusiastic pilot of the small spotter 'plane flew Moorhead's camera rather too near the Border. For the first time, Chinese anti-aircraft guns opened fire upon the West. It was the moment Hong Kong had been dreading.

Luckily their aim was not good and the startled pair hastily returned to land, feeling as though Biggles had escaped the Red Baron. They faced a panic-stricken Colony which lived in fear of a Chinese avalanche.

Newspaper reports disagreed as to whether the aircraft had been hit. The Government impounded the film and the Sherry-wine-Sir dried up; we had rocked the boat and were not popular. Peking was officially assured our fluttery little Auster was not the spearhead of a mighty invasion to free the Mainland.

To escape Establishment outrage we went by hydrofoil to consider excitement – vice, even – in Macao. Upon investigation the Portuguese colony seemed as wicked as Leamington, with gambling. We took a few shots of casinos and nuns amid crumbling baroque, and flew on to Tokyo.

There I made the first of several reports I was to undertake through the years on cosmetic surgery. The world craze for the improving knife was just starting and Japanese secretaries would go to a small private hospital off the Ginza during lunch-hour, to lose face. Some 30,000 Japanese women had already bought a Western look: £10 for the nose, £5 the eyes. To reinforce the bridge of the Oriental nose, small splints would be inserted, and tucks in the eyelids gave what was believed to be a Caucasian look. The operation took only a few minutes and was considered trifling, but the endless re-assembly line was too gory for me. Fortunately Moorhead had filmed major heart surgery in England and had a stronger stomach; but finally the Japanese surgeon got to him too.

'I've not seen that much blood in amputations,' he said, leaving the theatre to gulp a cup of Japanese brandy. The girls just got a cup of tea and, after a brief rest, went back to their shops and offices believing that beneath the bandages their appealing Butterfly look had gone for ever.

In Hawaii my something-for-nothing side was delighted by the free pineapple juice gushing on-tap at a cannery. I was less enchanted to find the carefree hula-hula girls belonged to a trade union and kept their grass skirts fresh in the 'fridge. It would not have done for Fletcher Christian.

We considered the macabre Dream Deaths: within 18 months 170 Filipino plantation workers had died mysteriously. In each case some young healthy bachelor would begin to shout, groan and scream in his sleep – and then die. Doctors and pathologists told me there was no medical reason for the deaths. One worker who had been awakened just in time from a near-fatal dream told me: 'An ugly little man was trying to choke me.' The deaths remain unexplained.

In Mexico we had the usual trouble getting our camera

gear through customs. All that was required to defuse the Bite was a nice quick bribe, but I can never bring myself to succumb – whether in Rome or not. I always appreciate how foolish it is to draw myself up like some Lime Grove Canute and attempt to impose Anglo-Saxon morality upon another lifestyle, for south of Panama *la mordida* spreads money around like taxes are supposed to do for us; but still I stick my heels in, get indignant and do it the hard way: days of struggle and ulcer-making bad temper on all sides.

Finally, unbribed and resentful, they let us in to film in Mexico and Acapulco. Moorhead and Downton then went home, exhausted. I doubt whether two television technicians have ever worked so hard or so well. I carried on to Texas for further filming with American crews in Brownsville, Houston and New Orleans.

From my professional point of view one of the disadvantages of such a major three-month tour was that I never saw my own programmes or found out what I had done wrong, until too late. In order to feed the hungry brute and keep Tonight on air, every report was instantly transmitted.

After filming I wrote and recorded wildtrack commentary and editing instructions, and tapes and film were flown home. In the cutting-rooms the commentary was woven among the interviews and the mute we had shot – and out it would go, for better or worse.

We would record that commentary as best we could – sometimes with blankets over the hotel bedroom window and my head stuck into a wardrobe. At other times, if more appropriate for the report, at some quiet spot out of doors. One night Freddie and I tried to find a tranquil place without background noise – in Hong Kong. It was like looking for a carpark in downtown Venice. We were not very experienced in those days.

It is only when you seek absolute peace, and stand to listen, that you realise how noisy our world has become. In Eire we once drove miles into the soft countryside to find the requisite hush. A twilight stillness spread over lonely empty meadowland, and in the silence we set up the recorder. I took a deep breath and started the commentary – when a coach arrived and two shouting teams poured out and began to play Gaelic football.

As the furthest-flung member of the Tonight family, I relied on cables and letters from Lime Grove to keep me flying-right. Now when I read my 1958 files I am awed by the concern, ideas, analysis, advice and care that came to me from Tonight, deep as it was in the hurly-burly of a nightly programme. The producers even urged me not to work too hard – and that's unnatural! Today I can film in California for three months without hearing one word from Yorkshire Television on any subject at all; television has changed.

So my worldwide reports went out on Tonight, and when I got back to Lime Grove they were pulled together, re-edited, and I wrote a new linking commentary. The 45-minute programmes were then transmitted under the omnibus title Whicker's World. These compilations were, thank goodness, well received – indeed *Punch* called them: 'Tonight's most notable achievement' and the Sheffield *Star* said: 'Mr Whicker's stylebook ought to be handed to the Panorama team, which is weightily informative but never stimulating.' In those days, most critics seemed kind – or, far more likely, Tonight only kept the good ones for me to see!

One day my barber, busy repairing the damage caused by Tongan and Mexican scissors, asked if I had more overseas filming planned. I told him I was about to go round the world again. He considered that, the way barbers do, and then said, 'This time, why don't you go somewhere *else*?'·

I settled for going round the other way, and flew west to Canada, where our first programme was almost our last. As their hard winter ended we went to film the first ship pushing through the ice to reach Montreal on the break-up of the freezing St Lawrence. We were aboard the 3,000-ton ice-breaker *Ernest Lapointe*.

Somewhere near Three Rivers I persuaded Captain Marchant to let us down on to the ice, for an exterior sequence of the ship in action. The river was a mile wide there, the ice between three and 15 feet thick. We trudged ahead across that frozen whiteland and set up our tripod and gear, while the icebreaker went astern. It needed a long run-up at 15 knots to get enough force to break through another 50 yards of pack-ice.

Behind me the ship gathered speed, hit the ice with a tremendous crunch and churned and cracked and groaned towards us.

I was standing with my microphone 10 feet in front of camera, setting the scene. In the background the rumble and roar grew nearer. The ice shuddered and trembled. Bill Searle, the sound recordist, edged back as far as our mike lead would permit. I carried on, earnestly explaining what was happening behind me. Cyril Moorhead's eye finally left the viewfinder. He gazed up in horror, mouth open.

I gave in and looked over my shoulder. The enormous prow was bearing down upon us like a threatening ten-storey building. The shot was just what I had asked for – but fast becoming too good.

Up on the bridge the Captain, even more alarmed than we were, ordered Hard Astern. He feared we were about to be flung beneath the cracking, groaning ice into the black water, to be crushed or frozen or drowned. Possibly all three.

The bow kept coming, towering above us like the *QE2*. The deep-throated crunch was deafening. We stood frozen – you could say. The monster was inescapable.

The ship finally ground agonisingly to a halt, three feet in front of the tripod leg. We measured it. Had I not stepped aside at the last minute I should have been given a 3,000-ton nudge. Another few feet and we would have disappeared, probably for ever. Whicker's Luck had held, like the ice – but only just.

The Tonight producers were ecstatic about that long-held shot. It showed a mad reporter with a death wish and was far more classic than I had intended.

When people afterwards asked, 'What lens were you using to give the impression the icebreaker had come so close?' I would give them an icy look.

Moving west we travelled through windswept Winnipeg to Calgary and took the world's most beautiful railway journey aboard The Canadian on the last leg of its 3,000-mile four-day transcontinental route across Canada, through the

Rockies and down to Vancouver. In the Scenic Dome observation car passengers relaxed while the long train zigzagged up through the mountains, and stared in disbelief as our own locomotive approached us and passed – in the opposite direction! It was weird.

I spent that night lying back in a soft armchair looking up at moonlit snowy mountaintops and the stars above, next to a pretty young nun on her way to an ecclesiastical conference in British Columbia. It was rather romantic. North American nuns seem somehow . . . less remote. She told me she drove the convent car and one day, getting a puncture in town, had asked some men waiting in a queue to change the wheel for her. They agreed, provided she and her companion held their places. The line was outside a Labour Exchange and she heard a passer-by say, 'Things must be tough – even the Pope's laying 'em off.'

On Vancouver Island in Victoria I met Dr Brock Chisholm, Nobel prizewinner, former Director of the World Health Organisation and a man of definite opinion: parents should not let their children believe in Santa Claus or, faith undermined, they would never again believe anything Mummy said. Every important Commission in the United Nations was controlled by Catholics at a time when birth control should be limiting world population. Cemeteries were a waste of good agricultural land and people should be buried on top of each other, in skyscraper tombs. He was the ideal Tonight interviewee: pithy, concise, dogmatic.

We flew from freezing Canada and left the Qantas flight in the steamheat of Fiji. From Nadi we drove round the island to Suva and on to Mba, to film some firewalking. In a little guesthouse I stepped out on to the verandah in search of dinner – and stepped back again, smartish. The ground was crawling with huge and horrible toads: hundreds of the giant creatures, croaking and rustling revoltingly. They occupied the hallways every night, I was told. There was not much night-time tiptoeing between bedrooms in *that* establishment.

In a cold grey dawn I stood, clammy and sweating, beside the glowing charcoal pit through which devotees were about to walk on redhot embers; and so they did, several times. One old man told me he firewalked to cure his stomach ulcers. 'You only get burned if you don't believe,' he said, showing me the unmarked soles of his feet. I examined the redhot pit, and opted for ulcers.

We flew on to Tonga and down to the gentle islands of New Zealand where I met the grandfatherly Prime Minister Walter Nash, from Kidderminster. In 1959 his nation of 2,300,000 people still had no television; it was one of the few virgin viewing areas remaining in the world. In Christchurch I did a vox pop, asking a score of passers-by whether they wanted to join the rest of us in front of the Box. Only two were against it – and one of them changed her mind half way through our conversation. Soon after they got their television – and Whicker's World with it, lucky people. I wonder how they would vote today?

We carried on to Australia, where in one of the offbeat conversations that were an innovation in those days I nearly got filled-in by a Bodgie, on camera. Bodgies and Widgies were the Australian teddy boys and girls. I had persuaded my swaggering roughneck out of some pub and into a back alley – which seemed an appropriate background – to ask him about his alternative lifestyle. At first I had a little trouble with his monosyllabic reactions, while he decided whether to enjoy the flattering experience of being listened to thoughtfully – or to beat me into the ground.

Finally goaded into communication, he proved an excellent example of my theory that for interviewers, silence can be the best question. At the end of a reply I sometimes choose to wait that extra three seconds to see what else may emerge to fill the hush.

The Bodgie concluded a recollection of mindless violence: '. . . so our gang finished up with a party in that house we'd taken over.' Pause. 'It lasted three days.' Another pause 'When we left, we set fire to the place.' Long pause. 'I took it as a joke myself.' Longer pause. 'Can't see why the firemen didn't.'

At any of those endings I could have said, 'Cut' and we would have lost a small moment of his reality.

The day of the fearful 1960 earthquake at Agadir I flew out to Morocco, with a camera crew and Peter Batty as director. We landed at Casablanca but could not reach the shattered coastal town by air, so hired a great American sedan and drove the 300 miles through the Atlas mountains. On the way we hit a locust storm: millions of the loathsome insects, each several inches long, blackening the sky and crashing into the windscreen, clogging wipers and thudding against windows and roof as in some horror movie. They carpeted the road as I drove over them gingerly, skidding on squashed bodies.

At Agadir there were other and more tragic squashed bodies to face. We filmed all day amid the ruins and another sort of horror, trying to absorb and convey the disaster while hampered by Moroccan soldiers rushed in to deter looters. They had been told to allow no one into the stricken town, and were ready to use bayonets to carry out that uncomplicated order.

Having filmed as best we could, we started to race back to Casablanca Airport to despatch the report. Half way there, after 36 hours without sleep, a day's filming and 500 miles at the wheel, I could no longer keep my eyes open. We stopped to sleep in Essaouira. The hotel was deserted, apart from two silent figures in the lounge. They turned out to be Heather Jenner and her husband Stephen Potter. Lifemanship seemed a long way from Agadir, where people thought only of staying alive; yet death was about to approach us, too.

At dawn we got going again in the great bouncy monster of a car, desperate to catch the day's only flight home. We were driving hard along a precipitous road high on the mountainside when at 80 mph – one of the tyres blew. The car swerved and headed for a sheer drop of thousands of feet.

I struggled to hold it. We came to rest with one wheel through the broken wall we had smashed, spinning over the ravine.

It was a rear tyre which had burst. Had it been a front wheel we should surely have swerved over the precipice and toppled down into the valley below.

When we hired the car the tyres had been all right; that I

always check. Evidently during those few hours of sleep some Arabs had stolen all four tyres and, to make sure we should be far away when we found out, replaced them with a bald set . . .

IRELAND

Maybe in Ballybunion . . . ?

EVERYTHING that appears on television is going to upset someone. We might escape criticism by showing Niagara Falls for 30 minutes – though some viewer would object to the waste of water.

One of Tonight's early teacup-storms followed Slim Hewitt's visit to Nuneaton, where he poked a little gentle fun at the architectural wasteland and finished by recalling that one of its residents had been George Eliot – 'whoever *he* was.' The good people of Nuneaton rose in fury at such unkindly ignorance. For the first time – but surely not the last – Tonight underestimated local pride. Television is funny about other people's bus stations at its peril.

Since we were now part of the national fabric, even our imitators got into trouble. In a satirical revue Millicent Martin was to play Mrs Jacqueline Kennedy taking me on a tour of the White House. I was looking forward to the show, called 'The Lord Chamberlain Regrets'. Unfortunately, he did. The 11th Earl of Scarborough ordered: 'Delete skit concerning wife of Head of State.'

On such a public platform almost any statement of opinion will create an equal opinion going in the opposite direction. Should Tonight go to Bolton just before Wakes Week and in some club ask members what they thought of Blackpool landladies – as we did – there would be an instant outpouring of bitter truth: spam and kippers and one lavatory for 32 guests . . .

Then on to Blackpool to get the boardinghouse side, and have a landlady admit she offered beds to 50 guests, but had only one bathroom . . . Next day, of course, the massed landladies rise in fury, the Mayor of Blackpool protests to the Director-General of the BBC, and Whicker is in deep trouble again for everything everyone else said. Carrying the Can is the name of the television game – though I suppose you could say, we *do* ask for it!

Tonight's first major row with political repercussions was caused, needless to say, by me, and was quite another can of worms. In January 1959 I went to Ulster, where there must surely be more bitterness and bigotry per square inch than anywhere else in the world. I filmed eight reports, a broad spectrum of life in the Six Counties. Each was matter-of-fact and straight down the middle. None took more than a tangential look at religion or politics – for even 20 years ago the sad and bloody story of people killing each other in the name of God was already boring an appalled world by its medieval mindlessness, and centuries of history and hatred cannot be compressed into as many television minutes.

With Barbara Vesey Brown directing, we filmed in Belfast and Armagh and were in a Londonderry hotel on the night the first of our short series was transmitted. The opener concerned, of all things, betting shops. It was Tonight's usual topical look at an innovation, for they operated legally in Ulster and were just about to appear in the rest of Britain.

To start the series I set the Ulster scene briefly with general shots of the Stormont and the City Hall, showed the usual gabble of wallside graffiti – 'No Pope Here . . . Vote Sinn Fein . . Ulster is Ours' – mentioned that Northern Ireland, though intensely loyal and the birthplace of most of Britain's best generals, had armed police but no conscription. Then we went into the betting shop to show viewers how this imminent addition to the High Streets of Britain operated, and to talk with a few punters.

When the report ended there was silence in our hotel lounge. The man I had been drinking with turned to me: 'You can't say that sort of thing.' I was baffled. During the previous year I had reported in exactly the same straightforward way from 17 different countries without being told I could not get away with it. 'Why ever not? Every word's true.' 'I know,' he said, 'but that doesn't matter. You just can't say that sort of thing.' As I was to find out later – he was absolutely right.

Next day, driving through the lovely Ulster countryside, we stopped to buy the local papers to see whether our little report had won a mention. We skimmed the pages, studied the television reviews, but there was no coverage at all. That seemed odd. Only later did we discover we had missed their reaction because it was the day's lead story under banner headlines. We had not thought to look at the front pages.

The Ulster sky then fell on Tonight, and on me: a Bishop and a Senator flew to London to complain, Stormont threatened to remove broadcasting from the BBC, and the Corporation's Northern Ireland Controller replied with a craven statement grovelling at their 'distress and indignation'. The Chairman of the Tourist Board expressed outrage and a BBC Sportsview team filming a local football match was dragged down from its camera stand and attacked.

The papers wrote about that unimportant little film for weeks: 'There was no reference to the city's industries and the general bearing of the citizens,' said an editorial in the *Belfast News-Letter*, referring obscurely to that ten-minute report on Betting. One hesitant correspondent to the *Belfast Telegraph* did whisper, 'Are we ashamed of the truth?' and was promptly shouted down. The Unionist Senator Daniel McGladdery was invited on to Tonight, protested vehemently and at length – and in the Hospitality room afterwards mentioned he had not actually *seen* the programme. His companion, the Bishop of Down, Dr J. F. Mitchell, said it failed to give 'a well-balanced picture of life in Northern Ireland' – a rather formidable task in ten minutes!

Unfortunately the empty uproar in which they were participating prevented the following seven programmes – which would have broadened that picture – from being screened. Baverstock and the BBC were thrown into a funk by this unexpected uprising of the massed ranks of hypocrisy. For the first time the new-look BBC TV service kowtowed to silly sound and fury. It was not a glorious moment for the Corporation.

Twenty-two years later Thames Television took a five-hour Leftish look at Ulster, following a straightforward 13-hour series on BBC 2; the agonising subject required that kind of space. Professor Rex Cathcart told Thames' researcher of the lack of interest the media had always shown in Northern Ireland. One of the few attempts at coverage, he said, had been the Whicker Tonight series in 1959 – and that had been banned after its first report. He did not explain that such censorship was at the instigation of Ulster officials. The researcher went to the BBC and asked if she could see these upsetting programmes. They were not available: all had been wiped.

It was not until 1966 – seven years after my series – that English television dared attempt another programme on Ulster, for our uproar had showed the threat of all that empty anger awaiting release. Today when we see what has happened in the unhappy provincial armed-camp, with its massed armies and terrorists and bombs, its destruction of buildings and bodies, it is curious to reflect that so recently a television close-up of one constable's revolver could unleash such fury.

After that hysterical warning from Ulster, filming around Eire was strangely peaceful. I kissed the Blarney Stone of course, and a fat lot of good it did me. I reported on the anomaly of the Nelson Pillar, tallest monument in Dublin's O'Connell Street, and concluded by saying that despite the official unpopularity of the British, he had stood there for more than a century and was doubtless good for another one – thus breaking my rule that prophecy on television never does you any good. Five years later Tonight's successor Nationwide, then edited by a product of Trinity, Dublin, ran that clip gleefully – after the IRA had blown up poor Horatio.

Down in County Kerry I met an old professional Matchmaker with a long record of happy marriages behind him. His was not an easy job in a land where in the spring every young man's fancy lightly turns to thoughts of emigration.

He told me for his efforts he received 'a percentage of the dowry and a grand hotel dinner'. It seemed a reasonable deal, so I wondered if he would put me on his books: 'Oh – an Englishman . . .' he said doubtfully, fearing I was beyond his powers. 'That's difficult.'

On reflection however he thought there might *just* be hope for me: 'Maybe in Ballybunion . . .'

AUSTRALIA

Breasts that'd poke your Eye out . . .

I FIND myself filming in Australia every five years or so, always with delight, always staggered to realise that the first white Australian was born in that powerful land less than two centuries ago. Critics say no one who was tops at anything has ever gone there to live, that the place has too many Irish, not enough Jews and an excess of Pommie Commie trade unionists . . . but of all nations it remains the Lucky Land. In three months during 1959 we travelled 35,000 miles to produce 25 programmes there. In those grey days of austerity every viewer must have considered escaping from Britain into the sunshine, or envied someone who had. It might be an unoriginal land with a high level of mediocrity, but seen from the grey shores of Britain, Australia did not seem to have a low level of *anything*.

During those months we considered their sunlit way of life in every State, from koalas and the six-o'clock-swill to the farmer in Moree who hunted and killed snakes by grabbing their tails and cracking them like whips. We followed him timidly; after each lightning lunge and frantic cast . . . there would be a *snap* as the spine broke and the snake's head flew off.

In the red, dead heart of Australia around Alice Springs I drove out to meet an old fossiker, a Pom who had been looking for gold for 40 years without success but still relished his parched way of life – which few could have tolerated. That morning I had brought some ice-cold beer from a pub in the Alice, wrapped the bottles in damp newspaper and put them in the shade under our car seat. When we went gasping for a drink, the beer was as hot as a nice cup of tea.

For a proper brew-up we joined an old Outback character, the late Bill Harney of Two Fella Creek. Sitting in the shade of a coolibar tree he told me how he lived his life by the Law of Least Effort, which suited him – and certainly in that temperature had a lot going for it.

The old sensualist recalled the Aboriginal girl he had married: 'Skin like black velvet – and breasts that'd poke your eye out.' That telling phrase went out on the Tonight programme to ten million viewers, who doubtless relished it as much as I had. When the *Radio Times* later asked me for some reminiscent articles I recounted Bill's story. The editor left in the black velvet skin but censored the breasts.

At my protest he came to see me in Lime Grove, a cheery chap with a loud voice and louder Max Miller overcoat. His was a family magazine, be explained, and obviously could not print a word like 'breast'. This was in 1964. I wondered idly how he would set about describing his double-breasted coat . . .? He never became a bosom friend of mine.

Around the end of November – torrid high summer Down Under, when movement should be minimal – we arrived at Winton in northern Queensland, where 'Waltzing Matilda' was written, to film a Swaggie actually waltzing his around the Outback. In the town hotel I flung my bedroom windows wide for a breath of whatever air was moving through the warm clammy night, and collapsed into bed. Just dropping off, blissful, when the most deafening full-throated uproar, like a jet take-off, blasted through the room, shaking the furniture. It came from a distance of some eight feet from my unprotected right ear and left me lying rigid, eyeballs staring. Nuclear bomb? Earthquake?

Two trembling footsteps out into the throbbing din,

pushing through enveloping soundwaves, and it became clear that my bedroom overlooked the township's open-air cinema and its Giantscreen, backed by Super-Stereo-Living-Sound, was just outside. Anna and the King of Siam were playing against my wall that week. I could not see either of them, but I could hear them all right; they stopped thought.

It appeared that only late at night did the temperature drop to 90 or so, when it was cool enough for an audience to sit outside and see a film, so each night I was blasted to bed by the interminable Dance of those dreadful Siamese Children, at several hundred decibels. Each time they Whistled a Happy Tune, my eyes filled with tears. If, crafty, I dodged them by staying up during the first performance, they caught me at full blast, second house. I tried getting to sleep, heavily drugged, during the intervals while they changed reels, but all the cobbers, mates and sports would leave their seats to gather with glad cries at the temporary bar under my window to kill a few quick Frosties before settling back to the faces of Deborah Kerr and Yul Brynner, 18 feet from ear to ear, whispering throatily to each other in deafening bellows that vibrated my bed.

After the first few nights, lying there with fists clenched, I found myself joining in their conversation: it was so – predictable. If there is any part of the dialogue of that long, long film you would like recalled, just ask: it is indelibly imprinted. Forgive me if I shout.

Back in England and compiling the series, we knew Daniel Farson had also been filming in Australia for Rediffusion and thought it foolish to allow our programmes to be pre-empted. Tony Jay, adopting his Strine accent, rang up the Rediffusion Press Office and asked when Farson was to be transmitted. They gave him the date – and we put our series out earlier. In such simple, Machiavellian ways are schedules planned and ITV confused.

As might be expected the critics compared the two of us. Angus Wilson in the *Observer*: 'Farson is less critical than Whicker, more anxious to be liked by his interviewees; he is very popular Press. Beside him Whicker seems like the *Guardian*.'

In the *Sunday Times* Maurice Wiggin wrote: 'I used to think that the earthly paradise must be located in British Columbia or Vancouver Island, but Mr Whicker has made Australia attractive. I sometimes have waking dreams of that empty 1,000-mile road from Alice Springs to the coast, or of Cooktown, where time stands still.'

Despite such enthusiasm from all sides Australia House complained, predictably. The High Commissioner in London, Sir Eric Harrison, wrote: 'If these reports went out of their way to make ill-feeling between England and Australia they could not have done it better.'

We were exasperated. At that time Australia was spending a lot of money on newspaper advertisements urging Britons to emigrate, and after every one of my programmes I received sackfuls of mail from viewers who had been stimulated to go to Australia and wanted to know how to set about it. Goaded by such official ingratitude, I wrote to Sir Eric asking whether in view of his objection I should tell these hundreds of viewers to disregard the favourable impression of his country they had gained from my reports. Australia House fell silent.

I do not claim *all* the credit for the rush of Britons Down Under which followed, but since those early programmes Australia has received even more of us than they want. Immigration control and a visa system have been instituted. Australia House has cancelled its advertising. Sir Eric never wrote to say Thanks – though after I had encouraged them on their way, a lot of contented new-Australians did.

Readers of the *Dundee Courier* voted our Whicker Down Under series the Most Entertaining Programme of the year. Runners-up were Laramie and Bronco; you can't *get* more appreciated than that.

So Tonight was off and running, its apparently effortless success endlessly analysed in public. Anne Scott-James wrote in the *Daily Mail*: 'Although it has taken some beatings lately, the BBC is still a pretty influential outfit. When David Frost appears in a shirt with tabs under his collar, he creates an insatiable demand for shirts-with-tabs, and the Alan Whicker voice is the voice of the Nation.'

That seemed rather hard on the poor old Nation: I thought the programme's impact had more to do with professional style, coupled with the old axiom that you can be Anything Except Boring. Writers always seemed taken aback at the programme's wide appeal. When a few of my Specials were transmitted on US television an incredulous *Daily Mail* headline shouted: 'Look who America's discovered!'

In the *Yorkshire Post* Peter Jackson considered *Tonight's* overall impact: 'Its characters provide the highlights which stick in the memory, but the programme's success is due to the fact that it is sometimes serious, but more often than not mischievous, a flighty sister of the more ponderous Panorama. Critics frequently attempt to dissect the programme in an attempt to discover what makes it so successful. The most obvious answer is that Tonight is rarely dull.

'If at times Michelmore seems a little too smug, Hart a little too sneering, Allsop a little too earnest, Robertson a little too sour and Whicker a little too jolly, then regard these failings with affection and put them down to over-exposure, for I can think of no other team which could survive more than 1,000 nightly appearances and show so few of their faults. Such occasional failings, coupled with a high degree of professional skill, have made the names of the team household words. Whicker's reports on his world travels are slick, solid and informative.'

Flying off in all directions, I pursued slick solid information with uncertain success. A land as unpromising as Alaska would yield endless fascination; then I would fail to capture the essence of some place obviously begging to be on television. Italy was the perfect example. I have spent years of my life in that warm and lavish land among its attractive and voluble people. I speak their language, know my way around – yet never have I been able to capture on television the character and quality of their stimulating nation. No explanation.

Nowadays of course, Italy has moved close – Leonardo da Vinci Airport arrives more quickly than Weymouth Station, hijackers and strikes permitting. Air travel, once a jolly and intrepid expedition, has become a mixture of boredom and indigestion, interspersed by fear. Cross and bruised from the boarding stampede, you hurtle through space, speechless amid several hundred strangers. On a long-haul, the break for travel between airports is rarely more than three of four hours, when you get new passengers, new crew – and the pretty stewardess you have been chatting-up is replaced by an aloof girl in love with the navigator.

Impersonal as an international Green Line it may be, but at least – I keep saying – it *is* safe. In smaller aircraft on obscure local airlines, one can feel less secure. In Mexico, bumping along 7,000 feet above Guadalajara, some tiresome expert recalled that the aircraft to which we were entrusting our lives had been bought in a trade job-lot several years before when discarded as too old and unserviceable – by a Pakistani airline . . . Conversation lagged.

Another Moment of Truth came while filming aerial topsoil-dressing from an ancient DC3 out of Hamilton, in New Zealand. Nine tons of fertiliser waited to drop from what had been the passenger compartment. To make sure the farmer who had paid for it received it – and not the cheapskate next door – the pilot had to dive so low he kept landing with branches and grass and people's hats in his undercarriage. These flying farmhands took off anywhere and landed on anything, throwing transport-planes around like demented Spitfires and becoming, in my cautious view based on tabulated percentages, dangerously over-confident. Insurance companies average such Bush pilots at 10,000 landings and takeoffs between each crash.

My cameraman was resisting the G-force in the second pilot's seat and I, somewhat to my surprise, was standing up behind them, straphanging, white and strained. We roared up a valley and turned left through some trees. The pilot was telling us this must be about his 11,000th flight – which just showed you couldn't believe in the law of averages . . .

We dived between two chimneys, around a barn, dropped our load – and up with terrible shudders into the sky. As I

opened my eyes it came to me yet again that there was a lot to
be said for interviewing in a cosy Tonight studio.

At Darwin we had to charter a small aircraft to reach
Victoria River Downs, as Australian farm 25 times the size of
Middlesex. The place was proudly advertised in the local
paper as 'all-metal'. This started an unfortunate train of
thought – like foods which boast about being '98.9%' pure.
What's more, when we flew through a storm – it leaked.
There is something disconcerting and basically *wrong* about
being rained-on from the middle of a cloud.

More than such events and places, more than experience
and apprehension and delight, it is the Tonight People who
stay fixed in memory, who come wandering back when I
suffer feverish influenza: there were the Lugers – Carlo and
Otto – on their remote farm at Mulbach in upper Austria.
They trained trout to answer their names and jump through
hoops. Since fish flee at a shadow I did not really believe it,
either – even though I was sitting there watching. The leader
of the 25 tame trout was Henry. Jumping through hoops may
not be much fun for fish, but Henry and his troop obviously
considered it better than jumping into the fryingpan. Like
Otto said, cracking his whip – if they don't perform, they get
their chips . . .

There was Sir Compton Mackenzie on his 80th birthday,
convinced that a Tonight would have spared Europe the
First World War; 'Imagine Whicker and Michelmore ex-
amining the events which led up to it! The public would have
seen immediately that negotiations would have saved the
day.' The old author was a television addict, regretting only
that it stifled imagination: 'When I was a boy I used to dream
about a desert island – what it was like, who lived there . . .
Now all a child has to do is to switch on – and his desert
island is brought right into the living-room.'

The characters who people our various disasters stand out
even more, in those nightmares . . . One New Year's Eve,
Panorama borrowed me for an outside broadcast on The
Women of The Year. The producer decided we should leave
their peaceful studio and congregate in a nightclub which
had just opened near Trafalgar Square. I had no hand in the

selection of the deserving ladies I met just before the witching hour: Edna O'Brien, a writer coming into her fame; Tania Mallet, a lanky girl selected for the international spotlight as the latest James Bond bird; Antonia Fraser, the author, wife, mother and all-round phenomenon; Celia Hammond, a model whose face and figure had been inescapable that year, and the formidable actress and institution, Margaret Rutherford.

We settled uneasily around a table in the centre of the club beneath unnaturally brilliant lights, already harassed by celebrating Stage Door Johnnies who believed I had more than my fair share of partners on that festive night; indeed, I had several more than I wanted.

One trouble with an OB was that it was Live; no margin for error or confusion. I had to introduce and explain the situation to one of the cameras and go on to converse entertainingly with five different women on five different subjects, while accepting the usual off-camera stage directions and overriding bawdy comments from merry members gathering in the outer darkness. An OB was never easy.

To add to our harassment there was no sign of Margaret Rutherford, our Grande Dame. The director grew more and more nervous as transmission neared and her chair remained empty, for she was the weighty lady needed to counterbalance those young models. I was also anxious because we had never met, and I always like to establish some relationship before going On Air.

Five minutes before transmission I left my nervous Women of The Year and dashed up into the dark damp street in the usual silly hope that gazing anxiously up and down might speed our Star's arrival. Indeed it did. A taxi drew up and a furious Margaret Rutherford struggled out, gasping and gesticulating. She was, as they say, madder than a wet hen.

It transpired that the hire car had arrived late to collect her from Barnet or Totteridge or wherever; then she and her husband had grown steadily angrier amid the New Year traffic as the driver lost his way a few more times. She brushed past me and stormed down the stairs, squawking furiously about cab and Corporation. Spectators and crew parted before two white-haired balls of fury.

I thought at first she was doing her irascible Miss Marple or Madame Arcati act, and was ready to be delighted – but this was not acting. She was livid. She stormed in magnificent outrage up to our floodlit table, glared around the other Ladies of The Year and disliked them all, glared at me and disliked me even more. As the Floor Manager's arm went up to cue my calm and considered opening remarks, and in the distance I could hear Richard Dimbleby handing over to me, she made the final decision. Bringing her husband to heel, she flounced angrily up the stairs, still chattering protest – and away into the night. She left a carefully-planned outside broadcast in tatters, the Ladies of the Year upset, and me with my mouth open.

It was not a Happy New Year celebration, and illustrated the destructive power of a taxi driver – though of course she might have hated us all, anyway . . .

More peacefully, there were the Caribs of Dominica, fierce and triumphant man-eaters who once found Anglo-Saxons far more tasty than those stringy Latins, but now eat white man's meals in their Reservation – and dwindle towards extinction. Doña Romero of Tehuantepec in Mexico and the statue erected to the memory of this most successful whore by – presumably – grateful men about town. The Maroons in Jamaica's Cockpit country and their poetic 'Land of Look Behind', a 1,500-acre sanctuary independent since 1738, where no stranger could safely ride. Two regiments of Redcoats sent to occupy the area in 1734 were decimated; not by Maroons, it must be admitted – but by rum. The American who sued his wife for divorce on the grounds that she was childish and when the Judge asked why, told him, 'Every time I take a bath she comes in and sinks all my boats . . .'

Then there were those girls on the remote Pacific island of Tonga, who were not childish at all. It seemed that they found a white stranger such a fascinating rarity that the moonlit tropical nights had a new and interesting sound coming gently through the rasp of cicadas and the clicking of frogs: a soft and persistent scratching on bedroom window-screens as young native girls tried to entice Whitey outside into the sultry silver garden . . .

Other girls on the farm near Toba harvested the crop of Mr Mikimoto – the man who discovered how to make an oyster cry, profitably. Each crustacean in thousands of baskets hung suspended in 200 square miles of Pacific was opened and a tiny sliver of shell inserted; the oyster, reacting as we do to grit in the eye, covers this foreign body with a liquid and so creates another cultured pearl. The quiet American in his East Grinstead home: L. Ron Hubbard knew flowers suffered a nasty nervous shock when picked, and proved it with his E-Metre. He was then unknown but busy founding the weird religion of Scientology . . . The cheerful, charming Fijian chief who prepared a feast for us and thought my reciprocal presents were a down-payment on one of his daughters . . .

Clothes for several months of such international filming present problems: there is Martinique's Diamond Rock to be climbed, but afterwards dinner with the Chief Minister; a witchdoctor's sooty sacrificial cave, closely followed by the Ambassador's party in Guatemala City. I have views about this, and they can make life rather difficult. My reasoning: if people are good enough to invite me into their livingrooms regularly, I should at least be presentable. I can't be handsome, but I can be clean.

It may be insufferably hot and humid where we are, but on the screen it never looks it. Viewers do not appreciate our difficulties – and there is no reason why they should. It ought to look easy. Any television reporter who shambles into my home in a T-shirt and jeans, dressed for cleaning the car, is considering his own comfort and not concerned about the people to whom he has been invited to talk.

Food can be another problem: in Dominica, lush island of rain forest in the Caribbean, we ate a big dish of 'mountain chicken', a rich white meat fried in batter. Each succulent serving was revealed, too late, to have been the hindlegs of a giant toad . . .

In Central America violent stomach upset lies in wait for

every foreigner; our camera crew were so nervous they lived for months on black coffee, omelettes and coke. We could not drink the water, of course, but one day in Oaxaca my recordist was risking a beer when he noticed slivers of broken glass at the bottom of his drink. With the prospect of a sliced tongue and bleeding to death in some foreign field, he complained heatedly to the waiter who, after examination, reassured him: 'Don't worry – it's only ice.'

'My God,' said Freddie, aghast, 'that's *worse!*'

TEXAS

Open up – FBI!

My first major tour of the United States in 1961 was also, for its crewing, the last perfect tour. There were just four of us and we were good friends: Mike Tuchner as director, Alan Jonas cameraman, and Dave Zeigler recordist. With our camera gear, film stock and luggage we all squeezed into one stationwagon and set off from Houston to film our way right through Texas, New Mexico, Arizona, Nevada and into California. In ten weeks we drove 7,274 miles and at least earned an approving smile from Mr Avis.

After that crews grew bigger on every tour and required two, then three, four or more cars. Larger crews meant more airline seats and hotel bedrooms, which could be hard to find. Instead of chartering one aircraft we needed at least two. Worst of all, it meant the basic fun and friendship of the expedition could be replaced by aggro; a small crew was hand-picked but with a large number, one whinger often slipped in to surface, niggling, when we were 10,000 miles from base. My original crew of two has today grown into a Hollywoodian mob which requires its own unit manager to handle reservations, rotas, days off, expenses, overtime squabbles – and people who expect to be brought tea on location.

British film crews are now so vast that pairs of foreign television men working with tape gaze at them in amazed disbelief. Experienced interviewees like American politicians grip their executive armchairs in alarm as we troop in, man after man like an Italian opera chorus. They think the kidnappers have landed.

The overmanning rot set in, gradually, after my second tour: we had two extra men so consequently, a second car. Filming in New England, we made an early start one morning on a 300-mile drive to the next location, for there was a camera-call that evening. Mike and I were hurtling west down the freeway out of Boston in the production car when we saw the crew car coming fast *towards* us in the other carriageway, heading east. It disappeared behind us into the distance, passengers deep in their morning papers. Mike and I looked at each other: we knew this was the day the circus left town . . .

In Houston we considered the Marcus brothers and their Neiman-Marcus store with its concept of 'Wantability'. It was just starting its outrageous Christmas offering to the new-rich of Texas: His 'n' Her aircraft, ostriches, submarines . . . The phrase of one salesman has always stuck in my memory: at my protest over the price of a simple Panama hat he explained: 'It was woven underwater by virgins in Ecuador.'

We took a look at Texas justice. In those days cameras could film inside courtrooms and watch the faces of men as they were sentenced to death. Judges relaxed with their feet up on the bench, smoking cigars and casually administering frontier justice. The accused could escape the death sentence by pleading 'the hip pocket movement' – that he had seen the dead man's hand moving towards a hidden gun.

Percy Foreman, famous defence attorney with 700 homicide cases behind him, showed me how easily he could neutralise the Prosecutor's closing address to the jury. Seated innocently at his courtroom desk, he would start ostentatiously to roll a cigarette and, when he knew he had attracted the eyes of most jurors, would absentmindedly overfill it – so every one of them would be disregarding the DA's peroration and leaning forward to warn him silently he was spilling his tobacco . . .

Short skirts were also an excellent distraction. In one year Percy had defended 13 women on murder charges – and 12 were acquitted. Everyone involved seemed to be playing some sort of dramatic game; it was very B-movie.

Years later when I returned to Houston to film a Whicker's World on the city I found Texas courts had slipped into line with the rest of the States: cameras had been banished, if not the histrionics and the tricks.

One of our programmes came into fearful prominence four months afterwards; we considered the easy availability of guns – still, as they say, an on-going story. I took my camera into the street one morning and stopped passers-by at random to ask whether they owned a hand-gun. Every one did, including a priest – and a couple of nuns who carried theirs in the convent car glovebox. A newpaper seller had a dozen. This short but telling vox pop was repeated after the Kennedy assassination. In the *Listener* Anthony Burgess wrote : 'As to be expected, Tonight was tough and sensible, Alan Whicker dealing out facts that, grim before, are intolerable now.'

We headed west to Midland. Little known, yet the richest city of the richest country, and administrative centre for 600 oil companies. Some of the old cowpokes reading papers on the stoop outside the corner store were pointed out as multimillionaires. There was no second-generation money in that make-it-yourself town, and no one could ever accuse Texas ranchers or oilmen of putting their fortunes on their backs. Strangers have been known to offer small tips to casually-dressed Midland millionaires for performing some small courtesy – and Midland millionaires have been known to accept.

The uninspiring little place, rising like a castellated fortress out of the prairie 300 miles from the next town, suffered a prevailing wind of 20 mph and sandstorms so intense you sometimes could not see across the road. Residents built protective garden walls to keep the sand out of their barbecued steaks. To live in Midland, one needed an ardent financial attachment.

As usual, my reports from around the State were gathered together and went out under an unoriginal title: 'Whicker deep in the Heart of Texas.' I wrote this curtain-raiser for the *Radio Times*:

Texans are Americans, only more so. An improbable people still in the happy dynamic phase of getting and spending; their money has not yet swamped the human personality, as it always seems to in a few generations. Texas is a Super-America, a state of superlatives where everything appears in extra-high relief; a mirror in which fascinated Americans see themselves reflected – much larger than life.

Bigger than any European country except Russia, Texas has a nightmare climate and unrewarding scenery – but a black earth that has made its people more rich more quickly than any other people, anywhere. Theirs is the land of second chance, the last outpost of individuality, the stage on which the American drama, in all its weird extremes, is still being performed.

Every Texan is a frontiersman at heart, and life continues zestful, adventurous, and unexpected: in the past three years 24 of them have been treated in one Texas hospital for self-inflicted wounds of the lower extremities caused by shooting themselves while attempting a fast draw. The Lone-Star State is lightly governed, for Texas law is still frontier law; a blind man recently got himself arrested seven times in one month for driving a car while drunk.

It is not, as is sometimes believed, exclusively populated by millionaires, but it is a place where taxi-drivers dropping you at the airport ask, 'Your own plane – or commercial?'; where a car that is not air-conditioned is a 'special order'; where some golfers use putters with 14 carat gold heads; where on a scorched prairie millionaires' wives attend air-chilled parties in sable stoles and diamonds too enormous not to be real. Yet in this 20th century city British Consular staff receive a 'hardship' allowance.

It is doubtful whether that rich Texan did buy his dog a boy, but Dallas millionaires certainly hire maids to care for their poodles and oilman Sid Richardson did telephone oilman Clint Murchison to ask: 'What was the name of that Railroad we bought yesterday?' It was the New York Central.

That was in 1963; nothing has changed. Texans remain a distinct race, with an eagerness to please and be pleased. Six flags have flown over their State, which more than any other has seen violence and corruption and exploitation, drought and depression – yet has always moved on to new and staggering prosperity.

As a young Army officer, Robert E. Lee was stationed in Texas before the Civil War. It was then a howling, interminable wilderness. 'I can hear,' he said, 'the footstep of the coming millions . . .' Those millions are still arriving.

With mixed feelings we left the Experience that is Texas and headed for a mystery plateau even more dramatic, where high in the Jemez mountains of New Mexico 13,000 people were bent upon an ominous task . . . From Sante Fe we drove 35 miles north along the valley of the Rio Grande, turned left onto a minor road that swung up through canyons and scented pine forests. At the entrance to a small white town we passed the inevitable Drive-in dispensing sodas and hamburgers, and a small roadside notice telling what to do in the event of nuclear attack; evacuation roads were marked in colour. The terrible irony of that notice was that this was where it all began: Los Alamos – a gentle Spanish name which means 'The Cottonwoods'.

The main weapons laboratory of the United States looked much like any other well-manicured American suburban town with its shopping plaza of 73 stores and ice-cream parlor offering the regulation 31 flavours. White bungalows had barbecue pits and mail-order lawn furniture in their backyards. The workaday community enjoyed the usual civic organisations from the Flying Saucer Square Dance Club to the Military Order of Lady Bugs. Then, out across the canyons, high wire fences and armed guards came into focus – and suddenly it was not just Small Town, New Mex, but a place of infinite menace.

Los Alamos was born to follow its destiny in the spring of 1943, when 100 scientists – including Dr Klaus Fuchs – joined J. Robert Oppenheimer to work upon Project Manhattan in majestic mountain country where for years the physicist had spent his family holidays. Together they blew us all into the nuclear age. The code name of the first holocaust was – Trinity.

We found some security measures had been relaxed: the road up the mountainside was open, wire fences could be approached and some laboratories visited, though all nuclear weapons remained unspeakable. The men who created them, their cafeterias and wastepaper baskets were behind an inner screen. We spent a week 'on the Hill', talking to scientists like James Tuck from Manchester University who had attended at the birth. He was a cheerful, light-hearted man – as indeed were his colleagues. It was a most confusing place.

In one of their laboratories they laid me upon a white operating slab which then slid silently into a great white cylinder. I was wearing a microphone and the camera recorded my muffled but invisible anguish: 'It is not agreeable, lying in the dark in a lead-lined coffin having my radiation counted – but it is I suppose the story of the 20th century . . .'

Later, at his home near San Francisco, I talked with Dr Edward Teller, the scientist known as the Father of the Hydrogen bomb. Hungarian-born and of formidable intensity and brilliance, he had just resigned from the US Atomic Energy Commission to campaign for the resumption of nuclear tests, and had been much savaged by the media. He only agreed to talk before a camera if we would guarantee to transmit the whole interview, without any editing. It was the only time I faced such a stipulation. I sympathised with his cautious reaction, but tried tactfully to explain that a fast-moving early-evening programme like Tonight was not designed to handle a long and sombre conversation with one person, however significant. Happily when he got to know us and appreciated we were serious and responsible, he withdrew the stipulation – but even so, neither man nor subject was easy to handle.

I filmed further interviews with Professors Frisch and Rotblatt, and ended my programme on the bombmakers of Los Alamos: 'If one day the hydrogen bombs do fall and the earth rots, we who must die will know that the weapons that killed us were devised here – and in its Russian equivalent, wherever that unspeakable place may be – and we shall know that the very first step towards international suicide, towards the death of our world, was taken in this lovely and sinister place . . .' The camera looked around, slowly.

Our own nuclear reaction was one ot total relief when we drove down the mountainside and away from those cotton-woods towards Monument Valley, familiar to Western film fans from 'Stagecoach' days, and on to the Navajo reservation at Window Rock. We filmed in the garish hell-on-earth of Las Vegas, and finally reached Los Angeles, where there was still no escape from war talk. The city was in one of its 'the Holocaust is coming!' phases. In Hollywood, a large round steel shelter stood in the forecourt of Grauman's Chinese Theatre, like a stranded whale. It was For Sale, of course – home shelters were a hot product, moving fast.

In one of the endless suburbs I interviewed a well-prepared householder who had a deep shelter with air filtration plant and stock of guns, water and dehydrated food. The impact of our programme came when he explained that in the event of a nuclear war he and his family would have to keep unready neighbours out of their shelter – with guns if necessary.

'What happens if that little girl next door tries to come in – would you kill her too?' It was an impossible and unfair question; a shelter, like a lifeboat, will only protect so many people. He did not hesitate: 'Yes of course; she'd have to be shot.'

That candid answer stunned viewers. One of them, Elaine Morgan, was inspired to write a play she called 'License to Murder'; it considered whether such self-preservation justified killing. At the Vaudeville in London's West End

audiences watched the predicament of a well-prepared
homeowner who murdered his neighbour, in denying him
sanctuary.

Life seemed all too death-defying so we drove north to San
Francisco, hoping for more peaceful days. One afternoon I
was writing quietly in my hotel room when there came a
sudden and imperious pounding on the door: 'Open up –
FBI!'

My instinct was to leap for the fire escape, because I'd seen
it all on television. On reflection I played it cool, gave-in and
opened-up. I was tapped-down but not cuffed, and allowed
to sit. Then I heard the involved story that had brought
armed Feds to my door.

In Houston three months before, filming a report on the
aggressively lavish homes of Texan millionaires, I had planned to say as payoff: '– but of course, to live like that you
really need one of *these* at the bottom of your garden.' The
camera would pan off me . . . on to an oil rig. Simple.

We set off one morning to get this easy shot, but were
baffled to find all oil wells had vanished. We drove for miles
across the prairie, getting crosser and crosser. As we were
about to turn back, frustrated, and try some more prosperous
route – there on the wide horizon stood one lone derrick.
Beneath it, we shot the payoff.

We were about to leave when a man emerged and told us it
was in fact some sort of communications station, under a
signal tower. At that stage in the game, with a quite adequate
scene finally in the can, we were not about to be picky over
pylons. We thanked him, and headed back to Houston. After
we had driven away he evidently warned the local police that
some mad foreigners had photographed his secrets.

By then we had gone our innocent way towards months of
filming, of unplanned zig-zagging across America, changing
our plans hourly, never knowing where we should be next
day. We must have proved a tough task for the FBI's Most
Wanted section. Yet in the end, they caught up with us. I was
impressed. They, stern-faced, were less impressed by my
identification: a dog-eared membership card for the BBC
Sports Club.

Fortunately that week we had been filming the San Francisco police – indeed in the raunchy Tenderloin district had just had our zoom lens stolen, which must have established our unworldly innocence. Even better, I had interviewed the top cop, Chief Thomas Cahil; he spoke up like a man and saved me a spell in Alcatraz.

HEARST

A Screaming Woman with her Throat slit . . .

HEADING north up the coast road from Los Angeles to San Francisco our trusty, overloaded Chevrolet stationwagon began to show signs of distress. At San Luis Obispo a friendly mechanic performed in one morning the kind of major repair that at home would keep my car off the road for weeks. In America it is always easier to get a backaxle changed than a button sewn on.

While waiting, we visited the nearby home of one of America's most remarkable men and were so fascinated we returned next day to film. A couple of weeks later, in San Francisco, Alasdair Milne cabled urging us to go back and produce a second and longer programme. We were happy to return to that Enchanted Hill for its owner had been one of the Men of the Century, no doubt about that. He started a war. He made Presidents – and almost became President himself. He owned seven castles – one in Glamorgan – and ruled an enormous empire with savagery and tenderness. He destroyed men – and made others millionaires. He was an extravagant art collector with a perceptive appreciation of beauty and the money to move crated monasteries across the world; but also the Potentate of the Penny Press who debauched public taste. He was the Citizen Kane of Orson Welles' classic film: William Randolph Hearst.

His incredible kingdom of San Simeon, on an estate bigger than Bedfordshire, was crowned by the white marble castle he had begun to build in 1919 but left unfinished when he died in 1951. There, amid treasures and 87 bathrooms, wild animals and 35 cars – and never less than 50 guests – he lived an Arabian Nights fantasy in medieval splendour which the New World will not see again.

When we arrived San Simeon had just been demoted from kingdom to peep-show; it was being handed over by the family to the State and prepared to receive, not guests, but an endless procession of tourists. The Ranger guide escorting us round already had a proprietorial attitude and grew most upset when I referred to Hearst as 'a delinquent millionaire'. The family had retained one of the three grace-and-favour guesthouses, where one weekend I met his eldest son George. He afterwards presented me with a portrait of his formidable father, looking very mild indeed.

To get the flavour of those days I also tracked down a number of old Hearst men, but found most were too frail to be filmed. His gossip writer Louella Parsons was, with Hedda Hopper, one of the Hollywood harridans who struck terror into the toughest Studio boss. When we located her she was too shaky and alcoholic to appear, and was soon to die.

After all my research I found, along with every biographer, that Hearst defied understanding. He remained a triumphant failure, a kindly sadist, a timid megalomaniac, a puritanical libertine – a man of enormous power, ruthless and delicate, yet never quite great.

Fear of Hearst, fear of the dread summons to San Simeon, reached out across the world. His highly rewarded executives – some of them dollar millionaires – would journey tremulously to that Casa Encantada and wait for days before wilting under the straight bug-eyed stare of 'the Chief', penetrating and cold, and the soft, childish voice that refused to grow up with him. For all his formal politeness (he would allow no one to follow him through a door) his sarcasm could be devastating.

Only child of an almost illiterate multimillionaire Senator and his gentle aristocratic wife, Hearst inherited the crudity of one, the delicacy of the other, and the strength of both – a combination of talents that was to shape history and convulse millions with fright, enthusiasm and rage. Born in 1862, his stability crippled by an over-maternal mother, by an atmosphere of protection and adulation that left his emotions strangely jumbled, he was expelled from Harvard without finishing his junior year. A tall gangling pink-and-white young man, he asked for, and was given, a newspaper. He was just 23 when his father presented him with the shabby little evening paper he had bought for political reasons: the *San Francisco Examiner*. Journalism has never recovered.

A Hearst newspaper, it was said, was like a screaming woman running down the street with her throat slit. No other Press ever matched its flamboyance, perversity and incitement of mass hysteria. The appeal was not to men's minds but to those infantile emotions Hearst never conquered in himself: arrogance, hatred, frustration, fear.

He invented the comic strip, gossip columns and often – the news. He copied, then exceeded, Joseph Pulitzer, his main competitor in New York. Journalism became a super-spectacular business operation combining the peepshow, the foghorn and Grand Guignol as he chased circulation by letting readers know they could depend upon being startled, amazed and stupefied every day – simply by buying a Hearst newspaper. Here he was confronted by a journalistic truth: stupefying things do not happen every day. He solved this problem by creating them.

His methods and morals remained those of San Francisco in the 1870s and '80s, and his most staggering achievement before the altar of circulation came at the turn of the century when his papers manoeuvred the United States into an unnecessary and stupid war against Spain, over Cuba. When the 24-gun US battleship *Maine* exploded in Havana harbour with the loss of 260 of her crew, the Hearst coverage was ruthless, truthless newspaper jingoism. That explosion – almost certainly accidental – represented two things he wanted intensely: war with Spain, and more circulation than Pulitzer. The stigma of this utter abandonment of honesty never left Hearst, though he still had 53 years to live.

When one of his 35 writers and artists in Cuba, Frederick Remington, asked to return to New York, Hearst sent his notorious cable: 'Please remain. You furnish the pictures and I will furnish the war.'

Sure enough he did, and his papers printed 40 editions a day. He offered to equip his own regiment and provide the Navy with an armed steam yacht. Upon a rumour that the Spanish fleet might sail through the Suez Canal to attack the Philippines, he instructed his London correspondent to buy a large British ship and sink her in the Canal and, presumably, put it on his expenses. They don't breed Press Lords like that any more.

Later he urged war against Mexico – this time, without success – though he howled against wars which did not have his authorisation. He was anti-British and pro-German in the First World War, anti-British and isolationist in the Second: 'It is no part of the duty of this English-speaking nation to support the British Empire in her ambition to dominate Europe, absorb Africa and control the Orient.'

Along with his political recklessness he always retained a juvenile worship of size, noise and display. Quiet quality bored him. He wanted to shock, or stupefy. 'To put out a newspaper without promotion,' he said, 'is like winking at a girl in the dark – well-intentioned, but ineffective.'

He had no scruples, nor could his reporters afford such delicacies as they discovered, daily, the secret diaries of killers and sex-fiends in lovenests . . .

One of the *New York Journal*'s sob-sisters, returning from a colliery disaster, started her report: 'I sobbed my way through the line and the sternfaced sentinels stood aside with a muttered "The lady is from the *Journal* – let her by." I was first to reach the wounded and dying. "God Bless Mr Hearst!" cried a little girl as I stopped to mop her brow. Then she smiled and died. I spread one of our comic supplements over the pale, still face and went on to distribute Mr Hearst's bounty . . .'

Live bullets flew and dead bodies fell in the circulation wars of New York and Chicago, and above the fray strode this Paper Emperor, this journalissimo with his rough-hewn body, clumsy bones and huge face – a wondering face, rather kindly, rather simple, though unhappy and haunted.

With his journalistic genius established, he went into politics, and got married; in neither of these activities was he a success. He was 40, his bride Millicent was 21 and a 'hoofer' in a Broadway musical. They had five children, but their marriage remained a polite, sustained armistice. His political life was more violent. He wanted power and being Hearst, ultimate power; but as he set off towards the White House the many enemies he had acquired closed-ranks against him. In almost Hearstian prose the *New York Evening Post* declared:

'It is not simply that we revolt at Hearst's huge vulgarity; at his front of bronze; at his shrieking unfitness mentally for the office he sets out to buy. All this goes without saying. There never has been a case of a man of such slender intellectual equipment, absolutely without experience in office, impudently flaunting his wealth before the eyes of the people and saying "Make me President". This is folly. This is to degrade public life, for there is something darker and more fearful behind. It is well known that this man has a record which would make it impossible for him to live through a Presidential campaign – such gutters would be dragged, such sewers would be laid open . . . It is not a question of politics, but of character. An agitator we can endure; an honest radical we can respect; a fanatic we can tolerate; but a low voluptuary trying to sting his jaded senses to fresh thrill by turning from private to public corruption is a new horror in American politics . . .'

They also don't write editorials like that any more!

Hearst failed to become Mayor of New York by a mere 3,000 votes out of 600,000. His campaign for Governership of the State was just as close – he lost by only 58,000 votes out of almost a million and a half – yet his short day as a politician was over. The United States had been spared its President Hearst, though some believed that without his newspapers Theodore Roosevelt would have remained a frustrated minor politician, Dewey a nobody, and the Presidency would have eluded Franklin Roosevelt.

So he retreated to the West to build the unimpaired monument to his unrestrained dreams: San Simeon, where we were filming. With his usual contempt for money, he adorned his magic mountain-top with treasures worth millions – a richness that was used daily and lived among, for despite his other castles and mansions, this was Hearst's real home. San Simeon was where his children grew up, where Winston Churchill, Calvin Coolidge, George Bernard Shaw and a procession of Hollywood 'greats' were entertained, where tomato-ketchup bottles and paper serviettes stood on refectory tables amid 16th century silver. He called San Simeon, which cost thousands of pounds a day to run, 'My little hideaway on my little hilltop'.

He met Marion Davies 14 years after his marriage, a pert baby-doll blonde in the front row of the chorus of the Broadway 'Follies of 1917'. He went every night to watch her and took two seats – one for himself, the other for his hat. Having captured her attention, he set about turning her into another Mary Pickford and the biggest movie star of the Twenties. Money of course was no object, but despite wildly eulogistic reviews in the Hearst Press, the American public was unimpressed by the virginal little-girl image projected by Miss Davies – a cheerful, loyal woman with limited education and a quick mind. So Hearst carried his princess back to his dream castle, where she remained during the rest of his life. The association was notorious – and touching. 'I'm not saying it's right,' he said. 'I'm saying it *is*.'

So if out of political ineptitude he failed to become President and the most powerful man in the world, he did not fail in a cut-down version of his dream: iron control over a great communications empire and possession of his own duchy in the West. It was as though he knew his newspapers were trashy, his political life a disaster and his films ludicrous, but longed to leave San Simeon as one unimpaired monument. This titanic man died on the morning of 14 August 1951. He was 88, shrunken, palsied and alone.

If Hearst the man continues to elude us, we can measure with terrible accuracy his influence upon journalism, which still reaches out and touches us all: it was heavy, lasting, often malign.

He owned 13 magazines, eight radio stations, film companies, news agencies, and 28 papers – though in that Yellow Age of American journalism they could hardly be called newspapers. They were printed excitement, the screeching, hysterical newsprint equivalent of bombs exploding, bands blaring, victims screaming, houris dancing. With Hearst as conductor, the song of the spheres became a screech. No man, it was said, did so much to debase the standards of journalism.

Back at Lime Grove we strove to squeeze that extraordinary life into the meagre 30 minutes the BBC planners in their wisdom had allowed us – before going on to the repeat of some football match. Our own pictures were supported by some unique home-movies belonging to an old friend of mine, Ben Lyon. As the young star of 'Hells Angels' he had been a frequent guest at San Simeon. His candid footage showed Hearst romping on the beach in a rare unselfconscious moment, and other sidelights of the picnic-and-saucebottle life among the stars and statues upon Enchanted Hill in the Thirties.

Ben would accept no fee for the film, so we filled his Holland Park home with flowers for his wife, Bebe Daniels. Later he lent this remarkable footage to a London collector of Hollywoodiana. Just before Ben died we met on board the *QE2*. He told me that when he asked for his film back, the man denied ever having had it. So if the BBC has junked our film, all that remains of Mr Hearst at play is now in that illicit archive.

We called our programme 'Megalomillionaire'. The critics were knocked all-of-a-heap. Too much talk, said one; more detail, asked another. Raucous . . . poetic . . . strident . . . superb . . . cruel . . . memorable . . . their reactions covered 180 degrees. Each was exact, for each applied precisely to the many men that were Hearst.

ALASKA

A Summer of Love, without Sleep . . .

SOME situations on television seem to have disproportionate impact upon viewers – though even after a quarter of a century in the craft I find it impossible to be sure what will catch the passing fancy, what will imprint upon memories. In our ephemeral medium, most events disappear instantly and without trace; others are constantly recalled. Viewers still come up in the street, for example, and say, 'Remember when you stopped that train in Alaska . . . ?'

I do indeed. We had been filming at Clear, the Missile Early Warning station with its giant ears – each larger than a football field – where men of the US Air Force stood ready as space-age Paul Reveres to sound the alarm at a Russian nuclear attack. Similar stations were later built at Thule in Greenland and Fylingdales in Yorkshire.

That morning as we prepared to fly back to Anchorage I recalled the unlikely tall-tale that in the vast emptiness of Alaska – with only 250,000 people, in 1962 – lonely Home-steaders could stand anywhere along the State's one rail-wayline and halt a train by holding out an arm, as though flagging-down a bus at a Request stop. In an empty land where snow can be 70 feet deep and temperatures 70 degrees below, where from his cab the engineer sees more moose than people, it had been pointless to build stations. So one morning in the empty wilderness 80 miles south of Fairbanks, we bravely prepared to hold-up the Aurora.

I stood by the line in the bitter cold, waiting for the one train which daily covered the 356 lonely miles of single track between Alaska's two towns. ('The train now standing at the platform is the train.') As we set up our camera, we heard from behind the mountains in the distance the mournful wail of the great diesel locomotive, heading south through the wilderness. In an anxious gabble I confided to the camera what I was hoping to do and, like Billy Brown of London Town – faced the driver, raised my hand, and hoped that he would understand.

The Aurora bore down upon us relentlessly and, after some moments of suspense – he did. With a terrible grinding, the great towering monster obligingly slowed to a halt. We grabbed camera, tripod and gear, and scrambled excitedly on board. That is the hold-up remembered by many viewers. It certainly made an impression on me: never again has any gesture of mine been as effective!

Alaska had been selected for this early Tonight tour in our usual haphazard way – probably with a pin – for this was in the years between the Gold-rush and the Oil-rush when the majestic and almost uninhabited State seemed merely an Arctic wilderness, a refuelling stop on the trans-Polar flight to Japan. As luck would have it, this Last Frontier produced 15 of our most interesting reports, compiled afterwards into Whicker on Top of the World, twice. It supported my contention that the success of a series was usually in inverse ratio to the pleasure and comfort in which it was filmed. Nightmare weeks of cold or heat, fear or frustration usually produced excellent television. When we found ourselves comfortable and having fun on location, I always began to worry . . .

In Alaska, any risk of happiness was soon dispelled. After the flight from Copenhagen and a couple of nights in Anchorage, we were leaving the hotel to go north in a US Air Force C47. I helped the crew with their equipment while our director, Jack Gold, looked after our suitcases. As baggagemaster, Jack was an excellent director: without any trouble at all, he left my suitcase standing in the hotel lobby while we flew hundreds of miles into the icy wastes. I started filming in that winter wonderland without a sweater, clean shirt, razor or any comfort known to man. There was a distinct chill in the air.

Alaska was then the last place in the world where they were giving away land – perhaps because there were 272 million acres of it, vacant. Any American who promised to develop his patch could be granted 160 acres for a registration fee of $12.80. At eight cents an acre Alaska was not a bad buy, even without oil.

In a small chartered aircraft we banged down to a wobbly landing in a valley clearing, and jeeped up the mountain to reach the home of Bert and Su Lum. A schoolmaster and secretary from Boonton, New Jersey, outside New York, they had been married a year and were brand new Homesteaders in the wilderness. It was considerable transformation. He had to clear and cultivate at least 20 of his 160 acres and build a habitable house within the three years stipulated, and was struggling to do that while living with pregnant Su under a tarpaulin. Together they made a century-old pioneering scene.

As we were leaving that evening after filming they asked for a memorial photograph, so we posed as a human totem pole, one upon the other's shoulders against the tall treetrunk which was the main support of their home-to-be. The unexpected result of that joky picture was that it put out the back of my recordist, the bottom man on the totem pole. He had been selected because he was the tallest – though, it transpired, not the strongest. I could tell he was in trouble when, back in Anchorage next day, I saw him bent double like Old Father Time and using a mike-stand to lever himself, groaning, along the hotel corridor.

A local doctor gave him pain-killing injections but, determinedly orthodox, he refused manipulation by an osteopath: 'Don't want any of those quacks messing me about.' For days he lay in considerable discomfort, while we carried on filming. One evening the Commanding General of the US Air Force in Alaska told me he had been helped by an exceptional local osteopath. I reported this to our recordist, still twisted and growing bitter. He finally agreed that since the chap treated three-star generals he might just be acceptable – even though not recognised by the BMA. The manipulator came to the hotel next day and fixed his back in a couple of minutes, with two dull cracks.

The absence of the recordist had merely meant inconvenience and more work for the remaining four of us. Today the whole unit would be out of action, for the union would not permit anyone 'unqualified' to undertake the not-too-demanding task of switching on a tape-recorder.

Soon afterwards, in an even more unrestrictive practice, cameraman Geoff Mulligan and I flew 900 miles out to the Pribilofs, the islands lying under permanent drifting fog-banks in the Bering Sea, north of the Aleutian chain. There were only two seats in the aircraft, which meant I was going to interview while operating recorder and microphone, and he would handle everything else.

We flew for a whole day, bumpily and with much unhappiness, before reaching the gale-swept rock. We had gone to watch the Alaska fur seals returning as they do each year to the beaches of their birth – an extraordinary scene. For several blustery days we filmed this enormous colony – 15 noisy rookeries within seven miles and, with two million fighting and fornicating seals, probably the greatest assembly of wild animals on earth.

Each 50-stone bull seal or Beachmaster in the densely-packed colonies is five times larger than the 60 to 100 females in his harem. For fear they may disperse to other males, he stays on guard and neither drinks nor eats for three months. He also gets very little sleep. It is hardly surprising that during his long summer of love, the Beachmaster loses 200lbs and suffers from exhaustion.

We filmed Dick Petersen, from the Johns Hopkins University in Baltimore. He had spent two years observing the seals' social and reproductive behaviour and, while there was almost no one on the island to talk to, he at least had plenty to watch.

The value of sealskins taken from this remote grey island

each year about equals the price the United States paid Russia for the whole territory of Alaska: $7.2 million.

We then embarked upon the lonely flight back across the Bering Sea, having completed without any problem at all a programme which today could not be attempted without six or seven men, at least; sometimes, 13.

Filming in Alaska meant a succession of such dodgy flights, but there was no alternative. The State, with its one short railway and few roads, was even then the flyingest place in the world. With an aircraft for every 30 people in Anchorage, flying visits meant just that. Aircraft were used as cars – to pop down the road for shopping, pick up the mail, visit friends. The air way was often the only way.

While we were there Roger Waldron, 41-year-old gravel company executive, set out in his three-seater 100mph float-plane for a day's fishing, taking his 16-year-old son. They did not return.

If aviation is suited to serve Alaska, Alaska is not suited to aviation: weather conditions change abruptly, clouds hide mountains, magnetic compasses go crazy near the North Pole . . .

We filmed the Civil Air Patrol searching for the missing Waldrons. Like lifeboatmen, this group of local volunteers lend their aircraft and themselves in any emergency, and fly to search and save – each pilot knowing that tomorrow, he could be the one in peril. In the Operations Room we waited with relatives and the Mission Commander, while the Air Patrol anxiously criss-crossed the skies.

Days later we learned that remains of the floatplane had been spotted not far from the mountain lake where they had gone so happily to fish. Their bodies were recovered.

We flew on to Nome, like which there is no place. This windswept settlement 40 miles from Siberia is the last town before Tomorrow. Jack and I shared a room above Nome's café. It boasted a juke box and one Elvis Presley record, which Eskimo youths played all night. Upstairs, trying to sleep, we could not hear the melody, just the thudding base. It vibrated the bedsprings. I never felt quite the same about Elvis after those endless Arctic nights.

Then north to Barrow, the ultimate howling, freezing wilderness on the outside edge of civilisation – the last place on earth. In this largest Eskimo village in the world, the night lasts 100 days.

One of Barrow's noticeable problems was that there was nowhere to dispose of the detritus left by 1,500 Eskimos. Junked vehicles and mechanical rubbish did not rust and crumble away, but remained frozen-fresh indefinitely. Garbage could not be buried because the ground was always icy, so lay around above the permafrost and made life interesting for the dogs. Beautiful it was not. There was the same distinct problem with sanitation. It was a hard place to enjoy – so I had every confidence the programme would be interesting.

At least it stimulated interest in Northants; after we had considered the multimillion-pound ballistic missile early-warning station at Clear, a *Rushden Echo* writer reflected in his Irthlingboro' Notes: 'As I watched that much-travelled Alan Whicker standing pensively near huge radar masts in Alaska which will give America a few hours (sic) grace in the case of a nuclear war, I found myself thinking about the Civil Defence training centre at Irthlingborough. I wondered what plans had been made at the premises at Wellingborough Road, as Russian ships churned their way towards Cuba . . .'

We escaped from Barrow with considerable relief, but left Alaska spellbound by its beauty and empty immensity. I did not return for 15 years – when Alaska had struck oil and was rich and famous.

Back in the Lower Fortyeight, we found Seattle in the throes of a World Fair – one of those vast international bazaars rare as eclipses of the sun and equally inclined to stay in the mind. They break out at intervals, because ever since Man learned to make things he has enjoyed collecting crowds to show off his achievements; the most sophisticated Fair remains the noisy market place at the end of the caravan trail with sideshows and spangled dancing girls, full of swank and wonder.

Seattle's Fair had already drawn nine million people to its 74 acres – yet was only 'second category'. Brussels, in the top rank, had been five times as popular and eight times as large.

Just as the Paris Fair of 1899 left behind the absurd Eiffel Tower, Seattle had its Space Needle, a teetering restaurant 60-storeys high which we could never reach because of the queues. The British Pavilion, designed by the man responsible for the Regent Street Christmas decorations, was thought to be the best at the Fair. It exhibited orbital engines, X-ray micro-analysers and the undercarriage of a Vulcan. Despite such overwhelming technology, when I stopped American visitors and asked how they saw Britain, they all reflected upon Beefeaters and thatched cottages. Not even Concorde can remove the transatlantic conviction that we are a quaint real-cute country. I recalled that two prize-winning American exhibits at the last major British Fair in 1851 were chewing-tobacco and false teeth, and decided it was better to be cute . . .

In the middle of a report from the Boeing aircraft factory outside Seattle, the Tonight office urged us to hurry across the 3,000 miles to New York. There at the United Nations building on 18 September 1962, still slightly breathless, I conducted the first two-way Telstar interview seen on television, talking with our Minister of State for Foreign Affairs Joseph Godber and the American Secretary of State Adlai Stevenson. Our conversation continued happily until the satellite dropped down below the horizon and switched itself off. The pictures were reported in the Press next day to have been 'impressively clear'. It may not have been Alaska yet we were, in a way, pioneering.

ALABAMA

Off to see the Imperial Wizard . . .

WHILE we were filming among the quiet volcanoes of Guatemala, the Negro Revolution had been erupting in the United States. Black Muslims and Martin Luther King were in full cry: 'Black people have been dying for nothing all these years – now it's time to die for something.' So they faced snarling police dogs, sat at forbidden lunch-counters, marched and protested, and in turn were clubbed and bombed and went to jail by the thousand.

Amid the angry turmoil of black-haters and white-haters, the University of Alabama was to be desegregated and two black students were about to be enrolled, by force if necessary. Tonight asked us to hurry north again to cover the expected violence.

The cable from Shepherd's Bush appeared to believe – as would any red-blooded Fleet Street news editor – that all we need do was step outside and call a cab. In fact we had to detach ourselves from the witchdoctors of Atitlán and move from the Sierra Madre down through the national state-of-siege roadblocks, back to Guatemala City. There, amid the turmoil of a Central American airport, we required room for five and a mountain of gear on the Pan Am flight to Panama, changing to a Delta flight to New Orleans, where we dozed the night away in the departure lounge before piling on to a dawn service to Birmingham. We just made it, the day before Governor George C. Wallace was due to 'stand in the schoolhouse door' to prevent Coloured enrolment. We hired a stationwagon and set off for Tuscaloosa, where it was all happening.

It was not an enviable assignment. The year before I had filmed a similar confrontation at the University of Mississippi – 'Ole Miss' – when a Black, James Meredith, was to be enrolled. Southern whites rioted, and turned to vent their racial fury also against northern newspapermen, whose reports they found too sympathetic to the Black cause. They were even more hostile towards foreign Press and television who were spreading the shameful scene around the world. A French correspondent who had a ginger beard and collar and tie – so even at night was plainly no Southern redneck – had been selected, shot and killed. Other correspondents were roughed up.

To the carloads of cheering, jeering youths riding around with Confederate flags on their aerials, a camera or a notebook – even an out-of-State look – meant Criticism. It felt strange and horribly wrong to be at the receiving end of anger and hatred from such generous and easygoing people. For a few violent days they seemed to belong to some other nation.

The University of Alabama also stood in strong Ku Klux Klan territory. We arrived in the furnace-heat of a Southern summer, driving past banners which declared: 'Keep 'bama White'. The atmosphere was eerie; roads normally used by the 16,000 students had been blocked off by armed guards. It was far quieter than 'Ole Miss' for the campus was already ringed by State police – burly big-bellied men in bright blue helmets with revolvers, dangling truncheons and 'Heart of Dixie' flashes. They were assisted by the only other armed State force: the more peaceful Commissioners for Game and Fishing, in helmets suitably green.

After Martin Luther King's 'Battle of Birmingham', President Kennedy had ordered Governor Wallace – how ill-starred, that trio – to stay away from the University. However in the 1958 Gubernatorial elections this arch-segregationalist had been, as he put it, 'out-segged' by an opposing politician. He was not about to be out-segged again, no sir. So the five-foot-seven Governor, former Golden Gloves bantam-weight who called himself 'a professional Southerner', stood in the schoolhouse door as he had promised and blocked the way of the tall US Deputy Attorney

General, Nicholas Katzenbach. We filmed the confrontation as they made speeches at each other while the two students, Vivian Malone and James Hood, waited in a back road, guarded by four carloads of US Marshals.

The little fighting-cock of a Governor refused to stand aside, so within minutes Washington reacted inexorably: the Alabama National Guard was Federalised. This removed 17,000 State troops from the Governor's control – though his armed police still occupied the campus and awaited his orders. The prospect of Americans fighting each other seemed unthinkable, yet in the livid steamheat of that tense and angry campus, everyone awaited the first shot.

Troops of the 31st Dixie Division arrived, all of them Southerners whose sympathies no doubt lay with the Governor. We watched their Commander, Brigadier-General Henry Graham, go up to Wallace: 'It is my sad duty to ask you to step aside.' The Governor made another speech, reading this time from a crumpled scrap of paper – and walked away.

He was the third Southern Governor to defy the Federal courts, and then surrender. Soldiers escorted the two Black students into the auditorium, to enrol. 'Bama had been desegregated, without violence.

As tension drained – for that day at least – I recorded my pay-off and commentary and we drove fast back to Birmingham Airport to despatch the urgent film to London. We were relieved, and triumphant: it had been a splendid and revealing story, full of fear and drama and hatred – but with an unexpectedly happy ending.

At London Airport the package of negatives was collected by a waiting BBC car and rushed to the laboratories, so it could be edited next day and transmitted in the evening. Then the car went on to deliver to the studios the six rolls of recording tape containing the sound of the confrontation, the interviews and my commentary. The commissionaire on duty in the middle of the night received the tapes and placed them for a moment on the wall outside the Lime Grove entrance. While his back was turned, some passer-by stole them.

Those tapes, worth a few shillings, represented thousands of pounds in airfares and effort – not to mention nervous energy and anguish. The mute film, all that was left, was never transmitted. No one called us in 'bama to tell of our stolen triumph.

In blissful ignorance, we were off to see the Wizard – the Imperial Wizard of the Ku Klux Klan. We did not travel the Yellow Brick Road, but the same old Turnpike from Birmingham to Tuscaloosa. There the Wizard – a mild man otherwise known as Robert Shelton – sold car air conditioning. Our hired stationwagon was loaded with the five of us and a mass of camera gear. With assistant cameraman Henry Farrar at the wheel, we barrelled down the dual carriageway towards the Klannish Konfrontation.

The director, cameraman and recordist were dozing in the back seat and I was sitting in front with a typewriter on my knee, preparing my intro and having some thoughts about the questions. Gazing around vacantly and seeking inspiration, I noticed some way ahead along the empty highway a stationary car waiting in the centre to cross our lane . . . had started to move forward.

Henry stood on the brakes. We skidded 50 yards and slammed hard into the other car, broadside on. The old jalopy was flung into the air. It went somersaulting away, over and over. Our heavy wagon stayed upright, just, but the bonnet concertinaed in front of the screen like a visor, and we ran off the road.

Flung forward in the whiplash, my typewriter was squashed between the dashboard – and me. It was never the same again. In the back seat our cameraman saw the lenshood of the Arriflex on his lap driven back into the camera body – but fortunately, not too far into his.

After what seemed a long time, screaming brakes and tortured tyres and scrunched steel fell silent . . . and from the other car we could hear merry music. It was on its roof, wheels spinning.

Gingerly we clambered out of our crumpled wagon, feeling for anything broken, and staggered over to the shattered car.

Father *(left)*, Mother and an Egyptian friend travelling in a manner to which I was reluctant to become accustomed . . .

Mother and my Godfather – evidently *after* that ugly scene over the toothpicks . . .

An early Whicker getting it together on the seafront at Brighton – and even then talking to-camera . . .

Wartime: John Amery, Cabinet Minister's son who was the Lord Haw-Haw of Mussolini's radio, arrested with his girlfriend in Milan. He was later sent from the Old Bailey to be hanged . . .

Left: Warriors' relaxation – fooling around for the camera with Captain Alf Black in our villa at Taormina, Sicily, before the invasion of Italy . . .

Opposite below: Christmas dinner 1944 in my requisitioned Florentine HQ with unused mistletoe. Cameramen, mechanics and drivers of the Film Unit waited upon, traditionally, by Major Lord Stopford, Lieutenant Craig, Captain Whicker *(centre),* Lieutenant Groom . . .

Above: After the Fifth Army's Salerno landing, General Montgomery's first meeting with General Mark Clark and his Chief of Staff, General Gruenther; Captain Whicker (*extreme left*) the correct few paces behind such a galaxy . . .

Fleet Street – and in New York a thoughtful reaction to President Truman, whose finger was hovering near the button . . .

Kim Philby, the Third Man, proclaims his innocence before a sceptical reporter and a maelstrom of photographers . . .

Television – and the on-camera chemistry that in 1957 got Tonight off and running: *left to right*, Geoffrey Johnson Smith, Derek Hart, Rory McEwen, Whicker, Cy Grant, Cliff Michelmore . . .

My first television interview: before a blitzed building at Ramsgate . . .

My first world tour, in 1958. An intro from among swaying hula girls on Kauai, microphone lead buried discreetly in the sand . . .

My early BBC titles in 1965 set the highflying tone: a VC 10 moved across the tarmac, its tail revealing our enormous lettering – which we had to paint out before they let us go . . .

WHICKER'S WORLD

Frugal fare amid a splendour of candlelit silver: lunch at Sutton Place with J. Paul Getty, the Solitary Billionaire . . .

007 at his peak – and my best side to-camera. Sean Connery was prickly about photographers on the set, so for stills we used this frame from our film . . .

Olga Deterding 'bought the ship' to join us as we filmed that 1965 Christmas cruise . . .

Anne from Notting Hill took her harp to a party and found herself flying over the Chaco with Whicker's World in a DC 3 of the Paraguayan Air Force . . .

The driver was hanging upside down, unconscious and pouring blood, while a transistor dangling from his driving mirror rocked-and-rolled happily.

With sirens and flashing red lights, the State police and a long low ambulance soon screamed up to the scene of highway havoc. They could see from wrecks, skidmarks and blood exactly what had happened, and were quite relaxed about another everyday accident. The only thing that seriously upset them was the discovery that Henry was not carrying his driving licence – a heinous offence in the United States. Blood and guts, injuries and ambulances, cars totalled, unconscious figure on stretcher, wrecker trucks with flashing lights, battered camera gear, shaken Limeys, lawsuits pending – nothing seemed to matter except Identification. Henry, standing weakly amid the wreckage, winded but thankful to be alive, was promptly and grimly fined $50, in cash.

After all that, the Imperial Wizard seemed something of an anti-climax.

SWITZENSTEIN

You don't get to be a Gnome by sleeping late . . .

AFTER witchdoctors' incantations and campus racism, I went with great relief to film among the clean and well-ordered charms of Switzerland and Austria, where food was delicious, lavatories worked and there was no daily hatred. In Zurich we started at the deep end with a programme on a secretive group already known as the Gnomes. We were acting upon Voltaire's advice: 'If you see a Swiss Banker jump out of a window, follow him – for there's money to be made.'

We followed Dr Alfred Schaefer, then Chief General Manager of the Union Bank, tracking behind him as he drove from his lakeside home promply at 7.45 am. You don't get to be a Gnome by sleeping late.

There were few chauffeurs in that rich land and, as the dignified Dr Schaefer explained, rather to my surprise, 'It's more sporty to drive yourself'.

We filmed his vaults, looked thoughtfully at the ledgers wherein 10,000 numbers showed where hot and cold money had come to rest in respectable anonymity. Dr Schaefer was correct, pleasant, reserved – and could have been sent to fill his significant role by Central Casting. We talked at length, but needless to say I learned few secrets – only that the tradition of thrift was holding up well. His nation had always loved money – and indeed there is no doubt the Swiss franc can be extremely lovable . . .

Along with clean trains, watches and milk chocolate, the world's oldest Democracy also specialises in hotels, so we considered their largest private hotelier: Fritz Frey, a charming man with the face of a fallen cherub. He owned the Burgenstock Estate, a sort of holiday camp for millionaires on top of a mountain promontory 1,500 feet above Lake Lucerne. His three hotels formed an island in the sky, disturbed only by the comforting clonk of distant cowbells.

When he inherited his kingdom in 1953, Frey stunned his frugal Swiss colleagues by covering his hotel floors with Persian rugs and adorning walls with Aubusson and Gobelin tapestries once owned by the Empress Eugénie and Frederick the Great. In halls and diningrooms he hung his father's collection of paintings by Rubens and Tintoretto, Van Dyck and Breughel. Among the antique furniture in daily use by residents were Maria Theresa and Louis Quinze pieces – indeed his hotels exuded such good taste and breeding that even the noblest guests were hard put to keep up with the furniture.

Frey told me that despite such man-made and natural grandeur, Burgenstock had no winter season, so earned money for a mere 18 weeks a year; and with 360 employees and exacting guests, he made a profit during only six of these.

In such fragile and esoteric surroundings the only unexpected amenity was the Submarine Bar, next to and below the swimming pool. One wall was glass. Residents, if they chose, could sit with their drinks and watch the bottom-halves of swimmers.

It became evident that male guests were congregating to watch the frolics. Finally, exasperated wives objected. Their husbands were paying a great deal of money, they complained, to stay at Burgenstock for a *rest* . . .

Amid such growing tension, something had to give and one day – it did. It was the elastic on a pair of swimming trunks. They came off in the water before interested spectators. Horrors.

The bar was promptly closed. Shocked management hastily backed down and agreed with the wives that watching such activity while actually drinking alcohol was somehow . . . unchaste. From then on the bar was demoted to Submarine *Room* and used merely for meditation. This offered voyeuristic husbands no legitimate excuse for daily visits.

As we headed for our next location I suffered one of those indignities that descend like some terrible punishment from above upon the best-intentioned traveller. Perhaps I had spent too much time in the Submarine Room.

As usual we had let the camera-gear ride comfortably in the boots of our overloaded cars, and tied our own suitcases to their rooofracks. Driving fast along an autobahn through a fierce rainstorm, we suddenly noticed people in approaching cars were waving. We stopped to see what could be causing such friendly demonstrations.

We found all that remained of my bulging suitcase was its handle, still neatly roped to the roof. The rest of the case had been wrenched away in the gale and, when it hit the ground, burst open. Looking back down the valley, we could see its contents being blown across the countryside, and disappearing fast. I noticed in a detached sort of way that all my careful notes and scripts formed an effective snowstorm. As we stood in the rain, my clothes and possessions were being distributed fast across a great deal of Switzerland. *How* we laughed.

My director was Jack Gold, who had misdirected my belongings in Alaska. While we scrambled around the fields I gave him a few damp looks, but this time he was relatively innocent. Thankfully it was Switzerland, so passing motorists stopped and helped. I got most of my soggy things back. My notes were last seen heading for Austria, and I waved them goodbye.

When so brusquely interrupted, we had been on our way to film in Toyland, a tiny sovereign State controlled by a police force of 14 men and one dog where if they need more money, they print another stamp. It was the 25th Anniversary of the marriage of the King and Queen of Ruritania or, to be precise, Prince Franz Josef II and Princess Georgina of Liechtenstein. Most of their 17,000 people came out to celebrate in the capital, Vaduz. Sodden and mud-stained though it was, it was pleasant to dance in the streets.

Since the State is only 60 square miles and most of *that* occupied by 24 alps, their cathedral is the size of an English country church and their whole compact Whitehall contained within one building. In its basement, the jail had only five cells – and they always sent prisoners home for Christmas. On the ground floor, the police station. First floor: offices of the prime minister, attorney general and various authorities. Second floor; magistrates court and the Westminster of Liechtenstein, its parliament.

The nearby post office was far more important. It was the headquarters of a highly profitable business with an output rarely put to use: it had standing orders from 40,000 stamp collectors around the world and its issues usually went straight into albums. Then there were the nameplates: since names of directors were not disclosed, many thousands of companies operated under the Liechtenstein flag of convenience. This simple dispensation provided local lawyers with a fortune in fees each year. Income tax started at four per cent, they said, and climbed *right* up to eight per cent.

Their ceramic industry was also, I discovered, the world's

largest manufacturer of black false teeth; most of those smiles-you-can-never-forget went East, where living teeth could be stained by betel nut.

Liechtenstein, sole survivor of the 343 states that once made up the Holy Roman Empire, is so neutral that during the last war they would not even allow Swiss soldiers to enter – and *they* were supposed to be defending the place. Its Army last went to war against Prussia in 1866, on the side of the Austrians. Their 58 soldiers marched bravely away to do battle but, far from fighting to the last man, 59 soldiers came marching home. After that, the Army was disbanded. They never did discover who the extra chap was – but he was plainly no fool.

We were entertained up in Castle Vaduz by the Prince, a shy, modest man and one of 11 children of a Hapsburg Archduchess – a group known locally as 'the football team'. When talking with this gentle man it was hard to remember that his person was 'sacred and inviolable' and his power so awesome a mere word could 'bestow titles, suspend sentences and halt pursuits'. He and his statuesque Viennese wife showed us around their 700-year-old castle – a perfect setting for the remake of 'The Prisoner of Zenda'. On their walls were 16 Van Dycks, the only Leonardo da Vinci in private hands and 77 Flemish Masters. The others were in the cellar. I asked how many Rubens he had, but the Prince could not remember. He thought it was 17.

I also met his cousin, Prince Hans, who was driving a local sightseeing bus. He never told tourists he was a Royal Prince, he said, because if he did they never gave him a tip.

AUSTRIA

Vienna is not the Wild West . . .

AUSTRIA has been one of my favourite lands since its stricken
post-war days and, when I returned in 1963 with a camera
crew, did not let me down. Our tour provided excitement,
sentiment, horror and fun – a predictably theatrical cross-
section of emotion running all the way from a celestial choir
to an undiplomatic car chase.

In upper Austria we considered Braunau, a charming
medieval town upon the River Inn. It had achieved an
unwanted niche in history which it has not chosen to claim in
the guide books: it gave birth to Adolph Hitler. Tactlessly,
we raked around those unhappy embers for a while. In the
peace of a smalltown afternoon I stood in the sunshine
outside the Schickelgrubers' backstreet home and reflected
upon the path that began at its front door and led directly to a
cataclysmic conclusion in the Berlin bunker, with half the
world aghast and the rest in flames . . .

For comic relief we went on to film one of our most happy
reports at Hellbrunn Castle, an hour's walk outside Salzburg. The magnificent garden of the 17th century mansion
stands full of michievous water jets; visitors, while solemnly
conducted around the grounds, are at every pause for information – drenched.

The Pleasure Castle and its waterworks were designed
about 1615, probably by the Italian Santino Solari. He must
have been a delightful madman. His gardens are full of
streams, ponds and traditional waterspouting Tritons; some
fountains operate mechanical figures, others balance balls,
cause organs to play, activate great jaws, or merely display

prettily. It is his hidden waterspouts that cause the fun and fame and hysterical shrieks. The graceful park lives in a perpetual tumult of screams and laughter for, as circuses and early movie makers knew, nothing creates higher spirits than misdirected water.

In one open-air theatre visitors obediently sit upon stone stools listening to their guide – until he gleefully activates 87 sharp jets which rise from the centre of every stool, except his. There is no escaping the ingenious, wayward little jets. Anyone hanging back craftily from the group gets drenched from an unexpected direction.

After submitting ourselves to the tour and getting suitably soaked, we spent the afternoon trying to film others undergoing that hilarious water-torture, while keeping spray off the lens. All this merriment sounds childish – it *is* childish – but I do not recall ever laughing so much in one day. We returned to our hotel, damp and aching. Almost four centuries ago, that naughty architect well knew how to bring out the happy urchin in us all. He created a frivolous garden and, through the ages, as much innocent laughter as any man has achieved.

For less-innocent waterworks we went up into the Syrian Alps, to brooding Lake Toplitz. The Nazis' hidden treasure is said to rest in its black depths. In the heart of their Alpenfestung, the Alpine Fortress they were to hold against the Allies, witnesses reported that during the final upheaval of World War II three separate armed convoys had unloaded and sunk mysterious cylinders into the lake.

Three years before our visit a team of divers working for a German magazine had raised 15 crates from its dark depths. They contained forged English banknotes with a face value of some £9 million. Then the Austrian Government's authority permitting salvage work was suddenly withdrawn.

Beneath a thick layer of submerged logs and treetrunks, more than a ton of gold is believed to lie in the dark lake at a depth of 300 feet, in 22 cases dropped in by Otto Skorzeny's paratroops. Another 24 containers are said to hold some of the looted treasure Hitler was planning to put into a museum in Linz, after his victory. Perhaps even more precious, or dangerous, the Nazis' ultimate secrets: sealed cylinders full of lists of numbered Swiss bank accounts, spies and sleepers around the world . . .

Attempts at salvage have always been diverted, for various and curious reasons, and investigators have suffered a number of rather odd accidents. No one would discuss the subject with me, but it was a good story, so I stood up to my knees in the icy lake and recounted the few facts and theories we could discover.

Some time before our arrival, for instance, three Austrian 'tourists' had set out into the surrounding alps upon a mountaineering holiday. One returned alone in a snow-storm, saying his friends had taken refuge in a mountain hut. When the weather cleared a rescue team reached the hut and found two frozen bodies, one fearfully mutilated. The stomach had been cut out. It was later reported this man had a sketch showing the location of hidden gold, and surmised that during a quarrel he had swallowed the map . . .

There was no doubt Toplitz was a sinister setting: secret-ive, hard to reach, unwelcoming – a place of dark mysteries. We were happy to return to the *gemütlichkeit* of Vienna; but even there that creepy, haunting lake inspired me to attempt a report on Spying – which brought our tour to an abrupt and violent end.

From the days of the Austro-Hungarian empire, Vienna has always been a city of intrigue; now this bridge between East and West was crossed by an even heavier traffic in espionage. In the tiny European cul-de-sac that was Austria, the Russians had their third-largest Embassy in the world – and those hundreds of diplomats were not trading in *petit point*.

The official estimate of the Austrian Minister of the In-terior was that 200 full-time professional spies were operat-ing. A Viennese newspaper, *Die Presse*, believed that with part-timers, messengers and pin-money amateurs, the num-ber was nearer 50,000. While not exactly encouraging such clandestine activity, the Austrian Government found spying a useful source of foreign currency. Their Supreme Court had ruled that espionage activities not directed against Austria were not illegal, so since the Third Man city had few home-grown secrets to offer the world, everyone could legitimately carry-on-spying on everyone else.

While in custody in Vienna, a Hungarian counter-intelligence agent had just died, rather too suddenly. Bela Lypsynik had escaped across the Hungarian border on a motorcycle. He and his information were about to be flown to a welcoming America. Then in a guarded room, he suddenly became violently dead.

It was not unreasonably assumed he had been murdered. Official Austria, much embarrassed, claimed his death was due to 'damage to heart and liver caused by repeated inflammation of gums and tonsils.'

Clearing our throats nervously, we drove to the Soviet Ambassador's so-called country residence, a large and anonymous villa on the outskirts of Vienna where, it was believed, all their European agents were debriefed. We set up and I told the camera about the web of espionage extending from that rather bland building. We completed our filming without spotting any movement around the place. This was, in a way, rather a disappointment.

The problem with the report was that, while there was plenty to say – much of it, of course, conjecture – there was little to see. It is not easy to film a spy spying, and even if achieved would not make much of a picture.

For a few additional and relevant shots we went back to Vienna's diplomatic quarter. The Russian Embassy stood in the Reisnerstrasse, not far from the British Embassy. After another short piece to-camera there, I left the crew to shoot mute establishers of the building and the district, and returned to the Astoria Hotel to prepare our next day's story. When my back was turned there was an extraordinary outburst of activity in that melodramatic city: my crew were chased through the streets by furious Russian diplomats in two black limousines. They tried to ram the BBC car. On that quiet Saturday afternoon our wordy background report had become an action Thriller.

As Peter Hall and his assistant Reg Pope completed their filming, Russians had appeared at the windows of the

Embassy, looking angry. Deciding the time was right for a tactful withdrawal, the crew began to load their car, nonchalantly but quickly. As the tripod went in, two agitated diplomats rushed out of the Embassy and tried to grab the camera.

With the help of Don Martin, our recordist, the crew pushed them off, leapt into their stationwagon and drove away fast. Convinced of guilt by such frantic flight, the Russians ran back to their garage, jumped into two Embassy cars and tore after them, tyres screaming.

Reg Pope, struggling to pep-up the old green BBC wagon, headed for the city centre – for want of anywhere else to go. Twice the Russians attempted to stop them by ramming. Then they tried to block their path fore and aft – and the way they do it in films.

Regrettably the crew were not in the mood to record from inside all the real-life action happening around them. It would have been award-winning footage.

In those tense moments Pope saw with anguish that the fuel indicator was empty. This was an in-joke: I always complained that they deliberately waited until we were in a hurry to get somewhere before deciding to fill up and check tyres and battery, in our time. They were learning a lesson, the violent way.

Fearing the car might gasp to a halt in some lonely street, when they would be grabbed by two carloads of Volga diplomats, Pope with presence of mind squealed to a halt alongside a Viennese traffic policeman. They all leapt out and appealed for protection.

There was a confused mêlée as the Russians rushed up, shouting. The bewildered Austrian, his weekend ruined, radioed for help. Police cars loaded with local Special Branch arrived from all sides – and played no favourites: they arrested everybody.

At police headquarters the crew were permitted to call me. Their message took a little time to penetrate. I arrived to find them much shaken by such James Bonderie. As the excitement of the chase waned and they absorbed what had happened, their alarm grew.

After a furious display of anger, the Russians went home, threatening an Official but doubtless more diplomatic protest. The Austrians had baffled them by pointing out that there was no law against taking pictures of an Embassy from the public highway.

Outraged that foreigners should have attempted to take the law into their own hands, the police had no intention of being leaned-upon: 'We are a free country now,' the Chief told me, with some heat. 'The Occupation is over. We will not have this behaviour in our capital. Vienna is not the Wild West.' I gave him my admiration and in turn, he gave me my crew; we parted with mutual expressions of good will.

Though they had emerged unscathed from an International Incident, the crew did not see it as a happy ending. They were convinced Soviet Heavies were now out to get them, and were totally unnerved. They explained to me that since they had been seen and identified, the Russians certainly believed them to be spies – MI5 and CIA, or worse. Hit men of SMERSH, the GPU and KGB must already be on the way.

The trouble, I realised, was that they had obviously been listening to my to-camera pieces that afternoon. That was the trouble with a good crew – they absorbed things; to bad crews my chat was just distant rhubarb. These gallant lads were already fearing for their gums and tonsils.

They had pregnant visions of stern men with spray guns that caused instant death without puncturing the skin, and poisoned needles jumping out of cigarette cases and umbrellas. They decided to drive back to England.

I counselled mildly against such a dramatic retreat, but they already felt themselves marked men, tragic but innocent victims of the Cold War. 'The risk may be only one tenth of one per cent,' said the normally phlegmatic Don Martin, 'but it could be fatal. I owe it to my wife and children to go home.'

Kevin Billington, the director, and I joined them for a farewell meal, after arranging with the hall porter that a waiter should come in during dinner and tell Peter Hall two men in long overcoats were asking for him.

When he did so Peter rose a foot out of his chair, eyes

staring. In appalled silence, they all pushed their food away and, ignoring our attempts to make-it-better, packed and drove West. They gave us wan little goodbyes and asked that we contact all police stations along their route into Switzerland, to make sure they had last been seen alive.

Next day Kevin and I engaged an experienced Viennese cameraman, Sepp Riff, and went back to the Embassy to complete a report that suddenly seemed much meatier. The *Sunday Mirror* headline screamed: 'Reds Chase Tonight Men. Drama of BBC Team in Vienna.' The *Observer* murmured 'The Next Tonight Nearly Wasn't.'

As I up-dated our reinforced story, the Russians peeped through their shutters. They were already, I suspected, regretting such uncharacteristic impetuosity in public, which must have meant Sibera for Some. Now they remained peacefully within. It was just as well – I had some distinctly loaded questions for them.

SILENT NIGHT

A marvellous Misfortune . . .

THE mountains of Austria can be magical in wintertime. One December night I went to a friend's wedding in a little mountainside church high above Innsbruck. As we rode through the snow in horsedrawn sleighs, churchbells were ringing across the valley and distant village lights sparkled across steep meadows, crisp and white. In the moonlight the spire stood silhouetted against a dark sky of stars. It was a storybook scene to weep over.

In a more businesslike mood, I took a film crew to Oberndorf, a village on the banks of the Salzach just north of

Salzburg, for a report which turned out to be even more emotional. We were trying to illustrate one of the world's perfect vignettes: how that touching 'Silent Night, Holy Night' came to be written.

It was dark and wintry as we filmed in the church of St Nikolaus – the original had been destroyed in an 1899 flood. In the memorial chapel a solemn little girl sat at her zither and played *Stille Nacht* for us. Then, haloed by candles, an angelic choir of children gently sang the evocative carol – and we were all swallowing and blinking.

The programme – 'Christmas and a Mouse' – was transmitted on Christmas Eve. The sound had to be wonderful, of course; but so was the little jewel of a tale which, if you would please hum 'Silent Night' to yourself, I will recount as I did standing there in the snow, where it all happened:

This is the scene of a true Christmas story that has in its way affected much of the world and brought nothing but delight – delight we owe . . . to a churchmouse. Into this church one Christmas Eve comes a young parish Priest, Joseph Mohr, to beg help from his friend, Franz Gruber, the local schoolmaster and organist. What has happened is as simple – and as comic – as many a minor tragedy: the organ of St Nikolaus has been put out of action by a churchmouse which has gnawed a hole in the bellows, so Father Mohr's Midnight Mass must be held without music.

That hungry mouse has initiated a chain of events which are to resound around the world, starting with this distress-call upon Franz Gruber, this attempt to save a devout congregation from a sad celebration upon a night of rejoicing. Father Mohr brings with him six verses he has written while trudging through the snow in the moonlight, upon some midnight visit to a sick parishioner. The organ may be out of action, he says, but at least he has his guitar. Could Gruber set the verses to a simple theme for their two voices? The organist reads the words, feels them already unlocking some melody, and promises to do his best.

They have been friends for years, these two men – opposites in everything but their natural gaiety. Father Mohr is 26

and in his third year as an assistant parish priest. He is the
fourth son of a Salzburg woman who never married. His
father, a soldier, deserted the family five months before his
youngest son was born, and Joseph never knew him. At his
christening, a man called Franz Wohlmuth stood as his
Godfather. Wohlmuth was the Public Executioner of Salzburg – a dark and unloved creature who had chopped the
heads off 90 people, including his own Godfather.

Joseph spent his childhood in poverty in the narrow
Steingasse – Salzburg's red-light alley. A delicate child, un-
exceptional save for his love of music, he studied for the
Church at St Peter's Benedictine Monastery. After ordination he found his way to Oberndorf, on the frontier with
Germany, while waiting for the parish that was never to
come his way. He was popular with parishioners, though his
superior, Father Joseph Nöstler, found him insufficiently
solemn. He was musical, yes, he sang and played – but
unfortunately, not always religious songs. What is more, he
was cheerful – an odd characteristic for a priest in those
narrow days.

So here's Mohr, that jolly young man, worrying about his
silent Midnight Mass; and here's his friend Gruber, who has
enjoyed as happy a childhood as Mohr's was forlorn. Franz
Gruber first played a church organ at the age of 12. His father
wished him to follow the family trade of weaving but he
preferred to teach and compose, and in the village of Maria-
Arnsdorf did both for many years. So he takes the six verses
back to his room in the schoolhouse and works through the
afternoon. That evening he delivers his composition to
Father Mohr – and at Midnight Mass, before a surprised
congregation, they sing to a solitary guitar. It is Christmas
Eve, 1818.

Across the world 'Silent Night' may have become the Song
of Christmas, most beloved of carols, but on this night it has
no such success. No single soul in the congregation – least of
all the minor poet and minor musician who put it together –
can imagine that one day it will be sung around the world,
whenever the Christmas Story is told.

The people of Oberndorf enjoy the carol and then forget

it – or, *almost* forget it. One or two choirboys remember, and sometimes whistle the tune. After Christmas, the organ-mender who has come to repair those bellows carries a copy of the song home with him to the Tyrol. Fifteen years later it appears in print for the first time – as a folksong in a book of Tyrolean songs: 'Author and Composer unknown'.

Father Mohr, with his cheerful, simple faith, never knows the success of his 'Silent Night'. Thirty years after that Christmas Eve, in 1848, he dies a pauper's death – at the end of his life as poor as at its beginning. There is no money for his funeral; a village charity must pay for the grave. He leaves only his patched priest's habit – and his almost forgotten Song of Christmas.

The composer outlives his friend; but it is only when 'Silent Night' has been attributed to Joseph Haydn's brother Michael that, in 1854, he writes to tell the story and give credit, finally, to the anxious young priest then lying in an unremembered grave.

In 1863, Franz Gruber also dies. He is 76 and merits only 12 lines in the Salzburg newspaper. He has written 90 songs in his lifetime, none of them remembered – except one, which earned him not a penny, though it was to become one of the world's best-loved songs.

The two gentle countrymen lived ordinary and uneventful lives, lightly brushed by glory only during those few hours of serene inspiration on Christmas Eve 1818 when they were prodded into a glorious epitaph by a marvellous misfortune – and a hungry churchmouse . . .

SOVIET BLOC

Hot Pants, well received . . .

ONE of the penalties Democracies pay for freedom is that international television and Press may observe and perhaps spotlight any shameful national defect. Urban violence in American streets is continually on display, as is life within British slums and prisons, riots in Brixton, unemployment on Merseyside, vandalism in the Gorbals. No distressing situation remains hidden – indeed since bad news is usually seen to be interesting news, it will probably be the front page lead.

The Police States of Eastern Europe of course offer no such freedom to observe and record to their nationals, let alone to foreigners. In Russia a major air crash will be ignored as something that just did not happen. A crime wave or a march by unemployed would be as officially unthinkable as a trade union. Even to comment upon such events could prove an offence against the State, offering the possibility of prison or, if repeated, some therapeutic injections in a guarded hospital. Straightforward reporting is impossible. It is hard to visualise a Whicker's World around some Siberian labour camp, in a nuclear submarine of the Red fleet or filming a hectic couple of weeks inside Moscow Centre police station . . . though merely the equivalents of our familiar Strangeways, Nautilus, West End Central . . .

Television pictures from within the USSR are rare – apart from that inevitable army parade through Red Square or those shots of fearful rocket-transporters. Until a few years ago any pictures that emerged had always been photographed by a Russian; foreign cameramen were not permitted to operate. It was a curious paradox that the British television technicians' Union, run by an English enthusiast for all things Russian, would in turn not permit ITV companies to use foreign cameramen – so two closed minds met head on, and there was no chink in that stern curtain.

Then it was conceded foreign crews might operate provided a full Russian crew stood alongside, its 'cameraman' closely watching the foreign photographer – the USSR was not slow in absorbing our restrictive practices. Today it relies upon the strictest supervision of subject matter and locations, right down to the selection of who may be spoken to, and what may be filmed.

In the winter of 1964 I took a non-union BBC crew to Czechoslovakia and Poland, less suspicious lands with perhaps less to hide. In both countries we were escorted by 'interpreters' who would on occasion demand a squint through the viewfinder to see what the camera was observing. Wherever we filmed, they telephoned their bosses to report our activities. We had to travel in the bus supplied, so could be contained and watched. However, our film was not censored and no attempt was made to influence what I wrote or reported. They soon observed we were in no way hostile – merely embarrassingly straightforward. In turn, our escorts were friendly, not to say envious. Their control was not harsh; we were merely permitted to know Someone was always there.

I had flown from London in a BEA Trident with 90 seats – and seven silent passengers. Even before take off, the whole expedition had a different feel. Prague Airport in the early evening was gloomy and deserted. My escort drove me 70 miles through the night to the spa town of Karlovy Vary, once known as Carlsbad. The great of the world had also travelled to the West Bohemian hills to take the cure amid its florid baroque; Emperors, Kaisers, Czars – even Kings. Edward VII had introduced the resort to golf; a local intimate of his, a dressmaker, had only recently died.

I joined the traditional procession beneath the porticos, strolling along sucking hot mineral water through the spout of my porcelain pot and hoping to feel much better. The 600 gallons bubbling up from the spring each minute contained a substantial concentration of sulphuric acid and chlorine ions, which sounded alarming but proved merely agreeably salty, without the bad-eggs taste of Bath or Harrogate. The waters were said to have done great things for digestions for more than 900 years.

On the surface not much had changed since the Communist takeover. The river Tepla flowed between cliffs of elegant houses which had escaped the war. Hotels were now spartan, but in use. The old patrician ways of the spa had been overturned and banners proclaimed, not a coming concert but the achievements of the Socialist Brigade of Bath-workers.

A brochure by my bed in the dusty splendour of the 800-room Grandhotel Moskva-Pupp was lyrical, yet schizophrenic, about the change of status of a hotel famous since 1782. The local sub-editor came in rather late with his revolutionary condemnation of a splendid past: 'What do you hear if you press the shell of bygone time to your ear? The distant echo of measured footsteps, gallant speeches, solemn oaths, polonaises and minuets, the tinkle of glasses and goblets, exotic language, the speeches of statesmen and diplomats, soldiers and adventurers, commercial and industrial magnates, artists and charlatans, scientists and ignorami. How many famous and more or less important people from all parts of the world has this hotel welcomed within its walls since its foundation? But for a long, long time it did not consider those through whose work, drudgery, privation and sweat this proud enterprise was created – the simple, working classes, the heroes of commonplace everyday life, for they existed only to serve the upper classes. Today, however, the Grandhotel Moskva belongs first and foremost to them, the true rulers of this country.'

The hotel might belong to them but of course they could not actually *use* it, nor even venture inside. It was reserved, not for the True Rulers, but for foreigners, Party bigshots and those rather More Equal than the rest, like Mrs. Nina Khruschev. She had been taking the cure when there arrived from Moscow the distressing news of her husband's dismissal.

During my weeks in Czechoslovakia I saw few uniformed police. The only time we were stopped was at a roadblock one dark and snowy dawn. The armed police who piled in among us seemed grim and threatening – but were only worried about our brakelights. When I wondered aloud what this stern militia would have done at 5 am in the remote Bohemian countryside if the driver's lights had *not* been working, a cynical filmcrew voice from the back of the bus suggested: 'Shot him . . .'

We found the Czechs agreeable and cultured; they told me they were the least-emotional race in Europe – apart from the English. They appeared to dislike the Russians, loathe the Germans and be influenced by the Americans: Scott Carpenter, the astronaut, was on one of their stamps.

We drove on to Rozvadov to take a look at the Iron Curtain from the *other* side, at the series of electrified wire fences and concrete teeth along the frontier, at spy towers, armed guards and dogs. Such defence in depth through several miles was intended of course not to keep people out, but to keep people in. The German side seemed unprotected, though Czech officers told me there was an American machinegun post on an opposite hill and sometimes GIs would emerge and urge their soldiers to desert, promising them various items in short supply, like whisky and pretty girls. We left the prowling Czech guards, for ever hunting their own countrymen, and drove across to Brno to join a more light-hearted hunt.

In South Moravia a French syndicate was shooting pheasant and hare. The empty country along the Austrian border provided some of the largest bags of game in the world including, we were delighted to note in the literature of Cedok, the Tourist Authority, 'the wary bustard', largest and most beautiful of game birds. The old bustard proved too wary for our French, though they massacred an enormous bag of other game, to their satisfaction. The group had last shot together in Spain and were enthusiastic about the Czech countryside and organisation. Cedok certainly gave that expensive outing of 14 Guns some strong Army support: 25

foresters and 120 beaters. Weary uniformed figures plodded across the horizon, as in a remake of 'War and Peace'.

Tweedy Frenchmen and their modish wives had been transported from Brno for the shoot in curious Czech back-to-front limousines. From coverts they happily shot the morning away with great proficiency until, at lunchtime, we were escorted by foresters along a woodland path into a forest clearing. There stood a long table, heavy with shining silverware, crystal glasses and elegant china on crisp white napery. From a service area discreetly hidden among the trees white-coated waiters emerged with mulled wine and schnapps. The lunch was excellent, the service unobtrusive and deferential, the whole scene superbly stage-managed.

I sat between two elegant and amusing Parisiennes in sables and, as we relished the *al fresco* banquet in that wintry glade, a few sophisticated snowflakes gently fell upon Purdeys and pearls and proletariat. It might be a worker's paradise, I reflected – but the Czar and the Emperor would have felt quite at home . . .

After the stolid Czechs and the stuffy oppression of Prague's Alcron Hotel, the Poles instantly appeared frivolous and stylish. Since they were the people we had gone to war over, I was pleased to find them so spirited. They were not permitted into our Hotel Europeiski, but could at least use the adjoining café where, as in the old days, the Warsaw smart-set lingered over its tea and aperitif. The added appeal for the various Available-Ladies, sitting smiling from their separate tables, was that the people next door were all rich and lonely foreigners, come bearing dollars and cigarettes.

By sauntering casually through to the cloakrooms at the back, they contrived to loiter profitably upon the hotel stairway. One of my colleagues gave way to some beguiling proposition, but upon its culmination found he had no money. In a moment of inspiration he presented her, tentatively, with an unopened packet of Y-fronts. She was enchanted.

Such women in reduced circumstances had joined the young and pretty students in tackling a new profession; along with businessmen diverting State meat and lorry drivers smuggling gold coins, they all had a sharp and skilled eye upon the easy-zloty. Amid poverty and slablike new buildings, the capital was still living upon its wits.

In a land always occupied by someone – Swedes, French, Russians – the alternative market was always directed against an unpopular regime, so corruption was acceptable, if not downright patriotic. Certainly they had suffered enough during the war. After rising four times against the Germans and then experiencing the Red Army's violent liberation, Warsaw had been 85 per cent destroyed. Nothing remained of the hideous yet glorious ghetto where the young took aim and were killed, and the old put on their prayer shawls and died in their various ways. Every Pole had some miraculous story to explain the mystery of his survival.

Even in 1964 the Poles were exhibiting their traditional suicidal courage. They were remarkably outspoken in their dislike and distrust of the Russians, about whom there was a string of pertinent jokes. Their own Communist leaders also suffered (Why is Gomulka the world's most brilliant economist? Because he knew as much about economics at the age of five, as he does today . . .) and conversation in the Warsaw Artists' Club was so counter-revolutionary I kept looking anxiously over my shoulder.

None of that hair-raising conversation and comment ever appeared in print, for the Press was muzzled. With their 800-mile Russian border and their capital the closest to Moscow, the Poles – 96 per cent of them Catholic – were resigned to both Party-lines: 'We *have* to go to Mass. It's a bit of a bore but if you don't, everyone thinks you're a Communist.'

In Czechoslovakia we had filmed Lidice, the mining village obliterated by the German SS after the 1942 assassination of Heydrich, Nazi Governor of the Protectorate. It had become a memorial to the massacred. Now in the old city of Cracow our Handler was anxious we should also film the nearby Auschwitz concentration camp. After consideration, we refused; it seemed official Poland was for ever looking backwards towards that horror with a sort of obscene relish, continually tearing the bandages off the fearful wound.

While we were there, a West German court hearing the case against some Camp guards arrived to inspect the scene of their crimes. The Poles went into a frenzy of organised publicity, offering jolly receptions at which books full of grisly photographs were distributed, with best wishes. Katyn was not mentioned. This constant parade of horror showed official determination that no one should forget to hate the Germans, but here they ran into half a problem: East Germans were now the Soviet bloc's Good Guys.

So I was sent to the saltmines. Not as a punishment, but as a sort of tourist. The mine was the largest and deepest in the world and had been worked for 1,000 years. Its pits and chambers stretched more than 100 miles, to a depth of 1,200 feet, and its underground lake was one-third salt – which meant it could be walked upon, almost. I was also informed the vast salt chambers could contain 400 cathedrals – the kind of improbable statistic you normally take with a pinch. We filmed some of the 1,400 miners in their salt-encased underground recreation centre and coffee bar, and had a snack in an efficient canteen. There was also a man-powered treadmill, as used in the days before saltmines got into the *Good Food Guide*.

I was down in that saltmine when I learned I had been voted the Television Personality of the Year by the British Academy of Film and Television Arts. Nobody had even bothered to tell me I was on the short list. On one of those star-studded nights of mutual congratulation and show-biz back-slapping in London's West End, the Award had been accepted by someone, in my absence. As I trudged thoughtfully upon my underground treadmill it seemed, somehow, symbolic . . .

One stormy December night as our visit ended, we drove a couple of hundred miles north, towards Warsaw. Our old bus sloshed through a countryside of almost Crimean poverty; candles flickered behind the glassless windows of gloomy hovels standing amid the mud and misery. It was a journey through the Dark Ages.

One incident encapsulated that whole stark, brave land,

but could not be filmed: we were reporting on the work of the brilliantly fertile Film School at Lodz. The students were out on location in the surrounding countryside, making a costume drama about Napoleon's Army in Poland in 1806: historic drama was at least politically safe. We drove around looking for their set, and finally spotted it: ragged extras playing the roles of peasants around an antiquated hay wain, a few fusty half-ruined shacks the art department had knocked up, some skeletal horses dragging primitive carts . . . an inspired and convincing location.

As we drew closer we found to our confusion that it was not depicting the Retreat from Moscow at all, not a scene from that wretched time two centuries ago – but just part of today's everyday story of Polish countryfolk . . .

PART FIVE

TURN OVER, CAMERA!

SUTTON PLACE

The Rosebud of Citizen Getty . . .

I HAD been growing restive within the straitjacket of Tonight's magazine format. This required filmed reports between five and 20 minutes long – usually about ten minutes – so whatever the subject, there was little time to develop theme or personality. In television, as in Fleet Street, we all believe we need more space and while Tonight editing was generally excellent, it had to be fast and furious. This ruthless pace often upset those of us out on the road. We would return to Lime Grove, view our films – and rage at the cutting inflicted upon our best bits, at those hard-to-get interviewees who had come over so well yet ended on the cuttingroom floor, victims of insufficient time and programme pressures.

After each foreign tour all my transmitted footage would be re-assembled and re-edited, and I would update with a new linking commentary. These compilations – the early Whicker's Worlds – had proved successful with viewers and the BBC was anxious all that free additional mileage should continue, with Whicker still securely upon the Tonight treadmill. However, after six years' Hard, I needed to take a few longer breaths, to preside with my director over more thoughtful editing, to be responsible for the strengths and weaknesses of the end product. I was struggling to draw away from the stop-press demands of our fast topical programme, while the producers were preoccupied with 'feeding the brute', nightly.

In the end we did a deal: I would continue under the stick of Tonight, but accept the carrot of an occasional series of one-hour Specials. These would be produced by our team, since the BBC's Documentary department was regarded by Tonight as staid and unadventurous.

The two curtainraisers we then rushed into, on J. Paul Getty and Baroness Fiona Thyssen, were seen in 1963 as television milestones: the first for content – a revealing profile in depth; the second for style and treatment. Both had unusual personal inter-relationships, as a television interviewer moved in to close terms with his subject and for the first time people were conversing naturally in natural situations, while the camera faded forgotten into the background.

Getty was unique, of course, and his slow and mournful delivery perhaps my biggest interviewing problem ever. The Fiona programme was far bubblier; we achieved the casual and conversational eavesdropping style I attempted in all Whicker's Worlds that followed, with varying success. They were cleverly directed by Jack Gold at the start of a career that took him through to major Hollywood films. Technically, both were breakthroughs, and as I went on to film in Mexico our producer Alasdair Milne wrote to reflect: 'Where can we now go, techniquewise?'

I received a certain amount of stick for being too hard on Paul, which may have been deserved. However, the nuggets of information and attitude revealed became public domain, quoted and requoted even today: Getty's extreme care with money, his modesty, his loneliness . . . That programme was later shown in most countries of the world. In America it made television history by being transmitted a second time within a few days – after which the poor man received 25,000 begging letters.

When I followed that famous duo with a Special on the Duchess of Alba I acquired a permanent and sometimes tiresome personal burden: I had imprinted 'millionaire' indelibly upon the minds of some critics – not to mention Monty Python and most impersonators. Until then I had for years been seen, I suppose, as some far-flung reporter struggling through the Australian Outback or the white wastes of Alaska – Tonight's man-around-the-world mingling with witchdoctors and terrorists, devious ministers and civil rio-ters . . . often in unenviable situations. A David Langdon cartoon in *Punch* showed me surrounded by shot-and-shell while a caring viewer asked her husband, 'Why don't they ever send Fyfe Robertson or one of the others to those dangerous places?'

The impact of our hour-long programmes, however, was so great that for the rest of my television career some of the less thoughtful or more hurried critics linked me automatically with the caviar-and-champagne set. A few later programmes, such as Monte Carlo or Palm Beach, reinforced this silly label – and I was lumbered. I have learned to live with it.

I remember chiding Martin Jackson, then *Daily Mail* television editor; he said he was truly sorry, but when he sat down to preview a Whicker's World he could think of nothing but millionaires. Few of my 106 documentaries for Yorkshire Television remotely concerned the Rich – indeed the preview we had just seen had been filmed within the enclosed Order of Poor Clares, those gentle nuns who live in absolute poverty. I wondered how he was about to overcome his mental block.

His column began: 'Alan Whicker, who *usually* interviews millionaires . . .' Later I chided him again, wearily, when once more he resorted to that tired theme after one of our most violent programmes. I had spent a month with my cameraman in the back of a San Francisco police black-and-white, arresting bankrobbers and rapists. He said, 'First time I've seen you in a car that wasn't a Rolls . . .'

I have given up chiding.

Getty was then a recluse about whom little was known, and seemed the least likely prospect for the invasion and total exposure of television. I had met him socially a few times, and was invited to lunch at Sutton Place one Sunday with mutual friends. He had bought the Tudor mansion in Surrey once owned by Henry VIII from the Duke of Sutherland for a laughable £65,000 – his buys were usually good – and moved into his country seat of power only three years before, in 1960, after living in modest hotel suites in Paris and London. Even then he kept talking about going home to

America, but was not much of a traveller. After being caught in a tornado 20 years before, he refused to fly again, and was equally fearful of the sea. This made returning to California something of a problem.

That Sunday he was as usual the thoughtful host. He preferred to listen, and his rare conversational contributions were hesitant. Amid an almost overpowering display of silver, our lunch was elegant but spartan; Getty was no trencherman. He later confessed to me his culinary weakness: buckwheat cakes with maple syrup, and corn bread. As a lifelong enthusiast for ice cream, I instantly warmed to him when he admitted he had once tackled three maplenut sundaes in a row. Dry chuckle at *that* small triumph.

As I drove back to London in the evening I thought I had detected within the shy man, then approaching his 70th birthday, a faint but unspoken desire for some public acknowledgement, some wider appreciation of his remarkable career. He was certainly a regular and informed viewer of my programmes, and had made some thoughtful comments. I confided my feelings to a wise mutual friend who had lunched with us, the actress Edana Romney; she had picked up the same vibes.

Next day I put before Getty the idea that he should be the subject of the first in-depth Whicker's World. After some reflection, he agreed. I then had to start thinking hard about the Very Rich.

The condition of the Poor has inspired literature, sociological investigation and government White Papers – and of course that large group is not difficult to join; almost everyone of us belongs to it, temporarily or permanently. I found the condition of the Rich, however, had been generally ignored by serious investigators. It was as though multimillionaires were the skeletons in our capitalist cupboard, viewed only with shame and envy.

Anyone who seriously wants to discover what the rich-rich are really like will find little reference material outside the aimless pages of the Glossies (where they appear fatuous) and the chitchat of columnists (marital upsets and silly scandal). Research in the BBC library produced a meagre

haul on Getty – indeed after the programme had been transmitted we had a call from the *Guinness Book of Records*, eager to
corral a few facts.

Everything about megamillionaires is so contrary to ordinary experience they can seem extra-terrestrial. For some,
their very existence is an affront. For others, the only objection is that their countless pleasures cannot be shared – the
Envy Syndrome is pervasive.

Though they suffer no restriction of choice, in reality even
multimillionaires soon reach the outer limits of purely personal gratification – which should be some satisfaction to the
rest of us. They can only eat so much food, however exotic;
only live in one house at a time, however splendid; only sleep
in one bed, wear one suit and one watch, ride in one car . . .
Personal lives which from a distance may glitter invitingly
can upon closer inspection seem thin, brittle and unsatis-
fying.

For just such an inspection Getty invited me to stay within
the sanctuary of Sutton Place, and subsequently film several
hours' conversation. As I had suspected, drawing him out
proved a formidable task, for he was the antithesis of the
pushy American oilman. His replies were slow and dif-
fident – so much so that I had to snap at his heels, verbally,
to keep the conversation moving.

Pursuing so hesitant and morose an interviewee through
the minefield of money was going in at television's deep end,
for everyone's reaction to the invisible barrier of great wealth
in others is intense and self-revealing. Few of us would be
what we are today if we could afford to be different; and
depending upon the viewer's attitude, any question of mine
was inevitably going to seem naïve or censorious, deferential
or aggressive. Appreciating this, I ignored the niceties and
we chatted man-to-man; but when the programme was
transmitted there was no doubt who had earned the Sympathy Vote. Getty was delighted. When we met afterwards
he told me with a husky chuckle, 'In every film there's a hero
and a villain – and *you* were the villain!'

That was true – certainly in America where television
critics at that time were unused to the direct approach. They

thought I had been hard on their favourite son, an original over-achiever. Some admitted that 'despite' the abrasive interviewer, Getty had come across far better than a poorer millionaire just featured on another programme, about whom the New York *Daily News* wrote: 'We know as much about Huntington Hartford after viewing CBS-TV's Chronicle profile, "The Reluctant Millionaire", as we did before it. It was an unimaginative, dreary dissection of a man who turned the surface of his life to the camera, and bored the bedevil out of us in the process. It was in startling contrast to Channel 13's candid interview Monday night with billionaire J. Paul Getty. The only question that came to mind as narrator Charles Collingwood listed the A & P heir's assets was: "Who cares?" ' Interviewing the Rich on television is never easy . . .

Huntington Hartford was certainly not a duller man than Getty, but he had been handled differently and allowed to present his own image of himself. The editor of *Punch*, Bernard Hollowood, reflected upon my problem: 'I have no doubt Whicker's new series of face-to-face set-tos will upset almost as many viewers as it will delight. Already I have heard people condemn his interview with J. Paul Getty as crude, insulting, and politically biased, when in my view he leaned over backwards to be courteous and fair. And if we can't ask pointed questions of a man tough enough to amass £500 millions and innocent enough to believe that he is "providing work" for thousands . . . well, the interviewing game can be written off. I hope Whicker will refuse to be dismayed and that he will continue to be courteous, fair and Whickerish.' I was further encouraged by the BBC Audience Research unit which noted many viewers had expressed relief that 'this familiar, cheery and confident figure added a bit of life to the proceedings.'

Such proceedings were filmed almost 20 years ago now, well before the oil wealth of the Middle East took off, yet even then the riches of the Solitary Billionaire – as we called our programme – were phenomenal. I struggled for some way of indicating his incalculable worth verbally, so it could easily be grasped by viewers: 'To be as rich as this man you'd need to win the Pools every Saturday for 800 years. He is several times richer than the total reserves of the Sterling area. He could pay this year's income tax for everyone in Britain – and still have millions left over. He earns much more each day than the average man earns in a lifetime . . .' And so on.

Getty's wealth could only be calculated, with difficulty, to the nearest hundred-million pounds, and still sounded like the mileage to Mars; yet as a three-dimensional man of likes and dislikes, hope and fears, qualities and defects, he was little known. No key to his confusing character had been found. A ruthless entrepreneur who ruled an empire with icy decision – he was also a gentle, bookish intellectual who loved his fearsome German guard dogs. He refused to pay more than the going price for anything and had changes made after calculating it cost 6d each time his oiltanker lavatories were flushed with fresh water – yet almost absent-mindedly paid a fortune for a painting. He owned better 18th century furniture than the Louvre – but had lived out of one suitcase in an hotel room. He built huge ships but feared the sea; owned an aircraft corporation but would not fly; controlled luxury hotels but preferred bed-sitters. Most expense-account businessmen would have found his lifestyle too frugal.

Getty was also an absolute monarch, owning 81 per cent of his 70 companies. No directors or shareholders influenced his lonely decisions. The international empire controlled from his rambling home in 700 acres of Surrey was linked to the Guildford exchange by just two lines; there was no telex, no teleprinter, no tension.

Upon our confrontation he seemed genuinely baffled by his own staggering success: 'I really don't know of any quality I have that many others don't have. I'm hardworking, I like to think, but I know others just as hardworking. I'm intelligent, I like to think, but I know others just as intelligent – or more intelligent. I'm imaginative, but I have many friends and acquaintances just as imaginative. I have always wished I had a better personality, that I could entertain people better, be a better conversationalist. I have always worried I might be a little on the dull side, as a companion.'

We deliberately put that disarming admission at the top of our programme. I was anxious viewers should not be so hostile to the Richest Man in the World that they would not give him a fair hearing. I need not have worried: most of them were *sorry* for him!

While intruding upon his private life, I tried to avoid the more personal areas. Getty liked the ladies, and if he had not known much success with them it was not for want of trying: in 17 years he had married five times. At Sutton Place I had usually found an attractive companion in residence, but in the background. Sometimes two. When we were filming it was a Rubenesque Frenchwoman, bored to distraction by a country life where even the modest pleasures of Guildford, a few miles away, were unattainable. I did not mention Madame Tessier or her alternates in the programme – nor his facelift, despite those small scars behind the ears. Such facets, however revealing of character, then seemed to me to be none of my business – even though Getty, to his great credit, had made no stipulation about untouchable areas.

He had a European background: his ancestors on his grandfather's side were from Londonderry, his mother was half-Scots and half-Dutch. He was never poor, never the traditional barefoot-boy selling newspapers. He and his millionaire father had decided shares were overpriced in the Twenties, so after the 1929 Crash they were among the few Americans with money in the bank. They watched the market all the way down – and then bought.

It was a relief to learn he was not infallible: he had withdrawn from the Persian Gulf in 1931 when the East Texas oil wells came-in and oil went down ten cents a barrel, and did not return to the Middle East until 1948. 'Had I stayed in the Gulf I would now have an industry many times greater than I have today,' he told me, apologetically. I boggled, having trouble enough coping with him the size he was.

In the desert Getty had once met the King of Saudi Arabia and the Ruler of Kuwait – who had also come up in the world through the oil business. They learned with surprise that, in more ways than one, the quiet man from Minneapolis could speak their language: he had learned Arabic from gramophone records. Mr Getty was always prepared.

His biggest business triumph? 'Oh, I suppose just being patient . . . Waiting for the oak tree to grow. Drilling oil-wells, there's always some grief, some catastrophe. There's always what we call "a fishing job" – tools lost in the hole, some unfortunate thing always seems to be happening. I made up my mind when I first started that if I carried my troubles into the bedroom with me I wouldn't sleep, so I just dismissed them. During the day I would worry, but I wouldn't worry at night.'

He told me, reasonably, that he had never been interested in selling out because he would not have known what to do with the money. I suggested he might just lie back and beachcomb. He liked that thought: 'I've always believed I was quite talented as an idler. Yes, if I had the opportunity to idle, I could do it pretty well.'

He was wrong there, of course. He had a fearful compulsion to work, and enjoyed nothing better than retreating alone to his sittingroom after dinner to disentangle a balance sheet – far more enthralling than a detective story and second only to his hidden passion: the Victorian author for boys, G. A. Henty. Those stirring adventure stories were the Rosebud of Citizen Getty: 'They take my mind off commercial things. There's not much about business or money-problems in Henty. He's a very good example of the best type of Englishman – and that's a pretty good type.'

The solitary billionaire often retreated into that simple cleancut world, absorbing again and again stout volumes by his bedside with titles like *Winning His Spurs* and *Bravest of Brave*.

I asked who else he admired, and with hesitation he offered Julius Caesar – 'Possibly the ablest man who ever lived' – Charlemagne, Mussolini, Winston Churchill – 'an example of what the human race can produce' – and President Kennedy. He did not care for Napoleon: 'He was too inclined to get into wars.'

From his peak of achievement and acquisition, was there anyone he envied? 'I envy people who are younger and stronger and more cheerful than I am, people who have better characters than I have. There is also a lot to be said for the ordinary man in the street. He has many advantages. Large financial responsibilities are not the key to cheerfulness.'

The charm of the very rich, it has been said, is the slightly hangdog look they wear; Getty certainly took his life and his pleasures with morose preoccupation and melancholy. He was a doleful man; smiles did not come easily. His passionate interest in his own business appeared joyless, though for him it had the enduring fascination others find in fellowship, or love.

I reflected that though some might think him fortunate, others would see him as a cold calculating machine; how did he see himself? 'As a tennis player, just trying to volley the ball back.' But who was serving? 'I get 50 letters a day where I'm supposed to make the final decision. I get maybe 1,000 letters a week, sometimes three or four thousand, from strangers. When you're President of a company, you can't very well pass the buck.'

He was no gambler: 'Gambling is risk-taking. It might be said the owner of a casino gambles, takes risks, but he has the odds in his favour, so that's intelligent gambling. If I wanted to gamble, I'd buy the casino.'

I wondered whether his wealth had made him sceptical of people, since almost everyone he met wanted something from him, and recalled an art dealer had told me he was unusually wary: 'Well, I try not to be suspicious, because that's a bad road to travel, but I find you can go into a man's house and criticise him or his wife, criticise his children, and he might still love you like a brother – but if he shows you a picture and tells you it's a beautiful so-and-so and you say it's a fake, you've lost his friendship for ever.'

Most millionaires obtain relief from the unease, suspicion and distrust that tends to characterise their relations with fellow men by philanthropy, by the wholesale distribution of some of their fortunes. Getty was not known for his benefactions, other than one annual Christmas party for a few Guildford children: 'I think a man is doing worthy work if he builds up his business, gives employment to large groups of people and so renders a service to the public, rather than delegating somebody else to do it for him by giving money to charity.' He recalled that Rockefeller – a much poorer multi-millionaire – had told him his policy was never to help individuals.

I asked about the pay-telephone at Sutton Place which we visitors were supposed to use for trunk or toll calls, thus saving him the odd shilling. 'Right-thinking guests would consider that was a benefit,' he said, firmly. 'It's rather daunting if you're visiting somewhere and have to put in a long-distance call, and charge your host with it. You did a programme on William Randolph Hearst some time back? When I first visited Hearst I was told there was one thing he did not like, and that was guests' phone calls on his bill. Anyone who put in long-distance calls – they went through his switchboard and they were accepted – when that particular person went back to his room, he found his bags packed and placed just outside the door.'

I doubted whether Getty would have asked his butler Bullemore to be as ruthless – but was careful to keep plenty of change handy. There was no doubt he could retreat into a cold basilisk stare when affronted.

I recalled, rather unkindly, that he often waited outside entertainments until he could get in at the cheaper evening rate, that he would queue outside a restaurant to avoid paying the supplement for the orchestra . . . 'I might have done that occasionally, because that's what a great many people do,' he said, quite unabashed. 'You probably do it yourself. If you know the cover charge in a certain restaurant is off at 10 o'clock and it's a substantial charge, would you rather go in and maybe spend ten or fifteen dollars for the sake of a few minutes? That would be splashing money around and showing off.'

As he had more money than he or his most distant descendants could ever possibly spend, I suggested there was no reason for him ever to accept the slightest inconvenience at any time. 'That's true – but don't you think it's something to do with human nature, to be careful? My idea of a good place to spend my money is right in my own business.'

When I reflected that lesser millionaires seemed to have much more fun and lead more satisfactory lives, he recalled: 'I went to St Moritz once and it was suggested I give a large party – they said for prominent men it was more or less customary. I was told a certain famous millionaire had just given one for 80 people, so before I committed myself I went to see him and asked how many of his guests were friends. He said, about five. There were 75 people he hadn't seen before. So I wouldn't do it – I didn't see the sense in giving a party for a lot of people I didn't know.'

I took his point; but could he not afford to be generous to his friends, at least? 'I don't think I'm ungenerous, but I think when it comes to helping a friend, one has to be sure one is actually being helpful. Sometimes you can help a person 'til you make him dependent – then they're worse off than before. There's the old story of the dog telling the wolf about all the wonderful benefits dogs have – a fine kennel to sleep in, regular meals, a warm house to go into every day, always a pan of water. The wolf listened and then said, "Yes – but what's that thing round your neck?" You never do anyone a favour by making them dependent.'

My own theory, the charitable one I offered when reporters afterwards questioned me about Getty, was that he was careful with his money because he needed to retain some nailhold upon reality. If he did not observe the little economies along with the rest of us, money would stop meaning anything. His unlimited funds would remove him from the human race and his senses reel before all his zeros. He was already different enough, so the only thing the solitary billionaire could not afford . . . was to lose that last touch of normality.

What had he sacrificed to become such an immense financial success? 'Oh, a lot of things I wanted to do, a lot of trips I would like to have made and theatres I'd like to have visited and walks I would like to have taken . . . Money doesn't buy health, and I also don't think it can buy a good time. Some of the best times I've ever had didn't cost me any money – down on the beach, on a surfboard waiting for a big breaker to come in, waiting to ride it into the shore. You're not spending any money there. The breakers are free. The sunshine's free.'

His fears were those of other men: 'Disease, old age, being helpless . . .' I asked how he would like to be remembered? 'As a businessman. Maybe a footnote in history, some place.'

So what was left for the richest-man-in-the-world to do? A long pause. 'Well, just keep on with the business.'

I had to put the final question: at 70 he knew, of course, that he could not take it with him? 'No – and it's probably a good thing. Might be quite a burden.' Paul Getty gave me a rare, thin smile.

We went on to film him among his art collection, his magnificent Rubens, his Rembrandt, his collection of Veronese, Gentileschi, Gainsboroughs, Titians, Renoirs, Gaugins, Utrillos – all of them most sensibly purchased. We looked at his Alsatians and the two aging Cadillacs in his garage. We filmed his walks: three or four miles a day, always measured by a pedometer. He took the pool temperature before his daily dip. Getty was a great tapper of barometers.

When we returned later to Sutton Place for our exteriors, it had been snowing. This time we brought a helicopter, and stood the uncomplaining Getty in the still white garden of his lovely unfortified manor house. The chopper slowly rose up into the sky, away from the lonely figure standing gloomily at the heart of his last home on earth. He was indeed the Solitary Billionaire . . .

The opinions of this unassuming man might not commend him to everyone, for the world when coldly contemplated can seem rather bleak; but they were not dangerous opinions, and indeed they helped many. Surely, I reflected, in that remote world populated by employees and strangers where he was busily looking after the millions while the billions looked after themselves, it was better for the rest of us that he should care more for tankers than yachts, find his pleasure in refineries, not racecourses . . .

Some time later, after the programme had been transmitted, Paul dropped me a note, signed in his almost childish hand: 'Dear Alan, I hope you had a successful visit to St

Moritz and that I will be able to see Heini Thyssen face-to-face with you on television, as I understand you were putting him through his paces.

'I enjoyed my "ordeal" very much, though I did cringe when I got a lorryload of mail as a result of the show and the attendant newspaper publicity.

'I must say I think you treated me very fairly and handsomely indeed, and whenever you want to you can give me as a reference. With cordial best wishes, Paul.'

When I wrote to thank him for that generous reaction, I mentioned an artist acquaintance was anxious to paint him: Mrs Honor Earl, daughter of Lord Maugham. I got by return another characteristic little note: 'I will bear Mrs Earl in mind. However, I am too old and ugly to have my portrait painted. One of these days I hope you will come out for lunch or tea. With kindest regards, Paul.'

One night he invited me to dinner at Annabel's, in Berkeley Square. It was the last time I saw him before he died. I arrived at the club to find among the friends at his long table, he was entertaining four Duchesses. During the lavish evening I noted that, though he did not go out much, when he *did* entertain it was in considerable style! He gave me one of those wintry little smiles. Afterwards I learned someone else had paid the bill.

Paul was being careful, right up to the very end.

ST MORITZ

He said he Loved me because I was so Ordinary . . .

GETTY, though fascinating, had provided what one stern critic called 'An essay in gloom', so I moved towards Baroness Fiona Thyssen for light relief. Afterwards I realised the two programmes taught a vital lesson about television. The transcript of the Getty interview read so well, seemed so thoughtful and illuminating it could have gone straight into hard covers – yet because of his doleful delivery the programme itself was sometimes rather hard going. Conversely, The Model Millionairess transcript seemed disappointingly lightweight – yet to view, the programme was enchanting from start to finish and she was enormous fun. To worry an old phrase, it's not what you say on television, it's the way that you say it – strongly supported by how you look and where you are.

At her alpine home, Chesa Alcyon, we filmed Fiona having her hair fixed and trying on her multi-carated jewellery. What we discussed did not emerge as deathless prose, but the scene was so captivating to watch that at one stage she pulled me up rather sternly: 'Have you run out of questions?' she demanded. I had plenty, actually, but they had temporarily escaped my mind . . .

When I came to write the commentary I recounted her life as a Once-upon-a-time fairy story: it all began 31 years earlier when a daughter was born to a Scottish Naval officer's family at Takapuna, New Zealand. When he moved to Washington she went to an American co-educational high school at Falls Church, Virginia, where dress-sense and

poise were stimulated; then to a boarding school in Buckinghamshire, where they were not. She escaped that grey uniform at 18: 'I was the ugly-duckling of the family. My sister
was always the pretty one so I thought about other things,
like horses.'

Her family could not afford to give her a Season so she
became a model and one of the first girls to make that slinky
craft not only respectable but desirable. Her friend and rival,
Jane McNeill, set the uplifting tone by marrying the Earl of
Dalkeith. Ann Cumming-Bell became the Duchess of Rut-
land. Unmarried Fiona Campbell-Walter, spinster of the
Parish of Victoria SW1, had to be satisfied with her first
magazine cover: *Titbits*.

By the time she was 21 she had been promoted to the
Glossies and invited to model the Paris Collections for the
American *Harper's Bazaar*, girlish equivalent to being
appointed Lord Chancellor, or captaining England. She was
then earning rather more than her father, a Rear-Admiral,
who was discovering ruefully that not even the most steady
promotion could keep financial pace with merely being a tall
and well-ordered 36-24-37, having long titian hair and hazel
eyes and a slightly wonky nose.

She had a brief fling with an Italian who imported timber
into Egypt, but that seemed inadequately romantic in view of
what the other girls had achieved, and the marriage was
called off. She was elected Miss Spirit of Park Lane, 1953.
You might think it would be impossible to be more successful
than that – but wait!

One day a rich Baron – a *very* rich Baron – swept down out
of the mountains to claim her as his third bride and carry her
off to a place at the end of the rainbow where rich people go to
be happy: St Moritz. The moral of the story, so far, is that no
man whatever his background is any match for a nicely
brought-up girl of good British middle-class stock. Now read
on:

Our hero was Heinrich Thyssen-Bornemisza, a nephew of
Fritz Thyssen, the Ruhr steel Baron who financed the Nazi
party and helped Hitler to power. Heini Thyssen was born in
Holland, became a Swiss citizen and told me with some

irritation, 'Everywhere in the world they think I'm German except in Germany, where I'm a foreigner.' His conglomerate included ships and shipbuilders, banks and construction companies, Germany's largest coal mine and power station. Despite all this he was described on his driving licence as 'Hungarian student', and his Swiss passport said he was 'Administrator of a picture gallery'. The only filming stipulation he made was that our programme should not be shown in countries where he had a business – I could never understand why.

Baron Thyssen had first married an Austrian Princess, then a Paris mannequin called Nina Dyer to whom as wedding presents he gave a conglomerate of diamonds, a Ferrari, black pearls, a Simca with gold ignition keys, a West Indian island and a black panther. At their separation ten months later she collected money and jewellery and a French château. The Baron had custody of the black panther.

Many of the people to whom I have devoted programmes have been friends, or friends of friends. The Baroness I approached out of the blue. One cold winter's afternoon, feeling the need to talk to someone younger and lovelier than our Solitary Billionaire, I telephoned her villa in St Moritz – and next day was sitting in the bar of the Palace Hotel, trying to cope with her brand of assertive uncertainty and already enjoying myself.

I thought she was gorgeous, as I still do, and could well see why Annigoni named her one of the three most beautiful women in the world. She saw herself as 'a big healthy girl with one of those indeterminate faces that goes with any outfit and no one ever recognises. I'm the proverbial country girl. For me it would have been all right to have married a farmer, if he'd been attractive. They usually aren't, though.'

She had a certain wide-eyed caustic honesty, and fortunately became a friend. Afterwards she told me it was our filmed conversations that first set her thinking seriously about her life and her marriage; until we talked at such length, she had just been bubbling along hopefully. For the first time, and certainly not the last, Whicker's World had offered a blend of psychiatrist's couch, confessional and sympathetic friendship. To be lightly but persistently grilled, to be concentrated upon intensely, seems to flush-out in everyone all sorts of unexpected reactions and attitudes.

Later she wrote to me: 'Odd as it seems, I really *enjoyed* your questioning. I do believe it's the first time I've ever thought about my own ideas – the horror was how few I had, in relation to the available possibilities. I might be tempted to start up a GBS-Mrs Patrick Campbell correspondence with you.'

When all the furore of our programme had died away she would sometimes come to my home at Cumberland Terrace in Regent's Park for a quiet and reflective dinner. Today, as her daughter Francesca follows in her modelling footsteps, her brother lives a couple of bays away from my house on the north coast of Jersey, so we meet occasionally. On one of these visits she told me: 'I ran into Paul Getty one night and we decided that we were going to organise a television programme and both of us were going to interview *you*. Soon after that he died – so you escaped.'

She had not much enjoyed her early covergirl life: 'A lot of awfully ropey people in that business. I got bored stiff working in smelly studios with that unattractive lot. And my figure gave out.'

The marriage that followed had its compensations: at least she did not have to hand the sables back at the end of the day. However, she received one nasty shock soon after their wedding: her husband was going steady with a Telex.

'We had an awful row during the first week, because it was in the room next to our bedroom. The New York Stock Exchange prices used to come over at night and Heini would leap out of bed and go across to read them. It was not the kind of competition I'd expected. It had to go – it was either the Telex or me.'

She said they received considerable crank mail: 'The one that surprised me most was from somebody in Germany who said, "We don't mind you being rich and we don't mind you being beautiful, but we resent you being happy too." ' Public reaction to our programme, when it appeared, was not at all like that: everyone, critics included, adored her. There was not one disparaging remark about her wealth, her luxurious and apparently carefree life. I have a suspicion the response might be different in these less generous, more envious days . . .

Fiona was then seven months' pregnant so we could not film her skiing, but we talked in her aircraft, her BMW, her speedboat. We wandered through their art gallery, one of the largest private collections of Old Masters in the world at the Villa Favorita, their home on the shores of Lake Lugano. We strolled through the town, still filming, and she organised a garden party where we considered the new in-phrase which had just appeared: Jet Set. She was obviously an original and quintessential member.

'I wouldn't say we're divorced from the realities around us. I'm worried about how the roses are doing, or if they're keeping the swimmingpool clean, when the guests are arriving, if the meat's coming – all the things a housewife has to worry about. I never spend too much money – I'm Scottish. I have a small budget and find it quite easy to keep within it. Of course there's always the thought at the back of one's mind that if I *really* wanted something special Heini would probably buy it for me – but I don't calculate that in my budget. The fact that he could give me anything I wanted, I didn't even realise at the beginning. He makes general scenes once or twice a year, just to keep me in line, but I think we're both agreed that I'm not extravagant.'

The only upsetting thing was when he sometimes ignored her: 'For a man who's got lots of businesses and is very strung-up during the day, it's sometimes difficult to switch off at night and suddenly get back into the family – so one has the feeling of being a bit out in the cold.'

I well understood. Compared with her vulnerable effervescence, Heini could seem remote. Also, the aphrodisiac of his incalculable wealth obviously had powerful impact upon the girls of the après-ski circuit. He reminded me with a smile that they had been married for six years: 'Coming up to the seven-year-itch right now!'

Next day he was leaving for Brazil and since she was Expecting, travelling for the first time without her. 'It's a very strange feeling,' she said. 'A good husband's awfully hard to find, and I'm frightfully jealous. When we're out and he's flirting abominably with someone, I eat and drink and dance and pretend not to notice. The trouble is, I'm no good at flirting myself – but I like to sort of be there, to keep an eye on what's going on. I'm very calm but I quite often make a big scene when we get home. I tell him, "She's nice, but she's an alcoholic" – or something like that. It doesn't always work, but I do my best.'

I asked why she believed her capricious husband loved her? 'Well first of all, he's stayed married to me for seven years, nearly. And secondly, he told me so. He said he loved me because I was so ordinary, which I interpreted to mean that I wasn't neurotic.'

As we finished filming, her Baron flew away from their romantic alpine château into the sunset and Brazil, and I went back to London. A couple of months later she had their son, Lorne, making one-of-each and completing her Happy Ever After fairy story.

Next year they divorced. She got around £650,000, Heini got around a pretty Brazilian.

THE QUORN

Will the Pretty Ladies please Hold Hard . . .

AFTER years of reporting about Everything from Everywhere, I embarked upon a programme which I feared would outrage millions before one word was said. From the elevated world of St Moritz I returned to the fields of High Leicestershire to look at the 18th century world of the foxhunter, from within. I went to observe a winter pageant through the finest foxhunting country in England, following the Quorn, the best known Hunt in the world.

It was a subject on which everyone took sides – there were no neutrals. For centuries the pursuit of animals for sport, not food, has caused bitterness between classes, and between town and country. A foxhunter had just been killed in an accident in the field and his widow received letters expressing delight at his death.

The 'golden thread running through the tapestry of the countryside' was also the 'cruel ritual' which triggered fury, self-justification, vitriolic humbug. Like birth-control or bullfighting, everyone was for it, or agin it. In risking such a controversial programme, we could not win.

Strangely enough – we did. It was one of the few Whicker's Worlds which received nothing but praise. The Joint Master of the Quorn, Brigadier Robert Tilney, told the Press, 'The programme was very objective. We have no complaints.' The Chairman of the League Against Cruel Sports, Mr Raymond Rowley, found it 'excellent – a very fair representation. There is no doubt it will have done our cause some good.'

Earlier, I had lunched with 'Dolly' Tilney, formerly commanding the Leicester Yeomanry, and his Joint Master, Mrs Ulrica Murray Smith, to consider the possibility of filming. They were all too aware of the 'Unspeakable in pursuit of the Uneatable' image. Their sport had been receiving a particularly bad Press and the new Hunt Saboteurs Association was causing uproar at Meets across the country. They decided to take a chance that I would be fair.

I have never ridden to hounds, but from a distance suspected that most people who criticised foxhunting did so not out of pity for the fox, but out of dislike for the foxhunter. He appeared to be a relic of feudalism, a squire rich in money and time and, even worse, enjoying himself . . . His scarlet coat stood for peasants opening gates for their betters and touching their forelocks – though the modern peasant opened bank accounts, not gates, and anyone who tried to make him touch his forelock would doubtless get a stiff letter from his solicitors.

If it was the animal that saboteurs were concerned about I could not understand why they did not also criticise, say, rat-hunting. The rat, an intelligent and highly-sensitive creature, has no fewer rights than the fox – yet nobody parades with placards demanding Hands Off Rats. It was, I supposed, because the public image of the fox is jaunty: the elegant villain of the countryside, bold and cunning, with a handsome grin that belies his killer instinct and no enemies except the Hunt.

Once considered lowly vermin and not an object for high sport, the fox shot up the social scale when hunting took hold – the only meteoric rise in status in the history of the animal kingdom. It is doubtful whether the fox fully appreciated this compliment.

The Ministry of Agriculture handled the explosive subject of foxhunting with timidity, admitting only that foxes were officially pests, along with rabbits, hares, deer and moles. Of the 31,000 foxes then killed each year, the Ministry estimated 21,000 were destroyed by farmers, gamekeepers and hounds; about 40 brace (say, four a week) by the Quorn.

If the bloodthirsty Master of Foxhounds is debauched, I wondered, what about the patient and solitary fisherman? Salmon fishing can be most cruel, yet nobody calls public meetings to protest. There was also that personification of gentle timidity – the man who chases butterflies; could it be those terrible pins and killing bottles were cruel to Red Admirals and Marbled Whites?

Certainly you could make a case that humans should leave *all* animals alone, for they have a right to live; but then that should apply not only to foxes and stags, but to mosquitoes and tarantulas and cockroaches, to cattle and poultry and pigs. The quality of mercy ought not to be measured by size or appeal or food value. It seemed the only person who could justifiably stand against foxhunting was a vegetarian who wore cloth shoes.

Past Masters of Foxhounds had dealt with individual critics in individual ways, from fistfights to gifts of 'two gallons of gin'. Since the war foxhunting had successfully resisted a hostile Press, bitter demonstrations and attempts at legislation. In 1949 two Private Members bills for the abolition of all hunting with hounds – as in Western Germany – had been introduced at Westminster, but withdrawn. A Government committee decided merely that animals were fortunate if they were fluffy or cuddly: 'Many people are inclined to be critical of methods used for controlling the numbers of animals they consider attractive, and at the same time be quite indifferent to the fate of animals about which they know very little, or which they dislike . . .' However, the Socialists have announced that a future Labour government would curtail hunting.

Even a natural sympathy for animals can be selective: just before we filmed, the warden of a deer sanctuary owned by the League Against Cruel Sports had been fined £25, with 20 guineas costs, for causing unnecessary suffering to 15 lambs on a sanctuary farm. None of us is consistent, it seems – not even the professional sympathisers. Many foxhunters, including the joint Masters of the Quorn, belonged to the RSPCA and saw no contradiction in that, for while the Society could not approve of hunting for sport, foxes killed poultry and lambs and had to be kept down; alternative methods of control caused even more suffering.

From beneath her bowler, one Hunt member told me vehemently: 'The only way to keep foxes down is by hunting. If you start poisoning, shooting, trapping, it's the cruellest thing you can do. Many a fox has bitten his own pad off, to get out of a trap. Many a fox is picked up dying in a ditch, from gassing. Would *you* like to be gassed?'

I said I surely would not – but then I should not like to be hunted, either. 'Ah, but the world is yours,' she said, expansively. 'You've got freedom, you can go where you like if you're a good fox.'

A bad fox, I reflected, must have been that one which went to ground injured while, in an effort to get him out, the Huntsman poked a gun butt into the hole. There was a sharp report, and when the Hunt returned after taking the Huntsman to hospital, they found a dead fox with its paw on the trigger. It was grinning.

For a country activity affecting such a small number of

people, the lobbies of both anti-Blood sports and pro-Field Sports seemed curiously intrusive. When it was learned I was considering this programme the BBC received oblique approaches from a number of extremely high-powered Huntin' folk in Court and Cabinet circles who feared a fair picture might not be presented – an unfair attitude, of course, being one different to theirs. The BBC had not in the past been subjected to attempted nobbling about evidently less-worrisome subjects, like Defence of Capital Punishment or Nuclear Policy . . .

So we spent several weeks following the pack across High Leicestershire. Though I ride – just – I refused invitations to follow on horseback as I might have appeared to be taking sides. With Jack Gold directing again, we went out four days each week; Peter Hall's pictures of that winter scene were magnificent.

The Quorn hunted from September until March. It appeared a closed society, though in truth could harldy have been more open: anyone could hunt, without needing to be a member. Mondays and Fridays were the Smart days over the grass part of the county within 12 miles of Melton Mowbray, when up to 200 might follow the bitch-pack and make a pretty pageant indeed. The unfashionable days were Tuesdays and Saturdays, with the dog-pack, when the field narrowed to young people, less confident riders and those who could never miss a day's hunting, however unsmart. One enthusiast rode out 96 days during the 20-week season.

There were then some 240 packs in Britain, more than before the war when the countryside was open and the squire significant. The Quorn had the biggest country in the land; 600 square miles in the 'eye of Hunting England' where the sport had changed less than elsewhere; but even this open countryside was shrinking. A growing M1 tore up Tuesday and Saturday country, and dual-carriageways extended along Fosse Way. The Hunt also had 900 landlords to deal with, instead of the pre-war nine, and needed to tread lightly. It had to show concern for the public, for local councillors who loathed blood sports, for unsympathetic small farmers and impatient motorists. Public relations had become vital, and leaflets had gone out warning all Masters there should be no reference, not even in conversation, to anything as evocative as 'hounds deserving a taste of blood' or 'hounds killing a deadbeat fox'. A more suitable way of describing such an event, the Foxhunters' Society suggested delicately, might be a casual 'the animal was accounted for'.

For the same reason the Hunt had stopped blooding its children, that pagan passing-out symbol of promotion in the field. A little girl told me nostalgically how her cheeks had been smeared with warm blood from the brush of a fox just torn to pieces, when she was four: 'I never washed it off – I let it wear off. That's the tradition, you know.'

In deference to public opinion the Quorn quietly dropped this old ritual, though following children felt deprived. Most of those who enjoyed foxhunting seemed to have started with the Pony Club at a dauntingly early age. One enthusiastic chap we filmed upon his Shetland pony, Nicholas Selby, was 18-months when he began attending the Meet, wearing nappies beneath smart tailored jodhpurs.

The Quorn, dressiest and most fashionable Hunt in England, had been pursuing the fox relentlessly since 1698, and at every Meet I appreciated something of the attitude of the Antis towards this haughty stronghold. Mingling with the Horsey Set, it was hard to resist a pang of inferiority: there is something distinctly crushing about anyone on a horse. It may be just a question of height, but as you stand there trying to converse lightly while keeping the restless flanks out of your face, you cannot escape the impression that the rider is looking down his nose, as well as down the nose of his horse. What is more, foxhunters look dashing, carry whips, wear toppers and drink port and sherry from silver salvers. Their voices, booming down from the backs of great steaming steeds, are assured and loud and hearty.

Though no one actually shouted Yoiks or even Tally-ho in my presence, I had the feeling they very well might, and they always appeared ready at the slightest provocation to ride-me-down. Even the most elderly foxhunters exuded a whiff of rollicking Regency days when the squire laid-about-him with his crop and had his wicked way with simple village maidens.

Most of the local maidens were not back in the village, it seemed, but out hunting, looking very chipper and dashing. They outnumbered and outperformed the men. I had always heard the effect of a day galloping through the fresh air with a muscular, steaming beast between their thighs had a stimulating effect, and indeed we found hunting people most friendly and welcoming.

Many of the men who rode out during the week were either retired or schoolboys, so my crew of half-a-dozen strapping young men was most affably received, and much appreciated the social intercourse that followed. Their stirrup cup was overflowing, and every day an adventure. My recordist spread the canard that he had detected the marks of spurs in the rooflining above the rear seat of my Bentley – it was that sort of jolly, gregarious atmosphere.

For its Hunt Ball, the Quorn took over Thrumpton Hall, near Nottingham, after suitably insuring the 350-year-old manor. We were assured by disapproving Antis it would be a mixture of arrogance and debauchery, so braced ourselves for the rampage. On the night it proved a rather tame kaleidoscope of scarlet and non-vintage champagne, with a band in the library and foxhunters weary after a day in the saddle sitting out on a Caroline staircase. We uncovered no debauchery at all; my cameraman was livid.

However, with their tendency to live-it-up, Hunting folk have always undergone much publicised divorce cases. The night air over Melton Mowbray, it has been said, trembles with the sighs of adulterers. To be brutally accurate, the far more dominant sound of that dashing set is the dull crack of breaking bones.

We filmed endless falls, with and without dull cracks. After watching three refusals at one hedge the rider gave up and galloped away past me with a despairing and furious 'Wanna buy a horse?'

For those with more acquiescent mounts, the carnage of foxhunting could be considerable. Pursuers paid a far higher price than their prey. Most foxhunters recalled with quiet pride they had, broken almost everything, and recounted with relish the catalogue of daily accidents – some fatal, some gory, all painful. Every season someone is killed hunting in the Shires. During our filming in Leicestershire one woman broke her back, a man's skull was laid bare, numerous collarbones and legs splintered, three hounds were killed by a train and several horses died, or had to be destroyed, in the field.

While they were paying such a heavy price for the avid pursuit of their particular pleasure, only a very few foxes were, as they choose to say, accounted for. To my particular sorrow, 'Dolly' Tilney soon afterwards took a bad fall when his mare caught her hindlegs in wire. He was half-paralysed and unconscious for months, his brain was damaged and he remained a vegetable for the last 16 years of his life. After the accident his wife Fanny received letters saying: 'I hope he's suffering.' They were written, of course, by people objecting to cruelty.

His Joint Master, Ulrica Murray Smith, had a magnificent seat. This pleasant, gentle woman was, upon mounting totally transformed: incisive, fierce, commanding. I kept standing to attention.

MFH remains a significant country title: there were then 395 of these autocrats, 72 of them women, all digging deep into their pockets for their pleasure and esteem. Riders backed away deferentially from such masterful personalities. I particularly appreciated one gentle lesson in control demonstrated by a former Master of the Quorn, Algy Burnaby, who ordered: 'Will the pretty ladies please hold hard – the plain ones may gallop on . . .'

To the Antis, these enthusiasts were 'Teddy boys in pink', aristocratic sadists revelling in a cruel and snobbish sport – though most were hardly aristocratic, let alone sadists. Many worked in offices, shops and factories. Hunt followers had their own club and turned up at every Meet, following in cars and on bicycles. I talked with Harry, panting heavily because he did not ride but *ran*, to hounds. After the war his bicycle had broken, he told me, so he started running after the pack: 'I just go on in my own stride, and that's it. I can keep going all day – but I'm really tired when I get home night time. I could eat the fox myself.'

I suspected he had seen far more kills than the mounted field, which was usually behind him. We were also in that position, for after energetic weeks scrambling around the countryside we had filmed everything there was to see in the home of foxhunting – except a kill. We had heard the hounds speak – and the foxhunters, endlessly. We had followed conscientiously from a Find to a Check, from a Check to a View, from a View to – so far – *no* Death in the Morning.

On our last day, as we despaired of properly completing the programme, the director sent assistant cameraman Butch Calderwood ahead of the hounds while we watched another covert drawn, another fox gone away. Then the first fox of the morning ran directly towards him, with hounds in full cry. It was caught and torn to pieces in front of his camera.

Not pretty, but the culmination, the reason for the whole scarlet carnival. It needed to be shown. I noticed few of the high-paying foxhunters were around at the time; they duly arrived later at a gallop, and celebrated.

When the programme was transmitted protesters jammed the BBC's telephone lines for hours, but in the end both Antis and Pros approved and – more important – so did those in the middle: the viewers. After three months Death in the Morning was repeated, and went on to be the BBC's official entry for television's international Italia Prize. I received my script in French, as given to the Festival jury: *La Mort, un Matin.*

L'Innommable acharné à la poursuite de l'Immangeable was easy, but the translator had some trouble with my terrible puns, like Quorn on the Cob, 20th Century Fox, and One Man's Meet . . . They lost a little in the translation – if that was possible. However I must admit we had considered even worse for the programme title:

> D'ye ken Mrs. Murray Smith . . .
> The Ride of the Ulricas . . .
> The Leicester Fiesta . . .
> Eager Belvoir

You can see why even I had not the courage to use them. I toyed briefly with Kinky Boots . . . and also, following the terrible falls we had seen, reluctantly decided against: Hey there, you with the Mud in your Eyes . . .

IMMORTALITY INC.

Trouserless in Charlotte Street . . .

CASTING around for other interesting individuals after the success of our first Specials, I went one day to take tea in Upper Grosvenor Street with Margaret, 11th Duchess of Argyll. The only child of a Scottish textile millionaire, she had been a famous beauty in the Thirties, and was still remarkably handsome. In her days as Deb of the Year she led the glittering parade of Bright Young Things dancing through that brittle age, and had married and divorced an American, Charles Sweeney. It seemed to me her life – a reflection of pre-war debutantery and post-war complexity amid embattled nobility – could make an illuminating programme. She agreed, so I turned my thoughts towards High Society.

However in 1963 this rather glacial beauty was about to be presented at a different Court and submerged in a most sensational divorce case. The Judge was outraged by what he heard: the Duchess, he pronounced, was 'a highly-sexed woman who had ceased to be satisfied with normal relations and had started to indulge in what I can only describe as disgusting sexual activities to gratify a basic sexual appetite.' On top of this field day for the lurid Press, her memoirs were to appear in the *Sunday Pictorial*. All this was far too explicit for Donald Baverstock, then Controller of BBC 1. He backed away from the project, nervously, and I had to convey my regrets to the Duchess; so a television tale full of stimulation . . . remained unheard.

We then moved on to another friend of a friend, though this time extremely happily married: Lew Grade. I had dinner with him and Kathie at their nine-room flat above Cavendish Square and, from behind that eight-inch cigar, he told how the Winogradsky family of émigrés from the Ukraine had been upgraded to the pinnacle of Show Biz. His formidable mother, Olga, was then presiding over the family compound at Wimbledon, his brothers Leslie and Bernie were also moguls, running their respective constellations around town. Together they controlled three-quarters of Britain's entertainment.

Reminiscing about how it all began, he recalled dancing his way into a charleston championship as a young man and suffering scarred knees as he threw himself upon the floorboards at the climax of each performance . . .

Such zest led unswervingly towards his daily dawn drive in an enormous Rolls along Wigmore Street to a vast desk at Marble Arch and endless transatlantic deals in megabucks on a bank of telephones. One of the nation's master-impressarios, he was then Managing Director of Associated Television, home of Crossroads, and his share price had gone from one shilling to £11 in three years. He was sometimes unkindly known as Low Grade.

I wondered whether the BBC would be prepared to publicise so formidable a rival. My programme suggestion went through the hierarchy right up to the Director-General; everyone instantly accepted the idea that we should consider one of commercial television's new mandarins. It was going to be an illustrated lesson in entertainment tycoonery for me – though I was dreading those early starts.

Now it was our turn to be rejected. Not by Lew – he was delighted, and flattered – but by the ATV Board. The ITV contracts were coming up for renewal and in television's money-printing days every company was terrified its boat, which had come in, might be rocked. Norman Collins, Prince Littler, Val Parnell and his other directors probably felt he was getting too much exposure anyway. So he was reined in and we had no early cross-fertilisation of channels.

At that moment there arrived on my desk at Lime Grove a surprising request for the creation of a private-enterprise Whicker's World on one individual – to be produced as a favour, in an attempt to keep other programmes within our schedules . . .

A popular series at the time was Come Dancing and, as the BBC agreement with Mecca Ballrooms was due for renewal, newly-rich Independent Television was dangling large offers before that entertainment octopus, urging it to dance across to commercial. The head of the BBC department, Peter Dimmock, came on to me in a high old state to say that the man with whom he was negotiating, Mecca's joint-Chairman, had seen my Paul Getty interview and longed to be the subject of a similar programme – not for transmission, but as a personal record of his achievements. Since Mecca also owned Miss World – another television blockbuster – Dimmock was desperate to keep them sweet. He begged me at least to go along and see the man, just to show willing.

I was not at all interested; the whole exercise seemed to be some obscure businessman's desire for instant self-glorification – and I was not used to being *asked* to dance. However for the good of Our Side I reluctantly agreed to meet him. On my way home from the studio that night I peeled-off in Kensington and took a glass of wine from a tiny balding man with a strong foreign accent, of whom until that day I had never heard.

Carl Louis Heimann was 70; he had just married for the second time and, somewhat to his surprise, had a son – between his two children, a gap of 40 years. He had also suffered his first heart attack, feared for his second, and wanted to leave some pictorial memory for a boy who might never know him. This anxiety got straight through to me – the one television man he could have approached who had no memory of his father, because of an untimely death. He explained why he wanted to be interviewed, and it became to me a sensible and significant idea. He hoped to leave his family a walking, talking private memorial so that one day the boy could at least say: That's my Dad . . .

If only my father and television had been around together at the same time, I reflected, how fascinated and joyful I would be today to meet and listen to him in such a way, instead of having nothing but faded photographs.

I agreed at once that my own company should produce the film, and grew enthusiastic about creating an interesting memory for two-year-old Stuart, with whom I instantly identified. I even wondered whether I ought to move into the obituary business – and call my company Immortality Inc. Then I settled down, professionally, to discover Heimann's story . . .

It has always been my belief that we all have within us one great television interview, if only the deeply personal tale can be sympathetically revealed, layer by layer. As I questioned this dryly precise little man in his small neat house off Exhibition Road he revealed himself to be the perfect example: unknown, but fascinating.

Carl Heimann had taken his first job at the age of 13 as a commis waiter, or picolo, in his native Copenhagen. For three shillings a week he worked from eight in the morning until midnight, with an hour off at midday. Not unreasonably, he decided to escape to America, but could not raise the fare. By 1912 he had saved enough to get part of the way, to England: 'If you travelled steerage you had to show £5 in cash when you arrived – which I hadn't got. If you travelled first-class, you didn't need to show any money. After paying that fare I had exactly 27s and the address of a lodging house in Charlotte Street. They charged a shilling for a bed for the night, and in my room I found there were already three other people – a man, and a couple in the double bed. When I woke next morning they had all gone – and so had my trousers and my 27s. So on my first day in London, aged 16 and unable to speak a word of English, I had no money – and no trousers.'

From that daunting introduction Heimann went on to become a multimillionaire controlling a nationwide organisation of 8,000 employees providing Britain with much of its indoor entertainment. He ran 52 ballrooms, 70 bingo halls, six ice rinks, 40 restaurants, and catered to much of the land – from the Arsenal and Tottenham Hotspur cafés to the Ministry of Defence Luncheon Club and the Cabinet Office canteen. Everyone, as you see, has a story just waiting to come out . . .

We filmed several conversations and observed him lord-ing-it over some of his indulgent pink-and-gilt establish-ments: the Empire Ballroom in Leicester Square, the Café de Paris, various Locarnos and Lyceums, the Hammersmith Palais . . . Such soft-lights-and-sweet-profits were a long trudge from the job he went to when he could borrow some trousers: washing dishes in a Surbiton lodging house for 5s a week. On his day off, he lived on a pennyworth of chips. To become a steward on a liner he walked to Southampton, begging meals along the way.

So he worked and starved towards his first business: the Black Cat Café in Coventry. In 1921 that proud possession was smashed in a riot by unemployed, who assumed that anyone called Heimann had to be German. The café was uninsured – and again he was penniless.

Over the years he clambered back until he set cash registers ringing and ten million feet dancing across the land, when he was calling the tune in a Palais business where the profit came quick-quick – and even quicker.

Together we told that story – and Come Dancing stayed with the BBC. He was thrilled to see himself on our film and presented one copy of the hour-long programme to the Mecca Organisation, one to his wife Brownie – and one to Stuart. Four years later the second heart attack he had expected arrived – and killed him.

Ballroom dancing's Carl-Alan Award remains one mem-orial – but perhaps more significant and certainly more personal is that private and rarely-seen programme . . .

MONTE CARLO

The position of the Tents determines
the Quality of the People . . .

AFTER concentrating for so long upon People, it seemed time
to take a close look at a Place. Where better to go, I thought in
my innocence, than the incredible village of Monte Carlo,
commemorated in song and suicide. I flew out on a recce,
checked in without pain at the Hôtel de Paris where life was
lovely until the account loomed. I learned that it stocked
1805 Napoleon brandy, that yachtsmen had christened its
famous bar Poule Harbour – and that I was tackling the
whole *belle époque* frozen into immobility in one glacial Principality.

The arid Mediterranean patch seemed to proffer only
polite disinterest and other people's problems, yet was to
prove a forerunner to my Palm Beach programme ten years
later – that other gentle invasion of a disdainful enclave. Part
of its charm was an unbending weakness for the past. It
exuded an aura of Teutonic Grand Dukes and actresses,
American millionairesses and gigolos, English Royalty and
discreet villas – with Edward VII remembered as Edward
the Caresser. It was easy to see only a comic-opera world of
posturing policemen and toy soldiers parading outside a
ridiculous palace, and all the pompous protocol and backbit-
ing of a tiny caste society.

In the summer of '64 His Serene Highness Prince Rainier
was locked in conflict with the man who *bought* the Bank at
Monte Carlo, as a headquarters of convenience: Aristotle
Socrates Onassis. He controlled the Société Anonyme des

Bains de Mer et du Cercle des Étrangers à Monaco – in other words, casino and hotels. Paradoxically, the staid Divine-Right Ruler and his government were anxious to drag Monte Carlo into the 20th century, while the swinging megamillionaire believed the future of the Principality lay in its past. Onassis, to whom Monaco meant merely 5 per cent of his income, wished to retain the chandeliers-and-bathchairs image.

I invited the protagonists to take part in our programme, but the Prince only wanted to sell the BBC an American film in which Princess Grace had just appeared, made by a company owned by her agents – a rather stilted tour of their Palace. Onassis had nothing to sell, but feared I might rock his boats: 'It would only make the Communist case against me more strong,' he said, and went aboard the *Christina* and sailed for the Greek Islands with Maria Callas.

As they dispersed it looked as though our programme might become Othello, minus the Moor *and* Iago . . . I was not encouraged when I spent an evening with Max Joseph, whose Metropole was the only hotel of consequence outside the Casino group. 'Monte Carlo is a dying place,' he said. 'My son and daughter wouldn't come here.'

Against discouragement from all sides we went on to disprove that prognosis and film an evocation of luxury, a temptation of bikinis, a dazzle of diamonds. It was surely more fun to watch than the dark glasses of the diminutive duellists. The mini-Principality enjoyed plenty of history, but so little geography its frontiers passed unnoticed. They were only marked by flowers, anyway. Some 22,000 inhabitants crammed into a strip of shoreline a mile-and-a-half long and a few blocks wide, with every square inch developed and endlessly redeveloped. As you might expect from a country with three times more croupiers than soldiers, Monaco – neutral during the war – was too tiny and too rich to undertake much serious work for itself, so Italians crossed the border daily to labour for the 3,000 Monagasques, who were most unpopular. Even the Riviera French thought them too money-conscious and greedy – which, if you know the Riviera French, is being rude enough . . .

I met some of the 600-strong British colony; Charles Biron looked like Somerset Maugham's older brother and seemed defiantly typical. He was 91 and after living in Monte Carlo for 43 years could not speak one word of French. 'You've only got to wave a few francs,' he told me, firmly. 'That's your passport.'

The theatrical casino where he and his wife gambled daily had been inaugurated with splendid irony on April Fool's Day 1863, and could be viewed as sugarcake charming or seductively wicked. Its success had grown from a myth (Riviera air cured consumption) and a song (that first international hit, 'The Man who Broke the Bank . . .'). Today no one breaks the bank, though hopefuls wander in and out of the Salles Privées like lambs – fleeced but still gambling – and roulette wheels spin 32 times an hour. The painted ceiling of the bar near the busiest salon, The Kitchen – so called because English milords would see their servants gambling there as they passed through – displayed the regulation bevy of bosomy nymphs. To suggest these girls were naughty and Not All They Should Be, the 1870s artist showed them smoking cigars . . . Times change, and so do depravities.

There is no Commandment against gambling; indeed on 23 February 1887 there came what could have been construed as a sign of approval from the Almighty: an earthquake damaged every church within the Principality – but left the casino untouched. Lest the faithful took this sign too earnestly, no hymns with numbers lower than 37 were sung in the English church, for fear hunch-players in the congregation might rush out and bet the numbers.

The golden days when gambling was illegal in France ended in the Twenties; since then casinos around the world have tried to emulate Monte Carlo, but always without success, for Monaco owns the legends – and if they are not true, they *should* be.

Maybe a golden button did not come off the blazer of Sir Frederick Johnson back in 1913 . . . but it is said a croupier, thinking he had dropped a golden Louis, courteously placed another on his favourite number while signalling a valet to pick it up. Before the button was recovered, Sir Frederick had won a fortune.

Maybe a less lucky gambler did not go out onto the suicides' balcony, spread tomato sauce on his chest, fire a shot in the air and pretend to be dead. He believed officials would rush out and stuff his pockets with money so his death would not be blamed on wicked gambling. When they did, he came to life – and strolled back to the tables . . .

I would certainly wish to believe in the Captain of the Russian warship which anchored in the bay in the 1870s. One night he paid the casino a courtesy visit, and also paid over some 20,000 francs in gold – all his ship's money. Broke but purposeful, he returned to the warship, trained its guns upon the casino and threatened to blow it to pieces if the money were not returned that afternoon. The frantic manager cabled the French Navy at Toulon for protection, but no help was forthcoming. At 3 pm the warship fired a warning shot across the bows of the casino. The next shell landed on the terrace. Before the third could arrive, the casino surrendered. A white flag was run up and the Chief Croupier put out to sea in a rowing boat, carrying the gold . . .

Gambling is always a dramatic activity. An elderly Frenchman once put 1,000 gold francs on zero and closed his eyes in suspense. The wheel spun, the ball clicked into the slot. The croupier announced 'le zéro', but the Frenchman did not open his eyes then, nor ever again. He had dropped dead.

The casino management also almost dropped – at sight of our camera. Photography is never permitted anywhere near the gaming rooms, where there can be much self-conscious cash – untaxed money, criminal money. Few gamblers are proud of their weakness, and some might be hon secs of Slate clubs or company treasurers or bank managers.

They finally let us in to talk with the Director of Gambling, Jean Cruciani, across one of his fully-manned tables where a piece of coloured plastic was worth a year's salary. 'The casino has always been selling thin-air,' he said. 'We sell illusion, at a very high price – therefore we must sell it well. We must give perfumed air.'

He described the role of occults and physiognomists in detecting those who tried to cheat the casino, for just as there is a school for croupiers, so there is one for cheats: 'We are constantly playing Sheriffs and Villains, you know.' Who was winning, I asked – knowing the answer only too well. However you see it, the casino takes some beating.

'We are winning. We must be. Not 100 per cent, but we detect them quickly – usually the second or third time. Our occults are watching people's attitude, people's hands, people's demeanour. The physiognomist is in charge at the entrance. He must recognise the good ones and salute them – preferably by name, which makes them feel at home – and keep the bad ones out.'

Monsieur Cruciani was rather thoughtful about the unsmiling croupiers who sat around him with no pockets in their dinner-jackets: 'We make sure they are honest. As a comparison, it's like having daughters: they are of age, they are well-bred, they are good girls . . . but the family is not willing to close its eyes to what they do. They trust them – but they want to know who they go out with, what time they come home, and so on. That's the way we are with our croupiers. We trust them – but we keep an eye on them. For their sake, and ours.'

Recalling legends of blood-spattered boiled-shirts upon moonlit balconies, I wondered how they handled compulsive gamblers who became desperate. 'We try to help them, morally and – sometimes – financially, for I feel anyone has the right to enjoy his hobby, whether it's horses, stamps or gambling. Some people drink to the point of becoming alcoholics – they can't help it. Some people gamble to the point where they become desperate. Some people – very, very few, fortunately – do commit suicide, perhaps because they have lost too much, but I think such people are weaklings and would have committed suicide anyway. Gambling is as old as mankind. I'm sure they gambled in the caves, and our trade is as nice and decent as any other trade. We are not harming anybody. We only accept people over 21, and they should know what they are doing.'

There were too many answers to that, so we gave up and

went to film on the opulent Monte Carlo Beach – which is not in Monte Carlo and not a beach. There is no room, so it is over the border in Roquebrune. There is no sand, so rock and gravel and concrete have been graciously arranged into elegant artificial acres where the sun beats down upon surrendered bodies. Crowds are limited by the simple expedient of charging outrageously for everything.

The beach was run extremely well by Monsieur René Grinda, who had offered a bow and a gracious word to guests since 1921 and, like everyone else, was full of nostalgic regret: 'The place today has altogether changed. In the old days when we had clients like Mr Rudyard Kipling, the Russians, the Central Europeans . . . even in summer gentlemen would walk out with their stiff collars and beautiful cravats – though they may have been wet through underneath! Nowadays, people live nearer to nature. Frankly, Mr Whicker, I mean to say – they are almost *naked*! Wealth unfortunately has changed hands. There are very few people who can afford to be on holiday all the year round, upon our humble shores . . .'

He had given us our title . . . Months later on programme transmission an unkind critic commented that at this point 'Grinda hitched up his smile to freeze it in a fox's grin.' He indicated the cabanas arranged before us in careful rows across the well-raked imported sand: 'Of course the real craze here is for our tents. We have 160, with 200 de luxe cabins and 34 private salons – and we have to pick our clients Mr Whicker, for they are booked many *years* ahead. These tents are giving me more trouble than three hotels and five restaurants – for the position of the tents determines the quality of the people, and many of them become most jealous.

'Here before us you have the Royal quarters – these are the tents booked for VIPs. And money does not count here, Mr Whicker. I could apply for twice the charges and they would be too delighted to pay them. I wonder whether the Almighty Father himself would be entirely successful in the rather depressing job of allocating position . . .'

He went off shaking his head and shattering social status

with a deferential bow. We retreated into one of his Royal quarters to join Charles Chaplin's actress daughter Geraldine, and film another famous daughter who was less shy – Zsa Zsa Gabor: 'You know, I met *her* father when I'd only been in America two days. He came over to me at a party and said, "You're a pretty girl – can I take you out?" He took me out twice and of course I was in a daze – the great Charlie Chaplin! The third time, he says, "You're too clever for me." I was only 18. Then I married Conrad Hilton and four months later I met Charlie again and told him: "I'm not happy – what shall I do with my life?" He looked at me and said, "For a girl who's only four months in America, you didn't do too badly . . ." '

The Hungarian teacup of Zsa Zsa was always full of storms. She had landed at Nice the day before amid an immediate public spat with Hannah Marcow, daughter of Lord Marks: 'We were standing in line to get off the plane when she pushed my child aside – she wanted to be first. Then her husband insulted me – but I didn't understand the English word he called me. So he made a fisherwoman out of me, and I was not raised to be a fisherwoman. If I had a gun, I shoot her. If I had a riding crop, I hit her in the head.'

Such bloodthirsty threats were followed by a blonde giggle: 'But nothing happened, because she had long fingernails. I was afraid she'd scratch me.'

Monsieur Grinda would have been shocked at such talk in a VIP tent . . . Indeed Monaco, like some splendid old lady without make-up, or with far too much, no longer seemed quite equal to the ardour of the tourist love affair. To have a look at those Untouchables who now dared to approach her, we drove away towards Italy to intercept a tourist coach bearing down upon the Principality. Monaco had found herself, with slightly raised eyebrows, merely the 22nd day of the 28-day Grand European coach tour.

The jolly singing passengers we filmed took only a passing glance at the casino, and drove right up to watch them Changing the Guard at Rainier's Palace. The drill would have reduced any sergeant-major to tears, but it was a popular scene and the only free entertainment in Monaco.

Afterwards they filed around the public part of the Palace, hoping for a glimpse of Princess Grace. They were unlucky, of course, for the Rainiers were far more regal than British Royalty, the Princess exhibiting all the measured majesty of a Philadelphia building contractor's daughter who had been a Hitchcock star. We watched her, cool as a pearl and heavily guarded, performing an elaborate ceremony in which a narrow sidestreet 100 yards long was given a new name: Avenue Henry Dunant. Every street's an avenue in old Monte Carlo . . . Since there are so few, each must be accorded proper recognition.

A few days later we also saw her with Prince Rainier, a small shy man of hot temper, at the peak of the Riviera social year: the Red Cross Ball. Early in the evening of Monaco's grandest night, their Serene Highnesses stood at the entrance to the summer casino and for a few minutes permitted themselves to be photographed, free, before going into its garden to preside over the 900 diners who had paid heavily for their places.

Outside the floodlit function we filmed a splendour of guests arriving. They were guarded by Rainier's ferocious police, exhibiting guns, white spats, the swarthy glares of South American cops – and similar charm. The Gala, at the crest of the year, always unleashed an insatiable demand for tickets. Despite the prices, hundreds had been turned away. Before our eyes, managers and headwaiters achieved wonders of tact and discernment, nicely balancing wealth and rank against tipping capacity – for position was vitally important here too, if you intended to be Quality.

In the warm moonlight the band played softly, and amid the slightly raffish glitter, a magnificent dinner was served in the garden to guests hung heavy with jewels. In Monte Carlo such display was not vulgar: the place has a flair for excess.

The Gala's lavish golden decor had taken four months to create: three floodlit graces held fountains aloft and the whole façade of the casino ran with water. Miss Bluebell's male dancers had been hastily rechristened The London

Boys for the night, for their usual stage-name was quite unacceptable: The Kelly Boys.

The whole shining spectacle had an incandescence that would have made a magnificent climax to our programme, but the Palace forbade filming. Before we could relish the stunning starlit scene our camera was banished, along with all others, and we went to console ourselves with dinner at a nearby hotel. We sat mournfully listening to distant music from the Gala and feeling like The Little Boys that Santa Claus Forgot.

As we were discussing how to end the programme, I felt the first soft suspicion of a raindrop . . . I brushed it, and the idea, aside: rain on such a night was definitely not permissible.

We sat in silent incredulity as the cool, tentative sprinkle grew to a shower, then slowly and relentlessly into a drenching downpour. Nature had come to our aid. With fiendish glee we leapt for our camera gear and raced through the tropical torrent, back to the Gala.

It was already a scene of chaos, a Mediterranean midsummer madness. The fearsome guardians sploshed about helpless and dripping under the driving monsoon that was reinforcing expensively-contrived fountains and waterfalls. As make-up ran and upswept coiffures drooped into downswept rats-tails, it had become a night of tears among the tinsel. The waterlogged band desperately attempted a despairing gurgle of Titanic music – but finally Rain Stopped Play. Diamonds were drenched, ballgowns bedraggled – and it was getting Rainier every minute.

As raindrops kept falling into deserted champagne glasses, we filmed the Mighty, sodden and scrambling for cover, the Haughty humbled, the Quality with all dignity drowned . . .

I just *hate* myself for enjoying scenes like that.

ATITLÁN

The nine Witchdoctors had special Power . . .

THE people of Guatemala were resting quietly between revolutions when we arrived in their land of 33 volcanoes and flaccid, eternal summer. The government which had just issued our visas had been abruptly dismissed during a relatively gentle upheaval, the President had flown away to live nearer his numbered Swiss bank accounts, and a state of siege prevailed. The mild martial law kept US tourists – an unusually timid group – away from Central America, and we had Guatemala more or less to ourselves.

Armed revolutionaries guarding the roadblocks were all delighted to have someone to check. Since few could read and none could speak English, we had a slow but cheery drive from Guatemala City to Chichicastenango, 7,000 feet up in the sharp, dry beauty of the Sierra Madre mountains. There we filmed the Indians on the steps of Santo Tomas as they prayed to Pasqualaba in murmured, conversational tones above smoking censers of pine-cone incense. The blue smoke would reach the spirits of ancestors, they believed, who would intercede directly with the Divinities on their behalf. Then these reverent worshippers went inside the Catholic church to lay off their bets on the Hereafter by praying with equal fervour to the Virgin Mary.

With his life and wellbeing in the hands of so many supernatural powers, the Indian takes no chances: he worships the litany of heathen gods left by his forefathers and, playing safe, also pays homage to the Christian God imposed by the white man. This is not difficult, for much of the symbolism of the Catholic church was familiar to the

Indian through his Mayan heritage: the cross already sig-
nified the four winds of Heaven, the four directions and
everlasting life. Elaborate ceremony, incense, prayer, images
as symbols of deities – all these were known to the Indian
long before Christianity arrived on horseback.

Such heathen incantations upon the steps of a Catholic
church – in defiance of priests who have been fulminating
against such practice for four centuries – showed the Indian
had come undefeated through the age of colonisation, his
faith an unyielding paganism. Yet like most country churches, Santo Tomas is cared for by those same Indians, by
members of the Cofradia, the lay-brothers who carry silver
ikons symbolic of the Holy Sacrament through clouds of
pagan incense.

These solemn men in their ceremonial costumes of black
wool embroidered with tribal symbols, with scarlet sashes
and headdresses, had great importance, ritualistically and
politically. In Indian municipalities it is conventional for
candidates to refuse to serve and have office thrust upon
them – just as at Westminster they drag the Speaker to his
Chair. In Chichicastenango this is more than mere convention. There is real reluctance to call attention to affluence and
power which could bring down the jealousy of other villagers,
and even malicious spells.

The ruling clan of these Guatemalan Indians had been
wiped out by the Spanish soon after Alvarado arrived 460
years ago. There remained only the taciturn peasants, so
expert at concealing thoughts and emotions, traditions and
rituals in a life almost unchanged through 1000 years. Unlike
the Indians of Mexico, to the north, they resisted as-
similation. Their language and costumes, their bizarre
fiestas, their rocket-born prayers to fierce idols came directly
from the splendid nations of Maya-Quiche, Tzutuhil, Cachi-
quel. The date of their origin is pushed further back into
pre-history with every turn of the archaeologist's shovel. The
bone of a mastodon believed to be 30,000 years old had been
discovered nearby – and it was *carved*.

The Ladinos of mixed blood who now rule Guatemala are
more gentle than were the Spanish, so in the remote high-

lands the Indian has contrived to preserve his identity, his pagan gods, his inner fury. He rarely smiles, though sometimes giggles in a foolish way in the presence of tragedy. Submissive, suspicious, hidden, never-to-be-reached . . . except in church, where there are more important matters to consider than instinctive withdrawal from a white stranger. Thus we were able to film them at prayer, so totally absorbed by devotion that, though respectful, we stood discomforted at our own intrusion.

They were urging their saints, seriously and at length, to bless their activities in the market and protect them from unfriendly neighbours, to sustain their pigs and chickens. They had also to consider the saints' shortcomings, as well as their own, and if necessary rebuke them for any reluctance to grant a prayer, despite the proffered candles and rose-petals.

The revered and dusky saints – Indians can never quite believe in loving kindness from a white skin – their brown saints have often been taken from the church by angry parishioners and left on the sun-scorched, arid ground outside to teach them a sharp lesson not to ignore a reasonable and humble request for rain . . .

On one momentous day we drove on another 30 miles to discover Atitlán. I have never forgotten this magic lake amid its mile-high volcanic landscape among the clouds of the Sierra Madre. Within sight of its almost hypnotic beauty I found it impossible to read my research books. After every few sentences my eyes would be pulled back towards contemplation of such splendour. It had a haunting and moody perfection, a handsome people – and witchdoctors.

On that first night I talked for hours with two archaeologists about the power of these witchdoctors who, they said, could curse a man to death for $15. At 2 am I left the bright hotel diningroom to stroll along the lakeside to my chalet in the garden. A tropical moon shadowed three immense volcanoes across still, silver water. The scented night was warm and silent.

Then, high up upon the black mountainside, I saw the glowing unblinking eye of a great fire: the sacrificial cave of the witchdoctors of Atitlán. Up there in the night they were performing some dark ritual. The still beauty was at once flawed and sinister.

Emerging in the morning, I looked up apprehensively towards that threatening mountainside. It was another place: bright with sundappled lime and lemon trees, orchids and bougainvillaea, with fluffy clouds decorating a blue backdrop. The witchdoctors had gone. Whatever it was they had to do . . . had been done. So – the light and shade of listless, evocative Atitlán.

During several weeks I found this dark and perfect place unique, and disturbing. Beauty unsurpassed, eternal spring – yet behind it all a strange and pervasive malevolence. There seemed no escape from the halfheard murmurings of halfseen witchdoctors; healing, perhaps – or bringing sickness and death upon man and beast.

After all these years in television I am often asked which is my favourite programme and always recall this as perhaps the most satisfying. I was profoundly affected by the potent blend of magical beauty and dark drama, by the goodness of a simple Guatemalan doctor and the sinister rites of his Indian counterparts. There was also the achievement of penetrating a truly private world, for to the Indians a white skin remains an official uniform signifying cruel authority. Few outsiders had ever witnessed the sacrificial ceremonies we filmed while composing the picture of Atitlán we called . . . A Sort of Paradise.

Professor George Guillemin, Swiss archaeologist who had been working in Latin America for 16 years, was the only white man I could discover who knew some of the witchdoctors. Once, he told me in some alarm, he had been visited by nine of them – a number which gave them psychological and magical power over him. They wanted him to hand back an idol he had excavated, but he was able to reassure them it had been immediately reburied, to avoid destruction by the Catholic priest.

They operated the 260-day Mayan calendar, he explained, which indicated the correct day to cast each spell. There were witchdoctors who cured, and those who did only harm: 'The one who casts bad spells is very specialised and generally

feared – but also despised. Indians will go to him when they
want revenge, when they are jealous, or when they want a
man killed, for a fee. The witchdoctor asks the deities to do
the harm – but I wouldn't exclude the possibility of poison,
down here on earth.'

In this age of space travel and nuclear power, the Indians
of Atitlán still believe there are two ways to kill a man
without touching him: by appealing to dead forefathers –
and by sorcery. We filmed one using the first method, which
is legitimate. He was praying at the shrine of Pasqualaba,
'weeping before his ancestors' in their world of the
dead.

His candles begged them to hear the case against his
neighbour, to summon him to appear before them in that
other world. This way of causing a man's death is not
considered sorcery, but execution by due process of law. The
plaintiff we watched was openly calling for justice, by day
when all could hear, and his potential victim had the opportunity to defend himself

The second method, sorcery, is murder. We watched that
too, performed in secret by a witchdoctor upon a distant
hilltop. The weird and endless monotone of his chanted
prayer remains the most sinister sound I have ever heard.

Such filming had taken complicated negotiation to
arrange. During our week at Panajachel I had been handed
from person to person before reaching the witchdoctor. To
my amazement he agreed to be filmed, yet during the whole
expedition remained totally disinterested in us. Not once did
he look directly at me, nor address one word to us. It was as
though we did not exist, as though (as many believe) Indians
see all white men as insubstantial creatures inhabiting some
dream world.

We followed him to his altar, where his techniques
appeared to me to include much that is used in European
witchcraft: portions of a Black Mass, prayers recited backwards, the victim's name written upon a cross, and afterwards the burying of the bones that had been cursed near his
home.

All this may, or may not, be effective; at Atitlán no one

would scoff. We returned from that evil scene in silence: someone had been damned.

Every Indian believes he is.dogged by vague yet powerful forces of evil and must forever be alert to protect himself against spells that may kill – or at least insert a live toad into his stomach. For protection he has a pantheon of specialised Gods – a sort of celestial Harley Street he hopes capable of dealing with any ill that may befall. Despite such an array, only the strong survive to middle age. Life expectancy was then 37 years, and a sick child more often treated by a chant than by penicillin.

Some 200 witchdoctors were said to be practising around Atitlán – and one solitary GP. We travelled the Lake in the Red Cross launch of Dr Fernandez Soto. His gloriously-located practice among a dozen mountain and lakeside villages would excite the envy of British doctors – though they might be less enthusiastic about his panel of at least 50,000 patients.

We went to the medical centre at San Pedro, a whitewashed bug-infested room overflowing with sick Indians and their children, every one infected by endemic parasitic worms, at least. They had trudged for hours across the mountains for a surgery arranged by the calendar, not the clock, and when they reached the doctor could not explain their symptoms, since they spoke no Spanish. It was easy to see why most of them found it simpler to rely upon the village witchdoctor.

To observe those other treatments we followed a far less orthodox practitioner towards a cavern high in the mountainside overlooking the lake. It was known as the Cave of Judas. The witchdoctor was attempting to remove a curse that threatened the life of a child. We followed in solemn procession as he led the young parents, carrying their baby and a chicken, up an Indian path at the side of an extinct volcano. The roof of the cavern we reached was furred by the soot of centuries of sacrificial fires.

We watched and filmed as he invoked St Bernard, St Martha and 'Captain' St George. With candles and offerings of aguadiente – a fierce sugarcane spirit – in place of communion wine, the ceremony became a dark parody of a Mass. With a blunt and rusty knife the witchdoctor cut the head off the fluttering chicken. He sprinkled blood from its writhing body upon the altar, offering the Gods a substitute for the afflicted child. On the ground behind him, the hen's severed head still squawked.

So in the end, it seemed it had all been in vain: the conquest and the bloody slaughter in the name of Christianity, the centuries of devoted service by missionaries. The Indians of Guatemala still remained aloof, still carried out, with blind unreason, the commands laid upon them by priests and chieftains who died many centuries ago, still obeyed their silent gods of rain and corn and death. Their short lives took shape around the core of an empty and meaningless secret, within that Sort of Paradise . . .

THE DUCHESS

A few Castles in Spain . . .

SPAIN is a land of brown and magnificent monotony, cut off from the world by geography and temperament. No nation offers an image more vivid, for she follows no fashion, stands aloof from the world and its wars, unreconciled to the 20th century. Because she has style and is not afraid to be patrician, Spain is distinct. She has always had the arrogant and insolent grace of the Grand Manner and, though progress may be weakening her identity, still seems poised as once we all were before the machine came to shift our rhythms. The Industrial Revolution, which somehow failed to spark in that dozing 19th century land, has taken fire today – so such splendid isolation may soon be over.

One side fiesta, the other misery – Spain has no half ways. It is sunshine or shade, bitterly cold or scorching hot. You are a good man – or bad. Poor – or very rich indeed. The formal and reserved people are not at all class-conscious and remain enviably at ease with each other, seeing themselves 'noble as the King – though not as rich.'

The position of aristocracy in their land of poverty and great wealth has changed perhaps less than anywhere, for the nation was so long withdrawn from the world that in many ways its attitude can still seem Victorian.

Neither talented nor tolerant as a race, Spaniards live out their social lives in the café; the street is their drawing-room Family life is cloistered and private. Outsiders are rarely invited into the home, yet at No 20 Princess Street, Madrid, I was favoured by an invitation to take tea with one family.

No 20 is better known as the Liria Palace – a sort of Buckingham, set in six sunlit acres in the heart of the capital. My hostess was Cayetana, 18th Duchess of Alba, head of a family so impossibly aristocratic that since 1053 they have collected 68 significant titles. The most titled British family, the Dukes of Athol, makes do with 10.

The small blonde chatting with me politely in a husky monotone across the teacups was also 14 times a Grandee of Spain – which meant if she were a man she could have worn her hat in the presence of the King. She often received letters addressed Her Majesty – a confusion not hard to understand, for the Albas lived surrounded by more wealth and splendour than many Royal families and also stood higher in the Almanac de Gotha.

They had four Palaces, two modern homes, more farms and land than they were prepared to talk about – and several castles. The Duke could not remember exactly how many, and so gave us our programme title: 'I wouldn't say we had many castles – we have a *few* castles . . .'

Such a loose grasp upon possessions was not I suppose unusual in a nation where once a Duke could ride across Spain from the Atlantic to the Mediterranean without leav-

ing his own land, where the Albas still maintained the right
to name the priests of at least 300 parishes.

My visit to No 20 was television's early step towards the
humanising of Royalty and nobility. Today, some 20 years
afterwards, we are used to seeing Queens and Presidents and
Popes chatting normally in our living-rooms – indeed they
now introduce their own television programmes and a *Daily
Mail* headline can read: Prince Charles does an Alan
Whicker.

In those days they were seen only in newsreels getting in
and out of limousines, or for five minutes on Christmas Day
reading a stilted speech. So unused were we to observing
them behaving normally in everyday situations that after this
programme I was to get a considerable drubbing from
various shocked *Daily Telegraph* readers for treating a regal
Duchess as though she were a normal woman.

Her family tree, I must admit, was certainly not normal: it
read like a roll-call of history, descending from a 12th century
Chief Constable of Toledo. Christopher Columbus was
there – his son married the grandmother of the second duke.
The most famous duke was the 3rd, the Great Duke, who in
the 16th century conquered Portugal, became Governor of
Flanders, Viceroy of Naples and the greatest Captain of
Emperor Charles V. Another ancestor was a King of England – James II, whose mistress, Arabella Churchill, was the
cousin of the Duke of Marlborough. During the last war
Winston Churchill always addressed the Duke of Alba, then
Franco's Ambassador in London, as 'Dear Kinsman'. Spanish and Scottish arms of the family linked more than two
centuries ago, when the daughter of the 11th Duke married
Fitz-James Stuart, 3rd Duke of Berwick; today Berwick is
one of their seven Dukedoms. Despite this, the Duchess was
little known in Britain.

I had gone a'calling with some trepidation, for those who
displeased the Albas have seldom fared well; in the family
tradition the Great Duke took care of anyone who neglected
to take care of him. Asked on his deathbed if he had forgiven
his enemies he was able to reply, with quiet finality: 'I *have* no
enemies – I've hanged them all . . .'

The best known Alba was Cayetana, the 11th Duchess, loved and painted by Goya. She was 13 when she wed her Duke; he was sickly, and their marriage was not a success. She appeared cold and reserved until, at 33, her eye fell upon Goya – almost 50 and deaf, a rough peasant of genius. Their love affair was a scandal and a delight. She died at 41, and all the women Goya was later to paint resembled her in some way. The world still wonders whether it was the Duchess who sat – lay down, indeed – for her lover's nude portrait . . .

That 11th Duchess was as dark and tempestuous as her namesake and my hostess, the 18th Duchess, is blonde and shy. She loyally dismissed the legend – it was of course the Duchess's head upon a model's body. Indeed the whole Alba family has always protected its flamboyant ancestress against the suggestion that she posed for the Maja Naked – or come to that, the Maja Clothed. In 1945 the father of the present Duchess even had the body of the 11th Duchess exhumed from the tomb where she had lain, privately, for 143 years. She was examined by medical experts attempting to decide, by measurement, whether hers was the body in the picture. Their verdict was not conclusive, though one of the Duke's doctors ventured to suggest it was 'unlikely'. This was not quite the exoneration the Duke had been exhuming for, so back she went to her grave and her mystery.

Our Duchess, an enthusiastic artist, complained to me that in a busy life she had little time for her painting. It seemed, in a way, a belated revenge for poor old Goya – whose troubles all started because the other Duchess had too *much* time . . .

Living her life amid the treasures and splendours of her Palaces, she made efforts to reach the workaday world outside – and doubtless receiving me was one of them – but the relationship remained uneasy, though she was popular with the public in the manner of British Royalty. King Alfonso XIII and Queen Ena had stood as her Godfather and Godmother in 1926. Her mother died when she was five, and during the war when her father came to the Court of St James, she was mistress of the Spanish Embassy in Belgrave

Square at the age of 14, entertaining the young Princess Elizabeth and going to school in a Kensington convent.

She retreated from our drab wartime world of gasmasks and blackout in 1943 for her coming-out party in Seville, attended by 7,000 guests. In 1947, at the last great feudal wedding in Europe, the Duchess married a civil engineer, the 4th son of the minor Duke of Sottomayer. Six years older than his bride, Don Luis married into Spain's noblest family knowing his role would be that of Consort, with his wife sole heiress to all her Father's titles and property.

Her gown was a copy of that in which her Great Aunt, the Empress Eugénie, had married Napoleon III. She rode through excited streets towards Seville Cathedral and the Archbishop of Valencia in a carriage drawn by thoroughbred mules. Though held in the poorest part of one of the poorer nations of Europe, the opulent ceremony was enjoyed as a spectacle and seemed in no way resented by the people. In the bride's trousseau were 11 fur coats – not immediately required, as the honeymoon was in Hawaii.

I had flown to Madrid, after much correspondence and telephoning among Spanish friends and contacts, to discuss with her the possibility of a programme. She was extremely shy and, needless to say, quite unused to cameras or television, which in 1965 had little part in Spanish life. We had a tentative tea – and next day she agreed to take part. This was I suppose an achievement, of sorts.

What followed was harder, and during filming I found myself spending much of my time, off-camera and on, overcoming her bashfulness. When I finally won through and sometimes she even smiled, I instantly had the uneasy feeling she was ready to over-react and order, 'Off with his head!'

I could understand why the artist who had once painted the Duchess in her youth swore never again to paint a child – and never did. She had a challenging blend of imperious timidity, of autocratic reticence. She was also unpunctual, unreliable and moody – and had of course the perfect right to be all these things.

However, after she had agreed to invite me into her life, we had flown a film crew out from England and managed to

arrange, with some difficulty but to her satisfaction, a complicated shooting schedule. It was a considerable headache,
therefore, to be handed a Ducal ultimatum every few days
with a shrug: 'Don't feel like filming today. I'll go to the
country tomorrow – so we'll leave it for a couple of weeks.'

One could appreciate her point of view: if all your life you
have never *had* to do anything and could always please
yourself, if you have the grandeur of Royalty without its
obligations . . . why bother to get out of bed if you don't want
to?

They say that no Spaniard understands a machine and
even if he does, is not prepared to meet it half way. So with
the strange television machine which had materialised within her world, the Duchess was disinclined to make any
personal adjustment. For us she was, as they also say, a new
challenge.

She always greeted me most pleasantly, as though we had
both achieved our declared aim and already produced a good
and sympathetic programme – when we had merely shot a
tentative few hundred feet. It was I felt an example of the
Spanish art of compromise, which consists of avoiding effort
because it must end in failure, while at the same time
behaving as though the effort has already and successfully
been made.

Trying to instil a quite foreign punctuality and professionalism into the 18th Duchess was not only presump-
tuous of me, but one of those extra-curriculum headaches
that the viewer, happily, knows nothing about. Most of my
work in every interview is off-screen, which is the time when a
relationship goes well, or not so well. Though I got along
with her, just, she had taken a dislike to Kevin Billington, my
director, which was reciprocated. It was not a happy tour.

Sometimes, however, she was absolutely wonderful and
we could enjoy our work. She went into the nursery and
bathed two-year-old Cayetano for us – though this was no
chore since she adored her five sons. She dressed in what she
called her 'cowboy outfit' and rode superbly for us – though
this was no chore since she adored horses almost as much.
She put on her flamenco costume and danced barefooted for

us – though this was no chore etc. She painted for us – though this etc, etc.

Trying to coax her into a sympathetic yet illuminating light, we were anxious to film her occasional expeditions into the world outside her Palace walls. She was the main financial support of a Madrid school for 900 boys run by the Salesian Fathers, and we watched one of her three annual visits. She was President of the Spanish Blood Donor Service and at a clinic told me she often gave blood herself. 'Blue, of course?' I ventured. 'Not at all' – with some asperity – 'As red as anything.'

She told me, 'I'm shy, but I have quite a strong character,' and I believed her. In that she was not typical, for Spaniards understand reserve but are usually untroubled by shyness, and women carry themselves with boldness and decision.

'I used to enjoy being a public figure, but now all the time I like it less. People don't know me abroad, but here everywhere I go I'm noticed. So I occupy myself with my own things – dancing, the Red Cross, the opera, and I'm often asked to open something at the University.' She rarely travelled overseas: 'I don't fly, and that's a terrible handicap because it takes a week to go from one place to another. I have given up flying because I had so many bad experiences.' In Ireland during the war, a Messerschmitt had forced her airliner to land, and she had almost taken the flight from Lisbon with the English film star Leslie Howard which German aircraft shot down over the Bay of Biscay. On her way to Hawaii after the war she had flown through a typhoon, and once an engine had caught fire. 'Actually, I've quite lost my nerve in the air – but I'm not afraid of anything else.'

She was a complicated and uncertain Duchess, but had disarming moments. After our programme had been transmitted I had several pleasant letters from her; in one she sent me this Spanish poem, which I found touching:

El día que tú naciste   The day that you were born
todos reían   everyone was laughing;
tú sólo llorabas;   only you were crying.

vive de tal manera	Live in such a way
que, cuando mueras,	that when you die,
tú sólo rías	only you will laugh
y todos lloren . . .	and everyone will cry . . .

We left her to film the future Duke of Alba, 16-year-old Carlos, and rode around with him in the Family coach. Alfonso, 14, was at his guitar lesson, strumming under the stony stares of noble ancestors in a ballroom dedicated to Great Aunt Eugénie. We caught her third son Jacobo, ten years old and the extrovert of the family, painting in his mother's studio.

Then we drove south to Marbella, where the Duchess had a splendid villa on the beach which she called 'the Little House'. We went on to Seville, to the loveliest of the Albas' many homes: the 15th century Moorish Palace of the Duenas. God gives a house in Seville, says a local proverb, to those he loves – and so it seemed. In its courtyard, amid myrtle and orange trees, roses climbed the palms. The resident staff had worked for months to prepare for the family's annual two-week visit, and were reinforced by most of their Madrid servants.

Seville is the essence of Spain, and in preparation for its Holy Week we watched the Duchess, Madrina of two Cofradias, dressing the Madonna of San Romano, her local church. In a poor parish, this Virgin of the Gypsies was no poor Madonna, for she was adorned by ten diamond necklaces and five diamond bracelets, by pearls and emeralds and rubies – and a tiara that belonged to the Czarina of Russia. Four other Madonnas were also dressed in the Duchess's jewellery. Her better jewels were kept for an even more beloved Madonna, La Macarena, the Virgin of the Bull-fighters, who wore the Alba necklace of 41 diamonds. La Macarena also carried on her left cheek a scar from a wine glass thrown by a man in drunken ecstasy – a crime which he expiated by walking behind her float in chains each Holy Week for eight years.

Few scenes on earth match the holy parades of Seville – the most extraordinary religious spectacle to be seen in

Europe since the 14th century, and all the more haunting because dignity and reverence accompany an odd matter-of-fact detachment. In churches smelling of incense and bubblegum, we filmed Penitents busily preparing the floats and themselves, while spitting and chattering and smoking – yet the grandeur of the occasion threw over everything a kind of dignity. When bells, clanging like old buckets beaten by a spade, summoned them to worship and wonder, they showed a devouring fervour.

As processions formed up in crowded churches, each a jumble of magnificence and neglect, the Penitents were drilled by loudspeakers, sergeant-major voices dragooning float-carriers attempting to shoulder an impossible load. There were 92 golden floats in the Semana Santa devotions, and each moved out steadily and slowly to gasps from waiting crowds. Beneath every one, 30 or 40 men were stooped and huddled in the darkness, carrying a burden of more than two tons, their feet moving in jerky rhythm under the skirts, like a giant centipede. Through narrow streets and alleyways sticky with candlegrease, each was escorted in triumph by hooded barefoot figures from the Inquisition. The second float in each procession displayed the church's Madonna, her doleful pink polychrome cheeks glistening with plastic tears. Some of these adored Madonnas had 20 changes of elaborate clothing, and their peep-show prettiness was received with childish excitement. Outside every church each Madonna was greeted by a weird *saeta*, the 'deep song', half Arab, half gypsy, a falsetto cry of strangled passion and solitude.

Holy Week provided a personal drama for each Sevill-ano – though the citizens were not passionately religious and the Church had many enemies. The energy and money poured into the processions would have built a housing estate; yet before each Madonna, all eyes brightened and arguments vanished.

The Duchess of course did not go to the procession – it came to her, its Madonna floating through the night as her candelabra illuminated her diamonds. These were unin-sured but far from unguarded, for what better security than

thousands of adoring eyes? Outside the Palace, as we gasped
at the beauty of it all, the Virgin did her little dance for the
Duchess.

The Penitential week in the city of Carmen and Don Juan
ended with the annual explosion of the April Fair, when the
whole rhythm of the city accelerated, cafés were hilarious
and it seemed as though some civic blood vessel was about to
burst. In the midst of this enormous binge, Carlos led the
Alba contingent in the parade of horses, fashions and handsome Spaniards. Hour after hour, young Andalucians
showed themselves off with great style in a sort of ritual
mating-session – a *paseo* with horses.

In the 15th century Palace of the Dukes of Medinacelli the
city celebrated its release from religious fervour with a party
for 2,000 guests, including Orson Welles – looking like the
last act of Citizen Kane – and a secret passion of mine,
Audrey Hepburn. It went on all night amid a convulsion of
castanets and flamenco.

The wilful Duchess remained at home – but she did celebrate later by putting on one of her flamenco dresses and
dancing for us with a certain abandon, eyebrows arched with
all the haughty disdain of a Duchess imitating a gypsy girl
imitating a Duchess . . .

DIVORCE

I had to be Ruthless, in order to be Free . . .

THE Divorce Reform Bill – divorce by consent after two
years' separation – was coming before Parliament and
already being attacked as a Casanova Charter. Socially and
judicially it was accepted that marriage was not for ever, so
second or multiple marriages were inevitable. Statistically,
such remarriage seemed to show the same failure rate as the
first-time-around. Through the eyes and experiences of a

couple of Eternal Quadrangles we considered those who had loved and lost and loved again, upon their marry-go-round.

At the same time, and unexpectedly, we revealed another turning point for television. People talking naturally and candidly about their private lives can often be fascinating – but I did not expect the programme would become front page news around the world. It hit international headlines not because of content or innovation or topicality, but merely because during our conversation . . . Robin Douglas-Home wept.

I have always believed there was a reason why this touching and most natural act so stunned those people who write to and for the papers: it was the first time *upper-class* tears had been seen on television. It was all right, on occasion, for a successful beauty queen or an exhausted soldier to cry, for a guilty servant to snivel or a fearful miner's wife to dissolve into tears, but after all this chap was an old Etonian Seaforth Highlander and an escort of Princess Margaret, a nephew of the Prime Minister and a suitor for the hand of Sweden's Princess Margaretha . . . In the Stiff Upper Lip set, he had let the side down. We were not then ready for simple emotion from anyone in an Old School Tie.

The programme was of course castigated for intrusion: some critics called our straightforward look at such consenting adults at a time when the Law was being changed 'a public duty'; others found it a distressing peep-show. 'Bad taste,' complained *The Sun* – of all papers. 'One of the most revealing scenes ever screened on television' – *Daily Sketch*. 'Delicately handled – in no way distasteful' – *Church Times*. In the Shires the *Leicestershire Mercury* was shocked by this conversational programme into a resonant editorial: 'It was as terrifying and more deeply disturbing than scenes from the Vietnam War. Everybody looking in was forced to wallow in it. There was no reprieve. Nobody could turn it off either. It was too compelling.'

All that happened was, when we talked to Robin at his house at West Chiltington, in Sussex, he recalled the distressing circumstances that led to his divorce from the model Sandra Paul. After a while the memories became upsetting;

he faltered, and wiped away a tear . . . I paused, and we were about to cut when, after a moment, he recovered composure and we continued our conversation. During the editing afterwards the director, Fred Burnley, asked Robin as a matter of course whether he wished that sequence removed from the programme. He did not. It was as simple as that.

I do recall how emphatically Sandra and Robin brought home to me the confusing fact that there can be two *right* sides to any argument. We filmed Sandra at her new home in Chelsea; she was blonde, vulnerable and shy, with that soft slight lisp that made men long to protect her – and she had been wounded by marriage.

Since I often get too close to my interviewees to retain a perspective, I find the instant verdict of the five or six men behind the camera a quick and sometimes salutary reaction, for they have been silently absorbing the conversation. When we left the house, I asked the crew what they thought. As one man, they agreed Robin must be a Right Bastard to have treated that lovely girl so badly – how could anyone be so Bloody Cruel?

Shaking our heads over man's inhumanity to woman, we drove down to Sussex to hear Robin tell his version of their divorce. In the pub afterwards the crew all angrily wondered how that Spiteful Bitch could have been so calculating and ruthless to such a nice gentle guy . . .

Sandra Paul was only 18 but already a top model when she married Robin at St James's Piccadilly in the summer of 1959. It was a year since King Gustav of Sweden had rejected his request for the hand of Princess Margaretha. He was 26, and had been playing the piano in a West End club and at the Berkeley Hotel when he met and lost his Princess, met and won his Model. Headlines announced: 'Prime Minister's Nephew weds Cover Girl.' They moved into a cottage at Alton in Hampshire and he wrote a couple of books while she continued her photographic career. After a year things began to go wrong.

As we sat in her new home in Drayton Gardens she told me, with that slight but irresistible stammer: 'We had occasional money quarrels about who paid for what, because we were both earning. I suppose they were also connected with possessiveness. I wanted to know what he'd been doing, or where he'd been, and he didn't want to say – so we'd have a row. He thought I shouldn't need to know everything. I felt when you were happily married you should share things, and that he should at least take the trouble to make something up to tell you, so you could put it out of your mind.

'I thought about divorce for two years before I did it, and finally went to New York with my child for three-months' separation. He came out during that time and tried to get me to come home. He said he was sorry he'd behaved badly and wanted me to come back, when we would try again. So I said, all right – but when I came back he had a change of heart and decided he would leave me anyway. Then I went to see a solicitor. It was just one of those things where we were both trying to pick up ends that were hopeless – they were too sort of . . . threadbare.

'Robin had a sort of anti-divorce phobia, I think, because his parents had been divorced and he couldn't bear the thought of it, so he refused to give me a divorce straightforwardly. I had to go against him, and one could only do it by pointing a finger, an accusing finger and bringing out old, sordid things – it was awful.

'He blamed me for dragging the whole thing out and couldn't understand that there wasn't any other way, because he had been unhelpful about the grounds. I don't think I was unfair, because it was the only thing I could do. It was hopeless for us to stay in a separated state. Hopeless for me – I was being selfish. I wanted to be free. I *had* to be ruthless, in order to be free.'

Later I sat in Robin's home as he recalled the early days of a marriage on the rebound: 'I felt bloody angry about the way the Swedes had behaved . . . I met Sandra in February, and we married in July. She was incredibly beautiful and had a tremendous quality of innocence. She was, I thought, a vulnerable creature in a highly suspect world – the world of models and fashion which I despised then and despise even more now. And maybe in a sense I was trying to rescue her from what I thought was going to be a decline in her character, due to her career.'

When things went wrong and he learned she was intent upon divorce 'I went straight to the best lawyers I could find and asked what I should do. The first thing they did was to make the child a Ward of Court, because they said her previous history indicated she was quite capable of using Sholto as a weapon in the divorce case, and removing him from the jurisdiction of the English courts. And from that one decision, I think, probably all the bitterness followed.

'She didn't want a period of separation, trial separation, and then to come together. She wanted divorce. So I agreed to give her the grounds. That, I may say, is a very expensive and thoroughly unsavoury business, involving expensive and thoroughly unsavoury girls in expensive and thoroughly unsavoury hotels, and it cost me a bloody packet. I had to do it not once, but twice, because the detective who came in the morning of the first night failed to recognise the girl who was meant to be in the same bed as me. And a man less like a waiter you've never seen in your life! I mean, he looked like some sort of Inspector Lockhart in heavy boots coming in with the coffee. I pulled the bedclothes off the girl's face, but still he failed to recognise her. Anyway I had to do it again, and I couldn't do it with the same girl because she was too expensive. So I got a friend who was an air hostess under a different name, and she said she'd do it under her real name, which was kind of her. So we went through all the palaver again. Eventually we all ended up – two girls, me, two private detectives and a lawyer all in an office listening to each other giving affidavits – the whole thing was completely crazy. In spite of the fact that this was good for two divorces, not one, it was not accepted by Sandra or her lawyers as being sufficient evidence of adultery, and she insisted on continuing with this petition for cruelty. I can only describe one's feelings to you as, you know, as though a small bomb had gone off inside your head.

'The petition chapterised the marriage almost day by day and, incidentally, letter by letter, in the most vicious and unpleasant terms, with me as the aggressor, the cruel one.

Five years of one's life, say 70 per cent of which was very happy, reduced to a great wad of foolscap, typed out by leering little clerks in solicitors' offices. All your letters from the moment you'd met, typed out, your letters to your mother, her letters to her mother, her mother's letters to me . . .'

Here the memories became too much, and the unhappy man wiped away tears. Then, recovering, he went on to explain: 'I couldn't bear her to put a kind of tombstone on this marriage, reading the way that the petition read.'

As Sandra had married again, I wondered whether he might consider remarriage? 'I have thought about it and come to the inescapable conclusion that it would be a final mark of insanity. If you've failed once I think you are going to fail a second time – and I just don't want to be destroyed again.'

So Robin was divorced for cruelty and adultery. He had lost Sandra to David Wynne-Morgan, who ran a Public Relations company and had been previously married to Romaine, a former Fleet Street secretary. She was a devout Catholic, and David had left her with their two children in a Stanmore semi. They had married at 23. 'I divorced him legally, but that doesn't leave me any the less tied, where my religion is concerned. He was tugging very much at the tie of legal separation and I didn't feel there was any point in hanging on, just through bitterness. I felt in some funny way too that if he got the divorce he wanted, he might be closer to us, because there wouldn't be that awful atmosphere in every conversation, when he felt he was in limbo, neither married nor divorced.'

She still regarded herself as married: 'When you've been brought up with a certain set of principles, in your own heart you can't detach yourself as easily as that, but it's no good going through the rest of your life feeling resentful. I just wish I had learned to be a wife, before becoming a mother.

'The children were only seven months and 19 months when I first had to cope, alone. Fortunately I'm fairly practical, but the emotional side is very difficult when you're trying to be both a father and mother. I miss sharing affection with somebody. You can pile it on the children and they give an awful lot in return, but they're going away one day – and then you're going to be left with a very empty life.'

In every parting, it seems, someone is selfish. In every wretched divorce there is one who goes eagerly towards remarriage and a sort of happiness – one who is left behind, alone.

David told me: 'I don't think I could have made a go of any marriage at the time I first married. I was simply not husband material. I think I am today, because if there was a clash with my business, my marriage would come first – whereas the first time if the *Daily Express* clashed with what Romaine wanted, Lord Beaverbrook was a 25-length winner before the thing started.'

An old Fleet Street colleague from the days we accompanied Princess Margaret around East Africa, David recalled how his married life with Sandra began in the Kensington Register Office: 'We queued up alongside some very pregnant brides. Then, to signal the start of the ceremony, the Registrar put a green plastic carnation into his buttonhole. Afterwards in the middle of the reception our dog – which the children all adored – ran out into the road and was killed. Then we left for our honeymoon in Spain and got to London Airport *just* in time for the flight – to find it was taking off from Gatwick . . .'

The other Quartet: Elizabeth Jane Howard, the novelist, who divorced Peter Scott, son of Scott of the Antarctic, and after a brief second marriage, wed another novelist, Kingsley Amis, who had divorced his first wife; Peter Scott went on to marry his secretary, Philippa Talbot-Ponsonby.

Elizabeth had married Scott during the war and had a daughter: 'He was absolutely obsessed with learning to run a warship well, and thinking of very little else. He managed to get more Oerlikon guns on to an MTB than anyone else. My interest in Oerlikon guns was minimal I should say, even with good will. He was more interested in action, and in other forms of life – that's partly why he's such a brilliant naturalist and zoologist. People were not his main interest. He thinks they're all right in their place, but he's got a lot of other places, and he will think more about gekkos than you or I would.'

Peter Scott was running the Severn Wildfowl Trust at Slimbridge in Gloucestershire, where he mentioned he had accommodated 350 migratory Bewick swans without a single case of divorce. He was so profoundly involved with birds it was said he would be the first man to fly unaided. He had called his son Falcon and his daughter Dafila – the Latin name of a pintailed duck.

They had undergone a relatively painless divorce. 'I walked out of the tube station at Notting Hill one day,' Elizabeth told me, 'and saw the placards: "Peter Scott divorces ex-actress wife" and thought, Oh – that's me.'

Had she at that time considered remarriage? 'Absolutely out of the question. I was sure I'd never marry again, and that I was going to end up a rather nasty old lady who had written a lot of books.' Yet after two unsatisfactory marriages, she still came back for a third? 'Yes – but you see, I might have written four unsatisfactory books, yet I'll still go on writing . . .'

This quartet all shared quite pleasant memories. 'We are still very fond of each other,' said Peter Scott, 'but we made each other miserable when we lived together.' They were all as reasonable and accommodating as our other Divorcees were bitter and wretched. Before today's easy divorce by consent, the Law could seem inhuman, sometimes demanding the spectacle of cruelty-in-public before two people could legally bury a dead marriage.

I remained in touch with most of them. About a year later Robin telephoned from Sussex one morning for a chat, and I invited him to a party I was giving that Sunday on a boat in the Regent's Canal. Sandra was sending six-year-old Sholto to spend that weekend with him, so unfortunately he could not come. We agreed to get together soon, and parted cheerily. Within a few days he was found dead in bed, of an overdose. He was 36.

Some time later I was touched to read in David Bailey's book that, along with Princess Margaret, I was included in the list of people this young man of unendurable sadness had remembered kindly, and with affection.

Today one marriage in every three is the second time around; two-thirds of those involved in a break-up marry within a year. Since our programme Sandra Paul and David Wynne-Morgan have been divorced again, and both have remarried. Romaine is still alone. Elizabeth Jane Howard has left Kingsley Amis. Sir Peter and Lady Scott remain together.

JAMES BOND

You can't see your Husband as a Sex Symbol . . .

IAN Fleming's agent, Robert Fenn, was also a friend of mine. One day in 1964 when we were planning a Caribbean tour for Tonight, he suggested we should make a Whicker's World on the creator of James Bond, then writing at Goldeneye, his house at Ocho Rios on Jamaica's north coast. It seemed an ideal project: 007 was already an international institution and authors, however successful, love publicity. After some discussion the BBC agreed, and I wrote to tell Fleming I was looking forward to our meeting, mentioned a few mutual friends, gave him a rough schedule of our movements and a few thoughts on how we might approach the programme. By return I had the rudest letter I have ever received.

I should have kept it. It was after all from a Bestseller, and must still be burning a hole in some Documentary department file. He had not the slightest intention of giving his valuable time to the BBC, or to me, for little or no payment. In that short sharp vein he dismissed us as parasites upon the creative body. It was strong stuff. Since I had understood the whole project was his and we were merely being agreeable and falling in with his wishes, I was stunned.

I had an active sense of injustice and a tendency not to turn the other cheek, so was about to leap to my typewriter and shoot off an indignant rejoinder. However for some reason I stayed my hand. I have never been quite sure why. Instead I sent an unusually gentle reply, regretting our lines had got crossed in that way, and saying only that his decision was certainly my loss – as it was.

Weeks later while filming in Jamaica we visited Ocho Rios, and I went to stay with Jeremy Vaughan on his father's plantation, just above Goldeneye. They saw Fleming most days and were concerned about him, for he was drinking heavily and usually legless by lunchtime. His writing was not going well, if at all. I recalled what had happened. 'Don't take it to heart,' said Charles Vaughan. 'That's not like him – but obviously he's a sick man.'

Within a few weeks, Ian Fleming was dead. I was profoundly thankful I had not risen to the passing irritation of an unhappy author in his last days.

I recalled this passage-at-arms a couple of years later when it was suggested we might make a programme on James Bond – who had effortlessly outlived his creator. In an elegant house in Green Street, Mayfair, I had an exploratory and far more welcoming session with Cubby Broccoli, producer of the phenomenally successful series of films and soon afterwards was in a long black limo with Sean Connery and his wife Diane Cilento, being hotly pursued through the backstreets of Tokyo by five cars and a swarm of Japanese paparazzi, all determined to shoot Bondo-san.

007, licensed to print money, was even then the hero of 50 million books and, after four films, the all-time cinema box office champion. When President Kennedy revealed a weakness for his exploits the books had taken off, closely followed by the films. He had made Connery, an unknown actor, the most famous face in the world, for there are no geographical limits to the appeal of violence, sex and snobbery.

Cubby Broccoli and Harry Saltzman were producing the

Bond saga in uneasy partnership. Harry was small and explosive, Cubby large and generous; he had been called Harry's sense of proportion. Together they made a formidable pair: Cubby would give you a cigar – and Harry would knock it out of your mouth.

In his stately home at Iver, Harry told me: 'The Bond films came at just the right time. Kitchen-sink realistic pictures were over, and we gave them a new mythology – a modern Tarzan. Cubby and I went through 200 actors in 1962 before choosing Sean. We liked the way he moved. Only one other actor moves as well – and that's Albert Finney.'

Cubby's grandfather had introduced the family vegetable into America, but he had made much more lettuce by introducing a cult hero. He stoutly defended the Fleming formula – 007's famous Licence to Kill: 'You don't see him killing just for the sake of it. No, he always kills in self-defence or for a good reason – for entertainment, or to progress the plot . . .'

With such uncomplicated reactions, Bond had already triumphed onscreen in Jamaica, Turkey, Fort Knox and Nassau. In this fifth epic, 'You Only Live Twice', Ian Fleming had allowed lone-wolf Bond a friend: Tiger Tanaka, head of the Japanese Secret Service. It seemed the wily Oriental villain we had known and hated for years was out – so in Tokyo, they were celebrating!

The film, which followed the book at a considerable distance, was going to cost multimillions and be seen by megamillions. To observe the epic headaches of Bondiana in the making, the Whicker's World film crew joined the Heavy Mob from Pinewood in a Japanese Air Lines DC8 on its way to Tokyo. Film company charters, where everything is lavish and free, are traditionally jolly flights, so we hardly noticed Anchorage, but in Japan no one could escape the instant impact of Bond-hysteria.

Sean and Diane had flown the other way round, hoping for a holiday. During their progress towards Tokyo they had been driven out of Bangkok by crowds, chased through Manila by Filipino fans, warily avoided Hong Kong for fear of mobs and, on arrival at Haneda Airport, been smuggled with difficulty into Japan. By morning, word had spread that Bondo-san was in town.

It seemed every tiny Japanese identified with the brawny monosyllabic Scot, and the lobbies of the Tokyo Hilton were thick with jostling Japanese photographers, each small darting man almost dragged to the ground by the weight of enormous telefoto lens dangling like submachineguns from his camera slings. The swarm seemed more waspish and inescapable than the Roman originals on the Via Veneto, for they wielded newer and more aggressive cameras, with longer lenses. In an effort to get them off the back of his prickly star, Cubby compromised with a Press conference, attended reluctantly by Sean.

On this fifth Bond (he did only two more) he was now merely irritated by worldwide fame which I doubt has been equalled. For the role of 007 he had abandoned his fierce professional concentration and seemed indifferent to the film's progress. At Pinewood I noticed he retreated to his dressingroom whenever possible, thoroughly bored, to practise putting: golf was his one passion. Being 007 had become just a tedious job – not the knightly mission we all saw. It was the Monster deciding that Dr Frankenstein was unworthy of him.

Sean was wearily convinced he had already been asked every inane question in public, but the ever-innovative Japanese produced a few more. They were totally enraptured by the image of the suave, elegant St James's clubman about-town; Bond, like Fleming, was Eton and Sandhurst. Sean Connery, however, was born in an Edinburgh tenement, his father a labourer, his cot a wardrobe drawer. He left school at 15 to deliver milk, before becoming a bricklayer and coffin-polisher. When I first met him in the early Fifties he had been a Mr Universe contender and was then an ambitious chorus boy in 'South Pacific', supplementing his income by babysitting.

He arrived late at this conference before 300 neat little Japanese journalists in identical dark blue suits and white nylon shirts. Up on the stage he looked relaxed and casual to the point of falling apart. He was wearing an open shirt and slacks, but not his hair-piece or his socks. There was an indrawing of Oriental breath.

Connery suffers fools badly, so the basically shy, dour and unyielding Scot did not bother to dress up his replies to a succession of irrelevancies. Translations went solemnly backwards and forwards for an hour or two while he came to the boil: 'What is tattooed on your arm?' (Scotland Forever, and Mum and Dad). 'After your experience as Bond, will you start a Detective Agency?' (No). 'What do you do when your children misbehave?' (I beat them). 'Why aren't you wearing a tie?' (Why aren't you?).

We had only one night in Tokyo before flying south to the location in Kyushu. Sean, on his first visit to Japan, rashly asked to see something of the capital, so Cubby organised a highly secret expedition to an exclusive little restaurant just off the Ginza.

Besieging hordes of public, Press and cameramen were still camped in the hotel lobby so, protected by house detectives, we tiptoed from Cubby's suite (1007, of course) to a service lift. In the underground garage two limousines waited, engines running. Watched only by a few giggling girls from the massage rooms, we piled in – and the limos shot out of the garage in true James Bond style.

Before we had gone 50 yards five waiting cars crammed with crafty cameramen spotted us, and screamed in pursuit. Long lenses emerged from windows, like machineguns. I kept ducking, because I'd seen the movie.

We raced on through the night streets, tyres squealing. Sean was alarmed, unaware they always drove that way in Tokyo – though this time, he was the target. The camera-cars tried to box us in while paparazzi clicked away in a frenzy of high-pitched ejaculation. Sean just sat, looking rueful.

At the restaurant we pushed through another fusillade of flashbulbs while Cubby organised defence-in-depth at the door. Then in the dark half-empty room we all sank into a booth, already weary. 'I begin to understand,' I told Sean, 'why you get a bit brusque.'

'It's not only here,' he said. 'We have a marvellous house

in Acton in a wonderful situation – a cul-de-sac right by the park, but there are some real head-cases around. They just come up and sit on top of their cars, or knock at the door and say, It would be marvellous if we could come in and have tea, or take some photographs, or stand on your wall. There's only one way to solve it, and that's not to be there. And the papers don't help. I've got no Press agent and no Publicity Manager – the Americans can't believe it – but consequently one goes into a barbershop and reads all sorts of garbage that some tinhead has put out.'

Sean, unaffected and indifferent to his image as the world's hero, did surprise me by one casual admission: 'I've only read one of the Bond books – or one and a half. They lack humour, that's their trouble.' He was distinctly uncommitted.

We relaxed over a few Kirin beers as though life was normal, ate our crab salad in peace and were about to tackle some giant Kobe steaks when there was a sudden shout: 'Look out – *there's* one!' A man who for half-an-hour had been drinking silently at the bar in the corner suddenly revealed himself in his true flashlight.

Frantically, he grabbed a couple of pictures of Sean and fled, pursued by waiters. The tiny woman who owned the place leapt across to cut him off. From outside the door came muffled thuds and groans. When she came back, bowing and smiling, the diminutive girl was carrying his camera . . .

As we were finishing our steaks a second kamikaze cameraman leapt into action: a silent diner sipping *sake* at the next table was suddenly transmogrified into a frenzied, foolhardy photographer. There were more shouts, and tables went flying. The lady of the house went after him, too. He never had a chance, poor chap.

We sat there, flinching, and decided it was just like one of those action films. After a while she returned, triumphant once more. This time she was bearing – his wristwatch!

'Next time,' I said, 'it'll be an ear.' When later she came round to ask if our steaks were all right she got, as you can imagine, no complaints out of *me*.

The location of Bondo-san's intimate little dinner party

must have gone round Tokyo for when we left the streets were solid with a Cup Final crowd, pressing against rows of policemen. Unfortunately my crew were taking a day off to recover from their merry flight, so we never shot a foot of those remarkable scenes – or we might well have added to poor Sean's persecution . . .

Next day we flew south to the first location, outside Kagoshima. I checked in at an enchanting Japanese inn which I discovered was to be used in the film, as the home of Tiger Tanaka. Ken Adam, the brilliant art director whose gadgetry and settings probably contributed more than anything to the success of the Bond sagas, was outraged. A Berlin Jew who flew a wartime RAF Spitfire, he was not one to accept injustice: 'We're staying at this bloody awful hotel in town and Whicker's living in luxury in our *set* . . .' Working in that steamheat was like moving through a turkish bath, so I would invite them to sit on my tatami for placatory drinks, between takes.

They used Akime as the fishing village of Kissy Suzuki, one of Bond's girls, where Sean – six-foot-two of indisputable Scot – had to pretend to be a small and inconspicuous Japanese fisherman. Bond films always demanded the surrender of belief. To help him blend into an Eastern background he wore a Beatle wig and make-up to cover arm tattoos few Oriental fisherman could boast.

The unit instantly walked into an international incident, where East was reluctant to meet West. Kissy's Ama pearl-diving girls, needed in bikinis for Press pictures, went on strike fearing over-exposure. The publicity man was outraged, for they were not timid local divers doing what came naturally but well-paid professional starlets and models flown in for the job. One was a lift girl from the Tokyo Hilton, hitting the big-time at last. Despite their city ways, three of the eight had been totally overcome by bikini shyness. The problem went all the way up to Cubby Broccoli. Exasperated, he emerged to overcome their modesty with money, quite quickly.

Lewis Gilbert, who made the successful 'Alfie', was directing his first Bond and still staggered by the big-budget availability of everything: 'I've made 25 films and I've never known anything like it. We have one giant helicopter to transport the unit but I asked for another 25-seater – so the producer's gone into town to raise one. I don't think there's anything I could ask for that's not been given. If I said I wanted another 5,000 people from Tokyo, they'd be flown in.'

He already had giant airborne magnets which captured speeding cars, space satellites which swallowed each other, and erupting volcanos. It was lavish all right. We tried an armed minicopter just before it went into aerial combat. Soon afterwards it crashed, killing the stunt pilot. The famous Bond spectacle was not all done with models.

One of the other vital ingredients was the Bond Bird. In London we had filmed luscious unknowns arriving from all over the world to be tested, in the hope they might be chosen to go to some awful fate by his side. Bond girls seldom lasted more than ten minutes on screen before something frightful happened, but during their brief passionate posturing they happily braved pirhanas and death rays for the pleasure of sharing his bed and vodka-martini.

The screenplay orchestrating such sex, sin and sadism was by Roald Dahl, who also wrote books for children. He was standing by in Kyushu to provide any additional pearls required. This put little strain upon his creative ability, for 007 scripts were undemanding. 'You have to stick to the formula,' he admitted. 'Bond's just a tough insensitive fellow who's rather good at his job. When I inquired whether he wanted a woman to chase around, they said, "Three would be better." '

While they were filming Sean as the biggest little fisherman in the village, I went to the beach and sat on a boat with Diane, an intimate spectator on the set and then six years away from their divorce. 'You just can't see your husband as a sex symbol,' she said, 'at least, not all the time. He's not changed much because of Bond, though perhaps nowadays he's quicker-tempered because of the pressures – like being followed into the lavatory by photographers, and all that stuff. He's tried beyond normal limits, because everywhere you go there's always someone coming out from behind a tree. Big eyes follow you everywhere.'

Indeed when we went to film some scenes out at sea, the Press tailed us in motorboats. As a ploy they were warned through loudhailers that the whole area was mined, but chugged after us undaunted. They were finally discouraged by some well-placed and spectacular depth charges, as used in the film.

We climbed with the second unit, directed by Peter Hunt, up to the lonely crater of Mount Shinmoe. Within that volcano were the villains James Bond had to undo – and at its burning heart, the headquarters of the No 1 fiend Blofeld. The crater was reached wearily by foot or easily by helicopter, and 100 Ninjas went over its edge on ropes. These warriors were on Our Side and their arrival to do battle was then filmed from below – but at Pinewood. There Ken Adam had built a volcanic replica big as the Albert Hall. This one set cost as much as the first James Bond film, 'Dr No'. Each film had to out-spectacle those that had gone before – not to mention imitators who were scrambling on the Bond-wagon.

At the mouth of the artificial Buckinghamshire volcano a helicopter descended through its lake – a sliding sheet of glass – and landed on a platform beside an intercontinental ballistic missile, imitation but full-size. There was also an internal monorail from which I did the payoff to our programme. The whole stunning SciFi scene had been built among flat damp fields, using more scaffolding than was needed for the London Hilton. It demanded a prodigious amount of work and expense and in the end, of course – 007 blew it up.

We edited our Japanese and Pinewood footage and Fred Burnley dubbed some tremendous sound-effects. Then Cubby, Lewis Gilbert and Ken Adam came to Lime Grove to see what we had done to them. They were still shooting, for their film was not to open until the next year, and were stunned and delighted by our instant-version. 'We won't bother to complete,' said Ken, not too seriously, 'we'll just use yours.' Unfortunately it was the last Whicker's World to be shot in black and white, and their blood-and-eruptions needed the impact of colour.

Bond films went to endless trouble and expense to achieve that stylish, camp quality which neutralised criticism of their violence. They were not afraid to be ridiculous. 007 had been attacked by giant squids, hauled naked across razor-edged coral, touched-up by lasers, poisoned, pulled apart, scalded, exploded, electrocuted and regularly beaten to pulp. His famous gadgets acted like the magic shields Greek gods gave their favourites, and he always emerged with his hairpiece unruffled.

This hero of our times had come to represent the positive unneurotic life, and a world fascinated by Bondage followed breathless from improbability to impossibility until Democracy was saved and paradise regained. In his anlysis of the craze, Kingsley Amis decided we did not want to have Bond to dinner or go golfing with Bond or even talk to Bond – we all wanted to *be* Bond . . . who stood between Britain and Disaster and always won, who felt little pain and no compunction and regarded girls as functional and disposable, like Kleenex.

I wondered whether we might not prefer to be Sean Connery, without privacy but with his salary of many millions, backed by a hefty piece of the profits. He was still marginally closer to reality.

Curiously enough, he was one person who did *not* want to be 007; and very soon, he wasn't. Today I am sure Sean could eat his Kobe steak without being interrupted by a single camera-shutter or one silly question. He has gone on to different roles – while James Bond still marches triumphantly through the most preposterous circus of the age.

TONY HANCOCK

You learnt to die with grace,
with your eyes smiling . . .

DURING the Sixties we would unwind in the Lime Grove
BBC Club after the nightly Tonight, usually bleeding from
some fierce internecine post-mortem, but occasionally
triumphant. Amid those blow-by-blows I would sometimes
move from our mob for a change of conversation and join a
tubby, mournful little chap who looked as though he had
dressed in the dark. He was always on his own, and just on
the verge of going home. Lonely, defeated, morose – he was
at the time the funniest and most popular comedian in
Britain: Tony Hancock.

I remembered those conversations years later when we
decided to devote a Whicker's World to the vulnerable and
courageous men who go empty-handed before a back-drop
twice nightly and risk their necks – the stand-up comics. We
called our programme: If they don't like you, you're Dead
. . . It transpired that sometimes in the sad world of laughter
even if they *did* like you, you could still die.

Comedy is so serious a business that top comedians regularly pay for their popularity with nervous breakdowns and
heart attacks. As we went to film, Bruce Forsyth was recovering from a breakdown, following those of Spike Milligan,
Norman Wisdom and Stanley Baxter. Charlie Drake collapsed, Frankie Howard lost his confidence and Peter Sellers
had a heart attack; Eric Morecambe's was to come.

They lived on their nerves. Not even the most experienced
comic could always be sure to touch the national funnybone,
to hear the sweet sound of applause. Laughter is vague,

infectious stuff; it comes in waves and disappears, leaving no trace and little memory . . .

Recalling our discussions, I asked Tony Hancock to take part in our programme. He was the most accomplished clown on the English stage and twice TV's Top Comedian of the Year. His show had emptied the nation's streets on Friday nights. By then he had left Sid James, left his programme, separated from his writers, made a poor film and appeared without much success in cabaret.

One afternoon we filmed a long conversation; it was a rambling stream-of-thought, but contained some of the essence of a comic genius who had just come off the boil and was living through a new situation.

Soon afterwards I left for the Far East to film. When I returned to record our Laughter-Makers commentary before transmission, I discovered the director had dropped the entire Hancock interview. David Rea was bright and self-confident, but liked programmes to be punchy and full of short sharp messages. I used to say his ideal interviewee would merely declare 'Junkie sex fiend slayed six in love nest' – and then we would cut. With a mass of good material, David had decided Hancock slowed up our programme – which I am sure he did. He had been thoughtful and troubled, and I had found the interview sad, honest and revealing. However it was too late for a recut, so our 'ancock was lost for ever on the cutting-room floor.

I could imagine his rueful, gloomy acceptance of that last failure, the shrug of those overburdened shoulders at his final dismissal – had he ever known about it. Soon afterwards he went to Australia and, in a Sydney hotel bedroom, killed himself.

His cult lives: actors portray him, Hancock's Half Hour goes out again and again on radio, comedians imitate him, his records are played in every programme about funnymen. Fortunately from the last long interview he ever gave – which no one saw – I kept all my notes. I can see him now, scrunched-up despairingly in that Hospitality room at Lime Grove like an untidy heap of old clothes that was slowly absorbing white wine – and talking his own epitaph.

We discussed the craft and I asked what he had learned in that early job as stand-up comic at the Windmill Theatre: 'Oh brother! I learnt one thing: I could make a living out of it. The show used to start at 12.15 and I was on at 12.19. I'd heard of second spot, but that was ridiculous. Two, three rows of gentlemen reading the sporting pages, with U-boat binoculars on their laps. I used to go on to deathly silence. You learnt to die with grace, you see – you'd die smiling. Even your eyes, hypocritically enough, were smiling as you went on. Then came the smash.

'At two o'clock you appeared again, by which time you'd probably collected a couple of odd drunks who would make a little noise – though not the noise you wanted, particularly. And the same two rows of gentlemen with the U-boat binoculars and the papers. I didn't like it the first time, and I certainly didn't like it the second time either. But it was a great experience and we had quite a cast. Harry Worth was there – he was a ventriloquist. Morecambe and Wise, and me and a pianist. And either Harry, the pianist and I, or Morecambe and Wise had to go at the end of the week. I sat up worrying all night, but we managed to stay and they managed to go. It hasn't done them much harm though, has it?'

'Your Lad from East Cheam was one of television's richest creations, yet since you shrugged him off you've never stopped giving yourself these convulsive remoulds . . .?"

'I'm not remoulding myself, I've just got older. The British public is extremely loyal, but very against change. I mean, some of those serials that have been drearing on for years and years and years, you know – the dog gets killed and the nation goes into mourning. The loyalty is immense.

'I didn't change because I can't – this is all I can do. But the background should be changed. Railway Cuttings as an example, Dick Van Dyke for another. You make it like a cake: take one comedian, one pretty wife, and two funny people in the office. The scriptwriter's churning these things out endlessly – it would drive me up the wall. It's formula comedy – but where did Laurel and Hardy live? Nowhere. Chaplin didn't live anywhere.'

'Just as there are Cary Grant parts and Margaret Rutherford parts, so presumably there are Anthony 'ancock parts?'

'With the East Cheam thing we found a serious identity which is very potent and it became very identifiable, which was good. It also became more difficult to write and perform. And eventually we got a bit bored with it – at least I did.'

'Have you faced audience hostility?'

'Er – yes. They threw 7½d at me at Bristol. I picked it up, went over the road and bought half-a-pint of mild. I've had the bird in every conceivable. way. It's all good experience in a way, in retrospect.

'It used to be 12 minutes, or 15 minutes, but all of a sudden Danny Kaye ruined it. He came over here and did an hour-and-a-quarter, or a bit more. So instead of going round the country, as it was pre-war, doing a 12-minute solid act, getting your golf handicap down and putting your loot in the bank every week, we all had to do longer spots. People would ring up and say – would you do 50 minutes of concert. It's a long time to die . . .'

'So what sort of comedian do you want to be?'

'A funny one. We used to have a convention in England that if a bloke didn't get a quick laugh, he'd gone. You know, he'd come on with long boots and a revolving bow tie and a moveable feather and all this business. Then these gentlemen started wandering on in beautifully cut silk suits and just sort of said, It's very lovely to be here . . . for the first ten minutes. I'd think, He's going to die a terrible death, I'll have to go because I can't even watch my worst enemy die – it's a most painful experience. I remember seeing Danny Thomas, and for ten minutes nothing happened at all. I thought, how can I get out without looking rude, because it's an unprofessional thing to do and I wouldn't do it. And gradually he got it, and he got it, you know? And when he went off, there was stamping, clapping and everything. It was a different approach, just a gentle, seductive approach, as against the gimmicks.'

'What do you find goes best?'

'True comedy. Honest comedy. Things that are recognisable. Situations that are recognisable. It was interesting to watch repeats of my own show because we tried to get things that wouldn't date. The one-line gag does date, in my opinion. But we were happy to see that most of it didn't date at all. It was still a man in a particular situation.'

'You've had a sort of mish-mash of emotion in public: your divorce and remarriage and separation and psychiatric help was all publicised, along with your weight problem and your drink problem . . . How has your career been affected?'

'I don't think it's affected at all. In any case, very few people go through life without something of this sort.'

'With all this, you've been called "the master of the self-inflicted wound". That's not a bad phrase . . .'

'No, it's not a bad phrase; whether it's accurate or not is another thing. I think if you're trying to achieve as much perfection as you can, within whatever limits comedy should have, then you're going to go through certain experiences – not always particularly pleasant – or I don't think you'd be able to give whatever is necessary.'

'But you've had a fairly tortured time of it?'

'Who hasn't? There's a certain sensitivity demanded if you're going to make anything in this business, which is an awful word anyway. But it makes one a little more vulnerable, possibly. That's something you have to accept.'

'I'm wondering how this kind of torment, such as it is, has affected your work?'

'It's helped. For one thing, you have a deeper understanding of other people's problems – and that's all comedy is really about. I don't regret it, but I wouldn't want to go through it again. I do the very best I can – nothing is worse than to come off and disappoint 'em. That's awful, because you can't blame anybody but yourself.'

'I'm sure I'm typical of all the people who watch you, and if you're not doing well, I'm broken up . . .'

'May I ask *you* a question? Don't you think sometimes perhaps you ask for a little more than there is to offer?'

'Of course – we always want more . . .'

'Yes, and I'm trying to give more, you know, so we're mutually dissatisfied . . . "City Lights", which I think is the most exquisite full-length comedy I've ever seen, was panned you know. It was Chaplin's statement. I thought it was absolutely magnificent and I went to see it five times. Maybe sometimes the audience ask a little too much. We just try to give as much as possible.'

'A friend of mine was on a show with you and told me before you appeared, you were wandering around back-stage and muttering, "Professional idiot, that's what I am – professional idiot." '

'I give myself a bit of a coating before I go on. Sort of helps make my shoulders drop when I start. Takes about half-an-hour of abuse. Self-abuse. Some people think it's intended for them, which is a pity. The odd right-hander occasionally, but apart from that, no trouble . . .'

Poor Anthony 'ancock. Life seemed to bring insufficient joy and too many right-handers – despite the laughter he offered us so lavishly. He was the classic figure: a tearful, self-destructive clown.

The humour he pursued – valuable as oil, and as hard to find – is conjured up by some elusive combination of words and attitude. Comedians are always prospecting, and those who strike laughter become famous, for as a nation we have an enormous appetite for comedians and a passion for their jokes. We wait for the funny men as eagerly as foreign audiences wait for the nudes.

I talked with Johnny Speight, Mike and Bernie Winters and others; every comic we invited on to our programme was anxious to appear – except Charlie Drake – but none could successfully analyse the craft. Try to dissect humour and it disappears, for it is a wisecrack that knows its own father. Dignified Alfred Marks, with his usual air of menacing distaste, reminded me: 'There are only six basic jokes in the world – the others are just permutations. Most of them seem to start in law schools and medical schools, and universities.'

Women rarely succeed in the laughter business – mainly, it has been suggested, because nature encourages them to believe that life works, whereas men can plainly see that it does not.

For comedy at its toughest we looked at the 'booze circuit' and watched Ray Martine working the Ritz Theatre Club at

Brighouse in Yorkshire: 'This is one of the hardest jobs in the world – you're fighting alcohol. There's a casino, there's chatter from the bar, but I'm gonna stand up there for an hour and do my stuff and if after that they don't like me – well sod 'em.'

He flounced about near the knuckle, successfully offering raunchy jokes; indeed it seems the dirty joke, cleaned up slightly for public distribution, is the one that lasts. Some of Cicero's rude jokes are still going the rounds. He wrote them 2,000 years ago – and they were not new, even then.

The Permissive Age only recently arrived. Ned Sherrin told us about BBC Radio's Green Book, produced just after the war to warn comics about doubtful material: 'Well-known vulgar jokes (eg the brass monkey cleaned up) are not normally admissible. There is an absolute ban on the following: lavatories, effeminacy in men, immorality of any kind, suggestive references to honeymoon couples, chambermaids, fig-leaves, prostitution, ladies underwear (eg winter drawers on), animal habits (eg rabbits), lodgers, commercial travellers. Jokes about harems are offensive in some parts of the world. Jokes like "enough to make a Maltese cross" are of doubtful value. All such words as God, good God, my God, blast, hell, damn, bloody, gor' blimey, ruddy etc, should be deleted from scripts and innocuous expressions substituted.'

Times change . . .

Old comedians learned their craft slogging around the music halls. We remember some of their songs, none of their jokes but most of their personalities, for everyone loves an old comic who has built up his credit balance of sympathy over the years: familiar face, familiar voice, familiar jokes.

Charlie Chester told me cheerfully: 'The fundamental basis of comedy is cruelty. If you ridicule one person in the room, everyone else will laugh at his hurt.' In this love-hate relationship it seems we laugh with relief that we are not burdened with the misfortunes of others – that we are not deaf or impotent or drunk or falling flat, that we haven't got a spiteful mother-in-law or a nagging wife – but someone else *has*. Even in pantomimes, childish audiences expect malice in wonderland.

It can work the other way around. We went to film a would-be comic tackling a cold audience in a Peckham pub. During the day John Slattery worked as a clerk in a Labour Exchange and longed to be a Funnyman. Two hundred of his comedy scripts had been rejected, but he was still out there, dying the death. Audiences will tolerate inadequate singers and dancers, incompetent jugglers, musicians sheltering behind instruments and props, but with a comic the relationship becomes personal. If he is not funny it is an affront, a betrayal.

At Hove we talked with Peter Cagney, a solemn bemused man who had a collection of 25,000 jokes for sale. I said I preferred sophisticated humour, so he sorted out a joke which we then tried out on-camera, after he had carefully explained it to me: 'You say, "I shed a hundred pounds of ugly fat in a week." Then you wait for the tag to come in. The tag is "I divorced my wife!" Would you like to see if you can time it right?'

At the New Victoria cinema in London I stood backstage with Jim Clarke, a 40-year-old driving instructor from Rotherham, Yorkshire. He was one of the finalists in a talent competition and longed to leave the audience of 3,000 laughing hard enough to win him the £1,000 prize. In the wings he admitted he was a bit nervous. He went on second and desperately told a string of unconnected gags – one of them twice. He raised very little laughter, and came nowhere; but even amateur comics bounce back. Afterwards with Ted Rogers, who was top of the bill, we considered his performance. Clarke defiantly blamed a bad spot and the audience. A comic *has* to be confident: how else could he go out front alone and sell himself to 3,000 strangers?

Ted Ray, nearing the end of his professional lifetime after 35 years on the boards, explained it to me perfectly: 'Middlesbrough Empire some years ago: a little fellow walked on, second turn. He was wearing a faded old dinner jacket, you see, and had a few gags and a song. He was terrible. When he was near the end of his song, somebody threw a tomato. It landed just under his bow tie and slid right down the celluloid front into his waistcoat. You would have thought the old boy would have come off in tears – but for that ego. As he walked off he said to the stage manager, "They don't seem to think much of your conductor here . . ." You can't break 'em, you see. You can close the theatres but boy, you can't take the spirit away . . .'

PART SIX

CLOSE—UP!

TECHNIQUES

Fearlessly in favour of Mothers . . .

WE have come a long way together since the days when the
BBC regarded Documentary as an unappealing word, like
Education, to be banished to the afternoon or late-night
ghettos along with programmes on Safety at Sea. Now every
opinion poll reveals it to be the one type of programme of
which viewers want more. Certainly it has created more
public discussion over the years than any other form of
television.

When I moved from Fleet Street to Lime Grove in 1957 we
would devour the newspapers and react to them. Today it is
television which initiates public debate, and the authority –
like many of the journalists – has moved west. Fleet Street
has become an adjunct of the television industry, getting its
stories by following up programmes, devoting more and
more space to previews and reviews, listings and gossip,
background stories and personality pieces. America long ago
discovered the public's insatiable interest in those who
appear; the picture of some small-screen personality upon
the cover of *Time* or *Newsweek* or *People* will stimulate an
impulse sale of untold thousands more than that of the most
significant statesman or politician, surgeon, businessman or
warrior, for television familiarity breeds content – and in a
small way, I am not complaining!

As we know, people divide into Talkers and Listeners;
obviously, I am a listener. Other people have always seemed
more interesting – which may not be powerful praise – and I
have never felt the need to put them right. This is one reason
why in the past I have refused invitations to go on chat-

shows, even with good friends like Mike Parkinson, Eamonn Andrews or Russell Harty. I would much rather hear your story than tell you mine – though to look at me now, you might not think so! A book can have a strange effect . . .

My programmes have always concentrated upon discovering the attitudes of other people, rather than stating my own. This upset some critics who wanted me to take sides, to uncover a dozen burning issues a year and each time wag an accusing finger at the viewer. You know the outraged attitude: 'It's a scandal – why don't *they* do something about it?'

Resisting those who see current affairs TV only as a medium for causes, I have carried on looking into situations and people, presenting the position as upon reflection it appeared to the director and to me, and leaving the viewer to decide. In any interview I go not for facts, but for flavour. I can always put the case-history, quickly and concisely, but what I hope to get from interviewees is opinion and attitude. Fortunately there are lots of flavourful people around – which is probably why Whicker's World has continued to turn, helped no doubt by the fact that I try to present only my best side to the camera: the back of my head.

Apart from such a hindsight, I keep out of my programmes where possible. Under our title this may seem odd, but its convenient alliteration merely allows us to look at anyone or anything, anywhere, in a personal way – with someone to carry the can after transmission for what has been said and done. That is the point of a signed documentary.

In the old Tonight days each report began and ended with a piece to-camera, for in the magpie's nest of a magazine programme such setting up of a new subject was punctuation which became part of the grammar. In the hour-long Whicker's Worlds that followed I tried to avoid these statements, preferring to use the time for commentary under pictures. It was necessary to be seen occasionally in various situations and conversations, and sometimes useful to be established within a location – on that swirling mosaic at Copacabana or in a Bombay slum – to trail what was in store and for many other reasons, some as prosaic as showing ours were today's pictures and not bought-in library-footage.

When I left the BBC to go to Yorkshire, my old Saturday night spot was filled by new and doubtless better programmes, which I was intrigued to see were equally personal and alliterative: from an old correspondent colleague in Korean wardays, that superb writer James Cameron, with Cameron's Country – and the excellent Trevor Philpott, my old friend, with his Philpott File. I did not feel quite as flattered some years later when the BBC offered Wogan's World which, though fun, was another ballroom game . . . Down in his massive Thames valley mansion, Terry was known as the Whicker of Bray.

I usually researched my programmes when possible, before doing the interviewing and writing, took part in the filming, presided over all the editing and finally wrote and recorded the commentary . . . so it was galling to read I 'fronted' Whicker's World. That was Clive James the critic before he became, as he would say, 'a multi-media experience'. His own adventures into television were then on the Manchester programme Cinema, where he would sit in the studio with metronomic eyes before his autocue and introduce film clips. *That* was fronting.

He goaded the talented Robert Kee to complain: 'He can't say I "front" because that implies that I haven't constructed, written and supervised the editing, and I have.' Clive, an amusing gnome, is also enshrined as the professional television critic who could write such authoritative nonsense as; 'Action in front of a mounted camera *always* has to be planned . . .' Beware the Experts.

Needless to say I was happier with Maurice Wiggin, who called me 'the electronic Aubrey' and wrote that I 'inhabited' my programmes. 'He doesn't inhabit them,' said Mike Tuchner as we sat arguing about our editing, 'he *infests* them.'

The advantage of such a personal approach to a programme is that the reporter provides the viewer's eyeline, on the spot. He is there in the middle of everything, finding out and if necessary, preventing people getting away with it . . .

The visible reporter can also offer the only touch of reassuring familiarity: I filmed two programmes with the San Francisco police, travelling in the back of a black-and-white behind two cops – often women officers – as they chased or arrested bank robbers and rapists, junkies and murderers. Every sequence looked exactly like a clip from Kojak, or Starsky and Hutch. The whole exciting scramble seemed too violent, too bloody, too dramatic to be real – until I was seen to be there, hanging on grimly and asking breathless questions. '*Told* you to wear your running shoes,' said a tiny girl cop sympathetically after one hectic arrest.

In less violent programmes it is also imperative to have someone on hand to put the supplementary questions. Critics of the reporter on-camera believe he comes between subject and viewer; he surely does when the subject is offering an obscure statement, a questionable view. Real people are not actors and are seldom able to make illuminating statements directly to the unblinking unsympathetic eye of the lens, like some professional politico. They talk naturally to a person, not a machine, to someone who has established a rapport but is also able to query and probe. *The Times* said of one documentary: 'Instead of making prepared statements, if the various contributors had answered questions, the tendentiousness might have been resolved into some definite judgment.' Volunteered statements can also be self-serving. The supplementary that follows is the question that reveals: In that case, how . . .? But surely . . .? Perhaps the most useful is the simple: Why?

As my very first director Antony Jay observed, the process of question-and-answer has been accepted as a technique for uncovering the truth since the time of Socrates. Today's television interview is significantly different from a newspaper interview: the journalist is simply collecting raw material, whereas the television reporter is constructing a finished product. He must be an instant editor – particularly if the programme is live – steering away from the dull and complicated, supplying background, and all the time making sure his questions unlock revealing replies.

Questions put without thought – or occasionally with too

much, when they may become tortuously convoluted – can also kill any conversation stone dead as the recipient struggles up for air. For a genuine 180-degree stunner I enjoyed Russell Harty's inquiry of one bemused subject : 'How are things in Japan?' There are a *lot* of answers to that question. Bernard Levin also left John Osborne a wide field of reply: 'What do you believe . . . about ultimate things?'

The visible reporter – someone like the agreeable Julian Pettifer – also provides a vital yardstick of honesty and credibility. If you know the person presenting the programme, you know how far you can go along with him, how much reliance to place on his opinions and attitudes. You have his measure. It is not easy to trust an invisible committee of faceless axegrinders.

The programmes Whicker's World would sometimes replace on the air were just such documentaries-by-committee: Granada's World in Action, and from Thames, This Week – now calling itself TV Eye. Both offer a background voice and a cosmic view.

Paradoxically these topical programmes which presume to give objective truth unalloyed by the personal idiosyncracies of a reporter, are in fact the most opinionated and politically-slanted of all television series. World in Action is usually a sort of Marxist party-political, TV Eye the predictable protest of the militant Left.

On occasion they lay aside their political message and produce powerful and enterprising investigative journalism. More often they peddle the same old repetitive line and struggle to knock the pillars down: ridicule the Establishment, show the police as stumbling buffoons or brutal Fascists, support the wreckers working to bring down our freedoms to whom any riot or strike is a victory, attack all Centre and Right governments anywhere, avoid a constructive word about the US or a hurtful comment on a Communist state.

Industriously, they scour the world for some enemy of Britain to encourage, lavishing sympathetic understanding on the masked man with the rocket. No hostility to the West is too obscure or wrong-headed for their attention, yet some off-screen reporter will fearlessly heckle a stunned 19-year-old trooper who has just been blown up. It is like relying on the *Morning Star* for serious guidance and is thin fare indeed.

After a lifetime of objective reporting, I find political polemics hard to swallow, and particularly resent the dose when slipped to me without warning. The IBA has yet to insist upon a caption-card stating : 'Please stand by – we have temporarily lost our Objectivity.'

So TV's droning Disembodied Voice has replaced the cinema's soaring Heavenly Choir, equally irritating but less sincere. I do not know how much impact slanted programmes have upon viewers, whether in the long term they are subliminally corrosive, or shrugged off and dismissed. Certainly these two unreliable witnesses are almost never in the Top Twenty, which suggests most viewers have grown weary of being nobbled. Such powerful evidence of the hand-on-the-switch supports my long-held belief that viewers are not the mindless morons some propagandists and TV executives believe. We can even on occasion work things out for ourselves and see through the spurious.

Anthony Thomas is a director who handles cameras brilliantly, but seems less sure with facts: 'The problem with an ordinary documentary is that people don't say important things when the cameras are rolling,' he says. 'They are too nervous. Cameras change people and they lose their naturalness. But using actors to say the words you end up with a more truthful picture.' H'm . . . It depends, of course, upon who *writes* the words.

He was talking about his Death of a Princess, in my opinion one of the least truthful pictures to be transmitted on television. Of this collection of unsubstantiated gossip and hearsay dressed up as a so-called drama documentary, *The Times* wrote in a Leader: 'It exploited the atmosphere of mystery and romance with which many aspects of Saudi society are surrounded, in order to compile a salacious detective story fallaciously presented as fact.' It also wrecked our relations with Saudi Arabia and the Gulf for many months, caused a Royal visit and many business contracts to be cancelled, and added to our unemployment. A high national price was paid for Thomas's right to write 'important things'.

Few of us, I suspect, absorb the concluding credits as they unroll, so with no evident reporter to blame for far-out views emphatically stated as fact, many World in Action and TV Eye viewers presumably accept *that* is the way it is, when of course it usually is not – or at least, there is another side.

As we all know, no programme can ever be totally objective – not even those which try! As soon as the camera turns over, a view is being taken – even disregarding that fatal moment when the editor starts to cut. The best the viewer can hope for is an honest and professional director, reporter and production team. I cannot speak for others, but I do know we at least always travel with open minds and try our best to discover what is going on when we arrive.

Some series get their scripts written before they leave the office and then hunt for pictures and interviews to illustrate the chosen angle. Such cosmic programmes tell us with finality: '*This* is what is happening in South Africa.' Signed documentaries say: 'This is what I've seen happening, but after hearing all these opinions – judge for yourself.'

Slanted topical reports have regrettably become the norm today. There are few regular current affairs programmes on ITV that are not politically angled – apart of course from the magnificent ITN. Surprisingly, in the money-making private enterprise jungle of commercial television, little is heard from the Right-wing. You might expect those cigar-smoking Chairmen and MDs in their Rolls-Royces to be slightly Right of Papa Doc, yet if they are they rarely make their opinions felt. This can be put down to inertia, or to concentration upon the financial statement for the next AGM instead of concern for the impact their programmes may have upon us.

In my experience of television mandarins, only my old wartime friend Lord Bernstein of Granada was actively political; as a determined Socialist his views led to the bias of Granada's World in Action, which has now lost the right to

be taken seriously. Elsewhere political drive comes from a
relatively few militant producers and directors – once lightly
dismissed as slogan-spouting trendy-Lefties. Many have
power of decision within their departments and a
disproportionate influence upon the current affairs programmes we see.

They of course have supporters among the critics, who
lavish regulation scorn upon any departure from the Party
line. I recall the typical *Time Out* reaction to our romp
through Palm Beach – which I admit was asking for it! The
usual snarling Trot wrote: 'They should have sent Pilger
with a machinegun.' Objective he was not.

At least the news departments on both channels have so far
resisted the militant Left, though there have been attempts to
undermine even those strongholds of journalistic integrity. A
group including Mr Wedgwood Benn, 73 other Labour MPs
and 23 Union general secretaries, supported by a weird and
self-appointed 'media group' from Glasgow University, have
protested about the 'bias', as they see it, of television news.
Politicians are always too busy to watch TV, except to see
themselves.

Aware of the Left's domination of current affairs on ITV –
and that attack is the best defence – the extremely Left
general secretary of the television technicians' union, Alan
Sapper, has suggested that his members should black out
transmission of any programme which in their opinion
showed anti-union prejudice. So from his own position of
some power, this official believed any union member in any
television company should have the authority to censor what
we viewing millions watch!

At the time of writing we are only three years away from
the thought control of Orwell's Ministry of Truth . . .

Television also faces the attack-strategy of many vocal
pressure groups. You will have observed the technique –
perhaps with incredulity at its breathtaking cheek: the Burg-
lars' trade union protests in a wordy letter to *The Times* about
police persecution, the IRA is officially outraged when the
Army defends itself, the hijackers are furious at some Government's ungentlemanly reaction, the looters indignant

when interrupted, the masked firebombers complain of harassment . . .

It is surprising that the Independent Broadcasting Authority has so long averted its eyes from programmes which regularly attempt to discredit by attack or innuendo those institutions – like the courts, the Army and police – upon which our established order and freedom depend, without requiring balancing programmes or on-screen warning of bias-to-come. It needs a promotion as blatant as the intended presentation of an IRA Lying-in-State to cause them to put the World out of Action, that week.

The IBA has perhaps been deceived by the artful themes and slogans which may conceal a programme's true thrust. Double-talk experts enlist on their side God and apple pie to offer campaigns no wholesome person could resist. Marxism has been cleaned up under the acceptable Anti-Nazi banner, and who would not support those fearlessly marching Against Sin, or For Freedom? Stand up the viewer who criticises the noble protests of the Stop-Slavery group, the Down-with-Torturers, the In-Favour-of-Mothers . . .

Few professional critics publicly resist such slanted political forced-feeding from the small screen; perhaps by now we are all too used to it. However, some have castigated me for not taking sides in my programmes, for not always being seen to be For or Against.

The other ITV network companies at least name the bilious reporters who attack the values and efforts of a free society, so we can evaluate their opinions and know who is getting at us. ATV has John Pilger, an Australian and rabid anti-American putting polemics above reporting. Yorkshire has the humourless Jonathan Dimbleby, sneering at our police or presenting a child's guide to hateful warmongering US and benevolent peaceful USSR. Both practise the 'Bring out your starving babies' school of accusatory-sanctimonious television journalism – but they do at least stand up to be named for contentious views.

Fortunately viewers can usually turn to the BBC for considered and objective current affairs, to the admirable Panorama, and Newsweek, and sometimes to Newsnight, to the Roger Mills documentaries, to such first-rate reporters as David Dimbleby, Ludovic Kennedy and Robin Day who remain their own men, offer unprogrammed thinking and question *any* party line.

ATTITUDES

Any more of your Flattery and I'll Shoot myself . . .

IF impersonation is flattery I have been flattered up to the eyebrows or, to face facts, sent-up rotten by everyone from Alan Melville to Benny Hill and on to Stanley Baxter; he called his programme Whicked World and very clever it was too. His glasses and voice may have been a shade light but his script was excellent – if you *like* that kind of thing – and in its way, almost too close for comfort.

Facing all this, there are times when I have thought: any more of your flattery and I'll shoot myself . . . though such parady is a useful corrective, demonstrating what one ought to stop doing, if only one could. It can also work the other way. In Clive James' name-dropping celebration of the Royal Wedding, for example, I found myself once again being epic-poemed, or doggerelled, and following Malcolm Mothermilk (a Saint) and David Dross (a Phenomenon) into St Paul's, as Another Phenomenon. As the *Observer* ocker lamely lampooned merely my mellifluous but relatively rare alliteration (he didn't try the puns) it stimulated a perverse determination to do it more often – to give 'em something to get their teeth into . . .

Just as all babies look like Churchill, so anybody with a moustache and glasses looks like me – near enough. The most remembered take-off seems to have been the Monty Python mob on a desert island populated only by Whickers, interviewing each other in Whickeric and desperation. I watched, and fell about – though next day our managing director was rather sniffy towards such satire. He did not know what I had suffered in the past.

I wrote my congratulations to John Cleese, with a PS saying he would of course be hearing from my solicitors. By return came a signed still of the five Python Whickers under their property palms and a note saying, 'Here's some evidence for them.'

Just as many of the most hostile Press critics have gone on to attempt their own Whicker-type programmes on television and so reveal a reason for always putting ours down, when I ran into Cleese at Alan Coren's he told me he was going to leave Python and his ambition was to do some similar documentaries. I was saddened: lots of people could do my programmes but it would be a waste of a gifted comic should he go straight.

That year Monty Python won the BAFTA Award and of course the clip used at the presentation ceremony in the Albert Hall was of all those awful Whickers strutting their stuff under the waving palms of Felixstowe. I have to confess that, sitting up there in a box totally surrounded by thousands laughing their heads off at that idiot, my smile grew ever so slightly fixed . . .

One summer I noticed people approaching me confidentially and muttering accusatory remarks like '*You* just cost me a few quid' or 'You might have *told* us she was trying', before passing on into the crowd. After some bafflement I discovered there was a horse running on the Northern circuit called Whicker's World, which everyone assumed I owned. When she lost I was accosted by reproachful strangers and, on rare occasions when she won, accused by friends of being cagey. Later there appeared an equally unsatisfactory horse called Mr Whicker, and another no-win situation.

I wrote to the Jockey Club wondering how my good name could be stolen without a by-your-leave and received a dismissive reply: 'The name Whicker's World was granted because it did not contravene any of our restrictions . . . nor was it the name of a well-known person.' Well all right, we can't all be famous. It seemed Weatherbys only watched television direct from the course; but to an unknown outsider, the owners and that curious organisation seemed a mite cavalier.

A much happier equestrian event occurred when I was filming in the Australian outback and learned that 30,000 readers of the *People* had voted me winner of the TV Derby of 1970. The television editor, Kenneth Baily, could hardly keep his amazement out of the telegram. In his story he wrote: 'Who would have guessed Alan Whicker would turn out to be the winner of the Popularity Stakes?' I was equally surprised.

An equally acceptable acknowledgement came from a Cockney milkman I heard asking a neighbour, 'Got 'arf an Alan?' He wanted a ten-bob note, or a half a nicker. Now that *is* a compliment. There is also the calming 'Don't get your Alans in a twist.'

For the last 25 years I have been receiving letters addressed to Alan Wicker of Whicker's World, or alternatively Alan Whicker of Wicker's World. Having lost so many H's, I am always delighted to win a few. When Christopher Lee and Edward Woodward made a film called 'The Wicker Man' around the straw dolls used in black magic rituals, many reviews called it The Whicker Man. Best of all, in Harrods splendid Food Hall one day I saw a discreet placard offering a £30 wine and cheese hamper containing old port and Stilton '. . . packed in a Whicker hamper.' It seemed, somehow, that I had struck a blow for aspirates . . .

Television has climbed the national appreciation index since the days when everybody loved it except the Very Posh, who only admitted telly to the servants' rooms Downstairs. In his book *In and Out, Debrett 1980-81* Neil Mackwood wrote that it was 'Out' to watch Dallas, Crossroads, That's Life or Benny Hill, but 'In' to watch the Muppets, Panorama, Not the 9 O'Clock News – and the Alan Whicker travelogues. However late in the day, it was reassuring to be admitted Upstairs.

Just as there are critics who cut me down to size and rubbish programmes they know they could do better, so there are the occasional Awards which help to restore morale. Acknowledgement from peers is always sustaining but however comforting it is to have such hardware on the sideboard, I have a soft spot for the newer type of Award – which you can *eat*.

For some lucky programme which tickled Swedish taste-buds, I received from one of their newspapers an enormous box of exotic chocolates, an accolade which did not stay long on the sideboard. Following in that wholesome tradition, readers of the *Sunday Mail* vote each week for their best and worst programmes; my Californian series received an enormous bunch of red roses – *and* a tin of raspberries. No spectrum could get wider than that. Curiously enough, in JICTAR's nationwide Top Twenty ratings, their Rose programme was 19th, while the Raspberry was 5th. No accounting for reaction.

In 1978 while filming in Kerala, at the tip of India, the Whicker's World Cities series through America won the TV Times Special Award for the programmes which had stimulated the most correspondence from readers during the year. They might all have been complaining, I suppose, but I prefer to think positively. The magazine sent out a striking piece of statuary, air-freight, and asked us to film a sequence with it to screen at the London presentation ceremony – which as usual I was going to miss. The heavy marble and gilt Award ran straight into Indian customs, of course, and never reached us. Hearing of our problem, the chef at our Kovalam Beach hotel thoughtfully baked a celebratory cake for me to brandish on-camera. It was a sort of compensatory award, though more gooey.

With all such much-appreciated hard and software, the ultimate accolade is delivered, as it always has been, by the viewer's finger on the switch. The *Evening Standard* headline above the week's JICTAR ratings during our last Californian series was the most welcome of all: Whicker's Top World.

There is, however, yet another type of recognition which can also be practical: one came from the Hutt River Principality, that independent State in Western Australia ruled by Prince Leonard, with its own money and government. Soon after I had filmed in Princess Shirl's kitchen, I was summoned to a sedate ceremony and appointed the Principality's roving Ambassador. Prince Leonard presented me with my Diplomatic passport, a most impressive green document embossed in gold, promising duty-free delight and VIP attention. I plan to test my Diplomatic status one of these days when I enter a country where I might enjoy being privileged, but in which I could also stand being thrown in jail.

I was later knighted by Prince Leonard, and received letters from his resident Ambassador in Britain addressed to Sir Alan Whicker – so at least I can face Robin Day, knightly . . . Prince Leonard had a few protocol problems with an Australian Government which seemed reluctant to accept his sovereignty, let alone his passport, so he has not yet reached Europe to touch my shoulder again with his sword.

On another programme Kirby J. Hensley, D D, President of the Universal Life Church, made me a Deacon. In Los Angeles, he presented me with my Credentials of Ministry, an illuminated certificate and a clergy car sticker. Such ordination, he explained, would help my tax situation and parking problems.

His copperplate credentials authorised me 'to perform all ministerial services such as baptismals, marriages, funerals. The holder is entitled to all privileges and considerations usually granted a Minister.' I treated these rather lightly until I found myself sitting at a Beverly Hills lunch next to a senior Judge from the California Supreme Court, and mentioned my ordination and new authority. To my surprise he took it all most seriously and said that if he ever married again, he would be quite prepared for me to conduct the ceremony.

I looked at him closely, but His Honour was not joking and, with three marriages behind him, knew the form. I was taken aback, and am still braced for my first performance before some lucky couple.

That clever Jonathan Miller once looked into the Whicker's World office in the BBC's Television Centre tower. 'My God!' he cried, as he fled, 'they're all *talking* like him . . .' This could have been a local inflection, but was usually self-inflicted. On location I would find the whole crew talking Me, at me, and mighty disconcerting it was too.

Filming in Ireland, I was writing in my room at the Castlerosse Hotel on the shores of gorgeous Killarney while next door I could hear my recordist playing back and listing his tapes of the day's interviews. Listening with half an ear, idly wondering how they had gone, I suddenly heard myself saying things I could not remember saying. Fearing I was losing my marbles, I listened some more – then burst in to find them playing a cod tape recorded by the cameraman, John Wyatt. It would not have mattered had I gone sick; he could have done my script just as well . . .

However when I heard myself on radio explaining Funk in front of a heavy beat, I knew *that* could not be me. It was a record by The Evasions, confusingly called The Wikka Wrap. The voice, Graham de Wilde, told the newspapers: 'I loved the Python sketch, and do Whicker impressions at parties.' He did me discussing Funk styles, and the number went to No 1 in the Disco Top Thirty. Since I am seldom glued to Radio One it was a long time before I could make out what the reporters were on about. Then my windowcleaner grunted, 'Didn't think much of your last record,' and the company sent a copy and hoped I appreciated their 'little bit of fun'.

It was less funny when I was being used in my absence to advertise products to the advantage of everyone else. A travel agency in Twickenham publicised itself around the country as Twicker's World. Dissatisfied clients would address complaining letters to me, demanding that I make good some holiday disaster.

The Independent Broadcasting Authority had always

regarded me as ITV's personal property and refused to let me do commercials – while offering little discouragement to actors impersonating me. I would hear them on commercial radio, Whickering away. Ronnie Barker, for whom I have boundless admiration, was able to extol the virtues of Japanese watches in Whickeric upon the regulation desert island after his agency had politely asked for permission to do so, and been refused. I should not have been allowed to put across those commercials in genuine Whickeric.

I had been fairly relaxed about the IBA ban and for years turned down requests to advertise beer and hotels, cars and shoe-shops and soup . . . However, any restriction of freedom is hard for a freelance to take for ever. In the past 25 years I have actively considered only a few commercials which seemed at the time appealing or deserving: British European Airways, the London Docklands, British Leyland . . . The IBA refused to let me support any of these taxpayers' ventures, so Robert Morley, Cliff Michelmore and Jimmy Savile stepped in and did them. I had earlier stimulated Savile's career when he was a disc jockey by turning down the Clunk-Click safety-belt campaign.

Sir Brian Young, Director General of the IBA, carefully explained in one of his superb letters that I was not on a Black List, but indeed proudly included on a White List. Their restriction was 'expressing the view that Whicker is a central feature of serious journalism . . . an important objective voice on ITV.'

It was flattering, but it seemed I was being flattered a whole lot more than anyone else. After ten years or so, he wrote to reveal I had been unchained and was a free man: 'It's like the Emperor of Japan in 1945 – you are losing your Divinity.' Rather ruefully, I replied: 'Emancipation, even late in life, comes as a great relief – though I suspect you have defended my Divinity so fiercely and for so long that, after various expensive courtships, word has gone round that I am Unattainable. Impregnable, even.'

However, I was at last at liberty to relax and enjoy it; I could even imitate Ronnie Barker.

The Alan Whicker Appreciation Society, I am pleased to

Dictators are not used to questions: Ted Morrisby, my researcher, adopts the correct attitude while President Stroessner of Paraguay, last of South America's old-style rulers, puts us both right . . .

Interviewees come in all get-ups. Stone Age warriors on the Indonesian Isle of Nias, who sometimes wear metal moustaches to frighten enemies, being introduced to even more fearsome hornrims . . .

Face to face with Papa Doc during my conducted tour of
Port-au-Prince, closely watched by Madame Rosalee Adolph,
leader of his murderous Tonton Macoutes . . .

The interview viewers never saw . . . President Duvalier doing
his Christmas shopping and making offers no Haitian jeweller
could refuse – before our empty camera. In the background
daughter Di-Di helps herself . . .

Kathy Wagner, the remoulded wife who set a nation talking, concealing her much loved Mediums . . .

Plato's people getting acquainted in their 'Disneyland for adults . . .'

Some members of the evangelical Alan Whicker Appreciation Society giving me a hard time: If you *gotta* be appreciated, relax and enjoy it . . .

The evidence John Cleese and the Monty Python mob offered my solicitor . . .

Writing in Pago Pago . . .

Riding in Singapore . . .   Training in Utah . . .

TV Times asked which six objects people might take to a desert island; I dismissed their original idea with 'two blondes, two brunettes, two redheads'. They, however, were delighted – and in the end, so was I . . .

The Whicker's World theme gets the Evita treatment: Andrew Lloyd Webber composed, Harry Rabinowitz conducted, 60 members of the Royal Philharmonic played, I enjoyed . . .

The Bentley that crept into my affections in 1965 and still has a long way to go . . .

Circleville, Utah: Valerie in a diner with 94-year-old Lula Parker Betenson, sister of Butch Cassidy! It was like meeting Robin Hood's aunt . . .

Living happily ever after: with Valerie in British Columbia . . .

Back home and resting. The only picture I really like: adequately distant, relatively relaxed . . .

say, emerged from Sussex in good voice, imitating wildly.
'You may be flattered, or alarmed,' wrote its Chairman, a
surveyor called John Ferdinando. 'We believe there's
another group appreciating you up north, but our membership consists mainly of irresponsible young businessmen.
Our activities have included cricket matches with a whicker-
keeper in which we all wear horned-rimmed specs and
moustaches. At all our gatherings we talk in native Whicker
tongue – no other language is spoken. Our aim would be to
entertain you, one day.'

I have yet to face the massed Society, since I fear I could
not stand the competition: even the voice would sound
wrong, and I should probably come in fifth . . .

However having experienced so much appreciation from
Monty Python and others, I had learned the hard way that if
you gotta be appreciated – relax and enjoy it. This I did, and
the AWAS proceeded upon its evangelical work among the
uninitiated and less-aware.

The *Evening News* reported: 'You've heard of Beatlemania,
Elvis addicts, and Travolta Freaks. Now news of the Whicker
Worshippers. With Whicker's photo in their wallets, a special Whicker tie and even special Whicker stickers on their
cars, the AWAS men have yet to meet their hero. Says Philip
Dorman (a raw recruit whose accent is not quite up to
scratch, but he's working on it): "People may join the official
AWAS by invitation only. There's a splinter group in the
Crawley area, a pale imitation of ours, but we don't
fraternise." And Keith Smith explains: "It's been an important focus of my life. I spent three months trying to perfect
my Whicker voice. I'm not a natural, but now I think I've
mastered the twang." Says John Ferdinando: "The time has
come for a major Whicker movie called Whickerfinger or
Whickergate." '

I found it a mixture of fun – and not quite knowing where
to look. Then I met a few members and was relieved to
discover I could not have been sent-up by a more amusing
bunch. Even the Society notepaper under its flying saucer
insignia showed a significant worldwide spread of interest:
'New York – London – Paris – Sydney – Dorothy – Arthur.'

AWAS members appeared on the Nationwide programme, and with some success laid the good word on Russell
Harty. They went on Southern's nightly magazine Day by
Day doing pieces to-camera around Brighton, just as I had
25 years before. The host of that programme, by happy
chance, was Cliff Michelmore. It was generally agreed that
the spread of such a civilising influence was a most wholesome trend. I receive reports of their various jump-ups, like
Ladies Nights and car treasure hunts. They took over the
Members' Stand at Plumpton Racecourse for a Whickers
and Tarts party: 'Interviewing and soliciting to the strains of
Henry's disco,' said the invitation. I was in California and
missed my chance of going to a fancy-dress party without
needing to change . . .

John Ferdinando sent me a dark blue Club tie tastefully
embroidered with spectacles and tiny smudge, which was a
moustache. They had the fallback version *without* the glasses,
he said, should I take to contact lenses.

PARADISE

Waltzing my Matilda around . . .

MUCH of my life has been divided between unspoiled Paradise Isles and White Men's Graves. I am always landing
unprotected by background music on virgin beaches, and
pushing on through primeval jungles and, whatever it says
on television, the Farflung can be horrid. Given the chance I
prefer my Paradises ever so slightly spoiled; there is a strong
argument for the well-beaten.

Travel agents trail 'unspoiled' like some hypnotic blan-
dishment – in one mighty bound you get not only ahead of

the Joneses, but far away from them. So what do they mean
by the magic word? No roads or beds? Yak milk? Mule
trains? Blubber for breakfast? Do-it-yourself dentistry? One
stream for drinking, washing and lavatory? His Unspoiled is
your Nightmare is my Forget it, for most Undiscovered
Paradises on the Whicker's World flightpath have, upon
discovery, offered dengue fever, dysentery, slightly rancid
meat, nowhere to sleep, filaria, sharks, intestinal bacteria,
heat stroke and water that wriggles.

Dr Livingstone caught the exploration bug and relished it,
but wrote that he could find no room to place a finger
between the insect bites on his children's bodies; so take back
your Undiscovered Africa, for a start.

On the Caribbean isle of Anguilla I was filming the
Metropolitan police taking over in 1971 after a minor revolution. My tropical boardinghouse was run by Auntie Bea, a
noted but resistable Bronx negress with a fast insult who
turned off the generator on the stroke of nine. She once left
the British Foreign Secretary sitting in the dark, poor chap,
doubtless poised to make a big decision. It was the kind of
place where you woke in the middle of the night to find, by
matchlight, a giant squashed spider in bed with you. Its main
shack was a mile from the nearest track. No telephone, no
transport, no people, no town even – and no place for that
grumbling appendix to speak up.

Escaping from Auntie to the isle of Grenada, I found the
local clinic was also suffering, hit by the scourge of Eric
Gairy, then Prime Minister. On political grounds he had
banished the proficient doctor and nurses. The hospital,
which had never boasted too strong a grip on hygiene, then
offered any patient admitted with an ingrowing toenail the
possibility of discharge with leprosy plus bubonic com-
plications. It was deeply unspoiled.

I am not pushing bland international hotels where you
face the tourist torture of a Thousand Surcharges and live on
deep-frozen indifference – though some professional television travellers I know still film the whole farflung programmes within their gardens – but I find it difficult to detect
any virtue in discomfort. Only would-be Papa Hemingways

bolstering virility by doing it the hard way find it more masculine to tackle the sheer rockface, instead of strolling up by the path at the back.

I first reached the isle of Tonga in a fluttery little charter-plane gasping for fuel, slept with bats in a disused hut, dined on fruit and coconut milk, combed my hair by feel, and was relieved to be rescued. Today, a cool scheduled airliner with cabin service from Fiji, and into the Dateline Hotel – yet the Tongans are just as sweet, the Royal Palace just as ginger-bread, the flying foxes still hunt at twilight and the bore-holes still bore.

In Bali I trudged through rain and rivers for several hours to watch spontaneous dancing in a remote village where no white man had ever. I later saw similar traditional cere-monies organised for tourists who arrived by bus and sat in armchairs clicking away amid blazing torches. The tourist dances were *much* the better: costumes more dazzling, per-formance more inspired, atmosphere more exciting.

The Pacific isle of Stone Age men, Tanna, has still not been spoiled: you undress by candlelight in a banana-leaf hut and go to sleep amid a hungry whine of mosquitoes, trying to convince yourself malaria is no worse than a bad cold, like that skinny chap said – the yellowish one who was shaking.

One Trilander hop away, at the very end of the New Hebridean chain, the tiny speck of Aneityum was inhabited by a few thousand Melanesians and one white man – a Kiwi who had lived there for a quarter of a century. His name, which you could not invent, is Artie Kraft. His island is an Unspoiled Paradise if ever there was one. He stopped build-ing himself outdoor amenities because hurricanes always flattened them. He was telling me about the time he broke his leg, had to set it himself and then wait several days for a boat to carry him towards something more pain-relieving than aspirin.

On another Unspoiled day his neighbour fell from the top of a mango tree and impaled himself on a lemon tree. Artie sewed the man's stomach and testicles back without anaes-thetic while listening to short-wave instructions from a doc-tor a few islands away. Anyone for Paradise?

The first thing any skilled traveller does upon arrival in Paradise, or anywhere else come to that, is to check his Exits. You must know how to Get Away. Before leaving the airport you go to Departures and collect the timetable of every airline operating out of the place; then you know precisely which days the flights operate and can call with confidence to demand a seat on 'Flight 215 at 9.20 on the tenth, arriving 18.50.' Never allow yourself to slip trustingly into the hands of a hallporter, or a travel agency by telephone. That is how I once got booked, tickets written and paid for, schedule typed . . . to a South Sea island airport which did not exist. Now I study the schedules, do it myself – and know who to blame.

If you travel a lot and enjoy studying your fellow passengers, you learn quite quickly how to spot whether the chap in the next seat has been around and is used to flying. Little quirks of behaviour soon give him away. We were at 29,000 feet and nearing Sharjah when, in the middle of a pleasant flight, a murmuring group of pilgrims gathered by my seat and lit a small fire in the aisle to brew their tea. I could tell at once they were not Executive Club cardholders.

I don't much care for airline tea either – as you know, the water refuses to boil at that height. It may not be British to make a fuss in public, but when they started fanning the flames with their safety instructions, I had to sacrifice my champagne.

It is not only dwellers of the Empty Quarter, temporarily aloft, who can mystify; people of the Asphalt Jungle can also inflict a flightmare. On the way home from New York one night Swissair were starting off well with vintage champagne and smoked salmon. In the next seat, an American businessman was relishing both – but kept his cigar alight and puffed away between mouthfuls. Also, *during* mouthfuls.

I gave up smoking years ago and try not to be insufferable about it; but I could see, through thick blue clouds, that the fellow was ruining his palate – along with every other palate in the next ten rows. Only with difficulty did I resist going into my outpouring of champagne act again.

Another heavy smoker on her way to Singapore disturbed

a friend of mine: in that lavish Concorde departure lounge he noticed a brooding, chainsmoking woman in a wheelchair. She was wrapped in heavy woollen clothes and being greeted deferentially by every uniform. He first thought it a trifle odd when this fragile invalid leapt up and womanhandled an enormous metal ashtray across to her chair, where she slumped and continued puffing. Once on board she again recovered use of her legs and began striding energetically up and down. Well all right, he thought, there *are* a number of pseudo-invalids who find it easier to cope with Heathrow from a guided wheelchair; but during lunch she went too far.

From her layers of wool she slowly produced an enormous knife and with awful deliberation plunged it into the neck of the inoffensive passenger enjoying his veal in the seat in front . . . He may have been a non-smoker – or perhaps her pâté was off. The point is, you cannot legislate for fellow travellers.

Homicidal maniacs apart , they may generally be divided into Know-alls and Innocents. The Know-alls demand seat 12A on a 1-11 or 14A on a Trident III – that sort of thing. Their problem is, airlines will keep moving bulkheads about and switching aircraft, so even those with a little con-figuration-knowledge can find themselves with their knees around their ears and the emergency exit three rows ahead.

Know-alls may also be full of grand folly. A pop star recently flew from London to New York and, when his recording company failed to greet him with a white Rolls, turned round at the airport and caught the same plane home again. By then apologies had come through clenched teeth, so in London he relented – and flew right back to America. That is 21 hours over the Atlantic and a fortune in cash, to make a mindless point.

Innocents are happier, carrying their world with them and searching for the reassuringly familiar; this category includes the wealthy. I have a friend who owns a vast and beautiful yacht he uses only once a year, when he sails from Cannes to Majorca to eat at a certain fish and chip shop. After lunch he sails back to Cannes, and flies home. It works out at some fairly pricey fish'n chips.

While I filmed my cruise around Indonesia some fellow-passengers peeled-off at one port to fly inland for a few days to see the temples at Borobadur: an expensive but rewarding expedition. When they finally got to the site it was raining, so most of them refused to leave the coach. When you've seen one temple . . .

Another world-weary fellow traveller was a snooty but elegant woman on a flight from Paris to New York. She arrived on board, fashionably late, with her husband, spoke not one word to him during the eight hours, brushed aside luxury meals and drinks but accepted a little Perrier. She was deeply engrossed in a book which I assumed with so lofty a lady had to be Descartes or Tolstoy – but when I peeped, turned out to be an undemanding thriller by my neighbour Jack Higgins. I am her opposite: while in motion I want to talk to everyone and see everything, read everything, drink everything. This may be the perfect recipe for acute jetlag, but I can tolerate anything except boredom.

Sensible doctors urge you to eat and drink little and do nothing but sleep on long-hauls; so many transatlantic commuters take a pill before they are airborne and need a good strong shake to get them on their unsteady feet at Kennedy. Though I rarely sleep in aircraft, I prefer jet-lag to pill-lag; you cannot get hooked on the wrong time zone.

The only time I am tempted to stun myself into insensibility is when I find the folks around me have brought along the kids, bless them. Children are all right in their place – but their place is *not* in the next seat on a 17-hour night flight. Some friends took their family to Sydney, first class, and told me the baby cried for the entire 30 hours. Even the stewards were aghast – and they hold their parties in the galley, well away from the paying herd.

If children need to travel, I have always believed the airline should reserve one section at the back exclusively for happy families, rather than distribute them and upset the entire aircraft; then all the kids can romp and scream together, their parents can exchange horror stories – and the rest of us can read the magazines or settle down to work. The airlines could promote flying nannies as a new facility supplied regardless of expense. I am offering them a travel breakthrough – and the rest of us, a few hours' sleep.

Even those who let the train take the strain can be unhappy with their companions. Geoffrey Keating, my old CO, travelled regularly on busy lines yet always contrived an empty compartment. His method of repelling boarders was devastatingly simple: he took a window seat early and removed his false teeth, leaving the few remaining home-grown stumps dotted here and there between drawn lips. When travellers approached his carriage, he grinned at them fiendishly. It was out of Hammer Horror. People went white. The adjoining compartments were always packed.

There is no doubt that travel can increase tension and *angst*: just watch those white knuckles at take-off. I was flying to Vienna with one of my directors when with wide eyes he whispered urgently, 'Have you seen – my head is growing to a *point*!' I scoffed, urging him to concentrate on keeping the Trident suspended in the air and helping it round corners by gripping the armrests and leaning over. However when I sneaked a look at his head – it *was* growing a point. In Vienna, he bought a hat.

Clothes indicate the regular traveller. Comfort is the keynote, not style; my rig is usually a blazer, which gets hung up, cardigan, old slacks and loafers that will accept swollen feet at the end of a long night flight. One prim member of the Whicker's World team was so concerned about his appearance he believed a handkerchief – even a tissue – spoiled the line of his suit. With a cold he also carried a permanent sniff. We used separate planes.

At her dressmakers the other day a friend was offered, for a giveaway £850, a chic and elaborate gabardine outfit which they suggested would be 'perfect for travelling'. I relished the phrase. To think – there are still people who believe travel is glamorous! I could see her trying elegantly to check in at Bombay on a Saturday night . . . She bought it, of course.

Princess Mary Obolensky represents a Bond Street jewellers and sometimes must travel with a multimillion load of rocks. To discourage robbery she cunningly wears her scruffiest gear and distributes diamonds and emeralds below an old T-shirt, in the pockets of jeans, in a plastic bag. I noticed she tended to give the game away, however, with that mink coat and Gucci suitcase. Such luggage should be designed to confuse – other people. It has to be easily identifiable on the carousel, but not as promising as Vuiton or Cartier, which proclaim affluence and attract organised airport villains or the passing opportunist. Today, luggage is showing signs of inverse snobbery: rich folk are going for fibreglass, just as the German owners of top-of-the-range Mercedes remove metallic proclamations from their bootlids and thus suggest to the watching world theirs is just another utility model, and no Big Deal.

When I began Waltzing my Matilda around the globe my system was to take only one enormous case, combining all my little worries into one backbreaking load. This monster left an international trail of ruptured porters – apart from tiny Japanese who would casually hoist it upon their shoulders and stroll upstairs, leaving me fearing the bottom had fallen out en route and they were carrying an empty shell.

When porters began to disappear – like those chunky leather suitcases with fitted silver-topped bottles that were Wanted on Voyage – I settled for two medium cases of equal size, to balance the load. The crucial point: you must never have too much to carry yourself at one go, or the third case you have temporarily abandoned will disappear while you are outside shouting for a taxi.

I have now moved on to an American case with built-in wheels which take the strain – but coming back from Jerez the other day brimming with sherry it was too heavy to move, even on wheels. I am working on the next stage.

The joy of sea travel, of course, is that you can take all the luggage you like, without having to pack or unpack. On our *QE*2 world cruise the couple in the next stateroom bought so many hefty souvenirs – Thai teak furniture, Rajasthani chests, Balinese ebony statues – that their double cabin was jammed deck-to-ceiling with crates. They could only just squeeze into one of the beds, in a corner.

She told me it was the first time they had slept together for years. Some women will do *anything* to go shopping.

CRUISING

It's not part of their Seamanlike duties to Dance . . .

I FIRST met Olga Deterding at a dinner party given by George Weidenfeld in his theatrically-booklined pad in Eaton Square. Daughter of Sir Henri, the founder of Royal Dutch Shell Oil, she had worked for Albert Schweitzer at Lambarene, financed a university ski team and once, when her car ran out of petrol on the Oxford bypass, left it where it lay, hitched a lift to the nearest dealer – and bought another. With her Modigliani face and agitated discourse she was, it seemed to me, natural Whicker's World material.

She was intrigued, and wanted to view our look at her friend Fiona Thyssen. I arranged a run-through at Television Centre and, still seeing her as a possible programme, took her out a few times. Such of her background as I was able to uncover seemed often unhappy, sometimes enviable, always unexpected. She had been living at the Ritz, and I enjoyed her forthright reaction to some boyfriend who wanted to leave when she wanted him to stay: she threw his trousers out of her window, down into Piccadilly . . .

Despite such straightforward determination she could also be shy, and was so self-conscious that once when I pointed a microphone towards her in jest – she froze, speechless. I soon saw it would be impossible to coax any coherent conversation from her in front of a camera. At that realisation and in the ruthless way of television, I tipped my hat and was about to leave; but in a faint echo of her Ritzian reaction, she was not quite ready for that.

She suggested we might spend the coming Christmas together. Fortunately for my eternal bachelor status I had, as usual during a peripatetic life, the complete answer – which also had the supporting strength of being true. I was leaving that weekend to spend Christmas aboard the *Andes*, filming a cruise to West Africa. 'Then I'll come with you,' she said.

I was triumphantly apologetic: 'That would be lovely, but the ship's absolutely jammed. Royal Mail even had a problem finding room for my crew. Not one bunk to be had.'

Afterwards when I told Mike Tuchner of our narrow escape, he said shortly: 'She'll buy the ship.'

He was right. Olga contrived to get herself not merely a bunk but a superb stateroom. We were beginning to learn it was not easy even in the fast-moving world of television to shake off a determined millionairess.

When we saw we *had* to be joined, we gave in gracefully and spent a jolly working Christmas, punctuated by cables and radios from Fleet Street demanding to know if the Captain was going to marry us at sea, which caused my blood to drain a bit. Fred Burnley, who was directing that programme, was not sure how to handle the situation, on camera and off. Nor, I must confess, was I.

Fred was a conspirator, having originally chased Olga for the programme and put through the call on the public address system at London Airport that halted her in her tracks as she was leaving to live in Paris, for ever. She had flown back for a programme-meeting in her house off Belgrave Square, which eventually changed a life or two. Fred and I had a suspicion we had started something we did not quite know how to finish.

Olga's occasional loneliness, of which I was then unaware,

was heartbreaking. One of the saddest stories I ever heard was her admission that sometimes she had been *so* solitary at Christmas, that warm and loving family day, that she had taken a couple of books and caught a train to Scotland, and immediately returned. The long and pointless journey was to give herself the sensation of being as occupied as everyone else, of having something to do, somewhere to go . . .

This from a pleasing young multimillionairess who, you might have thought, would have been beating suitors off with a stick. I had not heard this admission at the time she suggested we get together over the holiday, or I would have been upset and disarmed; but she was happily occupied over Christmas 1965, anyway.

Cruising was then the emergent holiday, and Sea's answer to Air. The *Financial Times* announced: 'Cruises are the most buoyant sector of the holiday market.' That seemed good news; I am in favour of shipping staying as buoyant as possible, particularly when I am on board.

We sailed from Southampton on a bleak Sunday morning in the 27,000-ton RMS *Andes*, bound for the Canaries, Madeira and West African sunshine. For 490 passengers the one-class liner was not only a floating hotel but a resort, and for 17 days we had no thought of packing, waiting at airports, tickets or tummy-trouble, no hunt for hotel rooms and no greasy foreign food. We emerged doubtfully from our luxurious shell at various ports for a quick coach tour round town before returning with relief to the familiar womb.

In accordance with tradition, single women far outnumbered single men. A concerned Cruise Director told me: 'If a lady does not find some kind of male companionship, she thinks everything about the ship, including the food, is awful.'

So our film of the voyage began, fittingly, at the Lonely Hearts get-together, where merry widows considered the field and prepared for action against a number of willing victims. 'She's got plenty of money and I think I could have married her,' an elderly but relentlessly jolly Mr Bill Grant reflected before my camera, 'but she got hold of me passport and found out me age. I think she wants a younger man.' He had arrived late at the party to find the best-lookers had been snapped up, but was unmoved because of a conquest already made in the Lido Bar: 'I've just met a lady who's taken a great fancy to me – but she pinched me glasses.'

I suggested this might be because she did not want him to *see* her properly, but he was undaunted. She had redeemed her cautious action by an excellent opening move: she paid for the drinks. Cruising can be a Man's world.

Romance, or at least dalliance, did seem the object of much travel; my crew began referring to one hopeful and convivial passenger as PL. This stood, unkindly, for Pissed Lady. She was amiable but – even without my glasses – not very appealing. When we filmed a conversation, her complaint was that the young officers were not entertaining single passengers. 'We didn't come on board to look for husbands, we came on board to be sociable – but they run a mile when they see a woman on her own. No one's danced with me yet.' She fixed me with a defiant glare and demanded, 'I haven't got a face like the back of a bus, have I?' There followed the longest silence in television history.

Afterwards on the Bridge I considered her dissatisfaction with the Captain, Commodore A. J. G. Barff: 'Most of the younger officers are married and they've got young families,' he explained. 'It's not like the old days when I was cruising before the war, when only the Chief Officer and the Captain were married, and the rest of us were available . . . We *hope* they'll all dance, and we encourage them to – but of course it's not part of their seamanlike duties to dance.' He had given us our title.

As usual, the majority of the passengers were retired, but this was a Christmas cruise so there were 32 children on board, greeted with restrained enthusiasm. On deck I chatted with an enormous rug, from which a mature lady's head peered: 'One small boy's always racing about and when I asked if he was going to see Father Christmas he turned round and said, "You can shut your cakehole." Well, you wouldn't normally hear such a remark in First Class, would you? It's simply that in normal life one wouldn't quite mix with these people – you see what I mean?'

I took this matter up with the boy: he was disinterested in Santa Claus but enjoying the cruise. The food was quite good, he said, though there was a shortage of artichokes.

One of the other children was also suffering a shortage: she was a ravishingly attractive Lolita of about 14 who had cast a calculating eye upon my crew. They were fascinated but frightened, and also awarded her some initials: JB, for Jail Bait. Not deeply flattering, but an improvement upon PL.

We sailed down the west coast of Africa to Sierra Leone, known – though *not* in the Royal Mail brochure – as the White Man's Grave. At Freetown we watched the splendid bare-breasted West African dancers who had recently performed in London's Trafalgar Square, where they had been compelled to wear cardigans. That film – without woolies – was actually used in the programme, which was a 1966 breakthrough, of sorts. 'Black breasts are all right,' the BBC agreed, reluctantly, 'but not too many of them.'

After a gap of ten years I considered another floating Whicker's World – this time aboard the world's largest liner, the *Queen Elizabeth 2*. When I made my recce, she was on her first world cruise; it was like putting to sea in the Waldorf Astoria.

In that monstrous place we moved from Hong Kong to Japan, then across the Pacific to LA, down to Acapulco, squeezed through the Panama Canal (almost 30 inches to spare on *both* sides – be reasonable) to Cartagena in Columbia, a bleak reception in that awful Jamaican Kingston, and ashore in Port Everglades in Florida.

At sea, departures are always sad. You get a lump in your throat leaving unattractive places you loathe. A jet take-off is an outgoing adventure: you are up and away and eager – no time for regrets. When a ship sails it is a melancholy moment of mournful sirens and damp little hankies.

Yokohama, for instance, is an absolutely wonderful city to see sinking below the horizon – the cold, wet, gritty greyness of it all. Yet when in the twilight the *QE2* moved silently, imperceptibly away from the thousands waving upon its quayside . . . when the streamers went out and the band played 'Auld Lang Syne' with a Japanese accent and all the harbour craft tooted Farewell – not a dry eye on deck. You would have thought we all adored the dreadful place.

Take Long Beach: the US Navy had moved down to San Diego and left nothing but tatty topless bars, hard porn bookshops, and dusty cinemas showing Adult movies. Who could feel anything but relief, escaping California at its most yukky? We sailed at sunset as shore lights glowed beneath a crescent moon. Small craft followed us down towards the Pacific, car horns sounded a salute, flags dipped, waterside restaurants tannoyed emotional goodbyes while waiters stood to attention. Total magic. Leaving this fairyland full of loving, caring people, we kept gulping. Ever gulped on a Jumbo?

It could be memories of the *Titanic*, 'In Which We Serve' and 'For Those in Peril' . . . or just the slow silent stately immensity of it all; but who expects to get snuffly leaving Honolulu when an *Hawaiian* piper stands on the dock trying to play 'Will Ye No Come Back Again'? Yes, yes, you murmur mistily, any time . . .

Passengers exposed to such emotion find the slow-moving luxury life so aimless that trivia loom large. On an expensive world cruise with nothing to do and lots of people to help you not do it, complaints grow predictably ingenious: the *QE2* ice was not cold enough. The elephants in Ceylon were too small. Rio's marvellous statue of Christ the Redeemer was all right, but the one in Lisbon was a better likeness.

A dieting traveller from Indiana was petulantly practical: Why no low-cholesterol imitation eggs? 'How's that again?' said the baffled Cockney steward. Another refused a coveted invitation to the Captain's reception: 'When you've seen one Captain,' she told me, 'you've seen 'em all . . .' A Frenchman protested that an actor in 'Murder on the Orient Express' had called his countrymen Frogs, and an American objected when the ship's band played 'Second-hand Rose': 'That's my name, and there's nothing second-hand about me.' There is no come-back to that.

In this most inward-looking of communities, the Separate Tables syndrome is a progressive sickness; a cruise breeds a weird boarding-house paranoia, a suspicious they-have-more-toast outlook. One of our passengers had cruised round the world 19 times, growing harder to handle on each circuit. The crew had endless horror stories: one couple were put ashore and flown home when their stateroom was found to be so filthy it had to be stripped and rebuilt. A 15-year-old daughter broke-out upon sexual adventures and a singer with the ship's band was only saved from walking the plank by some Polaroid pictures of her performance in other cabins. Another couple, so quiet and refined they were selected by a senior officer to sit at his table, fell to cabin fighting. She would come to breakfast with a black eye and, reciprocally, hit him on the head with a bedside lamp while he slept. These emphatic marital gestures affected mealtime conversation.

The most vehement protests came from ashore. When the liner set sail from Southampton to earn Britain $15 million and keep a thousand crew in work, some Labour back-benchers, sensing publicity, complained of the extravagance of the lone RAF helicopter that had flown past in salute. This tiny gesture, the Minister's reply revealed, cost £100. In Kobe, heart of the world's greatest shipbuilding nation, our Japanese competitors thought *QE2* significant enough to put up a dozen helicopters and parade their Firemen's Band to play the River Kwai theme – at a time when foreigners were writing the British off as a nation of Closed-Shops.

Sensing a unique opportunity to bang the drum, our Yokohama Consulate at the harbour gates, with typical British get-up-and-go, got up and went. It remained resolutely closed during the liner's three-day visit.

At every port she visited around the world this magnificent product of the Clyde was greeted with ecstatic awe. During the three days in Yokohama half-a-million people queued to stand and gaze. In South Africa crowds jammed approach roads. In Brazil even Cariocas were reduced to stunned appreciation. In Honolulu thousands rose before dawn to watch her sail in. Only in her homeland did the *QE2* rate snide Parliamentary protest, bitchy comment in gossip columns and dismissive television coverage.

'How do you feel about deserting Britain?' a TV newsman asked a pretty young schoolmistress as she went aboard at Southampton; her husband had just died of cancer and she was gambling her insurance money on a cruise instead of a nervous breakdown.

Going on board in Hong Kong to face the passengers' indignation about British media, I had first met Dilys (ran a St Pancras pub, retired to Frinton) and Evelyn (delicatessen in South Shields). 'Spending our money before the Government takes it,' they told me cheerily. 'Worked all our lives to earn it, so who's to tell us how to spend it? Wish each day had 48 hours – we never go to bed until tomorrow.' On shore the jolly pair ignored expensive organised excursions and used public transport; a determined Geordie pensioner demanding directions from a Japanese bus conductor is worth overhearing.

A London Transport Inspector from Finchley Garage told me when he retired his children had urged him and his wife to put their savings into three months of memories. With 1,400 passengers, the *QE2* was a city and it was hard to see them all as 'idle rich'. Some cruisers wore white handkerchiefs on their heads with the corners knotted and probably paid their fares in cash; others were moguls with Swiss accounts.

Surprisingly in an international ship, it was the Americans who were the dressers. One Florida couple came aboard with 38 cabin trunks: 'We thought they were meant for the ship's shop,' said a steward. 'Then they went ashore and bought more.'

Officers and crew were happily stereotyped: the Captain, all gold braid and pipe, was from a Senior Service advertisement. The Chief Engineer, small and grey and twinkling, had six single but mature ladies at his table. My cabin steward was a rosy-cheeked George Robey full of comforting reassurance. Stewards brought tea and cakes to deckchairs and, if there was the slightest wind, tucked their occupants up in rugs. It was the last resort on earth with nannies.

Like the ship's drinks, shore excursions were overpriced and tour guides traditionally excruciating: 'That house is

owned by Dolores del Rio, that one by John Wayne – and
that one by the coach driver . . . The Spaniards built that
sundial 400 years ago – and it's *still* working . . .'

In Hong Kong, 600 of the more adventurous passengers
set off for a three-day tour of Communist China; one got lost
before she even reached Kowloon Station, and missed it all.
Chinese guides proudly showed them over a new hospital in
Canton, but an American was so shocked at its primitive
facilities he reached for his chequebook on the spot and
offered to buy them a new one.

It seemed the perfect opportunity for an over-privileged
adult to do something for under-privileged children, so I
raffled a Rolls-Royce for the Showbiz Car Club charity. I was
sure my £100 tickets would be snapped up – until I recalled
how many 'idle rich' ran small provincial shops. Nevertheless we sold 150 quickly; the next £5,000 was a struggle,
for we were nearing the end of the cruise. The final £1,000
was coaxed from the crowded ballroom just before the
draw.

The Cruise Director asked two passengers to observe that
every number was duly placed in the champagne bucket, and
announced this precaution to the assembly: 'The scrutineers
haven't got tickets,' he explained. 'No,' shouted an American
darkly, 'but they've got friends . . .' Then I understood why
the Captain had refused to let his crew buy tickets: if they had
won, the New York passengers would have rioted.

With my hand in the bucket, I stood to make one good
friend and 199 enemies . . . but the Rolls went peacefully to a
retired couple from Kent, with bottles of champagne for
the next ten tickets and £6,000 for mentally retarded
children.

In that slow-moving month I learned to appreciate the
QE2 as the nostalgic end of an era. I also learned how to
handle unsympathetic passengers: you put their names down
on the list of 'Autographs Required' for a children's shipboard Treasure Hunt, starting just after lunch . . .

Because of other assignments we were not able to undertake the *QE2* programme, but three years later I did manage
a second shipboard Whicker's World on an adventure

voyage around Sumatra and Java which put out from Singapore and crossed the Equator twice. In a tropical rain forest
on the isle of Nias we filmed Pasadena blue-rinses confront-
ing Stone Age warriors. It was hard to see which group was
the more bemused.

The elegant *Prinsendam* was only 9,000 tons, or one-eighth
of the *QE2*, so could put in to ports usually inaccessible. She
offered the only comfortable way of observing at close quarters a society still so happily primitive that children begged
for the flower in your buttonhole, not for money – there are
not many of *those* left.

Passengers taking this slow ship to the Stone Age could
play Sir Richard Burton or Freya Stark every steamy day,
and return in the evenings to take a hot bath and a cold
glass.

I made the 4,000-mile cruise twice – once on a recce to see
whether a programme was possible, and once filming. First
time around, the passengers were marvellous: there was a
young Irish couple who kept the bar open until four in the
morning and upset the professional artistes by being far more
entertaining. There was a collection of fairground Travelling
Folk with wallets full of readies. Their wives wore large
diamonds with bathing costumes and were determined to
enjoy at all hours of the day and night the biggest and most
exotic drinks, every tall glass stuffed with tropical fruit and
flowers. The reserved English were the most amusing group
on board, and I arrived back at Singapore delighted with the
prospect of a merry programme.

When we embarked upon filming a few weeks later I stood
at the top of the gangplank with Frank Berry, the Cruise
Director, as he greeted the passengers. They seemed to be
mainly elderly Dutch and Belgians who spoke no English
and were somewhat sombre. There were a few rather cross
French and some Germans obviously braced to grab the best
deckchairs. With every arrival, my heart sank further: our
fellow-passengers were just not Fun People.

That is how it can go with the best laid plans of television
and men. Everything had been well organised: the crews –
theirs and mine – were marvellous, the ship's officers agree-

able, food and accommodation fine, customs placated, helicopter organised, weather good, sea smooth. The one thing we could not legislate for . . . was the passenger list.

Making the best of a bad complement, we steamed north out of Stamford Raffles' marvellous harbour, filming from the ship and from our chopper, and heading for two of my favourite islands: Penang and Bali. In the past I had always flown to them, busy busy, upon some urgent assignment. Sailing gently up the coast of Malaysia past dreamy dark green islands dotting the Strait of Malacca is a far far better way to reach George Town. We were covering the only cruise on which not even the most world-weary sophisticate could be bored with the ports of call: 'On world cruises they don't even bother to go ashore any more,' said the Director. 'They've seen it all before.'

Passengers received splendidly laconic advice from the Excursion Manager : 'In Sibolga there are lovely beaches, and sharks, and no hospital – so enjoy yourselves. Every pedicab driver says he speaks English, so ask him if it snowed yesterday. If he says Yes . . .'

Indonesian roads remain a pageant: the transport system inherited from the Dutch in 1946 has not been modernised, or even repaired. There are few new cars and it seems every other vehicle is stationary at the roadside, its bonnet despairingly open. From Belawan we drove into the Kara Highlands, almost on the Equator but 4,500 feet up, so below a couple of volcanoes – one smoking – hydrangeas and chrysanthemums were in bloom. After three hours bumping around in an elderly bus we reached the Karo Batak village of Lingga. 'The villagers eat dogs and donkeys,' the guide explained, 'to keep their blood warm at this height.'

The visitors, blood slightly chilled, clambered through high stilted longhouses with horned roofs, making sounds of wonderment, and watched a ceremonial dance by small dark animists who had nothing to sell – they were *that* unspoiled. Both groups were grave, polite, and quite baffled by those curious people from the Outer Rim.

Indonesia has 200 main races and 13,677 islands, 3,000 of them inhabited. One of the most fascinating is Nias, cut off for centuries from the rest of the world, with its own language, culture and mythology, and even now visited only by an occasional motor boat from Sibolga, a fishing village already isolated enough. The natives came originally from India, bringing remarkable stonework; they still use stone chairs and tables. Their mountaintop village of Bawömataluo was reached in the back of gasping old trucks and, finally, by a great staircase up the last of 700 stones leading from the sea. These and the equatorial steamheat proved too much for one Belgian woman, who had a heart attack

At the top, magnificent longhouses on tall piles stretched away in two avenues. Outside the Chief's house local warriors unleashed a wardance: fierce face masks, shields and spears. Tiny but ferocious headhunters militantly resisting outsiders, the Niha were not brought under Dutch law until the beginning of this century. Even today, it was whispered, some still practised human sacrifice. We noticed their teeth were sometimes filed to points, and blackened.

'*Please* don't buy their costumes,' the Tour Manager begged, 'or they'll have nothing to wear for the next cruise.' These were made of crocodile and karabau skins dyed black, and so stiff they stood up on their own between dances like suits of armour – which, I suppose, was the name of the wargame.

The warriors made themselves even more fearsome by wearing metal moustaches. Well let's face it, a moustache *can* be quite frightening . . .

At their unique jumping stones, barefoot warriors proved their virility: once they had to leap their enemies' walls but now sailed over seven-foot stone piles as a military exercise, to the cruisers' peaceful Oohs and Aahs and camera clicks. A group of Niha women in ceremonial golden headdresses offered dishes of token nuts to cruisers who had heard what native food could do to the stomach, so took only token bites.

They then performed a welcoming dance into which bemused passengers were invited, like some ladies Excuse Me. The Niha women were, I had to admit, rather prettier than the passengers. Brides were still purchased in Nias, and widows and girls not virgins were sold off at half price.

A man could once lose his hand for touching a woman's breast, but the days when Nihas could kill their own slaves ended in the Thirties, and some have now become Christian. Since then their sexual morality has declined, for they feared these instant pagan penalties far more than today's Christian punishments, which only have to be settled in the next world.

The hilltop home of their megalithic culture was one of the most stunning settings I had ever seen; two lines of stately black terraces, audacious architecture towering 70 feet into the sky above the pillars and paving of the Stone Age men. Overwhelmed by the mysterious, hidden island, I asked an American matron sitting next to me on some sacrificial slab what she thought of it all. She considered the scene. 'Very primitive,' she said. 'Yes,' I said, after a while, 'you could say that.'

Java has 50 volcanoes, 15 of them still active. On a silent night so still that at 19 knots there was no breath of wind on the bridge, we glided through the Sunda Strait. Lightning flashed along the horizon. Java stood black and menacing, Sumatra silver and moonlit. Between them, Krakatoa, which has erupted a couple of times this century and in 1883 gave the world its biggest bang: a volcanic roar heard 3,000 miles away. The tidal wave that followed drowned 36,000 people and volcanic dust provided brilliant sunsets around the globe. We passed this lightly-sleeping volcano with respect . . .

Bali, dreamland of 10,000 temples, has seen a tourist invasion which doubtless my earlier programmes assisted. The artistic centre at Ubud had surrendered to a florid rash of art stalls – but Balinese village paintings are still enchanting. On my first visit eleven years ago I picked up a few of these primitives for $10 each and later, at Neiman-Marcus in Houston, saw inferior examples floodlit and offered at $1,000 up . . . Encouraged, I bought a few more.

Much remains unchanged; food in still awful – but going to Bali to eat is like going to Venice to fish. The Barong dance is still vivid, the Kecak Monkey Dance one of the sounds of the world. I returned to the Water Temple, with its lofty

Presidential House where Sukarno used to sit on his balcony above the women's bathing area. He was very fond of nature,' the guide explained, understandingly.

In Surabaya, where Johnnie came from, some of the city's 30,000 pedicabs clogged the road as drivers watched the Kuda Kepang Horse Dance we were filming. Driven into a trance by frenzied drumming, a man chewed grass, drank from a bucket of water and – the link with horses is obscure – popped and ate a trayful of electric light bulbs, munching with many a snap and crackle. (I was not worried about the glass – but how could he drink the *water* . . .?)

We went by ferry to Madura Island to attend the village race meeting at Bangkalan, where sleek, elegant bulls raced fast as horses for 100 yards. We filmed the face of the cruise passenger accorded the honour of presenting the Cup to the driver of the fastest pair as she learned without much enthusiasm, that custom demanded she kiss all three . . .

The last port of call, Jakarta, a city of five million – only a quarter of them employed – and growing by 11 babies a minute. At the Hotel Borabadur I bought a three-day-old copy of *The Times* wrapped in a plastic envelope like a dirty magazine and almost as expensive: £1.75. Across 150 acres just out of town, President Suharto's wife had founded an instant-Indonesia exhibition with pavilions from the nation's 28 provinces. The savage Asmat tribe of Irianjaya had a splendid longhouse and expensive tastes: 'They were the people who ate Governor Rockefeller's son,' the guide intoned, thoughtfully. 'He was looking for carvings. They *said* he'd been eaten by crocodiles, but . . .'

Food on the *Prinsendam* was less rich. At the midnight buffet a local dish was called Nasi balls. Another roguish item : 'Pearls of the Caspian Sea, garnished'. Just in time I saw through the cunning attempt to put me off the scent and on to the Soup of the Day.

Our 260 passengers came from 16 nations; at the Captain's table, a couple from Liechtenstein, two New Yorkers, and a pair of Mexican-Americans from Chicago – she about to go into the *Guinness Book of Records*, she told me, as the world's most travelled woman. We swapped preferred destinations and I trumped her Bora Bora with a Norfolk Island. Later, in a Surabaya pedicab, her husband's £2,000 Patek Philippe was snatched from his wrist, which should encourage her to stay home where she belongs.

As is legendary afloat, the menus were long, lavish and well-read. Shipboard meals were major events on the daily programme and all cruisers concentrated upon the serious business of masticating their moneysworth. I heard two Indonesian stewards having a vicious row: '– and what's more,' snarled one, delivering the *coup de grâce*, 'you eat like a passenger . . .'

OLGA

You can't have it all . . .

NOT getting married can become a habit, I have found. My friend Harry Hamilton, with whom I joined the Army, seemed to marry and divorce rather a lot; invited to one of his weddings when about to film abroad I apologised and promised to attend his next . . . He was not at all surprised. However, I *was* when my own marital status continued to fascinate sections of the Press, rating in the list of inevitable questions just below Where are you going next? and How rich are you?

I have always believed that from a reader's point of view it would be hard to find a subject more boring than my sex life, factual or fictional. When I pointed this out, reporters would always play the 'TV's eligible bachelor' card, and go on popping the question: So *why* aren't you married? I usually reacted with 'Nobody's asked me,' because I could never accept anyone cared a jot. However one man made a habit of calling on the first of each month to inquire, checking the market as though I was on offer – and a cliffhanger, with it. Others, at the end of some thoughtful interview about programmes, would cough deprecatingly and murmur, 'Er, sorry about this, but my editor particularly asked me to . . .'

If forced to face such an unrewarding query and become introspective, I could only lay the blame, if blame it be, upon a relatively solitary homelife as the only child of a widowed mother, upon a character and lifestyle which moulded me into a sort of gregarious Loner. I love being among people – yet am self-reliant and content to be solitary.

If the uncertain post-war days seemed a poor period in which to select a permanent partner, my career afterwards was an even less promising foundation. Covering wars and alarums around the globe provided no background for a happy marriage. A man who does not know for sure where he will be sleeping tomorrow night *must* be a bad bet, as most foreign correspondents' marriages indicate. Afterwards came the even more far-flung demands of television; so all my life I seem to have travelled light and impetuously, constantly moving on. This got to be a habit and, faced by any indignant female reporter, sounds like Excuses Excuses.

In exchange for a stimulating and rewarding nomadic life, something has to be sacrificed, for you cannot ask a woman to live out of a suitcase. In my case it was hearth, children and in-laws. With my temperament, I have not felt deprived, nor do I believe the world is any the poorer without lots of little Whickers – though I may be.

The most powerful woman in Hollywood, then running 20th Century-Fox, underlined this for me. Sherry Lansing said: 'You can't have it *all*.'

This lovely woman had made a decision about the direction of her life and career, and found the result fulfilling. 'Some people envy my money and position, but I work late – and I go home alone. A woman who has no working life but has a husband and children, she has things I don't have. I work hard and I like it, but I'm alone, and if she's envious of me – then I'm envious of her . . . It all equals out, on a scale of zero to ten, to an eight or a nine. Nobody's got a ten. I've learned, you can't have everything.'

The marital adventures of others offer little encouragement: it is a fearful reflection upon life today that I need to concentrate with my head in my hands before I can come up with two or three truly contented marriages from among all my friends and acquaintances. A good marriage *is* news today, sadly enough, because of its rarity. Few attain such happiness, however many times they try.

During a restless life I have been fortunate enough to be committed to some very special women – and all, I like to think, remain good friends. Some of these relationships were close for many years, until elevated into calm and secure friendships; somehow it always seemed a pity to confuse a happy love affair by marriage.

Since the spotlight of television is the most public of platforms, I have always attempted to protect my private life – you have to keep something back for your friends. Occasionally I would find my name linked with someone in the gossip columns. Most of these tiny revelations, true or false, could be sidestepped, but one relationship had such a high profile it became public domain.

Olga Deterding was an amalgam of those words the world's Press find irresistible: heiress, oil, diamonds Schweitzer, St Moritz, millionairess, Society, eccentric, lovers, champagne . . . and, best of all, Poor Little Rich Girl. Amid popping corks and jungle expeditions, this wild blend of Barbara Hutton and Hester Stanhope offered a reassuring aura of sadness. She smiled-through-tears into our calmer lives, and those titillating stories confirmed our right-minded suspicions that Money Does Not Bring Happiness.

When we came ashore from that Christmas cruise to Sierra Leone, Olga had evidently decided to move into Whicker's world. I was flattered and intrigued – and not a little apprehensive, knowing the mould if not the model. She lived in constant flight from her love-hate association with the international media, wanting to be noticed and then resenting the intrusion – amused, then indignant. Dutch, French and Italians, Australians and South Africans were as interested in her as we were. I grew weary of denying stories of our marriage, of facing the most personal queries when I only wanted to discuss my programmes. I was certainly not serious about our too-public affair, though any emphatic denial might have seemed less than kind and no compliment to her, so in public I carried on ducking and dodging.

As the publicity circus rolled on, I began to understand the Hollywood marry-go-round where those in the public eye are almost pressurised by the media into instant-romance. I felt egged-on by the constant attention of a million strangers, swept along by silly excitement over a non-event which reached a crescendo in May 1966. We were in Monte Carlo, filming a programme on the making of John Frankenheimer's 'Grand Prix', with James Garner, Yves Montand and an outburst of stars and racing drivers doing their all in that stunning setting. In the middle of that sunlit sophistication Olga, in an exasperated sort of way, made me an offer no gentleman could refuse: she proposed.

I was taken aback, but just resisted: 'This is so sudden.' It had never occurred to me that her intentions were honourable – and it was not even Leap Year. After a suitable pause and a couple of gulps I accepted, sort of.

'Right – you've had it now,' she said, with one of her Cheshire-cat grins. 'Try to escape and I'll sue you for enormous breach of promise.' We decided we were Engaged, at least – and looked around to see if anything felt different . . .

Reporters flew out from London. The clamour followed us to Geneva, where she had a pad, and Paris: 'Jewelled by Cartier, dressed by Whicker, groomed for the jet age,' wrote the *Daily Mirror* in a frenzy, 'oil millionairess Olga Deterding sat in a Paris hotel yesterday talking of life as the prospective Mrs Alan Whicker. She said, with a faint lisp, "I proposed to him. I don't think he would have got around to it . . ." ' The coverage was kind and approving, but over-ecstatic.

She had by then sold her house in Belgravia, closed her

Paris apartment, and moved into my Regent's Park home with little baggage but considerable presence. My assertive Leo character might not seem suitable casting for the role of rich woman's acquiescent husband, but in fact her enormous wealth never intruded upon our relationship. After Twenty Years Hard I was, as the papers said, comfortably off; my income could keep her in everything but diamonds. Her lifestyle was relatively modest and she blended into my establishment, living in my apartment, driving in my Bentley, using my clubs, attended by my housekeeper. She rarely had to open her handbag.

This may I suppose have been some of the secret of my success for, to be brutally honest, Olga suffered the affliction of the very rich: she was rather stingy. Like Paul Getty, she worried about the pennies, and would drive friends bonkers by traipsing round town to get the extra couple of cents for her travellers cheques, or buying the cheapest wine – Moroccan red – Fortnum and Masons could offer. However, since it was usually my money she was being mean with, this was easy to accept. She was domiciled in Geneva, where her tax-free investments had been endlessly accumulating for some 30 years, and doubtless her gnomes knew what they were about.

Quite soon, to my surprise, she changed her Will, leaving to me everything she owned, except a few small bequests of jewellery. It was one of those generous, lavish gestures that did not actually cost anything, but was nevertheless touching. Faced by all those millions that document was, I told her, a blatant invitation for me to polish the stairs . . .

She brought nothing into my life except herself, but fitted in admirably, for she longed to join, to be part of something, to contribute. She found it refreshing that I made no concessions to her: I went to the same restaurants and parties with the same friends, did the same work in the same way and constantly flew off in all directions, as always. Her arrival coincided with one of the busiest periods of my life. Every month for three years an hour-long Whicker's World went out on the BBC, with all the researching, travelling, filming,

viewing, editing and writing that entailed. I wrote supporting articles for the *Radio Times* and *The Listener*, and since our
programmes were transmitted on BBC2, had also agreed to
write a regular column for the *News of the World*; I did not wish
to disappear from the memory of 16 million readers who were
unlikely to view that channel, then remote and esoteric. I
need not have worried for our series later replaced Panorama
on BBC 1, and doubled its audience.

So whatever they wrote in the gossip columns, under such
pressures our so-called jet-set romance became for both of us
an afterthought. However the papers had announced our
Engagement, which was at least a step in a different direction.

From then on, despite newspaper prodding, there always
seemed some quite adequate reason for not taking the ultimate step. I used to tell reporters: 'We're waiting until we
have two clear days for a long honeymoon.' I suppose if we
had rushed in and got that piece of paper during the first fine
frenzy, things might have been different. In truth and at the
end of the day, we were just not the marrying kind.

Olga was classless, intense, dramatic and shy. Her striking
Modigliani face photographed poorly. She was unconcerned
about clothes or appearance, and was neither domesticated
nor a home-maker. Her idea of preparing an intimate dinner
for two was to call Fortnums and tell them to send a game pie
over by cab.

Our relationship was agreeable relaxed: when on Desert
Island Discs I was asked to choose my one luxury object that
was completely useless, I instantly suggested Olga . . . This
shocked Roy Plomley, but she was gleeful.

Active and eager, the least-vague person I have ever
known, she would sit and listen with such intensity I always
believed my words would be remembered for ever. Her
loyalty and delight at being part of the team was endearing.
She took a childlike and touching joy in simple things: 'I'm
proud,' she once said, 'when I make you laugh.' She seemed
forthright and quite unsentimental – yet I would always be
discovering little hidden love notes.

As solitary travellers through the world, we were similar in many ways. We had both lived wandering lives and had lost our fathers when young. Sir Henri Deterding had died in 1939 when she was 12. He had adored her and named their St Moritz home Villa Olga. Her Russian mother Lydia was beautiful and selfish, so she and her sister Lilla spent a lonely childhood at boarding schools. Olga told me how once a strange and lovely lady who turned out to be her mother had arrived at their school, disapproved of their clothes – and offered to *sell* them some clothing-ration coupons. That remote upbringing was not the stuff of which happy child-hoods, or lives are made . . .

Lady Deterding entertained us at her splendid Avenue Foch home in Paris. I was most hospitably received, for behind her charm she was still incredulous, still could not *quite* believe an apparently level-headed chap was prepared to take-on such a challenge. Daughter of a Czarist General and nudging 70, she retained all her vivacity and much of her beauty. By candlelight she could be quite distracting; I was greatly smitten.

She wore the giant 41-carat diamond ring once owned by King Joseph Bonaparte and known as the Polar Star – at least, that is what she appeared to be wearing. During dinner she confessed it was a replica created at a cost of several thousand pounds when the insurance became too expensive for the diamond to leave its bank vault. I suggested it would have been more economic and just as indicative to have worn instead a small badge saying 'I own the Polar Star', but this was not well received.

After her death in 1980 this one ring, a small part of her collection, was sold at Christie's for £1,960,784 – which shows what happens if you are beautiful and well-mannered and look after your ration coupons . . . Olga was to be her main beneficiary – quite rightly, since she suffered most at the hands of that fascinating ogre.

Our visit to my prospective mother-in-law was somewhat shadowed by an article I had just written strongly criticising the French. It was much quoted in Paris newspapers; one commented ruefully: 'M. Whicker does not write with the back of his pen . . .' Her servants were outraged, and throughout dinner I was tensed to receive the remaining *Suprême de Pintadeau Sparnacienne* over the back of my head. Fortunately all I received were dark Gallic glares, for I was protected by the obvious approval of the blonde Russian at the head of the table, the only Hostess for whom General de Gaulle would leave home . . .

Before the war, Olga's father had left £23 million, and her inheritance grew staggeringly by tax-free bounds. She in turn grew strong and fearless, seeking outlandish adventure. She attempted to cross the Sahara by car and was rescued by the Foreign Legion. She worked as a barmaid and deckhand in Tahiti. When her plane to Nairobi was delayed at Brazzaville, she went up to Lambarene for a day's visit and stayed 18 months. With no medical knowledge, she passed much of that time whitewashing hospital huts. Her most treasured possessions were a small wooden box which Dr Schweitzer had signed for her when she left, and my father's gold fob watch.

She had always been interested in photography, so on location became our unit photographer, taking excellent pictures with fierce concentration, and acting as an expensive Gofer. My crew found her a bit startling and dramatic, but seemed to approve. For some three years she was another television-team gypsy, camping out in the Kuwaiti desert as required, keeping waiting interviewees happy while I filmed, carrying the tripod and, when we needed more filmstock in the Philippines, thumbing a flight to Zamboanga from Jolo in a light plane piloted by a jovial monk.

Once when I was doing a programme about Sardinian bandits, she lost a cap from a front tooth. With that dreadful spike she was out of a horror movie, though indifferent to her impact. Since we laughed a lot, I threatened to cover her face with camera tape, like the Invisible Man. Finally I took her to the nearby mountain town of Nuoro where someone in a café directed us to a dentist. We climbed some dark stairs from an alleyway, fearing a Crimean experience, and confronted a man in a white coat with sinister limp and dangling cigarette. Doubtfully we followed him through his scruffy flat and into a room out of Houston – in that mountain casbah, a brilliant white space-age surgery. He did a splendid job, while that cigarette dangled. Olga could have chartered a plane and flown back to London, but never demonstrated such grand folly.

At home she kept our photographic albums and started a cuttings book she called Pick of the Whick. She was then thin as a rake and full of nervous energy. I had been mystified to notice that she was also sometimes plump and lethargic. It transpired she was a compulsive eater, the first I had known; this affected not only her silhouette, but her moods. Some weeks she would do nothing but eat, and lie in bed. She was deeply ashamed of this illness, and at first told me she was hooked on drugs – as though that addiction was more acceptable.

'Going to my dealer in Soho,' she would murmer, slipping furtively out of the flat. After some hours she would reappear, perspiring but sated, saying she had found a Fix. She had indeed – but only by making the rounds of spaghetti houses, stuffing herself.

She could put on a stone in a day – a physical expansion I would never have believed had I not watched the scales. At some point she would decide to stop 'pigswilling', as I called it in an attempt to discourage her, and would then starve on cigarettes and pills and black coffee, and become hyper-active.

Such chemical imbalance, and the resultant dependence upon tranquillisers and sleeping pills, meant she was not always easy to live with. Once in a rage, having taken wine after a handful of Downers, she smashed all my marble lampstands. She stood triumphant and defiant among the debris, strong and sinewy as a lioness, and as fierce.

I was aghast and concerned, but also exasperated at such determined and hopeless self-destruction. Throughout her life Olga had just not been loved enough, and I suspected I was her last chance.

When, finally exhausted and all-but defeated by the end-less dramas, I threatened she would have to leave . . . she could show a little-girl distress that was heartbreaking. Sometimes that cry for help grew more piercing: once she slashed her wrists with a razor. I found her in the bathroom, hysterically running hot water over the gashes. The bath seemed full of blood.

That was the darkest of days. Others could be bright and full of laughter, for despite the occasional brooding melancholy she could not escape and had always known, Olga had finally found within my world a mission, a satisfaction, a concern. In her way, she thrived. My friends worried about her, and hers had never seen her so contented and assured.

Yet through it all, something within her fought against every happiness. Gorging and starving, comatose and febrile, appealing and violent, she was always unpredictable and driven.

These black moods grew more frequent and intense. Finally they became insupportable for both of us. After three years we decided that for both our sakes, we should part – so that I could work, and she could nosh unnagged.

My professional life, which at times of anguish had become almost an afterthought, was also changing: the IBA had awarded our consortium the Yorkshire franchise, so I was leaving the BBC after 11 years and could expect to spend time in the north, working with new people – and Olga was not ideally suited to life in a Leeds hotel.

Early one morning in the summer of 1969 we said good-bye-for-ever, quite calmly, and I left for Heathrow with Tony Essex. We were flying to Sweden to film a programme on Count von Rosen, the pugnacious pacifist from Biafra. At the airport I was sadly buying my papers when suddenly she appeared before me in her old cashmere kimono, uncombed, distressed and wretched – and wanting to come with us.

As other travellers backed away nervously and loudspeakers ordered Immediate Embarkation, we tried to calm her hysteria. Then she stood in tears and watched as we were hurried through Immigration. In Malmo, desperately anxious, I telephoned home many times. There was no reply.

I did not see Olga again for nine years.

On my return, hesitantly unlocking the front door at Cumberland Terrace, I could sense something was different. There was a peace, a hollow emptiness . . . which was not only in my laugh. Olga had gone – and so had much of my home. I had told her if she would leave she could take anything she wanted – and she had been as good as my word.

The study bookshelves reminded me of her front teeth without those caps: my remaining books leaned forlornly against each other. Unfaded squares showed where pictures had been. In her distracted way she had taken her own things, and whatever else she thought necessary – right down to the Moroccan red . . . This was no doubt a blend of heiress scorned, practicality and, let us hope, sentimentality. She was after all half down-to-earth Dutch, half histrionic Russian.

My housekeeper recalled that on the morning of my departure to Sweden a solicitor and a pantechnicon had arrived; Olga, with a nice sense of priority, had first changed her Will, then loaded-up and lumbered-off. It was the end of the affair.

In the months that followed I kept discovering unexpected things were missing: whatever happened to the *eggcups*? However, a deplenished household seemed a modest price to pay for my sanity, career and peace of mind. I wished her well and happy, wherever she was, and started refurnishing with a light heart.

Cumberland Terrace had been rather a tight squeeze for us, so I was in the process of buying an apartment in a building going up in Piccadilly, facing Green Park on the site of the old Turf Club. I had designed the top three floors, and it was becoming a spectacular triplex. Through her solicitors she now asked if one of her companies could take this over. At that time I was about to face a call for a lot of ready cash for my new Yorkshire Television shares so was relieved to surrender an extra financial obligation, and most happy to be able to stay on in Regent's Park, which I loved. In 1969 the Piccadilly flat cost around £60,000; Olga later told me she had been offered £1 million for it. I should have given her custody of my Yorkshire shares, instead . . .

Later, as I prepared to leave for South America, she telephoned from Miami and wanted to join us in Haiti. At that time the Tontons Macoute were rampant and Port au Prince seemed dangerous for a woman. That's what I told her – though to face facts, our affair had run its course. I was not about to mount her uncontrolled roller-coaster again. Just as we had come together suddenly and decisively, so we had parted. Never go back.

One spring morning in 1978 I was in Air India's Maharajah Lounge at Heathrow waiting for a flight to Bombay. The door burst open and a striking figure swathed from neck to ankles in mauve cashmere swept in, escorted by airline acolytes. It was Olga. We greeted each other with warmth and enthusiasm. She was off to stay with the Maharani of Morvi, so we reminisced through the long flight.

After the usual nightmare of an arrival at an Indian airport, we said our goodbyes and I flew on to Jaipur. I filmed two programmes, returned to Bombay and telephoned the Morvi Palace on the off-chance. Olga answered; true to form, she had planned to stay two weeks but was still there after two months. She came dashing down to the Taj Mahal Hotel and we went to some celebration where she paraded me around with her old pride and concern.

We also met at Beaulieu. Lord Montagu was thowing a Blitz party, with everyone in wartime gear. He wore his Brigade uniform and my long-suffering service dress had been demothballed. Some guests were Dad's Army, others Italian camp followers – but all were outrigged by Olga. Dressed as a paratrooper disguised as a nun, she wore enormous boots under her habit and carried a submachinegun borrowed from Cartier, which the Germans had allowed the jewellers for protection during the occupation. It was an early *Must*, with Cartier stamped on its barrel and about as chic as a machinegun can get. We did not talk much that night, for she was preoccupied with Nigel Dempster, the columnist.

In the winter of 1979 I was in London for a preview of one of my series and, passing down Piccadilly, suddenly decided to call and wish her a Happy Christmas. I had heard the flat was often full of spongers, a weird collection of even-lonelier people Olga had begun to gather round her. She was alone.

Happily we shared a bottle of champagne, and a few toasts and memories.

She had, sad to say, grown less appealing, more eccentric, and was reported to be drinking – but remained in essence the old excitable, outrageous Olga. Recalling her Christmas sadness, I considered inviting her over to Jersey for the holiday, but decided she might prove too unpredictable, too dramatic for our calm island celebrations. I thought I would invite her in the New Year, anyway.

Home again, I despatched my Christmas present: an Anaïs Nin book called *In Praise of Sensitive Men*, with a card saying 'Well at least you knew *one*.' I was sure that distinctive voice would come crackling and mocking over the telephone: 'You don't think *you're* sensitive, do you?' I had my reply ready: 'No – I meant Schweitzer.'

Soon afterwards she did call to complain that she had organised a buffet party to see the scheduled Christmastime Whicker's World on our Indonesian cruise, but because of a technicians' strike it was not transmitted. Her captive guests had to watch a library film about the mating of spiders, which was not considered a reasonable substitute.

She was jolly and full of chuckles: 'The papers have been asking what I'm doing over Christmas,' she said. 'I've told them I'm spending it in bed with Alan Whicker.'

She knew how exasperated I was each time the columns reported her lunatic adventures: arrested for zigzagging in the Rolls and spending a night in the cells, trying to buy the *Observer*, going to China by train with some clown, being mugged in Clarges Street, sitting naked in a Brasserie window . . . Whatever was reported, they *always* dragged me into the story. After ten years apart, our names were still linked.

Olga had seen me quoted as saying her escapades were 'one of the crosses I have to bear', so her present to me was a book about society gossip in which we both appeared, with the inscription 'To Alan, with love from his Christmas cross.'

Next night, alone, she left her flat to see the New Year in at some nearby club in Shepherd's Market, choked on a steak – and died.

It was tragic . . . for she *almost* made it.

Certainly it would have been out of character for Olga to end her days in a rocking chair, wearing a shawl and stroking an old cat. I had always believed she would leave spectacularly: a plane crash in the Himalayas, a poison dart up the Amazon . . . To collapse in a Mayfair club with a glass of champagne in her hand was, I suppose, a relevant way to go – suddenly, without pain or apprehension. From her point of view, a reasonable exit – though she passed through it too early in the performance.

I shall always remember her, always wish her well on her travels through that other world where I am sure she arrived quizzical and quirky as ever – curious and fascinated and dauntless. We shall meet no more Olgas.

PART SEVEN

MONTAGE!

DISNEYWORLD

The Pixie Dust was coming down sour . . .

ALONG with the disruption of what was left of my private life which came and went with Olga, I had in 1968 experienced the redirection of my television life. After 11 years with the BBC I sustained a professional separation and was hustled across to ITV, protesting feebly. It all took place, I suspect, because a friend of mine reversed his phone book and started calling people from the Zs, backwards – and illustrates what can happen if you just can't say No.

In 1967 the IBA was awarding new franchises for the fourth time. The authority had decided to split Granada's vast northern area, and eight consortia were after the new territory east of the Pennines. At the very last moment one of them, Telefusion, found it had no television names among its worthy array of bankers, businessmen and professors. Hugh Thomas, former ITN newreader then working for the PR company Voice and Vision, was asked to rustle up some expertise of which the IBA might approve. With his address book back to front, he came upon me quite early.

Since I was so happy with the BBC I was not much interested – though it did seem one of those rare no-lose situations: I merely had to lend my name, and take up the allotted shares in the unlikely event of our receiving the franchise. Then I would make programmes for the new group, for a year.

Front-runner in that contest was a consortium headed by Lord Goodman which seemed to boast every significant television executive – plus a number of the more timid, who were waiting in the wings to step forward shyly upon victory.

After deliberating the IBA evidently decided that so many Chiefs attended by so few Indians could only bring discord. To everyone's surprise and my discomfiture, our consortium won.

When the BBC read in the newspapers that I might be leaving, they replied with a lavish lunch attended by the full panoply of Controllers and powerful initials. They offered me Repeats, a better office, another glass of wine, a sticker for the executive carpark and all my heart could desire – money, even – and urged me to carry on in W12. It was flattering and hard to refuse. I had no written contract with Telefusion – merely a perfunctory verbal agreement – but with great sadness felt noblesse obliged me to say my farewells to the Beeb, and drive north.

Yorkshire Television was being born in a rented clothing factory in Leeds, with a lot of effort and not much joy. The only other person with creative television experience in the original consortium was the drama producer, Joan Kemp-Welsh. The Managing Director was a former Granada salesman, G. E. Ward Thomas, a Machiavellian figure who had descended from the diminutive Grampian station in Aberdeen, and was not popular.

From the start Yorkshire Television was a curiously unhappy company. Within days of its first programme in 1968 the technicians went on strike, and we were off the air. It was a sad omen. Almost all its newly-recruited senior executives soon died, resigned or were fired. Taking his leave after a short career, one of them bleakly told Ward Thomas, '*You* won't have to hand out many gold watches.'

Nevertheless the network company took off in the marketplace and the 10p shares reached 80p. At one of my previews the *Daily Telegraph* television critic Leonard Marsland Gander looked at me oddly and demanded, 'How does it feel to be a millionaire?' Then the IBA mast on Emley Moor collapsed. YTV had neglected to take out insurance against such an improbable disaster, so it seemed the company might be still-born. The 80p shares eventually became 8p. At another preview Marsland Gander asked mournfully 'How does it feel to have *lost* a million?' Since I had never shared his touching faith in the power of paper, I did not experience his acute sense of my loss.

Fortunately most of my work was away from YTV's Television Centre in the Kirkstall Road. On an early tour I flew to Florida to consider another centre of unreality and its newest, richest and most famous immigrant. To be brutally honest, I did not really take to him – but how can you be mad at Mickey Mouse? Don't think it's easy. To restrain enthusiasm even slightly is not only unAmerican, unBritish and Unkind, it's kicking Peter Rabbit's cottontail – you feel such a brute. However I came to discover that at close quarters, Disney can cloy.

Now 52 and very rich indeed, Mickey moved his billion-dollar business to the Sunshine State in 1971 and unleashed a social revolution – a project of such magnitude it stunned even that rich flatland so used to space-billions, moon shots and Shuttles departing on time from Platform 2 at Cape Kennedy, just down the road from the House the Mouse built. For the first of the series I drove north from Miami to watch the birth pangs of Walt Disney World, largest private building project ever known – and was suitably staggered, not to say put out.

Disney had quietly bought 27,000 acres of swamp and woodland between Kissimmee and Orlando in 1964. Not until 17 years later did other Hollywood studios, appalled at the price of Californian property, decide to follow him east, and by then Walt had set his 'Imagineers' loose and their incredible playground across 43 square miles stood large as Manchester, 80 times the size of Hyde Park. Against such a fibreglass fantasyland, Blackpool is Lilliput.

Cinderella's Castle alone cost £2 million, and would make Ludwig even madder. The Haunted House was almost ready when I arrived – they were just moving in the ghosts. It stood near an idealised 1890 Main Street. Alongside manmade animals, 37 lifesize Presidents 'authentically garbed by Californian tailors' were in action, computers controlling 24 body movements a second. Some of these grotesque living dolls talked. Seven-foot audio-animatronic bears in Grizzly Hall sang about Davy Crockett. Artificial lakes heaved as arti-

ficial waves pounded manmade islands. They were building
Cambodian ruins, while knocking them down elsewhere.

Walt created this vast spread because at his Californian
Disneyland, opened in 1955 and inspected by ten million
visitors a year, outside promoters make four times his profit
out of *his* crowds. Their surrounding motels, Spaghetti
Heavens and gas stations press-in and cash-in along concen-
tric circles of ugliness. Visitors must pass through them all,
twice.

In Florida, determined this time to contain his captive
audiences while they had any cash left, Disney decreed
they should stay, as well as play, so built 'a total destination
resort'. Phase 1 had five giant hotels – the first so vast express
monorails were running right through a fourth-floor lobby
big as a football field and silently disgorging passengers at
Reception. I watched the last of its 1,057 modular rooms,
prefabricated down to the wallpaper and bathroom mirrors,
being slotted in.

Another four motels, camping and trailer parks, hotel for
pets, 200 ships on five lakes, a submarine fleet, two railways,
park for 12,000 cars, two golf courses, a nature reserve . . .
were imagined and created. An $800 million Community of
Tomorrow is about to open and amaze us all.

Though this time held at a distance, developers flew
towards Disney's honey. In satellite new towns for 80,000
inhabitants, 18-storey motor inns grew overnight to siphon
off the crowds. Hot-dog-and-motel strips surrounded his
phantasmagoria, hungrily. The gentle countryfolk of those
ravished countries were slow to realise the magnitude of
Disney's impact. Kissimmee, once a trading post and the
State's Cow Capital, even had a gallop-in bar. A magazine
called it 'Bovine-orientated Kissimmee'.

There, and at the senior-citizens community of Winder-
mere, residents discovered Disneyland brings profit to promoters and real-estate men; to others – increased taxes, Cup
Final traffic every day, roads jammed solid for 25 miles,
crime, drugs and general disruption imported by the
onrushing millions. 'We're overwhelmed by people-
problems,' an apprehensive County official told me. 'If

everyone only drops *one* gum wrapper, we're knee-deep in wrappers.'

So central Florida had greatness, of a sort, thrust upon it. In the fastest-growing area of the United States, Disneyworld brought the wildest statistics since space flight. To the Florida domain it adds £3,000,000,000; at least 1,000 hotels, restaurants and service stations; 80,000 jobs. The frantic landrush sent promising one-acre scrubland sites up to £125,000. Disney's take in the first year was more than £40 million – much of it from concessions. The Florida Citrus Commission paid £1½ million for the ten-year right to sponsor a pavilion selling orange drinks; Gulf Oil put up £7 million, Eastern Airlines £4 million. Big Business hoped some of Disney's wholesome mystique would rub off on their customers and that under his childish spell visitors would be in the right mood 'to accept the Corporate message'. Could be – for the international institution peddles instant-happiness to a passive public which empties its mind and queues contentedly to buy.

Disney 'Imagineers' are chillingly efficient, they improve upon and tidy up nature. On Swiss Family Isle a giant tree spreads magnificently; only when you touch do you find branches are fibreglass on steel, leaves vinyl. It's creepy. Clouds of pigeons wheel around sunset ceremonies, their primary feathers pulled out until they learn to straighten up and fly right! Dissatisfied with all available pansies, they bred a longer-lived strain that is *faceless*. There's Disney for you.

My reaction to his original Californian operation was, I think, typical: I went to smile tolerantly, stayed to be mildly enchanted. Florida is the same, only more so; impossible not to succumb to such homespun charm, however phoney and oversweet. Not a child's world, but a middle-aged view of what a child's world might have been . . .

The man himself spun fantasies and relished an innocence that did not mix with the times. Walt Disney, a sort of genius, ignored the difference between children and adults. His sweet and harmless vision – mawkish, sugar-coated – reconciled generations and awakened old, warm dreams. The

Montage!

man-child who never tired of toys died of cancer at 65. He has not gone short of memorials.

In his work he escaped criticism by being resolutely cleancut and against sin; but his patriotic nursery whimsy is also waxen predigested nostalgia and a caricature of American history. The individuality of man and nature lies smothered by plastic, controlled by computers. Man dehumanised, nature defiled – but there I go again, being rude to cute mice . . .

At close quarters the insufferably sugary front displayed by this pushy industrial complex left me a trifle queasy. A sharp sense of double-entry book-keeping pervades, and all is artificial – even those stunning white smiles, switched on and off with chill discipline. Over the whole dollar-hungry scene hangs a Jehovah's Witness sense of mission and drive.

The simple mass psychology taught at the Disney 'University' in California aims at keeping Audiences in a spending mood. In Euphemismland crowds are Audiences, customers Guests, concessionaires Participants, uniforms Costumes. Hosts and Hostesses learn how to be 'People specialists'. This seems to mean constant grins and canned answers.

One of the blonde all-American Hostesses told me: 'When you work for Disney the glory falls upon you and you start to glow – it's Pixie Dust!' She did not smile when she said that, unfortunately, but she was glowing all right.

'Remember the story of Peter Pan? That's what Pixie Dust is to us. When we spread it, we spread happiness and the Disney feeling over employees and Guests. To me Walt Disney is my life: he's given me seven wonderful years!'

Indeed, he seemed about to be canonised. Though far from popular in his lifetime, employees' eyes brightened at his name and legends grew more loving as the years slipped by and good works proliferated. In discreet corners throughout Disney's ever-growing empire, small portraits now await their candles.

All his Hostesses seemed blonde and appetising, with lots of white teeth. 'You have to be screened to make sure you fit the Disney image,' one told me, 'that you don't get spots, that your hair's not too long.' I admitted a growing suspicion that

I would not get through their golden gates, and she studied me critically: 'Probably not. You could do with quite a bit of renovation.'

It was the truth. Rashly I asked what I needed to do – and got the Disney message straight between the eyes: 'Shave off your moustache, your sideburns and have a haircut. Your glasses *might* be all right if you were behind the scenes, but in front of the public you shouldn't really wear them. It would help to polish up your teeth. Also no limps and no pimples.'

I was thankful to win two points, however low on the list, but ventured defensively that surely Walt Disney had a moustache?

'The thing is, it's uncontrollable. Once you allow an infringement of the basic rules, you'd find your moustache would become a long walrus . . . The compensation is that with the Pixie Dust, you're honoured and respected in the community and you automatically become an Accepted Social Person.'

My realisation that I could never handle such dizzy elevation, with or without a walrus, was reinforced when a Host who had been expelled showed me one of Disney's secret backstage bibles, thick with confidential damning instructions to hire-and-fire executives: 'Height of hair from face to crown of the head should not exceed one inch. Shaving eyebrows is considered an extreme and not permitted. Men are requested to wear black shoes and black socks. The only permitted jewellery is watches and approved tie clips.'

The approved clip, I discovered, was one with Mickey Mouse on it. The watches were not required to have little gloved hands . . .

Our pilgrimage as Unacceptable People was suitably humble; we had set off to see the Wizardry, to look at a world about to be asPixillated – and emerged perplexed. This was not only due to a surprisingly inept public relations department. After driving 500 miles to Orlando we had received a guarded welcome from a clean-cut marketing man called Sandy ('This is a first-name operation, Alan'). They had their own television film to sell, he explained, so although my multi-million audience around the world might be useful,

'We prefer to control our publicity.'

Indeed they do. Chosen groups are brought in for an organised tour, lecture, brief word with selected personnel – and away, clutching files of handouts and pictures. What they cannot control, they fear – and here was this unchosen Englishman, about to say and ask goodness knows what. When you wish upon Disney's star, it makes a *lot* of difference who you are . . .

After much charming hesitation and a lot of wholesome telephoning, Sandy allowed we might film, provided not more than ten minutes of Disneyworld appeared in the programme. (We eventually used seven minutes.) We began filming carefully, to do the extraordinary place justice, but next morning a gritty PR man called Charles ('Now lissen here, Alan . . .') abruptly ordered us to leave the site by midday. It seemed Mickey Mouse had had second thoughts.

I found it almost a relief to meet someone being thoroughly nasty – at least there was nothing bogus about *his* attitude. He did not say 'These 27,400 acres are too small for both of us' but he did imply, with a stern stare over my left shoulder, that if we were still there, come sundown, we should be run out of town. It was High Noon in Fantasyland, and the Pixie Dust was coming down sour.

We departed, meek but sorrowful. Who can fight a Snow White army? Our hardhats were taken away, sadly and symbolically, and Disney's uniformed cops gave us brief automatic smiles as we drove out and away, into the sunset . . .

Let not the unsure Organisation Man's fear of the committee above cloud our reaction to Disney's staggering achievement. His earnest army makes the world's most significant attempt to solve problems of expanding leisure time – and incidentally, any problems of surplus cash in Guests' pockets. Imitations in the US, and attempts in Britain, have so far proved pallid and unappealing.

The Disney organisation is wholesome, well-disciplined and (usually) friendly – even the 45-minute funfair queues remain good natured. Within the Magic Kingdom the outsider will find no alcohol, no drugs, no litter, no sex, no uncut grass, no violence and − relief relief −no moustaches.

Instead, a reassuringly bland blend of whimsy, brilliance of imagination and cunning crowd control − a sentimental spread of antiseptic entertainment that delights those who love to get their teeth into a marshmallow-covered cream puff, artificially sweetened.

Sorry to be out of step, but this Guest (one fourteen-millionth of the annual Audience throughput) can do without such manipulation, however innocent. I'll glow my own way unDusted and unPixillated, thanks, if it's all the same to St Walt.

Let's face it, there's something positively *inhuman* about Mickey Mouse.

PALM BEACH

How can I lie about my Age
when my Son needs a Facelift . . .

TELEVISION looks best when it ventures where No Camera-man Has Trod Before − into Papa Doc's study, running the tar-and-feather gauntlet through the Australian union town of Broken Hill, getting in (and out) of a Gulag rehabilitation camp . . . Displaying bravado beyond the call of documentary I got in, and out, of Palm Beach − a closed society behind high walls if ever I saw one.

This improbable sandbar lies 65 miles north of Miami, but in another world. Miami Beach was the place I hated so much that once, waking in one of those white hotels totally surrounded by rudeness, I fled to the airport and asked for a ticket on the first plane out to *anywhere*.

On another visit, after filming Ben Novak in his giant Hotel Fountain*blue*, I was escaping north on the Floridas Turnpike on my way to Disneyworld. On impulse I peeled-off and cut through the grim reality of tropical suburbia towards the Atlantic and the golden ghetto of Palm Beach which, I had been told, showed what God could have done if He had money . . .

I was braced for wonderment, but once across one of the three bridges separating the island from reality, found it flat and unspectacular. Most homes on the neat and manicured sandbank lay behind the tallest, thickest hedges I had ever seen. Its impenetrable life was evidently lived behind impenetrable foliage – which was just the way the Civic Association wanted it. Unlike Miami's promoters, Palm Beach struggles to *discourage* tourists.

Some years later, filming a Cities series across America, I had looked at Anchorage as a Frontier city, Charleston for its History and Mormon Salt Lake City for Religion. Palm Beach had to be our ultimate Social city – if only those hedges could be breached. For a century it had been the Mecca of super-rich who felt improperly dressed without a yacht and faced only one money problem: how to spend it.

So, greatly daring, I went to take a close look at its outlandish population, and catch Society in the act. Not to do the old familiar television hatchet job: intercut poverty in the Bronx and Georgia, and cover with a few sneers. That would have been easy, but mindless. Instead, an inside view of the financial peak of capitalism, at the people who had made it and were dauntlessly standing up and spending it for good ole Private Enterprise.

A balancing interrogation of the families of the Masters of Russia would surely have been equally illuminating. I should love to carry the Whicker's World cameras into those private stores for Commissars stuffed with foreign goods, into the special tailors who cut those square button-three Politburo suits, and the vodka parties in country homes. What fun to watch them preparing for the Bolshoi and arriving in black limousines driven along reserved lanes . . . Unfortunately at the Soviet extreme they all live beyond guards and beyond observation. Frivolous Palm Beach is certainly no Kremlin, but in a happily uncontrolled world its inhabitants, though without power over millions, are similarly favoured and privileged above the rest of us.

Flying south from London on the long-hop to Miami to see whether such an intrusive programme was possible, I examined my attitude towards this secret society every American longed to join. To the tolerant, such Rich could be enjoyed as a pageant, a glittering entertainment. Like the Poor, they are always with us. Making money has ever been a proper American occupation, and rarely resented. It may be comforting to believe they have merely been lucky, but the secret of such success has usually been work, or intelligence.

In any land, when the hereditary-wealthy lose their spark, their financial genius, when sons and grandsons cannot match up to the Old Man and the blood thins and the family line shrivels . . . new Rich appear overnight to replace them, changing attitudes and blending into the froth of society. Few families manage to hold on to their money for long, so take the familiar economic rollercoaster: shirtsleeves to shirtsleeves in three generations . . .

As patricians become effete or are liquidated by taxation, we wander around their crumbling stately homes and, in a way, mourn them – as we do the dinosaurs. Their surrendered jewellery and displaced furniture stands on display in museums and their auctioned treasures fall into corporate or foreign hands. We read books about their lives and wonder why the intolerant merely focused puritanical fury upon their obvious faults.

Surely it would take a mindless militant with programmed reactions to resist an ironic laugh at the truly preposterous idiocies of Palm Beach? To entertain the Duke and Duchess of Windsor, Anita Young, widow of a railway tycoon, built a villa which even then cost £4 million, mainly because her French architect drew his plans in centimetres – which her American builder thought were inches. With more than twice the house she expected, Mrs Young went *un*metric in quite a big way . . .

When another resident died his servants stored him in the walk-in freezer and went right on drawing their wages every week. They would probably still be doing so had the bank not caught on when they tried to give themselves a raise . . .

I flew over the island, admiring its waterside backdrop of pale palaces and attendant white yachts. In such an extreme world, behind such high hedges, I doubted whether we should ever achieve our programme.

We started filming, tentatively. Then, with growing enthusiasm, the whole project became a happy challenge and fun to shoot. The scenes were scintillating, the subjects pleasant, the situation gloriously sunlit, the food awful, the crew content. It was good to be filming with Mike Tuchner as director again, for the first time since BBC days. More important – and breaking Whicker's Law that only discomfort and unease bring television success – the programme was well received. I had first recce'd seriously in December 1976 and filmed during the next months – yet ever since, whenever strangers come up to talk television, out of 106 Whicker's Worlds for ITV this is the programme they remember best of all.

Critics may condescend and Trots snarl, yet viewers evidently enjoyed this illuminating look at glossy, far-out people living extraordinary lives and saying silly and amusing things.

Our penetration of the hedges left TV programmers with a lesson which American networks, at least, were quick to act upon. NBC hurried to Palm Beach to cover our documentary. Though of course far better known down there, their programme was somehow short on understanding and humour, and left a sour taste; certainly it was not much fun.

Let us admit, the ridiculous place does invite attack. Even its birth followed a disaster: the Spanish ship *Providencia*, loaded with 20,000 coconuts from Trinidad, was wrecked one night out in the Atlantic. Its cargo floated ashore and provided an island 14 miles long and about half a mile wide with a splendour of stately palms. The first settler drawn to their elegant shade was a Civil War draft dodger, and by

1873 the population was eight. Then Henry Flagler built his East Coast railway and, to find passengers and spare the Rich their winter pilgrimage to Europe, created a great hotel. Just as turtles always return each year to lay their eggs upon the same Florida beach, so Society has come back seasonally ever since.

A writer who had been observing the social scene for the *New York Times* since 1963, Charlottte Curtis gave me her professional view of Palm Beach today: 'It's the American answer to Monte Carlo, a place to come to prove you've made it. If you're the hair-curler king from Tulsa, Oklahoma or wherever, how do you *know* you've made it until you're accepted in Palm Beach? It's a validation point for success in America, for living out the American Dream.'

I wondered whether she found it a silly fantasy world or a promised-land, whether she was envious or scornful? 'I'm amused and I'm educated. In today's cold wave I've learned that people sleep in sable coats, for even the rich get cold and diamonds don't really keep you warm – though their problems are usually at a different level. For instance, they have to decide whether to wear a diamond tiara or a ruby tiara to go out to dinner, to choose between seven or eight furs, to opt for the Lowestoft china or the Meissen china . . . They're the tastemakers.'

All wealth is relative, and sometimes – an illusion. John Jacob Astor observed, 'A man who has a million dollars is as well off as if he were rich.' In Palm Beach *everyone* is rich; it is full of run-of-the-millionaires who are not at all an endangered species. Ridiculously opulent, it remains one enclave where the rich-rich can enjoy something denied them elsewhere: insulated privacy. The place stands for Achievement in a society that invented Success, and even residents ask each other, 'Where do you live, in real life?'

That lifestyle is always extreme. There are 100-room 'cottages' with 10-car garages. A householder will spend £30,000 a year with a contract gardener, just to turn a dense foliage to the world, while beside his swimming pool four telephone lines reach out to reality. Overlooking Lake Worth, the $2,000,000 home of James and Zuita Akston had a glorious pool with 26,000 mosaic tiles, a marvellous art collection – and only one bedroom. He was unworried about thieves because his art was so massive: 'You would have to *pay* them to carry it out.'

On the Atlantic side, an earlier dreamhouse: a castellated fortress with 129 rooms and countless bedrooms which, when its owner Mrs Merriweather Post of Post Toasties died and bequeathed to a grateful State . . . Florida found it could not afford.

This was no shame, for the Federal Government in Washington had found it could not afford her boats. Mar-a-Lago had been built in the Twenties in the extreme Spanish-Moorish style much favoured in Palm Beach. It inspired a certain Harry Thaw, who had just killed the architect Stanford White in a romantic dispute over an actress, to exclaim: 'My God – I shot the wrong architect!'

Palm Beach always displays a nice sense of indifference to the outside world. The one big hotel refused to accommodate King Saud of Saudi Arabia because it could not cope with 'all those strange diets – all that publicity'. The island has been equally unwelcoming to Jews, excluding them from the stately golf clubs that are its heartland and forcing them to create their own Country Club with a particular exclusivity: no one to be considered for membership before donating some enormous sum to charity – a million dollars suggested.

Way out west in California, Beverly Hills houses today's overachievers – though once you stop achieving, nobody talks to you. On the steamy Florida coast, Palm Beach is for those who have *already* achieved and are resting on their pile. Perforce, most are elderly; the unkind call it God's Waiting Room and the scene can indeed make visitors Feel So Young . . .

The population of 10,000 goes up to 35,000 during the winter high season when residents return from their second homes and outsiders slip in to be seen, and to envy. I slipped in too, and the hedges proved less hard to breach than expected. I knew a few people living there and after a party or two, invitations snowballed. There was also the advantage of being a new face bringing a different smalltalk, another outlook, into a closed group that only met itself at every gathering.

The place seemed populated by Bathroom Billionaires known socially by their products, not their names. The life-pattern of Success being what it is, most of them were widows: Mrs Gillette, Mrs Listerine, Mrs Q-Tips, Mrs Absorbine . . . Among the few surviving Bathroom Men were Mr Kleenex and Mr Alka-Seltzer; Mr Borax had got fed up with his title, and left town.

I spent a typical Palm Beach day on the 92-foot yacht of thrice-widowed Mrs Mary Woolworth Donohue, blonde baton twirler and star of a 1948 Chicago television circus show. The *Mary Hartline* could sleep seven, carried her social secretary and, on deck, a small white car. She had just turned down $4½ million for one of her three Palm Beach homes which, when we went there for a drink afterwards, I noted was protected by bodyguards, five security systems and four great danes. It had been designed by Palm Beach's favourite architect of the Twenties, Addison Mizner, who was strong on balconies and bell towers but often forgot to put in the stairs. Today it is thought rather chic to own a house where the staircase is an afterthought. The mansion had 85 telephones, and was not cosy. There was nothing on display from Woolworths.

Palm Beach is a Girls' town, run by girls for other girls of a certain age, so its excitements concentrate upon the frivolous: shopping and dressing-up and parties and going-out. It is impossible to be overdressed. Its restaurants are opulent and noted for exorbitant prices and some of the world's worst food served with a condescending flourish and an open palm. I took Celia and Victor Farris to dinner at one lush clipjoint and raised my voice in outrage at the miserable food and service. The Maître d' was indifferent but my guests tried to shush me, muttering in anguish, 'They won't give us a table next time'. I thought this an undisguised blessing but in deference to their residential status, paid up and shut up.

It has, as you might expect, one of the best and most carefully regulated shopping streets in the world, full of famous names. Despite the tropical heat, no one may stroll

Worth Avenue from Cartier to Gucci to Van Cleef in too-casual gear; regulations insist upon 'customary city wear'. There is no ugly neon, no laundry or fishmarket, no hospital or mortuary. However, with an average age of nearly 60, Palm Beach has the busiest paramedics in the land. Their £50,000 mobile Intensive Care Unit, donated by a local widow, averages three emergency cases a day, usually men. Each represents a severe blow not only to the victim but to the resident regiment of women, for every time the siren screams they see another rare escort spirited away . . .

The matriarchal society, where the New Money spends it and the Old Money sits on it, has a stern pecking order. Only that Old Guard, its aged ranks thinning, stands aloof. Behind the reigning Queen, a number of aspirant Princesses jostle for position. In her retinue are the names you see in the columns, from Mrs Rose Kennedy to Lady Rothermere to Estee Lauder, for the place lavishly supplies that inescapable mainstay of journalism, the pub and, I suppose, life: gossip.

In this outpouring of society silliness there are two questions not even the closest of friends will ask each other. One concerns husbands. No-one casually inquires, 'How's George?' for during the boring summer low-season when everyone leaves town and looks at new faces elsewhere, George may have been turned in for a later model. The other is: 'Incidentally my dear, just how old are you?'

Juliette de Marcellus told me, 'It's against the law to be over twenty-five'. Hostess Helene Tuchbreiter was quite firm: 'There's *nobody* old in Palm Beach. I'm 39 and holding. Alternatively, I'm between 21 and death. I don't care how old I am, chronologically, as long as I don't *look* old. In America you don't find the European veneration of the older woman, which is a beautiful thing to see. We don't have it here. We just don't have it here.' Ann Hamilton's honest exasperation gave us our title:'How can I lie about my age when my son needs a facelift . . .'

So Palm Beach in its insular way ignores the passing years. Should it ever be forced to acknowledge that time is marching on, the most personal and indelicate of calendars has been created. Just as China has the Years of the Snake and

the Ox and the Monkey . . . so Palm Beach has The Year
One Side of Mrs So-and-So's Facelift Fell. The Year
Madame X went to Paris and Had All Her Blood Changed.
The Year Mrs Whatsername's Bottom Ribs Were Removed
(creating a wasp waist and an outstanding profile). Such
major events freeze the circulation of party life and are
recalled by other uplifted ladies with horrified delight.

The results of this expensive and painful quest for youth
can be remarkable. The only reigning social Princess who
refused to talk with me before my camera murmured she was
afraid her wrinkles might show. Leaving gallantry aside, I
could see no wrinkle – not even the scars she was actually
worried about. She looked around 32, or maybe 39 in a hard
light; then she confided that she had just become a great-
grandmother. Never underestimate the power of new blood.

The most noticeable aspect of life amid such rich and
rewarding reconstruction was the shortage of escorts. Even I
was in demand. Indeed it is said a man needed only a dinner
jacket and a little smiling smalltalk – and he was a social
success. Ageless matrons, overdressed and overdecorated,
waited in solitary splendour to emerge from their soft lighting, needing only an arm to hold, a hand to raise them from
the shadows of the Cadillac into the fluorescence of Life.

One afternoon we drove north up Ocean Boulevard and
past the Country Club, to chat with two darkly-attractive
divorcées: Ann Hamilton, mother of the actor George, with
four or five husbands to her credit, and Grace Brownlow,
who had done well with property in Arizona and scored
three, so far. We settled down in the art deco black and white
drawing-room of Ann's ocean-front house for a conversation
every viewer seems to remember, which of course went on far
longer than we could show.

We first considered that man-shortage. Even for gay
divorcées, it had sad undertones: 'I think we all get to the
point of desperation at times,' said Ann. 'We'll go out with
somebody we wouldn't be caught dead with in ordinary
circumstances. I used to say I couldn't understand people
being bored and lonely, but I *have* been lonely this last year.
You know, your children love you, but in a very selfish way.

You're sort of left alone and you think, Oh God. I mean, what do you *do*? Everything's fine during the day, but it becomes night and there you are, and you think – Do I go out with somebody I really don't want to be seen with? Yet it's better than sitting at home alone and watching television.

'I wish I could import the men I know in Hollywood, the ones who *didn't* make it in the movies but are absolutely divine, and sell 'em down here. I'd have a marvellous business. It's not easy in Palm Beach – it's dog-eat-dog. Sometimes you just have to call and say Would you like to go to this party with me? And of course the attractive men usually have no money. I won't pay anyone to take me out – I mean I'm not that desperate and I'm sure Grace isn't either, but there are a lot here who *are*, and don't mind. Well, they have enough money – so why not? If you are the age when you can't attract them, you must buy them.'

'After all,' said Grace, reasonably, 'what can you buy that's more important than a handsome man? But one of Ann's problems is that she's extremely critical, and if you're going to be critical you won't find anybody you like. I bring in someone who's an absolute knock-out and she'll say, "He was wearing suede shoes. Don't bring him round any more." '

'I'm a Virgo and I'm very picky,' Ann explained. 'I always look at the man's shoes first thing, and I can tell whether he's chic or whether he's tacky. When I get in an elevator or on a plane I look down – then I know whether I want to look up or not.'

Competition was so fierce a socialite needed to be tough – or fast on her feet. 'Someone was bragging at a party that she could buy and sell Palm Beach, which was ridiculous. One, who was lovely, said to the other, who was not so lovely, "I could help you quite a bit in Palm Beach." The other said "I really don't need you," whereupon the first one got up and hit her. So the other little lady, who really is a lady I can tell you but she's also 90lbs of karate expert, she got up too and knocked her off her chair. Used three karate chops.

'I find women are terribly nice to me now, which is frightening. Women hated me when I was young but now they like me, and that's awful. That means you're no longer a threat. They're sweet, but they don't include you because they don't need you.

'I was with George up in the Poconos and all these darling little old ladies interviewing me for the *Atlanta Journal* asked, "How do you manage to look so young?" I said, With a bottle of Nivea and a needle and thread. I'd much rather go to the cosmetic surgeon than the dentist – it's not nearly as painful. I think I encouraged an awful lot of them to go out and do the same thing. I just don't know why everyone doesn't have everything lifted. It makes you feel better, so I think you live longer. If you go to the mirror and this old creep appears, you think Dear God – why even *bother*? I would just love to lie down and have them lift everything from my feet on up to here, and whatever's left over – tie in a little bow at the top.'

She recalled a New York party attended by the old movie star Constance Bennett: 'She wanted her daughter to meet George. She had a marvellous face once, sunken but beautiful, but she was almost hiding from me – she looked like a road map, you know, just 9,000 wrinkles. I was talking to my son and I said, "My God, Bill, Connie's face has gone, absolutely gone."

'The next time I see her she comes in looking like her *daughter*. I'm really shocked beyond belief, 'cos she looked like she was in her prime, 20 or 30 years ago – and that's marvellous. So I walk over and I say: Connie, is that really *you* in there . . .?

'I first had *my* face done in Paris. I was 43 or something, but I was going with this attractive man and he thought I should. I had it done again in California – I had my face sanded, with a diamond needle. My skin loooked like a baby's. Then I had my bosoms done. I'd lived with these things since I had three children. They said I didn't need any transplants or anything, they were just going to make a brassière out of my skin, and I said, With my luck, I'll die tomorrow – but if I do I want to be buried topless, 'cos God knows if I've had 'em done I want somebody to *see* 'em.'

One characteristic of the matrimonial hurly-burly was that everyone seemed to have been married to two or three residents, thus confusing the outsider. 'In Palm Beach no-thing ever changes,' Judy Schrafft told me, 'except the combinations. It's always the same old faces – they just happen to be reshuffled every now and then. I really think everybody in town has had everybody else, at one time or another.'

One worrisome factor about multi-marriage was that the new husband or wife was not automatically endowed with the family membership at the Bath and Tennis, the Ever-glades, the Sailfish, the Beach . . . Such a privilege was not handed down, for if the club selection committee did not approve of the member's choice of a new partner – the marriage was irrevocably split.

Despite astronomical fees and subscriptions, the clubs were the core of existence and desperately difficult to infil-trate. Palm Beachers often went to their graves while still on some waiting list. So the newly-married members then had a terrible decision: a drop in social status, or a dropped spouse? It had to be faced: a new partner was more readily available than a membership . . . It seemed to me it would save time and trouble and family feuds if all broody Palm Beachers checked first with their selection committee before Popping the Question.

Palm Beach has always had its Queens. Queen Eva – Mrs. E. T. Stotesbury, a Philadelphia banker's wife – ruled during the Twenties and Thirties. Then Mrs Marjorie Mer-riweather Post ascended; she lived in that enormous Mar-a-Lago with a private golf course and 49 servants – and closed the place during World War II when she could only find 46. She had four husbands, flew friends in by private airliner and loved square-dancing. Though stone-deaf, she kept time by feeling the band's vibrations through the floor. Apart from providing music and a footman behind every chair, her hospitality was not lavish; guests summoned to appear and to dance with abandon for two hours after her regulation ration of two drinks, resorted to hip-flasks. She died at 86.

As we filmed, the Queen was Mrs Mary Sanford, a chorus girl and actress in the Twenties and Thirties who was still given to dresses slit to the waist, with see-through tops. After marrying the polo-playing 'Laddie' Sanford in 1933 she had been snubbed, but lived to exact revenge and see her regal position acknowledged by all – with amusement maybe, but nevertheless with deference.

I asked the Schraffts about Royal qualifications: 'You can't be a 90lb weakling and become the Queen of Palm Beach,' said Judy. 'A big name also makes a big difference. She needs to have lived here a long time. She has to have several houses around the country and possibly in Europe and be prepared for a big charity scene and some very publicity-conscious living. Some of the Princesses are quite frenzied – it's nothing but ego of course, but because Palm Beach is in the world's spotlight socially, being important here is being recognised, worldwide.'

I could hardly go along with that, since even as an avid collector of people and an international reader I had heard of few of their social stars – indeed some seemed rather bogus. 'I've been in Palm Beach, off and on, for 15 or 20 years,' Judy agreed, 'and every year has had its classic phoney who's come and tried to make a splash. Some day I'm going to write a book on the Phoney of the Year. There's always a Countess or a Duchess or somebody ploughing through the town – who turns out to be from Toledo, Ohio.'

Later George and Judy came to stay with me in Jersey to see how the other half lived without phoneys. Afterwards they were driving north to play at Gleneagles when our programme went out, and found people asking for their autographs. Palm Beach suddenly became fashionable on this side of the Atlantic and various villa-renting companies jumped upon the publicity. Since then its outside fringe has seen an invasion of visiting British, about whom Insiders have mixed feelings.

Juliette de Marcellus also came over to the Channel Islands to sample our simple life and stunned a friend of mine who lived at Inkerman Lodge by christening it Income-and-Dodge. Any island similarity ended there. She had been brought up in Palm Beach, was an articulate and attractive musician and her father a French Count – yet despite such impeccable credentials, bore one inexcusable burden in Palm Beach: she was single.

'I haven't been invited to a dinner party for six or seven years,' she told me. 'I have lots of friends, but I think hostesses are frightened I might make off with their husbands: but if you've been divorced or widowed from a rich man you've gone through the tribal initiation necessary to be a Mrs Somebody, so that's all right.

'Being French, we were always told by my father that a young woman wasn't interesting. He thought they were silly children until they were 40, but America hasn't learnt that. You have to be 25. Palm Beach is full of 70-year-olds putting stretchy things around their heads to make their faces look flatter and blonde wigs and all these extraordinary methods and means to try and stay just a few years younger. They're holding death at bay. They have nothing to do with their later years, they have no occupation, no thoughts, nothing to resign themselves to . . . so they just go on with the party until they drop dead – and then the paramedics emergency unit comes and tries to give them a few more months.

'But you don't get mugged here and the weather is lovely for people who are older and have arthritis. I suppose it's a land of make-believe. You can come here and be a European aristocrat, if you can rent a tux and grow a little moustache. You can be a conductor – we've had several symphonic conductors who may not have known which end of the baton to hold, but as long as you can pay for the merry-go-round, you can be anything you like.

'The Kennedys were unpopular here because they were rather vocal Democrats; also this very cutting anti-Semitism began to be rather shocking. As a musician I think it is staggering that when Leonard Bernstein came here with the New York Philharmonic they couldn't have a dinner party for him at the Everglades Club . . . Well, that's just savagery.

'When we first came here I was very little and nobody, for instance, would dream of having a photographer at their party. Then gradually the *nouveaux* came and blotted out the scene. Now I think the main reason for giving a party is to have the photographs, and people write to an advice column and ask, 'Is it right to have the photographer consummate the wedding?'

To me, this is the most curious characteristic of Palm Beachers: their craving for carefully-controlled acknowledgement. The attitude is agonisingly ambivalent: they hate publicity yet yearn to see themselves in print, being suitably social. Such validation seems imperative, for if they are not seen at parties, people assume they are dead – and if their pictures are not in the papers, they begin to believe it *themselves*.

The tiny sandbar where women dress up to go to Publix, their splendid supermarket, supports two papers and a number of giveaways. All are stuffed with scintillating people gritting their teeth at the camera. As usual, prints of the most flattering photographs go off to willing victims after every event, on spec, along with a bill for £6 each. After grand parties, the Hostess's great bound albums cost several hundred pounds. The photographs are almost always accepted. If the ladies do not buy there is the haunting possibility that next time they see their picture in the paper . . . they may look their age.

Such mutual-aid guarantees that only good pictures get released, for residents and photographers need each other. On the stage of Palm Beach, every night is a First Night. After a day spent titillating, a flattering flash of bulbs at each grand entrance is a reassuring culmination. To be ignored by a waiting cameraman is the ultimate humiliation. However, photographers are only welcome when every prospect pleases: hair, furs, dress, jewels, escort, stomach in, chin up, big smile. Candid pictures are out out out.

Mort Kaye, best-known local photographer, drove a Rolls-Royce and got kissed by victims who were suitably humble. He explained: 'It's a way of life – they *need* the recognition. You get to the point where, when you have everything – the accoutrements are not enough. You want to be recognised and you want your friends to know that you're important, too. It's also a marriage market. The other day we had a photograph captioned incorrectly: we said it was a Mr and Mrs, and it wasn't. Well, that woman was on the phone three or four times a day, wanting it corrected. The paper finally had to run the picture again with the right names to establish that she was *not* married, that she was still single – and available.'

The well-produced *Daily News* ignored events outside the island and covered only local socialising. Known as 'The Shiny Street', its publisher was Agnes Ash. 'The people who come here do have a lot of money,' she told me. 'Some of it is new and some of it is old, but most of them lack a personal image, and they count on building it through the Paper. Many of them only have a few years to go when they get here, and they have to make it Big. It's like building a monument – but they do it with pictures. When I arrived here I found I needed very durable clothes, for the sleeves were coming out of my evening dresses. At parties people who wanted to be in the paper, or to have their friends photographed, would be tugging on my sleeves all the time . . .'

We considered the formidable society leaders, who all seemed to me rather tough old birds. The Duchess of Windsor, who was impossibly regal and gave everybody a hard time, was sorely missed because no replacement had emerged haughty enough to provide a summit for the ambitiously ascending ranks. 'The Queen must have a set of standards – after all, if the ladder is an escalator there's no fun in climbing it. And once you get into Society, you never really know if you're *there*. You always feel perhaps there's some other tight little circle you don't even know about, where you ought to be. That's one reason why they follow the Queens, because they think Well, if I'm in her entourage, *she* won't go wrong. It's like following the platoon leader in combat.'

I said they never seemed to be able to decide whether they were queens or chorus girls. 'Some are both – that's the old American success story. They make the toughest hostesses of all, the most severe. They know how to put on a good party, because it's like a stage setting. Often they match their gems to the decorations. The most expensive ball decorations I've heard of cost $100,000, with feathers and monkeys. There was a real monkey too, but they finally had to abandon him for fear he might attack Bob Hope, who was their favourite comedian. You could say, why don't they just give the $100,000 to charity, but they have to make these great stage settings for women to show their jewellery and their clothes, and to get their husbands out – otherwise with their golf and fishing they tend to vegetate here, and leave the women alone.'

I asked what happened to the wife when her husband passed on to that great Stock Exchange in the sky? 'Well, she'd immediately better go through her whole list of nephews and find one available to come down here and take her to parties, or kind of rent-a-nephew.

'It's a great asset for any business to have single males on its staff – it's a business-promotion thing, not really gigolo although it is, kind of. If she's very rich she can get her lawyer to take her, her interior designer, even her florist. Her cosmetic surgeon would be perfect, of course, and then he could analyse all the noses at the table.'

For the *arrivistes*, breaking into society was the only preoccupation. I had never seen so many social climbers so intent upon the next rung, and wondered how they set about it? 'First you have to buy a house in the proper place. Renting is no good, unless you rent for two months as Kitty Miller does and re-do the whole house, even re-sod the lawn. It would need a saltwater pool because, though she doesn't swim, her decorator Billy Baldwin prefers a saltwater pool. She would re-do the drapery, move in different furniture and put in a taffetta or silk on the walls instead of wallpaper. Sometimes she would dig up all the garden and put in a different shrubbery.

'Then you ought to arrange a guest for the year. It used to be the Windsors – they charged a straight fee. Or you could just get the Duchess over for a party – she wouldn't allow more than 12 guests, and she chose the menu. Even that would cost you as much as $4,000, but, of course, you would get everybody's picture taken with her after dinner, to stand on the piano for the rest of your life. Then all your guests would remember you forever.

'Or someone like Princess Grace of Monaco. Hussein is

very popular. He's jolly and goes down to Worth Avenue and spends just thousands of dollars – and he is a King, a genuine King. They *do* like genuine things . . .'

I asked why some women wore tiaras and ball gowns for little dinner parties, or evening dress and enormous diamonds for the opening of some shop in the late afternoon? 'Yes they do wear their jewels for everything – often because they're afraid to leave them at home. One man who came to live here was worried, you see, because he had a *very* small Utrillo . . .'

I was transfixed by that misfortune, and suggested perhaps some local plastic surgeon could fix it for him? This became our running gag: 'He's a nice chap, but unfortunately he's got . . .' Mrs Ash explained that this tiny Utrillo was his most valued possession and he was afraid to leave it at home because he could not afford the insurance.

Such Art is the only heavy industry permitted in Palm Beach. Floodlit instant-masterpieces line its 36 galleries, and their Tuesday night cocktail viewings are part of the being-seen scene. Most of the offerings are overbright schmuck unworthy of the Bayswater railings; a few may be oldish Masters – or middle-aged Masters trying to show their age. At a gathering in one of these cultural centres, Wally Findlay, owner of a chain of galleries, told me how he had a stock of 10,826 paintings. His encyclopaedic computer print-out showed these to be on sale for exactly $21,738,134, or offer.

The Palm Beach attitude to wealth was that while they did not want to talk about it, no no, they *did* like everyone to know they had it. I went to see Mrs Betty Battin, known as Mrs IBM after her husband, its Treasurer, left her stock even then worth $40 million, or think-of-a-figure. She was reported to be 80. Soon after our visit, she remarried.

'The one thing I will *not* discuss,' she told me emphatically, 'is money. I don't like to discuss IBM either because they think I'm talking money – even though I own, you know, *piles* of it . . .

'These men come down here and read articles in the paper and when they think no one's looking, they'll come in and rob. Up to date I haven't been robbed, but I think if you keep a sum of money in your house, when they come in you just give it to them. But I feel safer here than in New York. Even if you take a taxi there, you're not safe because these Puerto Ricans drive cabs, and no widow goes out alone in New York at night. Here I have a chauffeur. He's a private detective. But many people can't afford that. He comes here at 4 o'clock and he watches to see there isn't anyone casing the house.'

It was a stiflingly hot afternoon as we filmed and friendly Mrs IBM asked my crew would they care for a drink? They nodded furiously and their eyes lit up as a trayful of cut-crystal appeared. Their eyes died down again when the glasses were filled with water.

Such a concentration of conspicuous expenditure can hardly escape attack at many levels, though it is hard to see what critics expect the Palm Beach rich to do with their money – except perhaps give it to *them*. Through hard work or good fortune they have far more worldly wealth than the rest of us, but are spending it as hard as they can and doing no harm – and occasionally, some good. Like winning the Pools, there seems nothing basically sinful in their windfall. After the programme the most frequent disapprobation I heard was that they jolly well ought to know how to grow old gracefully, to accept their shawls and rocking chairs instead of dressing young and behaving young.

I found something more gallant than ridiculous in the sight of all those elderly girls doing their utmost to defy the years, and kicking up their heels at the rest of us.

On occasion the pampered place could reveal its heart: a small happy house near Worth Avenue did not seem like Palm Beach at all. Christine Vollmer's seventh child Leo, born brain-damaged, was being helped to live by manual exercise performed by a group of 15 volunteers. Between them they spent eight hours every day moving his limbs in an attempt to teach his brain what it felt like to breathe properly. As we filmed one woman exercising the boy, his mother said, 'Each volunteer spends a whole morning or afternoon with him. I never would have imagined Palm Beach people could be so generous with their time, so punctual and so dependable.'

Living amid criticism, Palm Beach is ultra-sensitive. Every author who has dared write a book about the place has had to leave town, for anything short of adulation is regarded as hostility. John Ney was quite a long way short: he wrote that its social leaders were 'ex-chorus girls, ex-caddies, ex-policemen, ex-hairdressers, ex-beachboys and ex-callgirls.' *He* didn't last long.

I went to the apartment of that friend of Scott FitzGerald, the columnist Sheilah Graham, who had also written – though more gently. She recalled her first visit: 'In a Worth Avenue gallery I met Greg, who'd been my leg-man in Hollywood when he was 19 years old. He's 50 but he looked younger than I remembered him because he'd had several face-lifts and wore the most marvellous wig. He gave a dinner for me and suddenly I was being asked to every single party in town and I thought, Oh what a lovely place – they all love me. But it wasn't that they loved me, they love *anyone* who's a bit different, who's a bit of a celebrity. What I'd rather liked was that all the old ladies refused to be old. When you go to any of these charity things, you see them whopping-around, having a marvellous time.

'To succeed here you must have money and lots of it, you must be white, preferably Protestant, but you can be practically anything if you have enough money – though because that's common here, you must have attention as well. What's the use of having money if you don't show it?'

Gwen Fearon had been a local estate agent for 38 years and knew all about visible money: 'Ten or 15 million dollars is nothing in Palm Beach, absolutely nothing. One woman was telling people she considered herself very rich because she'd been left 50 million dollars, and a friend who lived right down the road told her, That's just peanuts in Palm Beach. You couldn't *possibly* get along on that . . .

'The people who buy my houses may want to give a party for eight hundred guests out on their patio, and bring in one or two orchestras. Very few people have more than four or six help, so they just call in the caterer, go off on their yacht in the afternoon, come home and get dressed – and the party's all set up. They bring in the tables, the linen, the silver, the crystal and the whole thing. Afterwards, it all disappears.'

I filmed one such party which Celia Farris, an aspirant Princess, was giving for 400 intimate friends in her lovely old home. It had a particularly elegant cloakroom which I was sharing with her tycoon husband Victor one day. He recalled a friend gazing around at the old marble and gold taps and subdued lighting during a reflective pee and commenting ruefully, 'This place makes my cock look shabby . . .'

The whole setting did have an aura. Before her marriage our Hostess had been Celia Lipton, daughter of the bandleader at the Grosvenor House Hotel, so she knew about presentation. An enormous marquee had gone up in her garden, the band was electrifying its instruments, drink and food and 30 waiters were arriving by pantechnicon. I walked around with Celia, already reaching a state of controlled panic: 'My husband is upstairs working on an invention while I've been doing all this work, bless him. Once he gets ready though, he really enjoys himself.'

During the preparations the musical Victor had been quietly playing the organ and doubtless reflecting upon the £10,000 tab he would soon have to pick up. However, the event was indirectly supporting the Norton Museum of Modern Art, which would soften its impact, tax-wise.

As the favoured 400 gathered in the twilight and 15 jockeys parked their cars, my crew jostled with a flash of local photographers recording the arrival. The Host and Hostess were submerged in a hubbub of greetings under palms in the carpeted courtyard, by now festooned with frivolity. The Queen, Mary Sandford, received a right royal welcome and an outburst of carefully-placed kisses. It was a relief to know we were at the right party. In the middle of such social ecstasy we captured one rather baffling exchange amid the barrage of camera flashes:

Celia: Victor? Victor!
Victor: Honey?
Celia: Nobody wants you anywhere but on the organ –
           right, Mary?

Mary: We want his organ.
Celia: Yes, we want his organ – er, *what* do you mean?

There was no answer to that question, except another
quick flash. It was a lovely party.

Since the object of Palm Beach life is to be seen, such
glamorous nights are regularly required to fill the Shiny
Sheet's daily schedules and keep people in motion. With
insufficient grand parties to supply the demand, art gallery
evenings and shop openings became significant; but the
major life-enhancing events are the Charity Balls, for which
hundreds dress up as never before, wining and dining lavishly for the underprivileged.

Every Ball needs a splendid lunch to launch it, followed by
regular fun-filled committee meetings. Newcomers use this
do-gooding treadmill as their entrée into society, but so many
people want to work and enjoy themselves for charity that
they have run out of Causes. There is no shortage of time or
money, merely a shortage of diseases. Palm Beach old-timers
have all the best ones tied-up, like the Heart Ball and the
Eye Ball, the Cancer and the Red Cross, Planned Parent-
hood and Mental Health. Ambitious newcomers can find
themselves eating in aid of an out-of-town Animal Shelter.

Robert Gordon, fresh from Boston real estate, had bought
a large electronic house on the Lake where the volume of the
overall Muzac softened automatically as you lifted a telephone and there was an eye-level television in the loo. 'We've
got five or six boats, counting the little ones, and a lot of
cars – two Rolls, two Jensens, the station-wagon . . .' He
also, we discovered with glee, actually had a rather small
Utrillo.

His blonde wife Arlette had just organised one of those
Balls: 'We did it for the Animal Rescue League. I think it
brought in about $60,000, for homeless animals all around
the world.'

We filmed a number of charity jump-ups, held for a variety
of good reasons.Each was spectacular. Tickets usually cost
£75, and many hostesses took a £900 table. The secret of
charity's success was that such contributions were tax de-

ductable. Food and wine and decorations – sometimes the whole dinner – could be underwritten by anybody looking for a big deduction.

At every Ball there was an auction, though it was a problem to find prizes sufficiently tantalising to interest people who had everything, several times. Even so, bidding was restrained for one donated prize: a certificate entitling the lucky winner to free open-heart surgery . . .

I spent some time with one 'high-profile social leader', Mrs Helene Tuchbreiter, a forceful and well put together Palm Beacher known as Mrs Truckdriver. She had run twelve massive Charity Balls so far, all of which called for months of work and the ruthless dedication of the General Motors sales director. Competition for the privilege of being Mrs Big was so intense rival hostesses had been known to slug each other in the Colony Hotel bar, after the Ball was over.

'When you deal with a group of women it's not going to be easy all the time,' said Mrs Tuchbreiter, soothingly. 'There are personality clashes and a bit of jealousy, and they usually say you make a lot of enemies. I've made, maybe, one or two, because I'm a hard Chairman, but I'm organised. In a few instances, which I'd rather not mention, there's been hair-pulling fights, but when you're dealing with women you're gonna have tension. I don't think we've had too many rough ones.'

As I considered that frenetic social scene with the well-arranged Mrs Tuchbreiter before a recent and even better-arranged portrait, our programme title sprang to mind, but for a variety of reasons was finally rejected: 'Balls I have held . . .'

PARAGUAY

*A truckload of Police,
for a truckload of Televisions...*

DICTATORS may not be easy to interview – but you have to
try. Sir Compton Mackenzie, you recall, thought we might
have avoided two world wars had television been able to get
its teeth into the men of decision and display them chatting in
chairs, not posturing upon balconies. Certainly Adolf Hitler
would not have remained the formidable ogre if, within the
security of our living rooms, we had watched him politely
interviewed: 'There are reports, Herr *Reichskanzler*, that
when frustrated you fall upon the floor and bite the car-
pet . . .?'

Such an amiable opening could have led to a small cell or
to a clearer indication of his personality and power. A closer
look at the loathsome Himmler or Streicher would surely
have alerted us to the possibility of Dachau, Buchenwald and
the Final Solution.

For those standing in the Piazza Venezia and looking up,
Mussolini must have seemed a commanding figure, but
Italian friends told me when making love in his Venetian
hotel his bull-like roars could be heard across the Grand
Canal. A piece to-camera with all that going on in the
background might have put him in perspective – or, just
possibly, increased his prestige. Impact can work both ways.

After the Goliaths of the last war had departed, television
came into our lives and the Mighty began to be seen in a more
accurate, more intimate light. Our leaders may still be as
great and as fearsome, I suppose – yet did we ever feel the
same way about President Carter after hearing him talk to

Rosalynn and Amy? About Papa Doc after we had seen him
throwing money out of the window of his Mercedes? About
the Colonel in the funny hat after he waved his pistol and
tried to take over the Spanish Parliament? About Khruschev
after he took off his shoe and pounded the United Nations
desk? A glimpse of reality can dispel awe, and posturing
becomes obvious. No man is a hero to his television
camera . . .

So in Latin America we went calling upon Dictators. After
a month in Argentina making a film on Gaston Perkins,
estanciero and racing driver, we flew north to Asuncion to
attempt a programme on His Excellency, General of the
Armed Forces Don Alfredo Stroessner, President of Paraguay. He was the last of the hemisphere's old style rulers and
since 1954 had controlled his little-known land, sternly and
absolutely, satisfying his countrymen's convenient habit of
obeying any order – and their weakness for a blend of ruth
less autocrat and uncle-figure.

The President's father, one of the early German arrivals in
the 1890s, had married a Paraguayan girl and started a
brewery. Stroessner, portly and blue-eyed, with cropped hair
and silk socks, still looked like a Bavarian brewer. He was in
fact the most skilled Dictator to have grasped and held power
in an unstable continent.

When we reached land-locked Paraguay he was in his
fourth term, his people were living under a permanent State
of Siege which he renewed every 60 days. The Constitution
had been suspended, yet he would doubtless have won his
elections even had they been free. His Germanic industry in
an easygoing land had earned him promotion to general at
the age of 37; his mother's Spanish-Indian blood provided
shrewd instinct and he was Commander-in-Chief when he
took over the country at gunpoint three years later. Since
then neither he nor the hard-faced and watchful henchmen of
his Colorado party had ever been seriously challenged.

One of President Stroessner's useful characteristics in that
continent of *mañana* was his ability to exist on two hours sleep
a night, after which he would telephone around his Divisional headquarters in the early hours to ensure no one was

plotting. He reached his Presidential desk at 5 a.m. Little wonder the Opposition never got going – no respectable South American Revolutionary is accustomed to working such hours.

The land he ruled so sternly was distant and forlorn, a medieval backwater with no income tax, no drainage, no traffic lights – and only three proper roads, with 275 miles surfaced. There was a military atmosphere of undisputed Generality: Paraguay was said to have as many flag-officers as the US. The Police Chief was a General, twin brother of the Mayor of Asuncion, who was also a General.

The Army ruled – and those to whom this was not Okay went abroad. It was estimated some 600,000 Paraguayans, or a third of the population, had fled. Movement in the other direction was believed to include Hitler's deputy Martin Bormann, Gestapo chief Heinrich Mueller, and the doctor from the Auschwitz concentration camp, a Bavarian called Josef Mengele who had taken Paraguayan nationality. Inquiries about new residents who had bought their way in were not welcomed.

We checked into the Hotel Guarani, a lone triangular skyscraper looming above Asuncion's peeling stucco. With the usual mass of research to be done and thoughts to be written, I borrowed a secretary-interpreter from a friendly bank manager. Anne was a London blonde, improbably imposing and statuesque – stacked, if you must know – who would have turned heads in Oxford Street. Striding around among small dark Paraguayan peasants, she was a sensation. Whole streets fell silent. Cars stopped. As usual with such wanderers, her story was unusual.

She had been a typist in Notting Hill but was desperate to learn, of all things, how to play the harp, the national instrument of Paraguay. She saved up and set off, and had reached Guyana when her travellers cheques ran out. Forced to break her journey, she went up-country to try to earn money capturing animals for zoos. She caught them all right, but they died in transit. She then married a man who owned the shack-hotel in the jungle village where she was staying, had his child, divorced him, and with a handful of settlement-money finally reached Asuncion with her son, and joined a bank. By the time we met she was an impregnable harpiste.

She warned me about the General's *pyragues*, his 'people with hairy feet' – the Political police who sat around the hotel lobby, eavesdropping upon any possibly-subversive gringo. It was typical of Paraguay that these Private Ears could not speak English, which must have restricted their reports. One Paraguayan in ten was said to be a paid informer, and the Minister of Justice admitted so many were employed they often ran out of information and had to make it up. It was a land where the Ministry of the Interior tapped your telephone – and you could *buy* the tapes . . .

I had spent enough time filming in police states to be careful about my documentation. I never take anything in to a Dictatorship that I would mind hearing read out at my court martial. I left my best-informed files, of which the political police would have disapproved, in Buenos Aires. I was careful to tear up copies of my notes as we typed them, and carry the originals. What I was not ready for – what I learned in Asuncion – was that my wastepaper baskets would be systematically emptied and their torn contents laboriously fitted together. I have never forgotten those pointless hours of work that so flattered my innocuous research notes – nor in future did I ever forget to flush everything, however innocent, down the loo.

One day, galled by our incompetent Shadows, we sent our assistant cameraman in a taxi in one direction to make a performance of filming general shots around town. When our Tails had dutifully gone off behind him the director, Michael Blakstad, and I took a skeleton crew in our hired car to film the Father Provincial of the 77 Jesuit priests in Paraguay. The Government regarded them as 'red fish swimming in holy water', but Father Manuel Segura, a courageous Spanish priest once at college at Chipping Norton, was the only critical voice I heard in that land.

'General Stroessner says there is a price you must pay for peace, and that is to allow military people, high ranking people, to do some smuggling,' he told me. 'Paraguay being a small country, he knows most of what is going on. Last year a General smuggled-in an aircraft full of television sets. They were loaded onto lorries at Stroessner Airport, but as the convoy was coming into town – the police arrested everyone!

'When the General heard this he sent out another lorry full of soldiers with machineguns and along the road they captured every policeman they passed. When they had collected 20 or 30 of them, he telephoned the Chief of Police and offered to exchange a truckload of police for a truckload of televisions. The Police Chief thought it was a fair deal, and everyone was happy.'

Father Segura told me the Government had bought from Spain four or five excellent river-ships to ply its lifeline – the vast Rio Paraguay – down through Argentina to the Atlantic, 1,000 miles away. Upon arrival their draught was found to be too great; they could only operate during four or five months of the year, when the river was high. They had been selected because they offered more commission than smaller vessels. An outraged Naval Captain made an official protest: 'Will you cut the ships in half – or pour some more water into the river?' He was then dismissed for 'disrespect' to the head of the State Fleet. The General hearing his protest was the man who had taken the commission . . .

Paraguay was the South American centre for the smuggling of black market Scotch and cigarettes, known concisely as 'goods in transit'. With fewer than two million people, it was officially the highest consumer of American cigarettes in the world. They arrived legally on scheduled cargo flights and paid a Government tax. When they left for Argentina or Brazil they were contraband, unofficially controlled by the military – a sort of generals' perk.

They went in an unmarked fleet of dark aircraft, from bi-planes carrying 200,000 cigarettes which pilots flew in sweatshirts and sneakers to keep the weight down, right up to elderly airliners. The Super-Constellation we filmed would transport nine million cigarettes, but had one disadvantage: it could not land in fields or on roads, but required a runway and well-bribed local officials. It was a risky business; one aircraft coming in to a darkened field put down on top of a 'plane that had just landed. Another, touching down on a road in the pampa near Buenos Aires, taxied to a halt outside an unlit building – which turned out to be the local police station. The Law came out, shooting.

As a sort of South American Tibet, Paraguay had lurched through the centuries, indifferent to the world outside. The 400-year-old tumbledown capital had never charmed travellers, and a century ago Sir Richard Burton wrote: 'The streets were wretched. Every third building, from chapel to theatre, is unfinished. Over the whole affair there's a thin varnish of civilisation, but the pretentions are simply skin deep. Drainage has not been dreamed of.' Paraguayans have still not had such practical dreams, and after flash rainstorms old pregnant buses ploughed through the floods like bloated gondolas.

Yet with all its man-made faults, Paraguay could still exude a sort of kindness, an air of magic. In a landscape often enchanting, it was a place apart. Strangers, softened by its improbable character, are said to cry twice: when they arrive, and when they leave. I found it a musical-comedy land always on the verge of musical-tragedy; the sort of place where you took your harp to a party – and got arrested . . .

Each year four Paraguayans qualified as engineers, seven as doctors, while 100 young men became Army officers. Apart from the possibility of profitable corruption, the Army had always required respect. Paraguayans were once forced to doff their hats to every passing soldier; country boys, who wore no clothes at all, were obliged to wear hats – so they could take them off.

Since 1811 and independence from Spain, the land has grown up in isolation, with its own language and legends. Its first President, Carlos Antonio Lopez, employed English engineers to build South America's first railway in 1858 and sent his son to Europe to buy armaments. Young Lopez picked up not only guns but – at the Gare St Lazare – a most remarkable mistress, Eliza Alicia Lynch. I cannot understand why this striking woman with her outrageous life has not become a central figure of films and books and dramas.

Born in Cork, she was married at 15 but left her husband and various protectors in Paris to sail to Paraguay with the Dictator's son, where the beguiling adventuress became in time the President's lady, and bore him five or six children. Though snubbed for years by those older families who married before their children were born, she dazzled Asuncion by her clothes, her parties, her courage.

Her President, Francisco Solano Lopez, had ordered Paraguay's Sacred College to elect him a Saint; the vote was unanimous – because the 23 members who said No were shot.

Fanatic and megalomaniac, he plunged Paraguay into the most bloody war: egged on by Madame Lynch, Lopez decided to fight three neighbours at once – Argentina, Brazil and Uruguay. At the beginning of this insane war of Triple Alliance, Paraguay's population was more than half-a-million. After five years, surviving men numbered 28,746 . . . Those the enemy had not killed had been tortured and executed by their own sadistic President until, before the eyes of Eliza Lynch, the Dictator at bay was finally hacked to death. Their country, stripped of crops and cattle and 55,000 square miles of territory, was almost wiped out. Paraguayans still talk of that war as though it happened yesterday.

Eliza had buried Lopez, along with a son, on his last battlefield, and returned to live in Thurloe Place, Kensington. Still later she went back to Paris and completed the circle as Madame of a brothel. She died in poverty.

Fifty years afterwards her ashes were returned to Asuncion to be placed in the Heroes' Pantheon – but even in a Dictatorial land there were objections, so in a casket in the Military Museum we saw the ashes of Eliza Lynch, the colleen who was amost a queen, still awaiting her final acceptance . . .

The bloodthirsty Lopez and his greedy, scheming Irish mistress are now almost sanctified; the passing of time – and a shortage of national heroes – has ennobled them. Only Paraguayans, who worship ruthless courage, could honour such blundering tyrants; other races would curse their memory for ever.

Then poor Paraguay went on to languish under a parade of

32 Presidents in 62 years, all of them instantly forgettable – yet whatever one may think of dictatorship or rule by the military, there is an argument for seeing it as the only successful form of government for the people of Latin America. Paraguayans in particular need a strong despotic control, or they fall apart. Faced with a choice, they fight among themselves. They only move ahead upon an order.

The man who gives that order, Stroessner, is a smiling autocrat who enjoys hunting, fishing and chess. One of his passions is the inauguration of buildings. He personally opens everything new in his country: schools, saw-mills, branch offices of banks. No detail of administration is too small for his bland blue eyes: the promotion of a private soldier to corporal requires his approval.

In an Air Force DC3 we flew north to the Chaco, an Indian word that means Hunting ground; larger than Britain, it was a fearful place indeed. The tired old airliner was brilliantly flown through windstorms, bouncing about in the rising hot air. The pilot would occasionally stroll back to remind me, as I sat hunched miserably in my bucket seat, 'Have no fear – God is a Paraguayan.'

Every time we landed in some unmarked desert wilderness among thorn trees and giant cacti, the scorching air outside the aircraft was so hot it was painful to breathe. We tried to film in the inferno of dust and drought and disease, of anacondas and lung fish, but the airless 110° left us gasping, and hot wind coated the eyes. The only people who could make the Chaco bloom were the Mennonites, latter-day Jesuits who arrived in 1929 and created an ordered Germanic community in a corner of the wilderness. There were 9,000 of them, riding buggies, growing beards and fearing God.

President Stroessner, who believed that a liberal Dictator and his Paraguay were soon parted, was said to have three active hates: journalists, foreign journalists and, worst of all, English-speaking foreign journalists. Back in Asuncion we reached the vast expanse of his regulation desk after the regulation hours in his ante-room

The well-filled waiting room is the Latin symbol of suc-

cess: in ante-rooms all over South America supplicants wait
upon Mr Bigger-Than-Thou who establishes his position,
his importance, his virility even . . . by the length of time he
keeps you waiting.

First you hang about in corridors on the wrong side of
armed guards. Then you mooch about in little rooms with
wooden chairs and small windows. Finally, the penultimate
promotion, you sit in bulbous chairs sipping black coffee and
waiting for admission into the inner sanctum. Folding money
can help, but you don't tip generals in waiting – not openly.

General Stroessner worked 16 hours a day, held a surgery
for his people two days a month, and was the only man in
Paraguay who could legitimately practise Ante-rooms-
manship. Eventually he permitted us in to film, but was not
an experienced listener and certainly not a man who got
asked many questions. Neither Ted Morrisby, my researcher, nor I ever finished a sentence.

His English was also inadequate for a filmed interview so
he asked for my questions, and provided answers in writing.
This was not what documentaries are about, but there was
little else we could do in an unwelcoming situation; at least
we had much film of him on his daily Dictatorial round.

To what sort of government was the Paraguayan character
best suited, I asked – was a strong man always needed? 'The
idea of a strong man, to which Europeans refer, is disparaging and unbecoming. The history of mankind was not
made by weak men. Europe in this sense acts as a universal
teacher. It would be absurd that a strong and virile nation
like Paraguay should have weak leaders with poor ideas;
Democracy without patriotism does not interest us.'

I recalled that his country had by then been in a State of
Emergency for 32 years and asked what, or who, was frightening him? 'The state of siege in some areas of my country
does not mean the suppression of liberties or civil rights. It is
only a means by which the Government keeps order, justice
and peace.' It was not inspiring stuff, but for fair play I read
out most of his answers.

Stroessner offered no fanaticism, no ideological justification for staying in power. He believed that stability and

development only followed strong rule: his rule. He took care
no heir-apparent was in sight – but when he does go it is
possible that, unlike earlier Dictators, he will leave behind
some achievement. He was slowly easing his control – so
much so that in the Asuncion newspaper *Patria* I bought at
the Airport only 16 of the 18 published photographs were of
him. The other two were footballers.

When our programme on The Last Dictator was transmitted I received a ten-page letter from the Ambassador of
Paraguay in London, who was putting himself straight with
the President. It was succinctly dismissed by Yorkshire's
Controller of Programmes, Donald Baverstock, who wrote:
'I don't think you can reply to this long-winded bilge.' I was
more affected by a letter from David Attenborough, the
Controller of BBC 2 which I had so recently deserted. In a
zoologist's reaction he wrote: 'I was brought up to believe, as
a basic principle of television, that to do a programme about
Paraguay without showing an armadillo was an act of
abnegation verging upon folly. To have managed to do so
and to have produced so smashing a programme demands
real skill. It takes qualities near to genius to break the rules.'

We left Paraguay behind to fly to Ecuador for a programme in Quito, and then on to spend some time with an
even more terrifying Dictator: Papa Doc Duvalier, President
of Haiti.

HAITI

Papa Doc – the Black Sheep . . .

In tropical twilight our aircraft touched down at Port-au-
Prince, and we stepped on to Papa Doc's Haiti. We had
landed in a despairing nation under the lash of a President for

Life whose years of absolute power had brought terror to his people and ruin to his country: We walked through the damp heat towards the decrepit Arrivals building of François Duvalier Airport and saw, seared across its peeling white plaster, a pock-marked line of bulletholes. That machinegun burst was the welcome Haiti offered its rare visitor, and it was right in character.

Inside the building, a friendlier reception from the President's official Greeter, Aubelin Jolicoeur. A small unctuous gesturing man with an ivory-handled walking stick, I recognised him instantly: he had been drawn to perfection as Petit Pierre in Graham Greene's frightening *The Comedians*.

He did his job effusively, and customs men fell back before the casual wave of his stick. He may have been smiling but other Haitians watched us, expressionless. The Tontons Macoute no longer stripped or frisked arrivals, but I was uncomfortably aware that the airport had just experienced one of those dramatic scenes that from Graham Greene would have seemed improbable fiction.

The eldest of Dr Duvalier's three daughters, his favourite Marie-Denise, had married the six-foot-three Commander of his Palace Guard, Capt Max Dominique, who instantly became a Colonel. Then Papa Doc, acting upon different advice, decided his son-in-law was involved in a plot against him for which he had just executed 19 brother-officers. After listening to the pleadings of his wife and daughter, then pregnant, he spared Colonel Dominique but sent him into exile, as Ambassador to Spain. As they left to fly to Madrid, the President and Mrs Duvalier came to the airport to say a sorrowful farewell to Di-Di.

The young couple stood at the aircraft door waving good-bye to their parents, to friends and staff. At that moment of parting, and at a sign from Papa Doc, their chauffeur and two bodyguards were shot down in front of them. Papa Doc, the master eliminator, had made his gesture of disapproval.

He turned and left without another glance at the three dying men on the tarmac. They lay in the sunlight under the eyes of horrified passengers en route from Puerto Rico to Miami, only 90 minutes away. The aircraft departed abruptly. An American airline man who had seen it all told me: 'The Captain practically took off with the door open. They just wanted to get *out* of there!'

There was no shooting upon our arrival: only those ominous marks of past executions. Outside, we were distributed among taxi drivers. They were all Tontons Macoute, Papa Doc's private army of heavy men, licensed to extort. Being a cabby was the best job in the land at the time – the only one in which a Haitian could get his hands on foreign currency. Theirs was the one Union Papa Doc permitted. My personal Tonton was a silent and sinister negro with a Gaugin face. He had the poetic name of Racine. He also had red eyes.

In the dusk we drove towards a bizarre experience, bumping through the sombre tumbledown capital and up the hill to the Castelhaiti Hotel. It was modern white concrete, but empty. That evening ours was the only occupied table in the gloomy dining-room. As we tackled some stringy chicken, a piano and violin were played mournfully in the shadows. Groups of waiters stood around in darkness, watching us and whispering. Below the broad balcony, the capital's few street lights glimmered, awaiting the regular power breakdown. It was a fearful town, hushed and tense – as though already flinching from the next blow.

We busied ourselves with preparations for a very hazardous programme. First we had to get to the remote and inaccessible Papa Doc. 'Once we've been seen with him, talking to him, we'll be all right,' said Ted Morrisby, who had arrived to research a few days earlier and had as usual tuned-in brilliantly. 'Then the Tontons and everyone else'll know he accepts us, and we won't get hassled or shot.'

In a land where people disappeared for ever, where there was no Embassy, no protection or asylum, no one to turn to . . . there was no argument against that convincing reason for trying to establish contact.

Those who live by fear, live fearfully; so Papa Doc was not easy to reach. He took care of that. His massacres had generated terror and despair and suppressed fury, so hourly he prepared for assassination. He rarely left the white American-built National Palace, the only massive building in town, which he had turned into a floodlit armed fortress – yet he was not secure even behind its walls and iron fences. The President he had ousted, Paul Magloire, had twice sent in old B25 aircraft on bombing runs. The grounds were now ringed with anti-aircraft guns and elderly armoured cars.

A murderous megalomaniac ruling a land paralysed by fear, the President also beseeched protection with a new prayer of which he was author: 'Our Doc, who art in the National Palace for life, hallowed be Thy name by present and future generations. Thy will be done at Port-au-Prince and in the provinces. Give us this day our new Haiti and never forgive the trespasses of the antipatriots who spit every day on our country . . .'

By a stroke of Whicker's Luck we discovered that Our Doc was next day making a rare excursion into the fearful city outside his Palace: he was to open a new Red Cross centre, a small building a few hundred yards away from that fortress.

We left our hotel at dawn and reached the area as troops and armed men began to assemble for the ceremony. There were hundreds of soldiers in their best khaki, with medals and white gloves and rifles. Militiamen wore blue denim with a red stripe like army hospital patients, and guns. Mingling with authority among them were men in thin suits, snap-brimmed fedoras and shades, casually carrying sub-machineguns – the Tontons.

As usual when overwhelmed by armed men enjoying a little brief authority, I adopted an attitude of polite, preoccupied condescension – like a prefect moving on a third-former whose mother was hovering. For a new and meaningful relationship with an unwelcoming guard, it helps to be politely patronising and to brandish a permanent smile. It is hard to shoot a man, or even strike him with a rifle butt, when he is smiling at you in a friendly way.

It also helps to press him warmly on the arm and say something impatient like: 'Do you mind standing aside *please*, British Television, we *must* do the President justice, thank you so much, just back a *bit* more . . .' It's the confident attitude that counts. When they expect you to be humble, a certain senior-officer asperity throws them off balance.

It is even more effective if the guards or police or hoodlums do not understand English. To attempt their language, whatever it is, instantly places you in a subordinate position of supplication and invites questions. Since adopting that haughty approach I am pleased to say I have hardly ever been shot.

So, surrounded by an air of intent professionalism and with tripod established inside their lines, we stood in the searing sunshine among what seemed like a sharpshooters' convention, waiting for Papa. After a while there was a distant roar of massed motorcycles.

First arrival was a chromium-plated Harley-Davidson, ridden by a large black dressed like a tubby boy scout; on his pillion a younger man, in a sort of beachgear. They were presumably powerful figures, and were followed at a distance by a horde of regulation military outriders, surrounding an enormous black Mercedes 600. The noisy procession had come all of 400 yards. A sort of shock ran through the massed troops.

Out of the limousine leapt a couple of portly officers with machine-guns. They stood quivering. After a long pause, a small stooped figure in a dark suit emerged, white frizzy hair under his black Homburg. Blinking behind thick lenses in the sudden silence, he asked in a hushed whisper for that Mace of Haiti, the President's *own* machinegun. It was handed to him and, reassured, he restored it to the guard. His gestures were those of fragile old age, and he walked with a slight shuffle. This was the man who had a nation by the throat . . .

He noticed our white faces and camera instantly, but without acknowledgement; he had presumably been alerted by Jolicoeur. After military salutes, anthems and ceremony, he entered the Red Cross building with Madame Simone Ovide Duvalier, a handsome Creole in a large white hat – closely followed by me, as usual brushing machineguns aside with a polite smile and a *Do* You Mind.

In the scrimmage Ted Morrisby and I managed to converge upon the President. We explained we had crossed the world to see him, and after some hesitant questioning received in return a murmured invitation to visit him in his Palace next day. We fell back with relief from the small surrounded figure. It seemed that at least we were not going to be shot – so far.

Later we learned that his Chargé d'Affaires in London was a Whicker's World enthusiast, and upon our request for visas had sent Papa Doc an approving telex.

Coming to power in 1957 with the support of the Army, the astute Dr Duvalier had thoughtfully observed that Dictators were in turn always overthrown by their own armies – so *he* overthrew his, quite quickly. He explained his attitude to me later, in an angry rasp: 'Only civilians can own a country, not the military men. The military man must stay in his barracks and receive orders and instructions from the President, from the King, from the Emperor. This is my opinion, this is my philosophy. To have peace and stability you should have a strong man in every country. Not a Dictator, but a strong man. Democracy is only a word – it is a philosophy, a conception. What *you* call Democracy in your country, another country could call a Dictatorship.'

The Haitian army once had 20,000 men – 6,500 of them generals; it was now reduced to ceremonial duties, and colonels. In its place the President had created his Volunteers for Defence – the evil militia of Tontons Macoute. It means 'Uncle Bagman', after the legendary giant bogeyman who strode the mountains stuffing naughty children into his knapsack.

In return for loyalty, he gave his armed bully-boys the right to lean upon the terrified populace, to tax and torment. Each nationalised hoodlum performed duties with which Papa Doc did not wish to be officially associated, and was licensed to kill. To provoke or deny any bogeyman intent upon stuffing his knapsack was to invite a beating, at least.

As all hope drained during years of sudden and unaccountable death, Haitians submitted to the gangster army which stood over them, controlled improbably by Madame Rosalee Adolphe. A Deputy and wife of the Minister of Health and Population, she had since 1958 been the Supervisor General of the 'Volunteers': 'They are not paid –

though I am paid because I am a Deputy. If we are attacked someone has to defend the Head of Government. I have always got my gun. It is always ready . . .'

The smiling little woman packed it, demurely, in her handbag. She proved her firepower to me, and then we all went up the mountainside to see some of her volunteers in action. We expected a mass of toiling figures, but found only a handful working on a road, watched by twice as many others; Tontons did not volunteer to work – they volunteered to supervise. That was the way of Public Works in Haiti: a few men with machetes, a lot of men with guns. I recalled a telling Haitian proverb: If work were a good thing, the Rich would long ago have grabbed it for themselves . . .

Papa Doc was believed to have executed 2,000 Haitians, and had certainly driven 30,000 into exile and the rest into terrified silence. In that manacled land it seemed to me a wonder there was anyone left to criticise, let alone attack. A missing Haitian would be unimportant and unnoticed, but the arrest or killing of a foreigner could only be ordered by the President – but there was little comfort in that for he seemed totally unconcerned about international opinion.

A foreign passport was no protection. The Dominican Consul was found with his throat slashed so deeply his head was almost severed. Cromwell James, a 61-year-old British shopowner, was arrested by Tontons and severely beaten – presumably for resisting extortion. It took ten days for his lawyer to reach him in jail – to find he had been charged with highway robbery! He died four days later from gangrene, caused by untreated wounds.

In a destitute land such extortion yielded diminishing returns, for there were always fewer victims to be squeezed. When Tontons began to demand money from foreigners, the British Ambassador Gerald Corley-Smith complained. He was thrown out, and the Embassy closed. Duvalier renounced the convention of political asylum and raided other Embassies to get at terrified Haitians. Washington was curtly told to recall its Ambassador Raymond Thurston – Papa Doc's financial crutch.

Though Haiti was officially Catholic, the Church also took

a beating; the Archbishop, Monsignor Raymond Poirier, was arrested and put on a Miami flight wearing cassock and sash, and carrying one dollar. Soon afterwards his successor, the Haitian Bishop Augustin was dragged from his bed by Tontons and not even allowed to put in his false teeth before he too was deported. A Catholic Bishop and 18 Jesuit priests followed them, as did the American Episcopal Bishop Alfred Voegeli who had ministered to Haitians for 20 years. Papa Doc accepted the Pope's excommunication with his usual deadpan equanimity – and went on to ban the Boy Scouts.

Next year, President Johnson agreed to send another Ambassador to Port-au-Prince, Mr Benson Timmons III. Papa Doc kept him waiting five weeks for an audience, and then gave him a stern lecture on how a diplomat should behave.

Committing international hari kari, antogonising the world while refusing to ask for Aid, may not have made economic sense, but to Haitians it made some sort of emotional sense: proud Haiti, first to defy the slavemasters, once again standing alone. From their point of view Dr Duvalier also had one thing going for him: most of Haiti's Presidents had been upper-class mulattoes with light skins – but Papa Doc was black as his hat.

In the years following the war some hundreds of millions of dollars were given or loaned this friendless land in Aid, much of it going directly to President Duvalier. The world finally realised Haiti was too corrupt and hopeless to help, and the dollars dried up. When we arrived in December 1968 the economy was in a state of collapse – finance in chaos, public works decaying, few passable roads, and a government so venal that all trade not offering officials a rake-off was at a stand-still.

With the lowest income, food intake and life expectancy in the hemisphere, the lives of the amiable, long-suffering Haitians had changed little since the days of slavery, two centuries ago. Shoes were still a luxury. I found it impossible to exaggerate the poverty of a land so out of step with the rest of the world.

From a workforce of two or three million, only 60,000 had

jobs – and most of those were on the government payroll.
The average income was about £25 a year, so hungry Haitians had little spirit left for revolt; the problems of living
through another day were enough.

They had also heard the President's personal physician,
Dr Jacques Fourcand, warn what would happen if Haiti ever
found the energy to rise against Papa Doc: 'Blood will flow as
never before. The land will burn. There will be no sunrise
and no sunset – just one enormous flame licking the sky. It
will be the greatest slaughter in history – a Himalaya of
corpses.' That benevolent doctor was a neuro-surgeon and
President of the local Red Cross.

Fear and violence were not new to that fevered land; the
cheapest possession had always been Life. It was once the
richest French colony, but after the only successful slave
revolt in history, in 1804, suffered a succession of tyrannical
Black Governors, Emperors and Kings. Toussaint Louver-
ture, Dessalines, Christophe lived and died by hideous bru-
tality: in half a century, 69 revolutions! They left behind the
world's poorest country – a mountainous, teeming tropical
land like a lush India, though only twice the size of Yorkshire. Nine out of ten of the five million Haitians were
illiterate, but they were a sympathetic and artistic people, the
women docile and graceful and, it is said, like panthers
dreaming. Port-au-Prince, tatty and sometimes even charming, was graced by gingerbread architecture and a dusty
crumbling elegance, with Victorian excrescences and curli
cues, a steam-heated squalor of peeling paintwork amid an
outburst of bougainvillaea.

My only pleasure in that cowed capital came from the
peintres naïfs. I was particularly taken with Préfet Duffaut –
a sort of Haitian Lowry who always painted his native
village of Jacmel and peopled it with busy matchstick figures.
I bought two from George Nader's gallery and gave the
better one to Cubby Broccoli, my Christmas host later that
month in Beverly Hills. I realised too late the simple primitive was quite out of place in his grand new mansion off
Sunset Boulevard – once owned by Papa Doc's neighbour
Trujillo – and was surely destined to rest in some distant loo.

I longed to ask for it back and exchange it for something more
fitting – say, a Rubens . . .

For anyone not offended by tyranny or destitution, Haiti
was a dramatic holiday-land. In those stricken days only one
cruise ship arrived each week and stayed a few hours. Most
passengers were too frightened to come ashore. To tidy
things up for the few who took the risk, all beggars were
banished to the countryside for the day. Jealous Tontons
stood waiting for the braver to file ashore and fill their
predatory line of ancient taxis. They were then driven up the
lowering mountainside to an hotel in the little resort of
Kenscoff. They watched some flaming limbo dancing across
their cold buffet, returned with relief to the ship – and sailed
away.

We recorded this sad little celebration amid despair, but
left before the performance was over to be ready to film their
dockside departure. As we drove down the hill, there in the
middle of the road was a brand new corpse, still bleeding.

The unfortunate man was obviously dead: a body asleep or
unconscious is somehow . . . different. I told Racine to stop,
so we could go back and at least cover the poor chap. He
refused, and drove faster. No Haitian would ever touch any
Tonton handiwork, for fear of suffering the same fate; that
was why those bullet scars across the airport walls had been
left uncovered.

So the whole motorcade which followed us down the
mountain had to drive solemnly and in procession around
that stark corpse. What the blue-rinses from Pasadena made
of it I cannot imagine, but it surely did nothing for the
Tourist Board's Come-to-Happy-Haiti promotion.

Haitians have seldom been able to summon up more
energy for imported Christianity than was required to bury
their dead, Tontons permitting. They may be 90 per cent
Catholic but, it is said, they are 100 per cent Voodoo. In
Haiti the supernatural is still alive. When a peasant dies,
before being placed in his coffin he will sometimes be dressed
in his best clothes and seated at a table with food before him,
and a cigarette put in his mouth – or, if a woman, a clay pipe.
Then friends and neighbours arrive, and the feasting and

dancing of the wake begins. Although by law the corpse is supposed to be buried within 24 hours, decomposition is often allowed to set in, to make sure sorcerers will not dig him up and make a zombie, a work-slave, out of him. The heavy stone slabs with which Haitians cover their graves are added insurance that the dead will not rise to slave as zombies for the rest of time.

In reply to my questions, Papa Doc angrily denied he was a *houngan*, a Voodoo priest – or even a follower of Baron Samedi, the most powerful, most dreaded god in the Voodoo pantheon. Baron Samedi personified death itself. He was always dressed in black and wore dark glasses. The similarity may not have been accidental, and was hard to ignore.

Certainly there were many weird stories about the capriciously brutal President, some terrible, some silly. It was said he sought guidance from the entrails of goats, that he lay meditating in a bath wearing his black hat, that he had the head of one enemy, Captain Blucher Philogènes, delivered to him in a pail of ice and sat for hours trying to induce it to disclose the plotters' plans . . .

Certainly he was merciless, despotic, malign; yet he received me in his study with eerie amiability. Behind him were signed portraits of the four men he admired: Chiang Kaishek, President Lyndon Johnson, the Pope and Martin Luther King.

He blamed the worldwide loathing he had earned on 'an international political conspiracy set up by several white nations who spend many millions to destroy our Fatherland, sending the North American Sixth Fleet to violate our national sea. Also, the USA has been sending *un*capable Ambassadors, so there is no talk between them and the President of Haiti. It is a question of men. The FBI is doing a good job but the CIA, not. It makes much trouble and must be blamed for the bad impression the world has of my country.'

He dismissed the bombing of his Palace: 'They are crazy. They will never reach their aim because I know who I am, and I cannot be killed by anyone. I have faith in my destiny. No other President of Haiti could stand up and do what I did in the past 11 years – facing eight armed invasions and three hurricanes.'

Though he was President for Life, and evidently convinced of immortality, I ventured to ask whether he had thought about a successor. He had not. 'All of them are at school now – they are the young people.'

His own son Jean-Claude sat beside us, a fat moonfaced 17-year-old, silent and embarrassed. I wondered what he would do with his life? 'That depends on him,' said Papa Doc, regarding the youth proudly. 'I hope he will follow the advice of his father, of his mother , and become a medical doctor.' (A couple of years later, Papa Doc died of natural causes – a rare achievement for any Haitian President – and Jean-Claude's career worries were over. At the age of 19 he became Baby Doc, the ninth Haitian since the 1804 revolution to decide to Rule For Life.)

Dr Duvalier seemed to me further evidence that no person is all good or all bad. He controlled his country's finances absolutely and was believed to have stashed $200 million in Switzerland, for his was a tyranny with no ideology except avarice. It was said that after dinner in his Palace he would go down to the cellars to watch his political prisoners being tortured, and on occasion would torture them himself. He was certainly known to slap ministers around his office, under the supporting gaze of the Presidential guard.

Yet he had been a selfless, caring, mild little doctor looking after the peasants and earning his famous nickname. A non-smoking teetotaller who loved his family, he was also a poet. He gave me copy number 892 of his *Breviary of a Revolution* and inscribed *Souvenirs d'Autrefois*, a collection of his poems, 'To the friend of the first Black Republic, Mr Alan Whicker, in souvenir of his short stay in the Island of Quisquetya, Sincerely, François Duvalier.' I had a suspicion I might not deserve the inscription.

Born on Sunday 14 April 1907, he told me his lucky number was 22. A man of moods, he was sometimes almost playful and anxious to make a good impression, at others glowering with suppressed fury. The only constant was the fear of those around him, which was unnerving and contagious.

I had played myself in tactfully during our conversations, slipping him the easy ones first. On our second visit I was intending to move on to some tougher questions, but at my very first he looked at me balefully during a long silence. Then, in a low menacing growl: 'Mr Whicker you are talking to . . . the President of the Republic of Haiti.'

I could hear the distant clang of cell doors slamming, and changed my line to something less controversial. There were audible sighs of relief from behind the camera.

Yet on another day when I reverted to those critical questions, he answered them all without getting more than slightly cross. It seemed to me that he might be diabetic, that his moods were medically influenced. On one of his jollier days he even decided to show us the town – and the best view of Port-au-Prince had to be from the President's bullet-proof limousine.

Papa Doc settled on the back seat alongside his gloomy bodyguard Colonel Gracia Jacques. We had no radio microphones in those days so the recordist, Terry Ricketts, rigged him up with a neck mike, with the long lead hidden round his body. On leaving the car he several times did himself a slight injury, without complaint. I sat opposite, ready to chat. Michael Blakstad, the director, and Ted Morrisby followed in one of the escorting police cars; and so we set out to talk our way around the sights.

He obviously wanted to show me how popular he was, and without doubt knew how to attract and hold an audience. A breathless cheering crowd chased our limo as we drove along – for he was throwing handfuls of money out of the window . . . Our pursuers, scrambling in the dirt, went frantic.

When we stopped he increased the excitement by bringing out neat packets of brand new notes, peeling off wads and handing them to anyone who seemed to have the right attitude.

In that land of destitution, the arrival of the black Mercedes amid a flutter of banknotes and a tinkle of coins caused far more ecstacy than Santa Claus, Royalty or the Pope.

With an annual income in every crisp wad handed out, it was well worth trying to keep up with the Duvaliers.

After a while he tired of that, and put his money away. The panting crowd thinned. We drove on. It seemed unreal to be riding around with one of the world's most feared men, broaching subjects which no Haitian would dare *think*. I wondered how he felt about Graham Greene and *The Comedians*? He had not met him, and brushed novel and gory film aside: 'He is a poor man, mentally, because he did not say the truth about Haiti. Perhaps he needed the money, and got some from the political exiles.'

He was more bitter about his predecessor, Major Magloire, then living in New York and threatening to return: 'He took 19 million dollars from the National Bank of Haiti and he uses that money to finance armed invasions and to bomb the Palace. He tried to kill me when he was President. I was in hiding for several years. Why did he not come here himself, instead of sending his young officers?'

He answered that one right away, and effectively: 'If he comes here he will be killed, because he is what you call a vagabond. A vagabond.'

Almost half of Haiti's revenue was spent on Papa Doc's personal security, so I questioned the use of his hated Tontons Macoute: 'It is a militia. They help me to clean the streets. They help me to cultivate the land. They help the Haitian Army and they fight side by side in face of armed invasions.' We were then standing among a bristling mass of them on a roadside high above the capital. When Papa Doc had got out of his car, they had all taken up defensive positions around us, as though assassination were imminent.

He could not understand why he was dreaded throughout the world, and found it quite unjust: 'I am the strongest man, the most anti-Communist man, in the Caribbean islands. Certainly the question is a racial one – because I am a strong leader the US considers me a bad example for the 25 million negroes living there. I should be the favourite child of the United States of America. Instead of which they consider me . . . the Black Sheep!' He gave me our title – and one of those ghoulish smiles.

Although his 500-strong Palace Guard now recognised us and knew we were accepted, they were all so permanently terrified that getting in to see him was a daily problem. He had invited me to return to continue our conversation and I had the forethought to arm myself with a laisser-passer sternly addressed to All Civil and Military Authorities and signed by the President himself. This got me through the sentries on the Palace gates, past a bristle of guards on various doors, up the stairs and along the corridor, right to the entrance to his chamber. There I was stopped by the Presidential Guard, a nervous group of captains and lieutenants who said that although they knew he was expecting me, they had no authority to disturb him.

The only person who could actually approach him was his secretary, Madame Saint-Victor, a formidable lady and sister to another son-in-law – but she was away ill. So we sat outside in the chandeliered ante-room and waited, and the President sat inside and waited – and nobody had the courage to knock on his door.

I finally broke the stalemate by leaving the Palace, muttering, and going down to the town's telegraph office. I had seen a telex in Papa Doc's inner sanctum and had noted the number – 3490068. I sent him a message, simple but direct: 'Mr President, I am waiting outside your door.' It worked.

Encouraged by our successful tour of the town, I suggested he might show us Duvalierville. He had ordered the building of this national showplace seven years before; it was to be a sort of Brasilia, and his memorial. He was not interested in going there, and said it was too far for him to travel. It was 20 miles away, in a village called Cabaret, but he had not been outside Port-au-Prince for years, probably fearing assassination attempts in the desolate countryside.

We later went out to look at Duvalierville by ourselves, and found he was not missing much. Like everything else in Haiti, his empty dream had died for lack of money. Crumbling and overgrown, it stood in wasteland populated only by a few listless squatters. It seemed a fitting monument.

However, he was willing to organise a visit to a nearby Health Centre. I listened as he pursued his daughter on one of the few working telephones in the land: 'C'est le Président de la République! Where is Di-Di?' His daughter had returned from Madrid, leaving the fortunate Colonel Dominique to travel alone into the security of Switzerland.

The Health Centre was quivering with nervous readiness when we all arrived, and upon the rigid form of a stoic patient with hepatitis, Papa Doc showed me he had not lost his stethoscopic touch. Across the body, I recalled that he was still a Fellow of the Royal Society of Tropical Medicine in London: 'Do you know that? Yes, I am surprising, eh? I am still interested in medical matters, and until I die I am first an MD and after that – President of Haiti. It was the best time of my life, when I was practising medicine.'

I wondered what he now did for relaxation? 'My reading and writing because, you know, this is another aspect of Dr Duvalier. He is a writer and a reader. Even when I am going to sleep I have a book in my hand. This is morphine for me. If I do not read, I cannot sleep.' Sometimes he was a hard man to dislike.

I had established an unusual relationship with him, and on occasion could even make him laugh. The crew sensed an Award-winning programme, which reconciled us wonderfully to the gloom and anxiety, to the unpredictable President's moods and the constant fear that at any moment . . . something could go terribly wrong.

Our other preoccupation was more practical: we were fast running out of film. On this tour we had already shot programmes in Argentina, Paraguay and Ecuador; Blakstad's service messages to Leeds calling for the despatch of filmstock were growing more urgent. Yorkshire Television had only been running a few months and administratively was still not sure what it was about. Our cables were ignored for several days because a weekend and Christmas were approaching. When stock was eventually despatched it was not sent directly to Jamaica, the neighbouring island, but via Pan Am's notorious cargo section in New York where, as we feared, it disappeared from sight.

Meanwhile back in Papa Doc's office we grew more and more worried, though our filming was going brilliantly.

Despite the fact that I was making the grim but courteous Papa Doc speak English – he was far more comfortable with French or Creole – it seemed he was beginning to enjoy being interviewed, being the centre of so much constant and flattering attention from foreigners. Ambassadors and Archbishops expelled, Ministers shot – but television entertained and hostile questioning accepted . . . Ours is a strange world.

All we needed for the documentary was a climax, and we got that when Papa Doc told me that next day he was going Christmas shopping with Madame Duvalier and Di-Di. Would I like to film their expedition? When Presidents start suggesting their own sequences, even I begin to feel quietly confident. The prospect of the terrifying Dictator considering festive gifts within his manacled capital was like a skeleton in a paper hat: macabre, but fascinating. It had to be the best sequence ever, the situation of a lifetime.

At that moment, we ran out of film.

As I had discovered with General Stroessner, filming a Dictator who does not want to be filmed can be quite dangerous. What is even more dangerous, however, is *not* filming a Dictator who *wants* to be filmed . . .

Back at the hotel we had a frantic conference across empty camera magazines. What to do? One way or the other, he was going to be displeased. This could lead to a sudden restriction of liberty – even to a spilling of blood. We could hardly say we were not interested any more, thank you Mr President. We could not stand him up, or we might be escorted downstairs to those dungeons. We could not leave the country without an Exit Visa – and anyway our movements were followed by a score of eyes. We had been anxious to establish a relationship – but now it seemed one could get *too* close to a Dictator . . .

On the morning of the shopping expedition I was half-hoping the guards would hold us up again, but of course for the first time we were swept straight in, with salutes. So I handed the cameraman my own pocket camera, a little half-frame Olympus Pen-F, and went on to spend the morning chatting with a marvellously relaxed President in various jewellers' shops while the excellent Frank Pocklington took happy-snaps, in anguish.

For a documentary, it was a dream situation – except that photographing us was a cameraman taking paparazzi pictures with quiet desperation, while the rest of the crew stood in the background, incredulous at what we were missing.

Papa Doc did not notice the absence of our Arriflex; he was too busy selecting the best jewellery he could find in the cleared and guarded shops, while behind him his womenfolk went through the stock with shrewd and practised eyes. I watched Di-Di riffling through the diamonds; she was a chip off the old Doc.

As our Presidential cortège arrived, each jeweller's face became a study because, on one hand, it was a great honour to be 'By Appointment to Papa Doc'. Such Presidential approval had all sorts of little side benefits – like the Tontons did not kill you. On the other hand, there was one slight but unavoidable snag: he never *paid* for anything.

He would make his selection with much care and then, instead of handing over the cash, would shake the shopowner's hand and award him one of those wolfish smiles. He got a few wolfish smiles back, but there was nothing they could do. At least he only took one item from each shop, and knowing The Gift You Carry Gets Home First, Papa Doc always had his with him, gift-wrapped, when he left.

We did not expose a foot of film on that unreal and unrepeatable scene. It was lost, along with the remainder of our planned programme climax. Papa Doc was spared my most pointed questions, which I had been thoughtfully withholding for the night before we flew away. What we had in the can was good, but the programme could have been so much better. For despair and frustration it was my worst television experience.

The programme was transmitted twice and afterwards submitted by Donald Baverstock for the Dumont Award, the international accolade for television journalists presented by the University of California and West Coast philanthropist Nat Dumont. The heavyweight judges were Dr Ralph Bunche, United Nations Undersecretary General; Norman

Cousins, President of the *Saturday Review*; George Stevens Jnr, Director of the American Film Institute; and Mrs Katherine Graham, owner of the *Washington Post*. Television services from around the world followed US networks to enter their best programmes. Out of 40 finalists, Papa Doc won.

The runner-up was a film by Austrian Television which dealt with the US Strategic Air Force. The Awards merited stern newspaper editorials complaining that foreign stations had walked away with their most prestigious prizes. The *Los Angeles Times* wrote: 'What is ironic is not only that foreign television is beating us at our own game – but with our own stories.'

By chance I was filming once again in the Caribbean at the time of the UCLA Presentation ceremony. I flew to Los Angeles, where the University's Melnitz Auditorium was crammed with distinction and champagne, and received the Award from the Chancellor, Charles E. Young. Afterwards, a grand reception and banquet at Chasen's, attended by stars, advertising agencies and network executives. Yorkshire had been desperate to break into the American market – and today, after ten years, has still not done so – but on this occasion failed to support me with even one handout; Lew Grade would have sent an army of salesmen and a ton of literature. In a golden moment when we were the target of every professional eye, I was absolutely alone. I spent most of the evening laboriously spelling my name to reporters who had never heard of me, or of Yorkshire.

After seeing the film everyone was most laudatory, once they knew who the hell I was. Amid the clamour Pat Brown, Governor of California who had just handed over to Ronald Reagan and become a lawyer, asked if he could represent me. I agreed to everything, flew back to the Caribbean – and was of course instantly forgotten.

Before I left to rejoin my team on location I had to face the dire penalty of the Award and deliver a lecture before the UCLA Faculty of Journalism. This was one of the hottest centres of professional instruction in the land. Knowing how intense American students can be, how eager and ambitious,

I had boned-up on the wider implications of our programme and its background, on the position of the United States within its Caribbean sphere of influence.

Some people dismiss television journalism as superficial, and of course mine often is; so as a Limey passing-through, I was anxious to hold up our end before these clever young Comers who had all seen the programme and could with some justification dismiss my kind of documentary as light-weight.

I was apprehensive, but the massed undergraduates were an attentive and appreciative audience with alert reactions, laughing in the right places and taking endless notes. I completed my *tour d'horizon* amid unaccustomed applause, gratified by the impact. The Dean made a few graceful remarks, and asked for questions. I braced myself for penetrating and informed demands beyond my knowledge.

There was a long silence. Then a plump young woman who had been absorbing every word with particular concentration stood up.

'Mr Whicker,' she began weightily, 'Is it true . . . that you married an heiress?'

Our whole Papa Doc experience was from start to finish full of light and shade, triumph and disaster, laughter and fear: a black and macabre tragicomedy.

PETER SELLERS

I think Albania's more Fun . . .

CALIFORNIA, that monstrous stretch of the American imagination, is a vigorous and blatant land of achievers and escapists where all America's promises and problems are exposed and exaggerated. New York may have been the melting pot of Europe but Los Angeles – that upstart Mecca on the Pacific – is the melting pot of America. The State looks back upon the rest of the world with cool indifference; go any further West, they say, and your hat floats . . .

Since the early Sixties I have regularly flown out to the Coast to film, always with delight and apprehension – for LA is where the New World really begins, where they spawn every fad and fancy the rest of us adopt five or ten years later.

When last I took Whicker's World there I feared that after such endless exposure on television viewers might have *had* California, up to here. Yet our series reached No. 1 in the ratings, which suggests we all have an insatiable appetite for the goings-on in that lavish, loony place on the far-out fringe of America.

Drawn into the last Western migration by climate and lifestyle, at least a quarter-of-a-million Britons have settled in Southern California – more than in any other foreign country. Every year another two or three thousand join the 50,000 living in Los Angeles, so the British accent is evident. I filmed a yard-of-ale contest in a pub at Corona Del Mar called the Five Crowns. It was modelled on Ye Olde Bell at Hurley and proudly declared itself as built way back in 1965; *there's* history for you. Tudor was suitably mocked, and service more Bunny than Barmaid.

There are 83 British clubs around LA and, though I found it hard to believe, Southern California supports 11 cricket clubs. Their skill seems adequate village-green, though rig and decorum have changed since the days when C. Aubrey Smith sent Errol Flynn off the pitch in disgrace because his shirt was unbuttoned to the waist . . .

The city has also changed; the dream factory of Hollywood was once controlled by men said to know only one word of two syllables: 'fillum'. Today California has cultural oases amid its concrete wastes: the Getty Museum at Malibu was endowed by poor old Paul with all that money he was so careful not to spend – oil shares worth well over £700,000,000, so far – and packs more financial clout than all British museums put together. If it ever flexed its money muscle, the art world would reel. Its amiable Director Steven Garrett, an English architect, told me that when visitors telephoned for directions to the world's richest museum, his operator told them to drive to the end of Sunset Boulevard, turn right on Ocean, and one mile north they would spot the Museum 'just opposite the restaurant called Ted's Rancho.' I wondered whether Ted gave Paul similar billing . . .

Despite the occasional rich museum and worthy cause supported by Angelinos with almost as much fervour as displayed on the other side of the continent by the Palm Beach charity brigade, Beverly Hills always seems to me to be populated by people afraid they are at the wrong table in the wrong party on the wrong side of Wilshire . . . I asked an expert on Horror about its Society life. Christopher Lee had escaped from Frankenstein, Rasputin, Dracula and macabre points Transylvanian to drop anchor in a condominium on the right side of Wilshire Boulevard. He drove me around the Bel Air Country Club in his golf cart, expounding upon the social scene: 'Bizarre! The only aristocracy that exists is that of money and power. If you want to belong – and personally I'm not in the least interested, nor are most Europeans – its a question of belonging to the right group. Do you go to the right restaurant, drive the right car, live in the right place, visit the right houses, have the right income . . . If your last picture made money, you have a higher social status than if it lost money. If you're working, if you're successful, then some people will think it's all right to be seen talking to you . . .

'There's a famous club just over there, the Los Angeles Country Club, which for years has had an unwritten rule that it will not accept as a member any person in show business. You could be a producer, director, writer . . . but if you're in show business, you're a rogue and a vagabond. It's rather ironic that as an actor who belongs to the oldest golf club in the world – Muirfield, founded in 1744 – I still cannot be a member.' I wondered about President Reagan, an actor now going straight; Christopher did not think he had made it.

'There's a tremendous amount of fear here, which stems partly from insecurity, partly from ignorance. As everybody knows, there *are* people in show business who in some degree or another are slightly ignorant. There are frightened people, because of the huge sums of money involved. Most incredible salaries are being paid out. The days of a million dollars being an enormous salary are virtually gone. When somebody talks about getting a million dollars they say 'Oh yes?' People are getting three, four, five million. One actor is getting ten million dollars for his next picture. I think it's wrong, mind you, though I've done 14 pictures in two years – which is one of the reasons I can afford to belong to a club like this, with an entrance fee of around £12,500 and fees of maybe £3,000 a year. Stratospheric figures, I grant you, but it's a question of proportion.' I took our programme title from his appraisal: 'Nothing is Utopia – but this comes pretty close.'

Another migrant, a Sheffield truckdriver filmed in a quaint 'mock pub', agreed fervently: 'You work less hours here and not so hard. You get a hell of a lot of money – and you don't pay so much tax. TVs and petrol and cars, everything is ever so cheap. I could've been a rich man if I'd come over sooner. I'm not in the union yet, but eventually I will become a Teamster because people are telling me I'd better be in it, or else I'll get shot.'

At the other and perhaps less-threatened end of the motoring fraternity – a gathering of the Rolls-Royce Owners' Club – an English schoolteacher mentioned that she and her psychologist husband owned five Rolls: 'We've cut our stable down. We used to have eight. When I was teaching in England I earned the equivalent to seventeen hundred dollars a year; now I get much more than that in thousands – but I miss the people and hearing nice British accents. I miss fish and chips and all those neat things. Good tea is hard to find here. So is Spode china and malt vinegar.' It seemed a limited sacrifice, for five Rolls.

At the Heritage Ball in the Beverly Wilshire Hotel we filmed local Brits and generous Americans supporting our National Trust. A portrait in oils given by the Ball Chairman, pre-war film star Anna Lee, still blonde and beautiful, was auctioned by Vincent Price as 'an instant ancestor' and instantly sold for $750. The lady is now doubtless proudly enrolled into someone's family history.

I sat with Juliet Mills, Los Angeles resident for ten years, and Samantha Eggar, 15 years, and wondered what they had surrendered for their sunshine? 'Chocolate biscuits, Mars bars, my family,' said Sam. 'We're all thoroughly Royalist here – I put the Union Jack up on the Fourth of July and all my neighbours called the radio stations to complain, but we've got the sun 365 days a year and we don't have to buy wellingtons or overcoats.'

I asked Juliet what might send her back to Richmond, Surrey? 'Stimulus. Here you have to try and surround yourself with stimulating people who can keep you mentally alive. There's a great deal of sitting in the sun and thinking about diets and money.' Sam added, 'There's a big television life here. Everyone glued to the box. Pret-ty boring . . .'

Indeed many flourishing expatriates seemed to grow more and more homesick. Over tea and fruit cake in her beamed mansion, surrounded by Royal family photographs, Anna Lee recalled mistily she had smuggled little packets of English forget-me-not seeds through customs in her brassière. In that lush semi-tropical soil I suspected they must immediately have grown six-feet tall, but they had not survived the harsh sun. Her husband, the poet Robert Nathan who was then nearing 90, observed that they must have been happier in her bra.

She was longing to return to her native Kent but explained, rather disarmingly: 'I grow so homesick, but every time I tried to go home to live, I usually married another American.' In fact she has only been married three times, while her husband has scored seven – 'but then you see, he's been longer at it.'

I had breakfast with Dudley Moore. Separated from his wife Tuesday Weld, he lived alone in an oceanfront house at Marina Del Rey. In his kitchen I noticed two enormous collections of vitamins and other pills in separate cupboards – one for him, the other for his dog. He had just experienced his first Californian earthquake: 'I was in the shower and I thought the house had been hit by the bulldozer that turns over the sand. I ran out on to the beach to complain, but there was nobody there. I thought Hello – that was not the bulldozer, that was God walking by . . .'

His career was just taking off, guided by 'Pink Panther' producer Blake Edwards whom he had first met among eight others in a group therapy session. He had been in analysis since 1964. 'Even if you're an achiever,' he said, 'it doesn't necessarily mean you feel comfortable about yourself . . .'

Another successful British actor understood that attitude only too well; one sunny morning we drove from the eye-watering smog of Wilshire Boulevard up to Summitridge, to spend the day with him. There on the heights Peter Sellers had rented the splendid blue and white house where I had often gone to the parties of Herbert Hischmoeller, a Beverly Hills socialite who was also, improbably, Consul for the Ivory Coast.

The house stood empty as we arrived but after a few moments Peter drove up with his new wife Lynne Frederick, then 24 and full of acquisitive triumph. They had been shopping down on Rodeo Drive and he had bought her some bejewelled *quelque-chose* she needed, and another toy for himself – the latest Polaroid. We immediately started taking pictures.

I had first met Peter 20 years earlier, when in the Tonight studio I interviewed his mother. In those days he was a tubby, square, adoring suburban son. Now after his procession of marriages and heart attacks he was slim and grey and elegantly casual, like a Gucci-lumberjack, but his feelings for his late mother were if anything more intense. 'Of course – you *knew* my darling,' he recalled. 'I still speak to her every day.'

The beautiful Lynne was concerned about him but not totally on his wavelength – surely a hard one to locate. There had already been talk of divorce. His marriages to lovely women usually ended unhappily.

With consternation he spotted the programme's working-title on our clapperboard: Brits. 'That's *not* a popular name here,' he cried, in alarm. He was at that moment braced for publication of a kiss-and-tell book by Britt Ekland, one of his least-favourite wives. He had also been affronted by *not* being included in Sophia Loren's memoirs, after what he regarded as their intense love affair. He was not an easy man to please.

We had a sunlit, happy visit, for he was relaxed and in great form. Roderick Mann was there too; he had been writing for the *Liverpool Echo* 25 years before when Peter was living in Penny Lane. Now show biz columnist for the *Los Angeles Times* as well as the *Sunday Express*, he reflected, 'We had no idea we were going to end up out here, playing the Hollywood game . . .'

Sitting there on the mountaintop, looking down through the cypresses at Los Angeles, we laughed a lot while I filmed a long conversation in which Peter was for once being natural and himself, and not retreating behind funny voices. Usually when interviewed he instantly became Bluebottle, Fred Kite, an Indian doctor or any of those characters filed away in that recording machine between his ears which provided instant and precise playback. He could not resist doing me, of course – the way everybody does – and then, unexpectedly, stood before my camera and ad-libbed a series of commercials about expatriate Hollywood. We eventually began and ended the programme with these. Afterwards I reflected upon the fee he might have required had Yorkshire Television commissioned him to do those four spots . . .

That thoughtful, funny day was unhappily soon to be the basis for my television salute to him in July 1980, after his fatal heart attack in London.

Everybody is a fan of somebody else. Roddy had been with Cary Grant when he whispered in awe, 'That's Duke Wayne over there!' One of the endearing things about Peter – then perhaps the most famous comedian in the world – was that he was so starstruck: 'I mean, to walk into James Stewart's office and see him *sitting* there. My mind goes like *that*, you know. It's all I can do not to ask for his autograph. I was always a big movie buff.

'When I first came out here they'd seen "I'm All Right Jack" or something, and my agent threw a party for me. Everybody was there. I was among people I'd only seen on the screen and I thought Oh my *God*! So I figured on taking round my autograph book, which I had in my pocket. I went up to Freddie Fields and said, "Would it be all right, because I don't see these people very often," and he says, "Listen, you're going to see them for the rest of your life. You've no need to worry about him, or him, or him – that's the *worst* thing you can do." '

His 'Prisoner of Zenda' was then being much attacked by the critics, while the film he believed the best thing he had ever done – 'Being There' – was about to be released. 'Fu Manchu' came out after his death. 'Yes, I'm known to be difficult, though I did have praise from Lorimar, the "Being There" people. Just the other day in a restaurant they told my agent and his wife, "If Peter Sellers is difficult, then that's the only sort of person we wanna work with." You see, I always arrive on time and know my lines, I don't fall over the furniture and I'm a professional. I can't stand the loonies, you see, I can't stand berks – this is the trouble . . .'

I reflected that not all Peter's colleagues were quite as enthusiastic; a friend had worked with him during one of his unworldly periods when he drove the unit to distraction by continually failing to turn up on the set. He would afterwards explain 'his voices' had told him not to work that day. This happened so often and so expensively that finally the producer took him aside. 'Listen, Peter,' he said heavily, 'it's very strange but I've been hearing voices too – and you know what they told me? They told me if you're not in tomorrow and ready to go, both your legs'll get broken . . .'

Despite his professional success, Roddy also disliked the place: 'I think Albania's more fun. When I lived in Great Portland Street I fantasised about Beverly Hills. Now I'm in Beverly Hills fantasising Great Portland Street. London seems absolutely wonderful, and I'm still outside the cheese shop in Jermyn Street. Here, I haven't walked along the beach with Raquel Welch. Not yet, anyway. I haven't got a white Cadillac convertible – they've stopped making them. It rained a lot last winter. The air is like poison gas most of the time, it truly is. For a non-smoker living here's like being a two-pack-a-day man anywhere else.'

I said it was surprising that someone who had been writing

about Hollywood all his professional life, and visiting often, should be so curiously unprepared for its impact when he arrived here to live. 'I think everybody is, because what you're prepared for doesn't exist. I mean, London never disappears for me when I'm here, but as soon as I leave Hollywood this place vanishes. It doesn't exist any more, except in a fantasy. I don't understand why that is, but I do know that all these people feel cheated. They've made their pile and come here and it isn't as good as they hoped it would be – so they resent it. One of the things I've found is that it's easy to feel underprivileged, because I don't know anybody who hasn't got a million dollars. There's just me and my maid – and my maid'll make it before I do, the way I'm paying her . . .'

Peter thought Hollywood was 'full of a sort of churning unrest. It's very energising, very charging to do some work here – but then I want to be off. There's an atmosphere I don't like. Rubs me up the wrong way. I'd sooner, for example, be at home and have somebody say to me, as they have on several occasions, "Saw your last film, mate, thought it was a load of shit." I'd sooner put up with that than what happens here: I remember going through a very bad patch and I came here for a while and found that several well-known people were crossing from one side of the road to the other, in order not to bump into me. That was terrible.'

A loser in LA, I ruminated, went to the lions fairly quickly . . . 'Like that!' he said, clicking his fingers. 'You really know when the skids are under you. Two films that don't do any good and it's *out* – the elbow . . . If you're a loser here they don't want to know, and if you're a winner you don't get a moment's peace.'

Roddy was also unenthusiastic about the social life: 'It's always the same people getting together. It's a repertory company. Once you've been to five parties, it's the same cast. One of the reasons life can be so dull I find is that there's no mix, as there is in Paris and to a certain extent in London, of politics and newspapermen and actors . . . The only way you'll meet an architect in this town is to hire one.'

'The British all sort of get together and talk about Harrods,' said Peter. 'That's about it really, unless you want to get caught up with the Hollywood set and get mixed up with those parties – but forget it, you know, not for me. Very private person, very private. A lot of people think I'm a right twit because I'm very quiet, but I can't take it. I work so hard when I'm filming that I like to be quiet and just think and meditate, maybe wander round taking photographs . . .

'I'm not poor and I'm well liked, so I can go into Gucci or wherever, and I just sign. Here they make life easy for you: you arrive at an Italian restaurant and the guy says, Luigi says, "Hey Mr Sellers, lovely to see you again, hey, wonderful, where is that beautiful girl you had with you – she had dark hair with beautiful lips and olive skin and beautiful eyes, I remember her very well, where is she?" And you say, "I'm no longer with her," and he says, "And a *very* good thing too – listen, I give you this table over here . . ."

'That's how I originally got Inspector Clouseau – from a conversation I heard between a concierge in an hotel in Paris and an American tourist. This concierge, believe me, was very sharp and used to tourists, a very patient, nice sort of guy, but there was a twinkle in the eye. This tourist was asking, "We'd like to take in the Lido show and right after that we want to go and eat somewhere good and then we want to go on to the Crazy Horse and we'll need a limo for that 'cos there'll be around six of us," and the concierge said, "I'm going to tell you what I'm going to do. I'm going to book you into the Lido. Six places at the best table, right? I'm going to book you into the Tour d'Argent afterwards, a nice table overlooking the river, everything – the best view. After that I'm going to book you into the Crazy Horse – you see all the girls, and there'll be a limousine waiting for you." This guy says, "Hey – that's *really* good of you." Now he'd only repeated what this man had asked him to do, yet he got a bloody great 500 franc tip. I thought to myself, that's old Clouseau, really. He just listens to people and tells them what they think. That's why he has to be one-up on everybody. Somebody says, "There's a phone call for you, Inspector" and he says, "Ah, yes, that will be for me." '

We recalled his clairvoyant, the late Maurice Woodruffe:

'I went to see a lady here the other day who deals in numerology and she told me of my various incarnations and what karma I had to work off in this life, which ends approximately by my next birthday, very soon, in the Fall.'

'Your *life*?'

'No, no – my karma. She said that in one incarnation I had been a priest in Roman days. You know, it's the old *déjà vu* thing, but every time I've been to Rome and wandered round I've felt it . . . especially one night in the Circus Maximus. It's now a car park, and about three in the morning I was sitting right in the centre thinking about all the Christians who had been sacrificed to the lions, and feeling that I must have been there . . .'

Peter was a strange, careful man. He would not sit in the sun, and drank only sugar-free Tab. He watched the load his damaged heart must bear, though did not spare it in his fierce work-drive: 'Financially I'm fine, thank God, but there's always that necessity to work – you can't sit on your arse too long. I could never retire. I don't know *any* actor who could successfully retire.'

He recalled the times of the Goon Show as the happiest days of his life. 'I don't have any friends here. I've only got, probably, I've only got two really good friends, or three at the most, in my life – and they're all in London. These people are acquaintances.

'You see, Alan, I don't have my books here. In a rented house, nothing I'd read – half of it's in Dutch anyway. I shall have all my stuff from Victoria sent over to Switzerland. My books should be there, you see, all me bits and pieces and odds and sods, you know, all me gear.

'We have a neighbour in Gstaad, Yehudi Menuhin, who lives most of the time in England and the rest of the time out there. He also does Yoga, and it's marvellous to see him in his garden, standing on his head playing his Stradivarius, which he does frequently. He breaks a lot of Stradivariuses that way . . .

'In the film game you're a bit of a gypsy, you know, you travel from place to place, which is a nice thing for you never get stale. But I happen to be one of those people who was

born and will die in England. I was born in Yorkshire but
I've been living in London all my life and I've sort of got
London *in* me. Although I can't stay there all the time,
there's something about the place that I can't get away from
and, you know, I don't *want* to get away from.'

He returned to London soon afterwards and, in the Dorchester, suffered his final heart attack. He would have found
it fitting to round-off his life as he had forecast. He left Lynne
behind in Beverly Hills – but also left her several million.
Within months she married David Frost. Within a few more
months, they divorced.

COSMETIC SURGERY

Mine are the Mediums,
and I love them very much . . .

Los Angeles is a Nowhere City. It is like living in a vast
motel where everybody is about to leave; no one has a past, or
cares what you do. There is no chance of establishing a
relationship with other guests, for they are all due to check
out in a day or two. Despite such restlessness, such indifference, its residents talk more than any people in the world
about 'meaningful relationships' – yet would not know how
to handle one if it took them by the throat . . .

When we wrapped for lunch in Beverly Hills on the first
filming day of another programme, I headed round the
corner for the Cheese-cake Factory and one of my many
weaknesses. At the restaurant a long queue stood before the
inescapable notice: 'Kindly wait to be seated.'

Suddenly I found myself escorted up the line to a window
table. Such favoured treatment was gratifying but surpris-

ing; I am not well known in America. When the waitress
appeared and went into the usual How was I today routine, I
understood: I had been spotted by a Cockney and a viewer,
who was being kind to an old familiar face.

Lil Simmonds had arrived in California a few years before
and in a land of non-stop talkers and extroverts, gave me not
only my cheese-cake with strawberry topping, but one of the
brightest interviews in three months of filming, full of com-
monsense and insight.

She was happy and earning well, though LA was no easy
ride: 'They work very hard around here – 18 or 19 hours a
day sometimes, with two or three jobs,' she told me, 'which is
definitely not the way they worked when I was in Oxford
Street, what with morning coffee-breaks and afternoon tea-
breaks and long lunch hours and leaving at five – and if the
tube's on strike you don't make the effort to go in. Here if you
don't work, you don't get paid.'

She had been married to her hairdresser husband for ten
years and Californian friends were telling her she had a
record: 'I say, people at home are married for more than 25
years – that's a record. Though in England we *do* put up with
things. We soldier on. People here don't. They think life is too
short. Why stay with someone who makes you unhappy, or a
home you don't like, or a car you're fed up with, or a rotten
job? People in England stick with jobs they hate – and dream
about two weeks in Spain . . .'

She had been staggered by the widespread use of one aid to
a better job or happier life: cosmetic surgery, for if not
everyone in California is young and beautiful, it is not for
want of effort and expense.

'You could walk down this street,' she said, looking
through the windows at the affluent parade, 'and out of 20
women, 15 would have had something done. Some of them
look marvellous – but the tops and bottoms don't go together.
Some have had their faces fixed, so you see this young face on
a body that's definitely a mum or a granny.

'I went to the toilet in a store here one day when I'd just
arrived, and there were two women. One was about 50 and
didn't have anything on from the waist up. Well, I went hot

and cold thinking I'd walked in on something I shouldn't have. She apologised and said she'd just had her breasts done, and did I want to see them? I didn't really, but she was so pleased with them and pointed out the scars and asked if I wanted to feel them, and all the time I'm worried the door is going to open and someone is going to see me in this situation. She said she was a nurse and her surgeon was a wonderful man, and did I want his telephone number?'

I wondered whether Lil feared the contented woman might have been trying to tell her something? 'Right – that's what came into my head: she thinks there's something wrong with *me*. I mean, people here have their bottoms lifted – there isn't *anything* you can't have done.

'None of the women dare get old, because their men don't want to look at an old woman. They can all afford to get a young one. I see guys in here who should be home caring for their grandchildren, but instead they're wanting young girls. Everybody's into looking the best they can. If your husband trades you in for a newer model, you've got to keep yourself in good condition to find your next one . . .

'I used to watch your Whicker's Worlds,' she reflected, slipping me another slice, 'and I'd think I bet he goes and sorts out all the weirdos. When I got here, I found yours weren't weirdos at all, but just ordinary people. I realised you'd picked the normal ones. Its the oddballs who *don't* have something done. The one I remember best of all, that people were talking about, was that blonde who'd had everything redone by her own husband – her breasts and chin and ears . . . You told him he must feel like Frankenstein and he said he'd like to think he was nearer to God.'

I was delighted my seven-year-old programme should be so exactly recalled, and on such a day. 'I've *just* left his surgery!' I said, pushing aside the cheesecake in the excitement. 'I've come back to see what else he's done to her – and whether it worked . . .'

Indeed I had that morning started to put the marriage of Kurt and Kathy Wagner under the microscope again, and was wondering whether viewers would be prepared to spend an hour on their matrimonial rollercoaster. I was still friendly with the cosmetic surgeon and his patient-wife, but it was not going to be an easy programme. My director hated such a close look into a household: too much talk. My cameraman hated it: no pictures. YTV executives hated it: too unconventional. In fact on transmission Kurt and Kathy were once again watched with amazement by 18 million viewers and came fifth in the national ratings – a triumphant position for a documentary.

This is not to say everyone found them sympathetic – indeed the programme won me the Raspberry of the Week from Scottish *Sunday Mail* readers who decided what Kathy really needed was a head transplant.

Some righteous woman from another Sunday tore into poor Kathy for not being a homespun Progressive, and into me of course for not spending the programme attacking every one of the Wagners' values. This would not have been hard to do, though the plaintive and resentful reporting she adopted and urged would have produced unrewarding television. Whatever one thought of Kathy, she was certainly not sitting back and dreaming about two weeks in Spain . . .

Our first programme in 1973 had been transmitted at the start of America's cosmetic surgery boom, which finally took off in Britain in the Eighties when the medical profession began to change its puritan stance which had always seen cosmetic surgery as piffling and trivial. Britons began to follow Americans in their search for a better 'body image'.

While we were filming, Kurt in his cool way had taken a critical look around my crew and offered to tidy us up, for free. There was plenty to be done: my researcher had standout ears, the producer a weird nose, and there was so much I needed doing, badly, that Kurt found it hard to know where his scalpel should stop. As I always explain, they're not making mirrors the way they used to . . .

We were all too scared, of course, so missed the opportunity of joining David Frost and Roger Moore in having our bags removed and becoming unbelievably gorgeous.

Many Californians, far less timid, far more desperate to win in the youth game, had decided it was not possible to enjoy the good life if their cheeks wobbled when they walked, and just-plain-folks were having facelifts. They could lose their wrinkles in less time than it took to get their hair styled. They seemed to be saying, 'I may die – but I'll never grow old . . .'

This nationwide trend had of course started in Hollywood, where looking young is the most important Social Security – not vanity, but necessity. It is, after all, the place where dreams *should* come true, where great beauties are made, not born.

We watched scores of patients submitting to a fast tax-deductible operation and, after a couple of hours starring on closed circuit in the recovery room, tottering shakily home – already looking forward to putting their new faces about. Following the purposeful submission of Presidential wives and the unusually firm chins of rejuvenated politicians, such surgery was no longer merely the narcissism of show biz, but a sign of sophistication – the red badge of courage.

Certainly Kurt and Kathy created remarkable viewer-interest and gave me my biggest postbag. After seven years I was still receiving letters about them from around the world.

In 1973 Kathy had sat up straight, preening in the sun-shine by her pool, and told me proudly: 'My breasts are at least *four* times as big as they were. I could have had Small, Petite, Medium, Large or Extra Large, but I had the Mediums and I think they're *plenty* large enough. I love them very much. By having them done before I'm in my forties, I have a jump on life.'

Her new Mediums had destroyed neither her sense of balance nor her cornering: she had learned to cope with them. 'They've helped me feel more secure with myself and my whole life has changed. I used to wear falsies – sometimes I had three falsies on each side. When I was in Florida on my honeymoon, swimming in the Doral pool, one of them came out and floated in the water . . . so I swam away! Then after we'd been married a short while, we had some special people visiting with us and while we were having dinner our little dog Napoleon came in flipping one of my falsies in the air . . . Next day I called Kurt's office and informed them I was coming in to have surgery done on my breasts.'

While Kurt was about it, he also increased the size of her chin, did her eyes and pinned back her ears. The thought that had echoed down the years for me – and the main reason why I had returned to the Wagners – was her remarkable assurance: 'He'll *never* have to divorce me, because he can always change me . . . every year.'

So after a tactful seven years I was back in Los Angeles, where nothing is permanent and two out of three marriages end in divorce, to see how the prescription was working – and if I could still recognise her. I feared by now she might have become the first android.

She remained a bubbly pneumatic blonde with a flip but telling turn of phrase. Kurt, small and bearded, had a thicker frizz of dark curls, but the same dogmatic attitude. He collected old French posters and was proud of his large goldfish.

They were still together after 13 years of marriage, which was approaching some sort of Californian record; yet Kurt came up to my hotel room, sat over a soft drink and poured out his feelings with such astonishing candour that I decided to consider, on film, the success of an improving knife when operated within the family.

He was born in Vienna in 1934, son of a Jewish father and a Catholic mother who escaped from Hitler and arrived in Brooklyn when he was four. His first wife died, and he married Kathy, a tall and buxom girl born in California in 1941 and then teaching black children in the Watts ghetto. He had become one of the best known and richest of America's 2,000 cosmetic surgeons catering to the national craving for rejuvenation.

'Plastic surgery is a marvellous tool, but it's an illusion, and illusion is short-lived. It's part of show business,' he told me in his hospital suite in a black glass building on North Camden Drive in Beverly Hills. 'I ask people what they expect from the surgery, and if they can't give me a good answer, I won't consider operating. I turn away those who come in with pictures of Elizabeth Taylor or Clint Eastwood and say, "Make me like that". I turn away people who hope to change their lives dramatically, who say, "I want my husband back, I can't get a job, I know I could be a foreign agent if I looked like Sean Connery." If a woman who is getting a divorce has a face-lift, she's not going to get her husband back – in fact, she may not *want* him back.

'Cosmetic surgery is just holding back the clock. People tend to blame failure on their external appearance, and very frequently after you've taken away their excuse, they can't deal with that either. All of a sudden they can't say "My life doesn't work because I'm ugly," for when I've stopped them being ugly, their life *still* doesn't work.'

I watched him operate upon a succession of patients. He had abandoned his old surgeon's skullcap with its jaunty query 'What's up, Doc?' for standard green, but his running commentary was as cheery as ever: '. . . and this nice lady is an old patient of mine who had her face and eyes done about ten years ago. She was able to be gainfully employed until she had to admit her age, whereupon she was fired for being 65 years old. She decided she wanted to work again – but couldn't get a job. So here she is, having another facelift. She's 60 now, and one of those people who think I make the world stand still, that she owes her existence to me – and perhaps to a certain extent she does owe me her economic existence. Of course some of these people do go a little overboard, as far as adulation is concerned.'

Most of his nurses and staff also seemed to regard him as a putative husband? 'I would say,' he looked round with some satisfaction, 'that Maria, Laurie, Robin, Vicki, Alex, Nancy, any one of them would snap me up tomorrow. If they wouldn't, they ought to have their heads examined.'

When his equally adoring 68-year-old patient awakened after the operation, I wondered, would she not feel she had gone 15 rounds with Mohammed Ali? 'Surprisingly enough, this is all relatively painless, because most plastic surgery is done underneath the skin. I cut the sensory nerves so the area's numb, and for any number of months they don't feel anything.'

Kurt obviously longed to be in showbusiness, proper. He was only content when the centre of attention and controlling the scene. As a dominant surgeon he was constantly on stage – except at home, where predictably he was least happy. After so many years reassuring patients, his conversation had a sing-song lilt, like a cowboy singing to calm the restless herd. Even outside his operating theatre he addressed people as though they were under twilight sleep.

His operations were fast and deft. Patients were wheeled out and in as the lilting cross-talk continued: '. . . now I'm just going to break this nice lady's nose with an electric saw. The nose is a secondary sex characteristic, and on this 21-year-old lady it goes to the right. We're going to straighten it out and make her look a little bit nicer, aesthetically. This saw sounds a lot worse than it is. Some people take a hammer and chisel, but this is a more humane way of punching somebody in the face . . .'

The girl's nose broke with an awful crack. There was a fair amount of blood. I gazed at the ceiling and murmured that it was not an easy scene for anyone not sharing his enthusiasm for surgery. 'I agree – I'm surprised you haven't fallen over on me yet . . .'

So was I. As someone who cannot watch an inoculation, keeping upright during such operations was an achievement. I found the concentration required for the interview, the worry about each answer and the next question, my concern for what the camera was seeing . . . helped take my mind off the gore. When the sights and sounds grew too bloody, I looked away for a moment and thought of mountain streams.

Editing was another thing: weeks later, sitting at the Steenbeck, those relentless colour close-ups of skin being cut and bones rearranged were far too much for me to take. The film editor found he could just manage to work on the footage for short periods if he turned off the sound.

'. . . now this is a 53-year-old man whose eyelids and eyebrows are beginning to droop, so we're going to arch-up the eyebrows within his hairline and then, to make him look rested and more alert, we're going to take out the extra skin and fat from his upper and lower lids and . . .'

After a reassembly line of operations, we sat in his mirrored office and considered the face-saving situation. Kurt had once told me we were living in the days of the ageless person, and I was beginning to feel Beverly Hills people could be divided into three classes: those who had undergone cosmetic surgery, those about to, and those coming back for the third time . . .

'Whether it's the Greeks, Egyptians or Romans, we've always paid a premium for looking youthful. At the zoo you'll notice most mammals spend a great deal of time preening themselves, so perhaps there's a genetic desire to look better. Today people are vying for a decreasing number of jobs in a very competitive market, so we do about 30 procedures a week. In addition we see somewhere between 40 and 60 patients a day.

'When people ask how long the results will last, I usually tell them as far as eye operations are concerned, it's any-where from ten to 20 years. Facelifts – the first one, five to ten years depending on the quality of their skin, and with each succeeding facelift, a little bit less. The oldest person whose face I lifted was 91 years old. She'd already had five, and looked quite good. She was a very active and aware human being.

'I talk with many of my patients – not necessarily at length, but incisively. A plastic surgeon has to be somewhat of a psychiatrist – after all he's doing psychiatry of the skin. One or two millimetres on the end of the nose can bring happiness or sadness.

'In that respect plastic surgery *does* sometimes change people's lives. There are two kinds: one is a restoration, as you would to a fine painting. You have an individual who is the picture of Dorian Gray, aging but wanting to be some-thing akin to the way they remember themselves in time gone by. The other kind of plastic surgery is a transformation, like a nosejob, a rhinoplasty, pinning ears back, making breasts where there were none.

'Yet I have the distinct impression that people only want to be normal – they don't want to stand out. I don't think people want to be too beautiful any more than they want to be too ugly. They just don't want to be noticed.'

It must be a wholly narcissistic attitude, I said, because nobody else gives a damn what we look like. 'Absolutely true.

The only people who really care are parents – and that's only because children are a projection of themselves. From then down it's a straight drop. Nobody looks at us the way we look at ourselves in the mirror.'

Once the only men who went for furtive facelifts were actors fearing for their livelihood; now, I recalled, I had talked with a 60-year-old retired builder who was having a facelift because 'I can take care of my body by working-out in the gym, but my face is getting away from me.'

Kurt nodded, snipping away: 'We have engineers, professional people, retailers, wholesalers, salesmen, movie stars, gigolos, homosexuals, you name it . . . A man can have hair transplants, hair flaps, nose done, chin done, ears pinned back, lobes made shorter, face done, neck done, stomach done, his arms, thighs, buttocks – most anything . . . Then there are the more exotic operations – many men are becoming women, and that involves a different kind of surgical procedure which I don't particularly like to do, but once a man has undergone a sex change operation, very frequently I build feminine breasts, change the adam's apple, the contour of the nose, the cheekbones and the chin to make them look more feminine.'

While we were talking a large gift-wrapped box arrived from a former patient, a junkie alcoholic prostitute. He had corrected her pendulous breasts, removed some tattoos and given her a tummy-tuck. She had afterwards dropped both her addictions and her profession. The thank you was a lifesize torso in chocolate, with small firm upstanding breasts and a grateful sugar-coated message.

I sensed that to such patients, and to the procession of anxious supplicants who daily waited upon him, he must appear a miracle-worker, for he was offering them their dreams . . .

'I may be the god of the outer skin but I'm surely not the god of the inner workings. I can't give a patient a new heart, a new liver or a new spleen, and I can't change her physiologically. If she thinks I can, she's playing games with her mind. But people see the results and say, 'I'm going to have some more of that stuff". It can become almost an addiction.

Anyhow, it never made much sense to buy clothes for hundreds of dollars and at the same time just let your face drag.

'I think individuals should look as good as they can for as long as they can, and not make a mockery of themselves. For instance I've given my father and mother some plastic surgery, but they don't propose to go out and be teeny-boppers and wear tight jeans. They just look well-rested and refreshed, and that to me is growing old gracefully. My definition of old is dead, and we have plenty of time to be dead.'

The bottom line of the narcissism of his patients was presumably the desire to be more sexually attractive; I wondered whether such insecurity was contagious? 'I had hair transplants myself, and I had my eyes done. I also had my chin done, a long time ago. I won't discount the fact that one day I'll have some more cosmetic surgery. I would assume that in ten or 15 years I would have a facelift, but I don't know. Right now it's not a problem.'

At their Sherman Oaks home in the San Fernando Valley, Kathy, was full of admiration for his restored looks: 'Did you notice all that *hair* that's on there? Eight years of transplants, and it's all growing. Of course he now has a permanent wave, which shows it off.'

Since our last visit his restored locks and looks had only added to her worries: 'One day in the mirror I saw a bit of sagging here and a bit there, so I decided – why not? After all I'm married to the best in the world and I might as well take advantage of it. I asked him to do a facelift on me. Remember, my husband has all these very special ladies who come in to see him, so I must be always one step ahead.'

She also submitted to dermabrasion, a wrinkle-removing operation which to the incredulous outsider looks like a faceful of third-degree burns. 'The acid takes the top two layers of skin off, but it's not painful. In the beginning you come out looking like a hunk of raw beef, and you need two weeks to recover. My son saw me all swollen, with all the scabs, and he said, A truck ran over Mummy's face . . . But I just stayed in bed and was waited on and found it most enjoyable – and it took some of the surface wrinkles and the freckles and the years away . . .'

She always recounted her operations with such breathless little-girl delight, as though surgery was fun. This I just could not believe. 'It's the *nicest* thing in the world,' she protested.

'It *can't* be,' I said, aghast. 'That's a neurosis, if you enjoy operations.'

'Not if you enjoy looking in the mirror afterwards, and seeing yourself nice and rested. That's a good way to make your world be.

'And remember – every single one of those women who come into him and whose faces he changes, whose bodies he changes, they love him. To them he's Doctor God. So I need to look good, for some day some beautiful lady could come into his office and he might run off with her.'

Pedalling away in her bedroom on their $2,000 exercise bicycle, she explained her tactics: 'You must work-out, you must wear bright colours. I don't even go out to the market without my eyelashes on. You must keep yourself a nice, pretty, cosy kind of person to be around.

'When he comes home at night I'm there for him. I have the outstretched arms and I'm in a nice-looking outfit and my hair's fixed up and my make-up's on and I've got waiting lips for him.'

Did she still see him as a romantic Viennese lover or as a man with an Oedipus complex who thought he was Napoleon?

'I see him as both those things. He may look at all those beautiful ladies that are about, but they don't always have such great things to talk about either, and as you get older you learn a lot more about life, you do have a lot more to talk about. I can be tired and sad and depressed too, but on the whole . . .'

'If you're tired,' I interrupted, 'you might just relax and be natural and forget to put on an act for him . . .'

'No, I'm always nice,' she said firmly. 'I think I was *born* being nice.'

'But he knows exactly what you look like because he's done

most of it himself. How your breasts look is no surprise to him, because he *made* them . . .'

'That's right,' she said brightly, 'and he didn't even want to do it. But now he's done them he loves them, the same as I do.'

Keeping their marriage together proved not merely a question of more elaborate cosmetic surgery; many of Kathy's friends looked for help in the Singles bars of Encino, while she had gone to two psychiatrists and a marriage guidance counsellor.

'I feel ladies have forgotten we were made to be soft and gentle and cuddly and cosy and nice. You still catch more flies with honey than with vinegar. Yes, I *have* learned to become a bit tough, because you have to be to make life work for you, the way that it should. But all those dumb-arsed ladies sitting out there doing stupid things with their lives, let 'em look at me in these nice surroundings with three Rolls Royces and beautiful furs and beautiful clothes and maybe they'll be able to score better. Maybe they'll find some bloke in some bar . . . and if they use a little bit of softness, eventually they'll be able to get that man they really wanted.'

Kathy was bright, direct, excellent company – but seemed to draw her reactions from television's day-time soap operas. She played all the stock characters: tantalising seductress, staunch companion, loyal wife, roguish mate. In basing her expectations on such simple dramas and modelling her emotions upon their clean-cut cardboard figures, she was merely following most Californians to whom an experience seen on television seemed more powerful, more sustaining, than real life. To *appear* on the screen could validate a whole existence. Kathy had little depth, but a firm grasp upon money and status, and her definition of a happy marriage was an interesting sex life. So she passed through her world as though reading from an open copy of 'Fascinating Womanhood'.

Still, it could not have been easy to stay married to a god – especially an unhumble one. She had started out upon her marriage as Little Miss Innocent, treating Kurt as the infallible master, teacher and oracle; now she learned to 'zap him back', for Kurt sent her and his favourite nurses to an Erhard seminar for EST – a sort of humiliation therapy. She absorbed more than he expected.

'We learned how to communicate with each other, which is something I believe women and men have not always known how to do. I'm not an unintelligible person but for a while in my life, being a homemaker and a housewife and taking care of the children and being a PTA President and working with children's groups and being a Brownie leader and then a Girl Scout leader, I had lost some of the feelings that women in the business world have. I found out that I really am very special, and all of a sudden he had a different wife who believed she had a real purpose in the world and that she could go out there and be a dynamite kind of person. Yes, I could give him hell – but in a very nice way.'

I wondered whether I was watching the marionette cutting her own strings . . . Did she ever want to shake up Kurt's self-satisfaction? 'Yes, I do have that feeling. I sometimes wish he would loosen up and drink a little bit, or smoke a little grass. It's good to rattle the bars, sometimes. But I can do that, because he can come home one night and I can just not be superglad to see him. Then he can wonder . . . what did she do today?'

'It seems Kurt did himself a bad turn when he sent you to EST. You began to get rather stroppy?'

'A *bit*! Not totally – but just a bit.'

'You'd been using cosmetic surgery in an attempt to make yourself a princess – now you found you could be a princess through your mind?'

'If you have a combination of both, there is no power on earth that can top those two things, working together. You just have to keep your mind aware of what's happening in the world.'

'You mean current affairs? That's a long way from water beds . . .'

'Happenings in the national news – that's why *Time* magazine is so useful . . .'

'The situation in Guatemala? That turns him on, does it?'

'Er, no, but a woman must keep herself abroad and abreast of these things.'

I went shopping with Kathy, her eyes sparkling through that hot-house of materialism. She coveted a low-flying Ferrari, the kind of car it would have been quite impossible for her to slide into, had she chosen the Extra Large. The Large, even.

She was looking for a present for a sister about to get married yet again: 'It's going to be fifth and best, I just *know* it.' I had been staggered by Californian multi-marriages: five or six was no unusual score. Her friend Terri, lunching with us in an open-air restaurant, was less ambitious: 'My mother was ready for me to have five husbands, but I'm going to stop at three.'

Pale and unlined, she had just had a peel. 'On the third day afterwards I saw a mirror – and I looked like an old Indian woman. My face was swollen out half an inch, and my eyes were slits. Kathy came and sat on my bed. I don't know how she could bear looking at me – though I suppose she's used to it. But within ten days I was out shopping with a new baby skin, and now it seems very tight and healthy. I think I'll do it every five years, until I'm ready for a facelift.'

Sitting watching the passing parade jiggling by, I reflected that all these new young girls arriving in town provided the male status symbol – you *could* get by with a utility model, but the luxury version got you a better table. In a society where a 25-year-old was a has-been, surely growing old must be the worst thing that could happen to a woman . . . ?

'Luckily, we'll always have Kurt to rely on.'

'But aren't husbands always turning their wives in for newer models?'

'We *are* the newer models, so it's OK. We go to Ron Fletcher's to exercise. We eat salads, we walk, and we think good clean positive thoughts . . .'

'That's OK as long as your *husbands* keep thinking good clean positive thoughts . . .'

'We can make them do that. That's easy. You just need a soft feminine kind of manner about yourself.'

'Now she's giving me her little-girl routine again!'

'Listen – we happen to be married to two of the hand-somest men who both have rather large egos because they're very talented, and because of that they're insecure, so they always need the compliments. When they get the compliments they just rise to the occasion.'

'I thought it was you women who were insecure, because of all these lush young 19-year-olds . . .'

'Have you tried talking to a 19-year-old lately?'

'Every chance I get . . .'

'The wind whistles through their ears.'

With his commitment to the Californian spirit of total self-absorption, Kurt worked-out every day, pedalling away on his exercise bicycle with a radio headset clamped over his ears, or rowing furiously. Unable to jog because of a bad knee, he used his gymnasium, and one outside activity satisfied his fitness bug while providing trendy family Togetherness: roller-skating. He was into every new craze, early. 'I'm a marvellous disco dancer – but for my birthday present I'd like a new pair of rollerskates.'

He and Kathy, the two daughters of his first marriage and their adopted son, all skated regularly in expensive and exotic gear. I went with them to a fashionable rink where sharp young blacks in day-glo satin danced backwards at 60 mph.

One Sunday morning we drove down to the Venice board-walk. Skaters wearing headphones glided about, exhibiting themselves. At one of the seaside stalls, next to a van selling Humphrey Yoghurt, we saw an earring salesman piercing a girl's ears as part of the deal. Kurt could not watch this outdoor surgery, and looked away. 'Hope you're not going to keel over on me,' I murmured, triumphantly.

Back in the surgery next morning upon his Empire couch amid all those mirrors, Kurt told me: 'I went through a critical period in my life: I became 40 years old. One morning I was getting up and I looked out the window and thought to myself, You know it wouldn't be so bad if I were dead, because I wouldn't have to make any decisions. Then I thought, You're such an up-guy, to even *think* that . . . there must be something terribly wrong. So I went to an EST psychological seminar and an analyst. Within a couple of weeks it became obvious that I was responsible for many of my problems, that nobody was *doing* it to me.'

He also went to an analyst, to find a confessor and father-figure. Los Angeles must have more therapists per square inch than anywhere else in the world, all listening intently for their Big Bucks. As people arrived at the end of the rainbow with no worries about rent money or how to pay the grocery bill, it seemed they looked round for other things to agonise about.

The Wagners provided the complete West Coast package: rich couple, healthy and not unattractive, with large home, regulation stable of Rolls and formidable income . . . retreating in superficial despair to their psychiatrists' couches.

'When I decided to go on my inner journey I knew it wasn't going to be easy,' said Kurt. 'It's not over, although I perceive that I don't have that much longer to go. I've been in analysis for five years, and I've gotten most of the answers I wanted. You see I'd never got straight in my mind who I was. I assumed the role people wanted me to play – a good son, a good husband, a good surgeon. I played for the audience, I never really played for myself. Everybody wants approval – incidentally, plastic surgery was another form of seeking approval: I wanted to make people perfect, so they would love me. Now I've come to the realisation that I'm not God, that I can't please everybody. I'm really just a sculptor of the living.'

In a town where no one felt significant without an interesting trauma, it seemed to me his analyst had merely helped him to rationalise his discontent; he now knew to his own satisfaction *why* he was so discontented. As a believer in the slow natural therapy of a sympathetic friend who was a good listener, I wondered what he would tell his psychiatrist that he would not, for instance, tell me?

'I wouldn't tell you about my masturbation complexes, or my dreams. That's none of your business. It's private.'

EST cost him around £70 a day for a six-day course, while the fees of the ubiquitous shrinks of Beverly Hills escalated to cover what the traffic would allow. I suspected he might have felt easier about our conversations had I been charging a ferocious fee. 'I've spent around $50,000, give or take, on my therapy – but it's far less than the last Rolls Royce I bought and it'll give me a lot more mileage. I fancy I'm a much more satisfactory human being.'

Their marriage? 'It's a retooling of a relationship. The ideal relationship between a man and a woman is one in which you're protected like a child, but are treated like an adult. Now, that's difficult to come by. Everybody yearns for the warmth of the hearth, yet likes to feel that if they wanted to, they could just run through an open meadow.

'Women no longer want to be subservient. They're looking for equality, they're right up there saying "I want what's mine" – and of course in California it's very well defined. Half is hers.

'I think Kathy is going through a transitional period in her life. After all, she's not 25 any more. There are a lot of women who go through this stage, if they've gotten where they've gotten because they're very good looking. When they start to see the twilight of their sexual attractiveness, they start to doubt the future.'

Kathy seemed concerned about his young nurses, yet I recalled he had once told me he would as soon be married to her mother! Certainly he had achieved the ambition of many men by changing his mother-in-law: he had cut more than 10 lbs, or the weight of my portable typewriter, off her stomach . . .

'Her mother has a characteristic that I perceive as being desirable in a male-female relationship – which is, not getting so much flak about things that I do, or not do. She would give me more space. She wouldn't give me the lip that I get from Kathy, and I'm sure she'd be more grateful than someone who still feels at the top of the heap.

'You see I did something with Kathy that was truly difficult: I took a woman who was pretty, and I made her beautiful. But I can't change her. I can change her physically, but only she can change herself.'

So the improving knife was not enough? 'No, it isn't enough. It *can't* be enough.'

He was right about that. In an outburst at once anguished and silly, Kathy later told me: 'If I could say what's real I'd be getting a divorce tomorrow, because I hate this fucking man I'm living with, goddam pain in the arse – thinks he's Dr God, breaks my nails disco-dancing with me . . . I'm a *much* better rollerskater than he is, but God forbid I should let him know . . .'

As though that was not enough, in 1981 Kurt faced three years in the State penitentiary. Before a Los Angles Municipal Judge he was charged with receiving art works stolen from an Arab sheikh's Sunset Boulevard mansion, where we had filmed statues with pubic wigs. It was alleged that in payment for cosmetic surgery performed on the chauffeur to Sheikh Mohammed Al-Fassi, Kurt had received model boats, electronic equipment, antique furniture – and a couple of juke boxes.

In all, art objects and furnishings worth $500,000 had been stolen and the mansion set on fire as a cover-up; Michael Ivan Luterlof, that chauffeur, admitted grand theft. Kurt pleaded No Contest. The Deputy District Attorney asked that counts of insurance fraud against him for conspiring to stage a burglary at his own home in Sherman Oaks and reporting a $227,000 loss, and a stolen property charge against Kathy, should be dismissed.

Superior Court Judge Jack Tanner found Kurt Wagner Guilty, after Luterlof had testified against him. He was fined $5,000 'the largest fine possible under the law' – and placed on probation for three years. He was also ordered to perform 300 hours community service, providing surgery for the poor at the Los Angeles Children's Hospital.

PLATO'S RETREAT

A Friendly way of showing Friendship . . .

WE devoted one of our series of six Californian programmes to Sunset, the broad boulevard that drives right through Los Angeles from the original settlement around Our Lady of Angels. This church opened its doors in 1882 in what is now downtown LA, yet looks and sounds like Mexico. On it way to the Pacific, Sunset cuts through Hollywood and Beverly Hills and, around the Strip, that ultra-Californian kaleidoscope of flaky people, urban shame and private splendour which exists on the fitful far-out edge of the West.

Sunset's 19 miles of visual fatigue say almost everything there is to say about the world's youngest Great City: the gracious and the grotesque, the splendid and the silly. We filmed a dog's birthday party at the Bowser Boutique. It was offering as a suitable present for a lucky birthday dog an £8 jogging suit, or a personal horoscope at £12 a sitting. Assorted animals perched around the party table were known by their owners' names, like Suzy Streisand and Mickey Rooney. Before them was a birthday cake with red icing in the shape of a fire hydrant.

For less elaborate everyday nosh, poodle parlours offered kosher dog food 'canned in kitchens so clean your dog could eat off the floor'. Your pet may not *look* Jewish, the tins warned, but who knows – he could have come from overseas and changed his name . . .

The party was interrupted by a singing telegram delivered by the usual resting actor who danced up in white tophat and tails and sang a long congratulatory message at

the birthday dog. We caught the occasional canine yawn –
though that could have been indigestion; it was certainly a
hard scene to swallow.

Tapdancing telegrams had been breaking out all over
Hollywood. A friend received a score of musical messages
at his birthday party, so his celebration never got off the
ground; every few minutes they had to stop talking to
listen to some forceful livewire who regarded delivery as an
audition. In Beverly Hills telegrams have become more of a
conversation-killer than television.

In the superb shopping streets around Rodeo I looked in
on John Isaacs, whose Michaeljohn salon in London cared
for the hair of Princess Anne. His Beverly Hills branch was
merely handling JAPs – Jewish American princesses – and
show biz. While we talked amid a giggle of crimpers Britt
Ekland arrived, looking crisp and cute. A bright funny girl at
any time, she is the classic cameraholic: when her eye catches
sight of a tripod she instantly revs up into top gear. As
scissors snipped in the background, we had an unexpected
threesome.

'This town only cares about two things,' she said, eyes
swivelling to flash at the fascinating lens. 'To be famous, and
to be rich. You can be either of them, not necessarily
together, and you're OK. I feel trapped in paradise here,
because it's so beautiful and I've got everything life could
offer – so there's no sense of struggle. No moaning about the
weather, no complaining about strikes. It's like one endless summer holiday – but it's essential to have a tan
long nails and blonde hair, and you must have a beautiful
white Mercedes. Unless you have a white Mercedes you
stand out too much in the crowd.'

We looked at No 9561 Sunset, which had managed to
stand out in its own particular way after a Saudi Arabian
bought it for $2.4 million, in *cash*. I asked the estate agent,
who was Jewish, how he handled the heavy payment? 'In a
large suitcase,' he said, 'and very carefully.'

As we talked tourist buses stopped outside the mansion,
because the new owner had planted plastic flowers and
erected tall green statues with painted genitals and pubic

wigs. It became a sort of pornographic Disneyland. 'A lot of
people advised him not to do it,' said the agent, shaking his
head. 'However, he made up his mind that he was going to do
it and – as you see – he *did* it!' Soon afterwards the Sheikh's
villa got even more publicity when it caught fire. The statues,
unfortunately, were not even singed – though Kurt Wagner
was.

At Jimmy's, then the in-place, we filmed Beverly Hills
lunch-time ladies in their hats. I had a date with Gitte Lee,
Danish-born and once a Balenciaga model. She had arrived
with Christopher in the film capital of the world as an
innocent from Cadogan Square SW1, but was aware how
many actors were ripped off by their company's Chinese
bookkeeping. She promptly went to the University of California to study tax and estate planning. 'I thought, I'm a new
kid in town – I'd better find out fast what it's all about. A lot
of people lose their cool when they suddenly make a couple of
million dollars.'

Tangentially, she also learned about California's lavish
Marriage Rights and community property laws. This must
have been a nasty blow to Christopher's straightforward
sense of decent English double-entry book-keeping . . .
which did not necessarily include 'half is hers'.

Gitte had brought their daughter over from her London
school. She had been unhappy and lonely in Beverly Hills so
her headmaster urged the LA cure-all: she should go to a
psychiatrist. 'She went four times, you know, at about two
dollars a minute, and afterwards told me all she did was get
him to help her with her maths. That homework cost me an
absolute fortune. The shrink told me he had children aged six
and seven up, as patients. He recommended she should go to
him two or three times a week, for about four years . . .'

Jimmy himself had been at the Carlton at Bournemouth
and the Savoy before becoming a social arbiter and power in
Beverly Hills, as Maître d' at the Bistro – the peak of the
colony's fierce determination to see and be seen. The position
of the table you get in any significant American restaurant
represents your billing, your place in the pecking order. It is
regarded as vitally important.

This has always baffled me, since I ask only for peace and comfort and, hopefully, good food. At the Twenty One in New York, a famous watering spot where the fare is always quite awful, we were led with great ceremony to a round table between the queue at the entrance-rope and the swingdoors of the kitchen. I started to protest but was shushed by American friends who whispered that it was the very best position in the house. They were pathetically grateful at being Chosen. As passing waiters jogged my elbow, I moodily, tackled a tepid hamburger.

'If people don't get the right table, their whole evening is disastrous,' said Jimmy, 'and it's vital to be able to place them correctly. Zsa Zsa Gabor, you know, usually arrives in mink. We have our cloakroom up front, but there's no way she'll check that coat. She has to walk right through the restaurant to a table at the end to let everybody see what she's wearing. Then she'll hand it over, and it's carried back. Marlon Brando comes in fairly frequently and Johnny Carson of course and Bob Newhart. We also have people like Mrs Chandler, who is a very important lady. She owns *The Times*. Then there's Mrs Bloomingdale and Mrs Ronald Reagan. They're not show business people, but they're still important in terms of influence in this community.'

When I considered the dover sole, Jimmy recalled one guest had just complained that $22 an order was a bit much. 'I explained we had to fly it in from England, but he said, "Did it have to come First Class?"' I could tell that cheeky upstart was due for a quiet table where all he would see was Zsa Zsa's mink, being carried.

Along Sunset, we filmed Hollywood's most powerful fans, the munchkinboppers – girls aged between eight and ten but hoping to pass for an aging 13 who think the Beatles and Rolling Stones are geriatrics and spend like crazy on records by any new boy wonder who takes their fancy in the pages of some fanzine. The magazine *Tiger Beat* had actually advertised for 'teenage idols', which reminded me of a Situations Vacant I once saw in an Adelaide newspaper in South Australia for 'television personalities'.

A queue of youngsters waited to have pictures taken. I found most of them hard to idolise: there was a lot of gum-chewing, acne and plastic sandals. Executives called their mass audition 'a cattle call'.

I observed that for the munchkin multitudes, the Elvis Presley truckdriver-look was dead. They did not wish to be threatened. Today's teen-idols seemed bisexual, for in a world of violence, kidnapping, gay rights and permissive sex, Hollywood had begun to repackage innocence. The winner of our audition was a boy who looked more like the *girl* next door.

Further along Sunset we noticed on the Strip a tattooist's parlour, something more usual amid adult bookshops near dock gates than among high-priced property. The salon of the Tattoo Artist of the Year was 'open noon til midnight, two shifts for tattooists, no waiting'. He had just given Ringo Starr a permanent star and Zandra Rhodes an indelible flower. When we arrived he was working on a young cabinet-maker whose skin had almost disappeared under blue and red swirls, like Chinese foulard.

He had already spent around $5,000 to be transformed into an illustrated man. He denied there was any kind of neurosis involved: 'I just get enjoyment out of having this beautiful artwork, and being different. I love the way people react to me, because of it. Makes me feel special. It short-circuits people's brains – they just haven't *seen* this sort of stuff. My wife's also tattooed. She had cherry blossom on her shoulder.'

Bent over his needle, the tattooist added, 'We refuse to do anything above the neck, or on the hands. A swastika would be just too, you know, too unpleasant. Sometimes penises are tattooed, but not often. Ladies put a tattoo on their breasts, or feminine things like hearts or rosebuds or butterflies. Traditionally, people also have the names of their lovers. Tattoo artists are happy to see this done, both for sentimental reasons and because if they change sweethearts later, you get repeat business to cover it up.'

He could see I was incredulous, so added defiantly, 'You've probably met *lots* of girls who've been tattooed but you just don't know them well enough. If we give a girl a suitable impulse tattoo, there's no big problem – nothing but unending fun until she's a grandma.'

We moved on cautiously, to consider Plato's Retreat West, a private club for swingers where *everything* was allowed except alcohol and unescorted males. The 5,000 members it claimed needed to be very heterosexual indeed, for they went to have sex with strangers – so they could be considered fallen Angelinos.

The club stood in a seedy Hollywood sidestreet and was active until dawn. Its amenities included a disco, cinema, buffet, jacuzzi – and 27 cubicles upstairs. The orgy room was called the Mat Room as though part of some gymnasium – which in a way, I suppose it was . . .

It had previously been a gay bath club. In California homosexuals have managed to weld themselves into a minority with political clout and at the slightest restriction of their particular activities would scream 'Police harassment' in outrage, like looters disturbed in the everyday act of smashing shop windows and emptying supermarkets. Heterosexuals of course are not organised, and therefore vulnerable. Just before my visit the police had raided Plato's, issued complaint applications for lewd conduct against its members – and cited the management for operating pinball machines without a permit.

In the end no action was taken against Plato's people, other than a stern warning about lifestyle; doubtless their names were fed into some hungry computer which would remember forever that they were aggressive swoppers, at least.

I am no enemy of gays, as several programmes prove, but it seemed unfair they should be protected for turning in a different direction, that the private 'gloryholes' where they practised their rituals should be sacrosanct – while heteros were picked on for demonstrating appetites that were relatively straightforward, even if over-active.

Filming in a sex club was an unlikely project, demanding a nice line between active porn and inactive boredom, between under and over co-operation. In our Sunset profile we had already looked at museums and star-studded mansions, talked with industrialists, society women and film stars; for a rounded picture we could hardly ignore the tacky – the outsider's abiding impression of Sunset.

David Green, my director, went to see Plato's management, and they agreed we might film if we came in early, before the serious activities of the night began. We went hesitantly on a recce, signing the temporary membership forms to admit we appreciated we were in for an Adult experience. Barbara Twigg, our researcher, and a girl friend stood as those essential partners who, in keeping with club regulations, had to be thrown into the central pool in an abandoned way. We kept an eye on our quid pro quos, but it was not a place where people were dragged upstairs screaming-and-kicking; more a scene of stealthy co-operation.

Next night we went back to film, set up our lights, stood the camera unobtrusively in a corner – and waited for the Action.

Nothing happened. A few of the staff acknowledged us with that special American blend of the remote and the roguish, like airline stewardesses in leotards. They were wandering around in the gloom, preparing a tired buffet, laying out piles of towels, straightening the mattresses.

Like any empty nightclub observed in the daytime, this Swingers' swapshop was not upon close inspection very seductive. It smelt of disinfectant and roasting popcorn. Its romantic centre was a misty enclave of couches and bolsters surrounded by transparent folds of slightly grubby white veiling, like a Japanese honeymoon hotel or the setting for a turkish delight commercial. 'Isn't that exquisite?' breathed the manager, who was escorting us round. Well, actually no. The cubbyhole cubicles were even less appealing; it must have been like making love in an airing cupboard.

The place was getting to me. I have a healthy appetite, but not even the free buffet seemed desirable. When I peered across the empty mattresses in a cinema which should have been showing raunchy blue movies, it was transmitting the NBC news. This was not erotic.

Beginning to feel undersexed, I moodily watched the

jacuzzi bubbling away to itself. After a while we felt the need to film *something* if only to break the monotony, so at the director's request I removed my shoes and they shot me strolling across the mattresses in the orgy room. I then suffered an instant desire to burn my socks.

A few couples drifted in. We studied them expectantly. They were mostly middle-aged middle-fat middle-Americans. They changed into something loose and came and hung around the bar, drinking cokes and being warily polite. I found myself making desultory cocktail-party chat with a group of unappealing people in towels. I was not sure what I had been expecting, but it was not *this*.

After a while I grew impatient to leave and get some fresh air. David, having invested a lot of time and effort getting cameras and lights in, wanted to wait on the off-chance something – anything – might happen. To cover all our trouble, he said, we ought to shoot a few more feet to indicate the club's potential, however boring.

They started disco dancing, so we filmed some of that. They were a nondescript group and could have arrived from any shop or office; not even their towels were distinctive. Some of the girls were quite pretty, some not very; some young, some not so; some mildly interesting, some Forget It. Then a few pairs mooched away into the jacuzzi and, through the steam, it seemed the evening was getting slightly warmer.

Clutching my notebook to show I was neutral, and working, I mingled with members and found one promising interviewee: a young nurse of 23 with a face like a nun. Suzie came regularly with her husband, and sat and discussed her sexual activities with such straightforward candour that I began to feel sheepish about *not* being a swinger. Encouraged, I urged her not to get too deeply involved with anyone until I could return to her with my camera, which by then was observing couples mingling in the jacuzzi.

This was evidently stimulating. After a few hundred feet of steamy titillation, David reminded them that the orgy room was empty, not to say unusually well lit. To my surprise they all instantly rose from the frenzied waters and strode past us purposefully, naked but business-like, and distributed themselves in small groups around the mat. It was not the kind of get-together one would normally be observing, so tactfully we left them to become further acquainted. When we returned – it was Hieronymus Bosch. I was still not sure what I had been expecting – but this, I supposed, was *it*.

Oblivious of lights and film crew, a confusion of moulded heaving limbs was spread out before us. Introductions had been effected and co-operation was whole-hearted. We were suddenly confronted by more Action than we could reasonably handle . . .

My crew stood, hypnotised and abashed; even the Sparks was fiddling shyly with his lights. This was a room, it seemed, where Anything Went – though it was all happening under a stern notice announcing 'No Smoking'. After all, there *are* limits . . .

We suffered a long moment of indecision.

However, the camera was ready and waiting – so we pulled ourselves back to reality and in keeping with my theory that nothing ever happens twice, began to film anyway. 'We'll think about it afterwards,' I said, with a small gulp. I did not dare ask Peter Jackson what he was actually *seeing* through his viewfinder, for the camera does concentrate so. Even glancing around the whole room with professional detachment, I was seeing rather more than I cared to, thank you very much all the same.

David whispered that perhaps I should go and sidetrack the owner, lest he come in and tell them to break up and get back to polite conversation, so with some relief I went and sorted him out. He was called Larry and had started the original Plato's in New York. This west-coast branch seemed a sort of franchise, and he had arrived to supply impetus and new ideas. His dark blue T-shirt announced: King of the Swingers.

I found what he had to say unusual, and decided to interview him in front of the jacuzzi. For cutting continuity, this would require our hyperactive group back in the steaming water again, where we had filmed them before they went into overdrive.

Back in the orgy room, my cameraman had by now shot more than enough. He was standing aside observing the turmoil with professional boredom – indeed the thrashing about *was* curiously unerotic. The crew had also recovered from their shock and were merely wondering how they were going to describe it to the boys, back at the studios.

Such disinterest should have been off-putting, but our members were now intent upon themselves and had stopped being camera-conscious or acting. They were oblivious of everything but what was immediately ahead.

'Tell them to stop,' I said to David, finally. After all, he was the director. 'We want them back in the jacuzzi so we can film some chat with the King. We've got quite enough of *that*.'

He ventured into the middle of the room among the various heaps of members, and coughed expectantly. 'Er – excuse me,' he said, looking round for attention. No interest. The fête continued.

After a long pause waiting for inaction, I joined him under our lights amid the toiling masses. 'We've got to break this up,' I said impatiently, across a heave of buttocks. Nobody noticed, or cared.

'I say, I said, stamping around the mattress. 'Just a jiff. Would you mind? Listen could you *hold* it a minute – er, that's to say, would you *hang* on a minute . . .' Not one of them even bothered to look round. They were just not taking Direction.

To be studiously ignored by a dozen adults consenting in private can be slighting. I was baffled.

We had a conference behind the camera. Someone suggested we might all go in and drag them out by the ankles – though that could have led to some dislocation and, it appeared from cursory inspection, two multiple fractures . . .

In the end we only got them to stop by turning off our lights and leaving them in the gloom to which they had once been accustomed. Slowly they grew aware the impatient world outside was trying to tell them something, and slowed up a bit.

David explained what we were trying to do, and they disentangled with difficulty, breathing hard. Nobody said anything. As a group, they were not strong on conversation. Standing up, shakily, they obligingly tottered back into the next room and the warm water, where we quickly filmed an interview with Larry before they could get started again and wreck the continuity.

Trying to rise above it all, I asked why he had chosen such a name for a club not noticeably platonic: 'We wanted something that was either Greek or Roman, because that's erotic,' he said. 'I decided on Plato's because it was the only one I could spell, actually. Afterwards I discovered Plato was gay, but then it was too late to change.'

He was articulate and voluble, a truckdriver with a sense of mission, and had been wounded by outside criticism. 'What we do behind these closed doors is really nobody's business. We're in our own private club and have a perfect right to lead the lifestyle we want to lead. No it's *not* franchised sex – it's a swinging club for free-thinking people, free-living adult couples. It's a club with everything included, with sex available if wanted – but people don't *have* to get involved sexually. They come here to dance, to meet other people and to socialise. We have backgammon rooms upstairs, we have many, many things – like pool tables. But if they desire to get involved with other people sexually, then it's there. So it isn't a sex club, it's a social club with sex available on the premises.

'On the East Coast we've had up to 1,000 people on the premises at one time, and we've never had a bouncer. We've never needed one. Men don't look to fight when they're going round in towels. They come with ladies, and there's no pressure.

'You see, a man and his wife may not believe in monogamy, they may believe in open marriage and want a total honest relationship. A man may love this woman, want to live with her, have children with her, and the woman feel the same about the man . . . but they may also feel they just don't want to be with only one person sexually throughout their whole lives. Some men believe that if *they* can do it, why not their wives? So they come here together, instead of going out cheating, going to prostitutes and saying they're home half-an-hour late because they missed the train.

'We're in a society where one out of every two and a half marriages ends in divorce. With swinging couples, it's one out of every 12. I don't know if it's the right way, but it's the right way for *me*. It's the right way for these people too – they're happy.'

I looked around. They may not have been happy, but they were certainly *occupied*. Surely, I suggested, the Courts could say that Plato's encouraged lewd, dissolute and degenerate conduct, that it was the camel's nose in the tent? 'I think sex is beautiful, absolutely beautiful, and when you see it done here, it's not lewd. Nobody's running around grabbing at anybody. It's a beautiful thing to see four or five couples in a room having sexual relations. There's nothing indecent, in my eyes. And if a person thinks there is, they've got a tremendous hang-up and a problem and they'll never be happy in life.'

I suggested that the members splashing happily behind us, all quite obviously into group sex, must be voyeurs or exhibitionists? He was shocked by my insensitivity: 'Group sex to me is ten couples in one big heap. Since I opened up Plato's three years ago, I've never yet seen a pile-up. Never!

'I've seen two couples together, or three couples in a situation, and it's quite beautiful – but everybody isn't into everybody else. Even on the mat area, where you can get 15 or 20 couples, there'll be just a couple here and a couple there. Everybody isn't piled into one big heap. We respect our women. Our women respect us.'

I stared around, watching them respecting each other like anything, in properly small groups.

'Nobody has the right to tell us how to lead our lives,' he said. He had been through this conversation before – probably with the police. 'A lot of people don't mind their own business. With all the problems in the world today, they worry about things like this! There's wars and violence and everything else – that doesn't bother anybody, but people get *furious* about Plato's. For what reason? We're here, happy, having a good time. This is our fantasy land. It's Disneyland for adults, that's all it is.'

So we filmed around their playground. It was hard to see where we could go now, techniquewise. Having lived through the hurly-burly of the Orgy Room, I found it impossible to *imagine* what they did behind the door marked Games Room . . . I went in with fingers crossed.

It was full of pintables. In its relative calm I settled down with Suzie, the nurse, who had obligingly delayed getting into the spirit of things. In her see-through mini negligée she was pretty and plumply provocative. Her husband Michael joined us; he was 27 and bearded. She told me she came to the club 'for sex, good conversation and intellectual variety.' You could have sex with many in an evening, or you could just find yourself spending the night 'talking to one interesting man, as has happened to me many times.'

However, on occasions, she added thoughtfully, she *had* made love with three different men during one visit. Her husband claimed a top score of seven women.

She was the more intelligent, and I wondered what would happen to her sense of loyalty to Michael, who seemed smug enough, if she met someone she preferred? 'That's interesting, because I *did* meet one man I had a lot in common with. In my field Michael's completely irrelevant – he's into electrical contracting and I'm into saving lives. This man was a clinical psychologist working with battered children, and I did a thesis on abused children in college. We went into a private room and lay down together and just talked for two or three hours, without having sex. He asked me if I would have an outside affair with him, but I said I would *never* do that. I swing – that's where I lose my inhibitions – but I could not go out and cheat on my husband. It's as simple as that.'

Michael revealed there were class divisions even in sex clubs: 'We went to one where the people had noses that wouldn't go below their eyebrows. If you didn't have a Mercedes or a Rolls, they wouldn't talk to you.'

It seemed to me it must be hard to be snobbish while wearing only a towel? 'You'd be surprised. Women have their ways of finding out about you – and telling you to get lost, in a very polite way. I saw one gentleman get a cup of very hot coffee spilt right onto his towel . . .'

Looking around with quiet despair I observed, rather unkindly, that perhaps California would deserve the earthquake when it came and the whole State slipped slowly under the Pacific. Were we not living through another Sodom and Gomorrah? 'I've often wondered what that meant,' said Michael, not too concerned.

'I don't feel what we are doing is perverse at all,' said Suzie, taking the point. 'Though I do believe there *are* things that deviate in sex, and they are extremely rude.'

But surely sexual activity in the club must be like making love in a cinema foyer and remove the last vestige of romance and affection from sex? 'Not really. You could go in a private room and nobody would disturb you. There're locks on some doors.'

Michael was in qualified agreement with me. 'I've never *really* been into groups. I like a one-on-one basis, or two-on-one. I've never been able to get going in a group room. For some reason I think, like you said, it takes the romance out of it.'

Suzie did not find her clubbable activities with strangers either debasing or cheapening: 'No, I'm not a sex object. He's letting me express my individuality by sleeping with other men. Sex exhilarates me, you know. I feel good afterwards. I don't have to go out and have an undercover affair. That would really bother me. My conscience would get to me. Sex between Michael and I is special, but sex here with other men is a fantasy. It's an ego trip – it's like dual infidelity.

'But it must be a couple. That's the basis of swinging, and you build a friendship from that. One couple we know are the Godparents of the other couple's children – but they swing together. It's just a friendly way of showing friendship.'

PART EIGHT

WIND HIM UP!

ISLANDS

They feed the Pigs on Passionfruit,
the Sheep on Wild Peaches . . .

I CAN recall the exact moment that led me to buy a house on a
tiny island and live happily-ever-after.

We had been filming in the Far East for several months,
covering 40,000 hot and humid miles and living the usual
gypsy life out of suitcases. After completing six programmes
we wrapped and I rushed towards the first plane home – to
be welcomed at last by my own bed and books. I loved that
apartment at the top of Nash's magnificent Cumberland
Terrace. At night when through-traffic was stopped, Regent's Park, in the very heart of London, stood tranquil and
silent as though in the countryside.

Next morning I got up and, ignoring the mountain of mail,
unpaid bills and Dear Sir Unlesses blocking my study door,
went down to the garage to see if the Bentley would start. She
did, in her usual well-bred way and I set off on those
too-familiar 200 miles up the M1 to Leeds, checked in at the
Queens, went on to the studios – and started editing and
writing the series.

It was a weekend, so the place was deserted. In the deep
deep hush that follows television's short week I worked at an
editing, Steenbeck with my old friend Tony Essex, Head of
Documentaries, getting the first taste of what we had shot.
Then I drove out of Leeds, north across the River Wharf to
the village of Leathley, to lunch with Stephen and June
Watling. It was flaming June and we sat on the lawn
drinking white wine and eating strawberries.

I absorbed the green peace, reflecting idly on the frantic

activity of my past months, the bumpy flights and hassles with oriental customs, the endless worries about programmes and crew hours and dawn starts and late finishes and constant packing and flying-on, culminating in 18 restless airborne hours getting home. Then immediately on to the M1, bucking all that traffic and driving too fast and arriving with sweaty palms to face suitcase-living for more months while editing and writing . . . before setting off around the world again on the same wonderful treadmill. I looked across the dale and into the future and for the first time wondered: what am I doing it *for*?

Certainly not for grandchildren. Not for ambition or money or fame or whatever; so – for habit? Since the end of the war I seemed to have been constantly working Away – but rarely playing at Home. I relished my television life, but it had meant seven-day weeks and only a few days each year in my own bed.

Sitting amid a serenity of roses listening to the chimes of the village church, I was suddenly aware that never in my life had I owned a garden – not even a windowbox. I finished my wine and decided: I'll find a piece of earth. I'll buy a home.

It was about time. That piece of earth was, after all, the object of all the effort. I longed to be near water, so as soon as I could get away from the studio for a few days took a wide detour on the way home and looked at millhouses in the Cotswolds, the Wye Valley and Dorset. Brave, tragic Kenneth Allsop with whom I had shared a Tonight office had just found a mill outside Bridport and was writing ecstatically about his bird-watching life. I hunted and viewed and discussed, yet nothing I saw seemed quite right. Then I realized the reason for my dissatisfactions: I was still suffering from Islanditis. If the anchor was going down, it needed to be in a certain kind of place.

I had caught that happy infection years before in the South Pacific, on a tiny speck of Switzerland floating in tremendous seas between Australia and New Zealand. In a paradise where nothing bites and nothing stings, they feed the pigs on passionfruit and the sheep on wild peaches . . . Norfolk Island, the distant home of the descendants of the Bounty mutineers. Its towering pines and little mountains stand above dramatic seascapes of blue ocean and white water; an unknown place fit for eagles, or angels.

I first reached Norfolk in October 1960, not feeling at all angelic. Qantas had to use an old DC4 on the island's short grass strip, which had a giant banyan tree as its terminal building. After a couple of frenzied days filming we had to scramble aboard the airliner again on its way back from Auckland or we should have been stranded for a week, and on our Australian tour had no time to spare. It was time enough to fall in love.

That gentle corner of paradise 12,000 miles from home and about 1,000 miles from anywhere else, was once Britain's Devil's Island, where convicts from the settlements of Van Diemen's Land and New South Wales suffered deliberate and calculated inhumanity: 'A place of extremist punishment, short of death.' Some 1,200 twice-convicted prisoners considered too dangerous to hold in Australia sailed into a regime so harsh some blinded themselves with the sap of the milky mangrove in an attempt to escape the labour gangs, or committed further crimes to find relief in a death sentence.

One group in leg-irons were building a bridge when, goaded, they smashed the head of a brutal guard with their shovels, hacked up his body and walled it into the stonework. That night it rained. Next morning a tell-tale trickle of blood was seen oozing from the wall . . . Ever since it has been Bloody Bridge.

The island was relieved of its burden of human misery in 1855, when the convicts were replaced by dusky families of Christians and Nobbs, Mills and McCoys, products of the most famous mutiny of the high seas. So the first invasion of remote Norfolk had been caused by the need for a secure penal settlement for 19th century hard cases, the second when the Bounty descendants outgrew Pitcairn. The island's third invasion was caused, it seemed – by me.

My original programme had been transmitted one miserable November night; on the strength of my enthusiasm for that sub-tropical speck in an azure ocean, some 50 British families sold up their homes and travelled across the world to start a new life in the South Pacific. The original Bounty families numbered 193 but 46 returned to Pitcairn, so our net contribution was considerable. As I flew from Sydney on my second visit it occured to me I was in for trouble if, when my lot finally reached Norfolk, they all hated it . . .

I need not have worried. They were as happy as Mutineers in their tax-free oasis, and threw a thank you party. One of them, Tom Elliot, composed some forgettable lines which he proclaimed with considerable flourish:

> Tonight it is the pleasure of the people gathered round
> To welcome Alan Whicker, he whose name is so re-nowned.
> He's here again we're glad to say, to make another picture;
> We hope his visit will become a firm biennial fixture.
> It's sad to think that he must pay such rates and taxes heavy;
> Australia pays those things for *us* – we never get a levy.
> So Alan Whicker come again: our greeting will be hearty
> We'll kill the fatted calf again, and have another party . . .

When television is blamed for everything bad from dandruff to drug-taking, it was a delight to find one programme at least had improved so many lives, if not their doggerel, and that so many contented families were indebted to the small screen. Indeed Norfolk offered such an idyllic life that when Tom Lloyd – editor, writer, printer and distributor of the local weekly – was involved in a legal dispute he was threatened with transportation for seven years – to England. That scared him.

Once again I surrendered to the languor and beauty of an island where it is always afternoon, where the grass is unusually green and scarlet hibiscus blooms big as plates amid guavas and frangipani, where blue and red parrots and white terns fly amid murmuring pines.

Norfolk's three-miles-by-five showed signs of advancing civilisation: 30 telephones, one street lamp and two policemen. Cattle were still treasured and had right of way; it was cheaper to hit a pedestrian.

We were there for Bounty Day, when most of the 1,200 residents put on period costumes and went tor a picnic within the walls of the prison. Their tablecloths were piled with suckling pigs, great red emperor fish, tropical fruits and flowers. They were honouring forefathers who in 1787 defied Captain Bligh and the Royal Navy to return to their Tahitian foremothers. By cruel justice most of Captain Bligh's party survived their 3,600 miles in an open 23-foot boat, while all but one of the mutineers died violently in various ways – though not before starting families.

Their leader Fletcher Christian and his Tahitian wife had a son called Thursday October Christian. He was among those transported to Norfolk which, because of its isolation and lack of a harbour, became a sort of unchanging 18th century storeroom of people. The whole population shared eight surnames. On my first visit there were 24 families of Christians, 12 of Adams, 27 of Quintals . . .

I spent much time with Girlie Christian, who had once come galloping up Middlegate to greet me. She was now 76, her voice a lilting blend of 18th century west country English, Gaelic and Tahitian. In time to come that conversation will be a goldmine for phonologists and phoneticists. She had 86 acres but had never married: 'Husbands steer clear of me, boy,' she giggled happily. She described everything as beautiful, and only herself as ugly. This was not so; she was unforgettable.

She had just lost a leg in a fearful riding accident : 'I pretty well lived on horseback, then. I was going off one morning to get ripe peaches, and it was the big chestnut's turn for a gallop. He'd been down there a million times before, but this time he turned round and bucked and I shot up in the air. I hit the ground harder than I wanted to, and he came straight down, saddle an' all, over me. When he stood up he was crushing my chest and my stomach – boy, I must have been strong. The doctor said I was made of iron. I couldn't move then, for a long long time, but I lay there thinking : I'll be jiggered if I'm gonna die and sleep down here with these ants, so I started to crawl up to the path, but it didn't feel right and when I turned round, I saw my right leg on the gravel over there, with the bone stuck down into the ground.'

She was finally carried in an open truck to the Island doctor, still clutching her leg: 'I said, Doc, before I go under, sew my leg on again, so's I can go to the ballroom. I'm old and ugly but still I love the ballrooms. They suit me good – they're beautiful.'

Sadly, Girlie's dancing days were over, though with only one leg she still showed spirit enough for ten. I called her from New Zealand in 1979 and learned the indomitable lady had gone to her defiant ancestors.

On the island she loved, whenever two cars passed along its 100 miles of narrow roads I was delighted to observe their drivers always waved. They did not need to see who was approaching, because on 13 square miles they *had* to know each other. For the same reason, everyone always said Hello to everyone else. Life moved at a proper South Pacific pace. Nothing got locked up: 'If you take the keys out of the car, you might lose them . . .'

Their barter system made financial gain unimportant. Riches were in personal and communal happiness. Time was to be ignored and work sidestepped. A Norfolk Islander is pleased to tell visitors he is an 'LAP' – 'as Little As Possible.'

Gentle dreamy folk, they live slow sweet lives as changeless as the empty ocean which surrounds them. Even their voices have the low musical murmur of those who for generations have never known hurry or anxiety. 'Whataway you?' they inquire politely, in greeting.

Their drowsy oasis, determined to remain a century behind the rest of the world, had no taxes or duties and offered one final gracious gesture: it was a great place to die. Burial is free to resident and visitor. The graveyard is two centuries old and must be the most beautiful in the world.

I would sit under its pines and absorb the tranquillity, wondering again how much sensuous serenity could grow from a history of pain and fear. In that most cruel of penal colonies many hundreds had died in violence and despair, purged of their wickedness by the lash and the scaffold. In other forlorn places of dread I have visited around the world, in Dachau and Devil's Island, the horror remains and can be felt; it has seeped into the stones and left an indelible emanation of misery . . .

The gentle peace of Norfolk which so affected me had also, it seemed, soothed away the torments of yesterday, placated the restless spirits of those unhappy men. It was now a place to laze and wonder – and listen . . .

> Between the soughing in the pines
> And the surging of the sea,
> Hear a far-off human sigh . . .

As an urban creature who had spent his life in cities and relished the protective anonymity of an uncaring metropolis, I grew captivated by the idea of living within a small community set apart from the rest of the world, where I would find myself absorbed within its borders. Under the pines in that graveyard overlooking the South Pacific, I caught Island Fever.

Returning to Sydney that evening, the lights in the packed elderly airliner were so dim we sat in gloom, unable to read for five unpressurised hours. With all the old treasure-island magic knocked out of me, I went slowly mad. I could not see myself doing that regularly, just to reach Australia, so started my search for another island.

My other favourites were almost as far-flung: Penang, in the Straits of Malacca, where deserted rock-strewn beaches are still and perfect as Japanese gardens and the people a warm mixture of Malay, Chinese and Indian – plus a few happy hangovers from the British Raj. The truly magical Bali, where one would always remain an outsider. Friendly Western Samoa, where I tore a ligament and the famous Bloody Mary – actually called Aggie Grey – gave me her stout lemontree walking stick; few men can say they have been supported by Bloody Mary . . .

None of these exotic green dots could fit permanently into Whicker's world. I wanted to lift the drawbridge slightly – not pull it right up, and goodbye.

Nearer home I looked at Malta, with its golden honeycombs of local limestone; it has a lot of character – most of it barmy. In the end I found an island where I could live and work: it had been waiting quietly, almost too close to see, while I gazed towards far horizons. With majestic coastline and slight French accent, it lay only 90 miles from Dorset – or 35 minutes from London Airport. Post and papers arrive at breakfast-time and I can understand the television, yet countryfolk speak a patois William the Conqueror would understand and customs he knew are part of everyday law. Britain's south sea island – Jersey.

I had kept half an eye on the Channel Islands since my first visit for Tonight in 1961, but property there always seemed out of reach. Then came an invitation from Channel Television to attend its tenth anniversary celebration. They had asked somebody from Coronation Street, from a comedy series, Sandy Gall from News, with me as the documentary man. Len Matchan lent me his penthouse at the Water's Edge Hotel and during that weekend I looked over houses and found that because of fear the OEEC might change Jersey's financial status, property values had levelled off when those on the mainland were inflating. Jersey's low tax, though hardly a disadvantage, made little difference to me: most of my income was taxed at source, I had stopped smoking, did not drink spirits and used only a limited amount of aftershave. Food was more expensive than on the mainland, and life-enhancing wine no cheaper.

That weekend I found my home in a glorious setting on a wooded hillside overlooking France, surrounded by three acres of roses, hydrangeas and pines. It had no pond or stream, but instead a superb view of the deep sea and the Dirouilles. The daily sight of some wide expanse of water as it changes from turbulent to turquoise brings balance and serenity, and is good for the soul. It was not quite Norfolk – but it *was* above the bay where they filmed 'Seagulls Over Sorrento'. How can you get more exotic than that?

Jersey was accepting 15 new residents a year, following careful vetting – a number about to be reduced to ten. It was a challenging sort of island, loftily dismissing many would-be residents for its own secret reasons. My bid for the house was accepted, so I was officially examined, investigated, consi-

dered – and finally admitted! The search that began in the
Pacific and crystallised in Yorkshire, had ended.

I am now, as I said, living happily ever after; island life has
proved everything I expected it would be – except that the £8
day-return flight to London has become £84, and still going
up . . . All that balances out in the end. Happiness does not
show in the double-entry bookkeeping, yet is everyone's
bottom line.

Just as it picks and chooses residents, so Jersey jealously
guards its independence. It was part of the Duchy of Normandy long before William set sail for Hastings in 1066 and
all that, and the Normans ruled the island for another 138
years afterwards. Considered carefully, those other islands to
the north – now known as the United Kingdom – really
belong to self-governing Jersey, still making its own laws,
running its courts, post office and airport, issuing banknotes,
controlling its destiny.

Sir Amias Poulett, a perceptive Governor of Jersey, wrote
before he died in 1588: 'I can now tell you by experience it is a
blessed life, to live in those little Isles. When I consider the
course of things in this worlde I pursuade myself that God
loveth those Isles and careth for them.' In the first book ever
written on the Islands, in 1629, Chaplain Peter Heylin found
Jersey 'exceeding pleasant and delightsome'. It *is* a caring
community where Church and family retain their old significance, still free from natural or man-made disasters, from
earthquake and tidal wave, anarchy and riot and terrorism.

Like that other island which started it all for me, Jersey has
time. People stop in the narrow deep-cut lanes to talk. Pause
to admire an outrageously pretty cottage garden and you are
liable to have cuttings pressed upon you. Stop a milk rounds-
man and, should you have no change, he may present you
with a pint. In the countryside, help yourself from wayside
stalls of flowers and vegetables and leave some money in the
tin. Does that still happen elsewhere? It is certainly the only
place in the world where I enjoy shopping, because in St
Helier stores the assistants, like Mr Kipps, are unhurried
and friendly and ready to step outside and point out the shop
down the road.

Jersey folk, so friendly and financially astute, may not always fully appreciate their own island; some have even expressed surprise that a professional world traveller should be so happy to come to rest on their 45 square miles. They have their own way of being nasty or nice: referring to one stuck-up local, a farmer's wife said, 'We say he fancies his goat.' There is no answer to that; nor to the ultimate compliment from a plasterer: 'We like you,' he said thoughtfully, 'because you're so *ordinary*.'

One Jerseyman, a former editor of *The Times* and Director-General of the BBC, Sir William Haley, describes their character as 'a mixture of British pragmatism and Norman shrewdness.' The French have always been in-and-out; from 1461 they occupied the island for seven years. During their Revolution and the Napoleonic Wars, aristocratic émigrés came to stay – and trebled the size of St Helier. Their final attempt was a comic and unsuccessful invasion in 1781 – the last land battle on British soil. Today the French get their own back as hordes land daily on shopping sprees. Some 6,000 of them live on this Isle de la Manche which Victor Hugo, a former resident, called 'a piece of France fallen into the sea and gobbled up by the English.'

There were already some 15,000 British residents 150 years ago, attracted by the climate and the cost of living. Income tax was not introduced until 1928, and when Hitler's Army took over in 1940 was still only 9d in the pound. To pay the Occupation costs of 12,000 German soldiers it was raised to 4s in the pound – at which tolerable level it has since remained. The Wehrmacht was dismissed in 1945, leaving only fortifications, a dearth of trees and the memory of a certain chill correctness.

Though nothing in the world gets better, except perhaps medicine (and not always that) Jersey has the peaceful lifestyle, the stability, the mainland has lost. It exudes tranquillity. What little crime there is comes mainly from itinerant workers from both sides of the Channel. Strikes are rare and quickly settled, for these are reasonable folk. Each parish had a perquage, a pre-Reformation sanctuary path from its 11th century church to the sea, wide enough to allow safe conduct all the way down to that getaway boat. If a capture was made despite such sanctuary, confessions were never extorted by torture; Jersey always hanged its witches before burning them. Guernsey burned them alive.

Despite the tiny population, Jersey still finds leaders of surprisingly high calibre – men who would make their mark anywhere. Hired professional advisers have proved successful, but all decisions come from the States, the 500-year-old parliament unburdened by the party system which plagues other Houses. Its members do not need to vote against their convictions nor make party points. They are 53 fallible but well-intentioned men and women, elected because their value is known.

In these brusque days the island's public servants are pleasant without exception. Postmen wait while you finish a letter and come back if they see it incorrectly stamped. Septic tanks are politely and euphemistically emptied by, wait for it, the Resources Recovery Board. The honorary police force is based upon the unarguable principle that local men know best what is going on in their own parishes. With their amateur status they remain easy targets for any snide journalist who wants to cover his holiday expenses, but in country districts the voluntary system works, as it always has, remarkably well. St Helier has paid uniformed police who seem more agreeable than policemen elsewhere. Even traffic wardens are friendly and helpful – and that's *impossible*.

As you may have gathered, I go about the world an eager ambassador, and flying over Burma have been delighted to find a Jerseyman piloting my Malaysian airliner. The Sydney fruit-machine factory sales manager was Tourist Officer when first I visited the island. The other luncheon guest at the Penang Club has, I discover, a home in the next valley. My Hong Kong hotel receptionist worked at St Brelade's . . . It always feels like a family reunion. Yesterday's Jerseymen also got around: Colonel 'Buffalo Bill' Cody, the cowboy whose museum I visited outside Denver; Jean Martell, the brandy-maker; Lillie Langtry and Elinor Glyn, raising temperatures around the turn of the century; Mr Cabot, whose family went to Boston to Talk Only to God . . .

Despite those even more famous ambassadors – the Bambi-esque cows with soft sexy eyes – the world outside does not always seem aware of the island. A letter from the US reached me after months stamped 'Not known in Nicaragua'. I was shocked. Were those postal workers not aware that Britain's first four pillar boxes, created in 1852 by Anthony Trollope, stood in St Helier? American telephone operators tend to connect you with the upstart New Jersey (wherever *that* is) or those obscure dots off the Californian Pacific coast which presume to call themselves the Channel Islands. When I wrote Trinity, Jersey on my Charleston hotel regis-ter, I noticed the clerk instantly demoted me to Trenton, New Jersey.

The real Channel Islands – self-sufficient for three centur-ies – have their own television service, all the more remark-able because with Jersey's 76,000 population it is as though Carlisle or Hastings or Stevenage had a station. There is a responsible evening paper which, for lack of competition, displays lofty indifference to hot news. It took them five days to print the results of our parish cattle show. The suspense was awful.

My new home not only spared me the motorway but to my surprise allowed me to work more efficiently. The studios at Shepherd's Bush or Leeds had always been full of distrac-tions; now on the garden floor beneath my hillside house, a large room with wide windows became a study. When I awake my desk is downstairs, not 200 miles away. From it I look out at camellias and hydrangeas, or across roses to the sea and the coast of Normandy. With telephone diverted, the only distraction from typewriter or Steenbeck is a sparkling invitation from the pool, or a crackle from the log fire upstairs.

At first I was hesitant to ask directors to make the journey and suggested film-editors should come instead. 'If anyone's coming', said Fred Burnley after one look around, 'then it's me . . .' So after a stroll in the garden and a quick swim, they absorb some Atlantic air, enough wine and a few non-canteen meals – and collect their duty-frees on the way home. We get through twice as much in half the time, for we work undisturbed as long and as hard as we want – a requirement which, surprisingly, television management and unions can combine to prevent.

Overtime bans and working restrictions are old-hat, but trying to write in YTV's London office I had faced a new and unexpected obstacle: at 7 pm every evening the caretaker chased us out into the street. The great building had to be closed and empty by then; something to do with fire regulations and insurance.

Once, working in our Carnaby Street office through the quiet of a Sunday, my secretary and I were securely locked in. In our exhilarating television business it was not assumed that anyone in the executive offices would actually *work* at weekends, so the caretaker bolted and chained and went home.

By the time we noticed we were cut off from the outside world, it was night. We considered attempting a dash for freedom across the dark rooftops towards the welcoming lights of Regent Street, but it seemed silly to break a leg, at least, for such an undeserving cause. I called West End Central and the police came and laughed at us through the glass, and went off to chase the keyholder. He had to come in from Stanmore or Kingston and was not well pleased. The long night did little to stimulate artistic creativity.

In my island home we sometimes work 18 hours at a stretch, oblivious of union hours or management regulations, indifferent to Bank Holidays and Boxing Days. I had not appreciated how communications had freed us from the need to remain physically at the centre of things. Apart from certain shops and airline offices, the only organisations which really need high-priced central offices are those whose bosses want to stay close to comforting expense-account restaurants – like advertising agencies or uncertain companies yearning to cut a dash.

Years ago I filmed Pastor Krogager running his enormous Tjaereborg travel empire from a tiny village in Jutland; with telephones and computer terminals, he might have been in the centre of Copenhagen. He was showing us that the day of the dirty, dangerous and overcrowded metropolis is over. In a micro-processor society we will perform our computer operation without leaving the old hometown. Today, even after seeing Paree, most of us would be happy to *stay* down on the farm and let those robot-run factories in town get on with it.

In my craft I was fortunate to be able to initiate a new work-pattern: I would spend three or four months filming six programmes in, say, India, and then fly home and await the rushes. After processing and synching-up, a daunting pile of cans descended upon my study with a terrible clatter. Days and nights of viewing and shaping, of delight and anguish, and the rushes would be freighted back to Leeds with a sheaf of editing instructions. As commentary writing and editing progressed and each pile slowly shrank towards the final-cut of two 26-minute rolls, it was the *film* that travelled backwards and forwards, not me. I just let the cans take the strain; must have added years to my life.

This is now spent in a house almost as far from the airport as is possible without falling into the sea, and on the rare occasions when I have to return to The Smoke, calls for a pleasant 20-minute drive. Zipping along the back lanes Jerseymen avoid in case they get lost, I often reach the runway and the 7.45 am flight before meeting another car.

One day I flew to London – a quicker journey than the dreaded motorway slog from Regent's Park to Leeds – to lunch at the *Punch* Table. An incredulous editor asked, 'How can you live over there, so far away?' There was no simple answer, except 'Far away from *what*?', so I recalled that the evening before the local carpenter had arrived at my home with a lobster he had just caught, accepted a glass of wine but refused payment. How often did that happen, I wondered, in St John's Wood?

Sweet Jersey lobsters and succulent Guernsey scallops are the best in the world. Island cream is totally sinful, and the rich yellow ice-cream tastes the way it did in my school tuckshop, though with no food subsidies butter is almost worth smuggling. Paris is less than 200 miles away, the Normandy coast 14 miles, so we flew to France for lunch the other day. I love to drop that into the conversation. It took eight minutes to reach Dinard. On the way home, rather heavier no doubt, it took nine.

On the island I have for the first time come close to the seasons. Within a city it is hard to know whether it is winter or summer. Now each natural phase becomes a personal event: goldfinches hatch in the honeysuckle; the koi carp are at it again; the first rose, raspberry, lily . . . Growing wild across the island, the hydrangeas which go so elegantly with granite – though my old Jersey gardener scorns them as weeds. Upon inheriting him with the house he observed, 'You have to summer-and-winter a person before you know them.' Luckily it all worked out.

Our southern skies are bright with swallows and wagtails, the stonechats, bluetits and bullfinches which are so welcome, the blackbirds and thrushes which eat the strawberries and are less so. Black-faced nuns tramp up my garden path, keeping both feet on the ground (they are doves) and magpies chatter villainously. Vast fields of daffodils seem so brilliant you can feel a warmth. There are meadows of anemones, camellias at Christmas, and a delight of wild flowers: foxgloves, bluebells, heather, pale yellow lupins, snowdrops, wild garlic, jasmine, Jersey orchids, sea lavender . . .

The Malays say if you drink the water of any place long enough you take on the characteristics of its people. I look forward to that, for happy is the man who finds his ideal, whether in work, love or home. It is a great joy to know I shall spend the rest of my days in the tranquil, contented *therapeutic* island where spring comes a little earlier, summer seems endless, and autumn hangs around. In due course I'll move on to the Trinity churchyard, where I shall be most comfortable.

CLIFFHANGER

The Start of the Best part of my Life . . .

THE television and film industry, exciting as it is, can offer a funny-mirror distortion of life, an outlook without much conviction or foundations – like the streets of Hollywood houses with no backs, the cutaways pretending to be part of the conversation and all those happy-endings followed by the casual impermanence of multimarriage off-screen. Whatever happened to reality? I was always bemused by their decision not to film 'Oklahoma!' in Oklahoma because Oklahoma didn't *look* like Oklahoma. Let me out.

Real life in the fast outgoing lane becomes a matter of judgment and reaction. Experts have proved to their own satisfaction that one in every four of us is unbalanced, so think of your three closest friends . . . Should they seem all right – then it's *you*.

Considering my own balance as I launched myself gingerly upon this ego-trip and refreshed my memory from old Press cuttings, I noticed that even back in 1957 one critic was writing as unkindly about each of my programmes as he is today. Whatever the story, location, subject, camerawork, situation . . . all Whickerwork has been knocked, by reflex. In thousands of programmes even I must have produced a few that were acceptable – but if the chemistry is wrong, it stays wrong. Anything I do – my next series, say, or this book – will inevitably prove as bad as he expected. Such people are rarely won over; more likely, antipathies are confirmed. So after 25 years you could say he at least is consistently balanced, over on the hostile side!

Reaction may also work the other way, thank goodness,

with kinder folk who can approve and enjoy, and those whose minds are receptive.

Looking back down the years, and taking my lumps, I detect that amid a mass of faults and foibles my own balance, right or wrong, has remained reasonably solid. I have been unusually cautious, not to say dogged, in my slow and pensive selection of the permanencies of life. Once chosen, however, they have stayed that way. The restless pursuit of 'improvement' has never appealed, for I observed that if prepared to be patient, there was no need to accept second best. I have always approached life that way and am not about to change – not even if I live to be 39 . . .

Take the everyday example of a car – that luxurious necessity some people turn in every few years for the latest model. I decided early in life that for my modest tastes, a Bentley Continental was just about right. I was delayed in my achievement of this simple target by one tangential condition: insufficient cash.

Nevertheless with eyes fixed I began to work towards that elegant hand-crafted machine, first exchanging my old Hong Kong Humber for an elderly Mark VI in mistletoe green with 73,000 on the clock. This wafted me around the country in some style during my formative Tonight years. While filming in a rainswept Welsh valley I would at every opportunity leap into the back seat, put the heater on and my portable typewriter up on a picnic table and sit back, thinking large thoughts. Interviewees would join me behind the steamy windows of that warm and welcoming roadhouse.

As the years passed I progressed resolutely up the Bentley range, through a steel grey R-type and into the S-types. I owned a I and a III, but dodged the II on which you had to remove the front wheels to change the plugs . . . In 1965 I could just reach my target: a two-door Mulliner-Park Ward SIII. They only made 110 of them, and 60 went for export. I bought one in dawn blue, fitted a deep sunshine roof and telephone and believed myself utterly mad to pay so much money for a mere car – even though it was the most beautiful machine on the road, and not all *that* mere.

It cost around £8,250 – which today would buy some

run-of-the-assembly line saloon. After 17 years' driving pleasure, I could sell it for three times what I paid. There are not
too many 17-year-old cars on the roads today about which
that can be said.

Since the classic retains its looks and the best lasts well, I
shall doubtless drive it for the rest of my life without feeling
the need for change nor any desire to trade-up to the latest
model with digital whatsits – which now costs more than ten
times the price of that particular madness . . .

It was the same with a home, when I got around to
wanting one. I could never understand the American idea of
a bi-annual upheaval of removal vans into something nearby
but different. I would rather go without, than make do; and I
did. I waited more than half a lifetime to buy the house that
suited me. Then I moved in – and dropped anchor for ever.

Advertisers creating dissatisfaction by flaunting their
crafty Wantability factor encourage us to covet built-in-
obsolescence. I find myself fighting back from the other end
of that value scale, without the least wish to keep up with the
Joneses. Let them worry about me, should they be foolish
enough to care.

Incomparably more important than anything else is the
question of a wife; this *has* to be the least casual decision of a
lifetime. I can never quite believe in those Las Vegas marriage parlours which couples visit after a night out to indulge
in a quick wedding on the way home. Surely inside that
neon-lit clapboard 'Wee Kirk in the Heather' they must all
be playing some silly charade, to canned music? It *can't* be for
real – not instant Grooms, not fast takeaway Brides?

Needless to say, I was ultra-cautious about Her too – some
would say, ridiculously so. I waited and watched for years,
went on any number of trial runs without finding the person
to live with for ever. All right – I will admit under questioning, if you'll turn off those bright lights, that I was *not* hunting
very hard . . . Nevertheless I went through the motions with
enthusiasm. All rehearsals were live.

One hesitancy stemmed from the fact that I have always
been acutely aware that, though what I had to offer was no
big deal, it was still no area for compromise.

I made no search for this paragon; destiny rarely operates that way. I have filmed enough programmes on marriage bureaux and computer dating in England and America to know that cold calculation rarely works – though the RA who once asked to paint my portrait, John Bratby, told me he found his second wife Patti in that impatient way, and they seemed to get along well enough.

In the selfless cause of television I have on occasion submitted myself to such a systematic and unemotional search, from the native chieftain who offered me the pick of a giggly line-up of dusky daughters . . . through the Irish matchmaker who had some promising colleens back in Ballybunion . . . to the Los Angeles computer which rattled out a batch of concrete-jungle names and addresses with terrible take-it-or-leave-it finality.

In sensible hands the computer may remove some of the impossibilities, some of the women you would never have pursued anyway. It will not offer you a Bolivian animist with filed teeth ten years older and much taller who has seven children, refuses to fly and hates television. The most simple-minded computer should be smart enough to deal her out, for it knows all the straightforward facts: height, religion, education, interests, professed character and given age. What it cannot provide is the *spark*.

Upon investigation and filming among these proffered partners around London and Los Angeles – I sent my regrets to the Chief – mine proved to be pleasant women one and all, though with perhaps a loose grasp on cold hard truth. However, each came as close to my ideal mate as a headhunter's giraffe-necked daughter from the upper Zambezi. They were all, I am sure, deeply disappointed in me.

With Life, I have found, you have to lie back and let it happen. Or in my case, not happen.

On Saturday 1 November 1969 I awoke in my own bed for once, having returned the night before from Bavaria and filming Prince Johannes von Thurn und Taxis in his Regensburg palace. I reached for the phone to start my English wheels turning again. It was dead. Help.

Cut off from the outside world, stricken, unshaven and

bedraggled, I stalked down to the Cumberland Terrace lobby in my bathrobe, muttering, and on the house phone called the engineers. It seemed that the GPO had acted upon my request for a telephone in the Piccadilly apartment I had been about to share with Olga and in so doing had unplugged my Regent's Park line, for good.

I was indignant they should assume no one, not even an itinerant bachelor, could have a temporary second home or even a temporary second telephone. While we considered their censorious attitude to life and I faced the prospect of my cherished ex-directory number going to someone else and having to throw away all my writing paper, engrave another drawerful and advise everyone I was still around . . . a petite girl with long dark hair came out of the lift on her way to some ballet class. She had not been expecting to confront a semi-naked man shouting furiously in the hallway, but seemed to accept the situation when it was revealed all I was flashing was the exchange.

She had, it transpired, lived for several years in the apartment below mine, but the splendid anonymity of metropolitan life had protected us from earlier contact. It was exactly like my discovery of Jersey, which had been there all the time – too close to see. At her sympathetic invitation I continued my calls for help in the calmer surroundings of her home, and later descended again for coffee and urgent attempts to confound the GPO and get my life underway. 'He looks a bit better,' her Portuguese cook confided, grudgingly, 'with clothes on.'

It was the start of the best part of my life.

Valerie Kleeman was tiny, gentle, shy, untidy, warm, honest and affectionate. She had a sweet character, a quick instinctive intelligence; she also came to love me – an inestimable gift accepted with wonder and gratitude.

I then had many other friends, but most of these relationships gradually fell away. When three years later I bought my home in Jersey and the following year moved to that island for ever, she came with me. We have not been apart since.

Our little island population is the perfect distillation of

every sort of person: among the locals who come a'calling – a farmer and the Lieutenant-Governor, Sir Peter Whiteley; a would-be writer and Jack Higgins, whose Eagle Landed nearby; a bank clerk and the ex-Governor of the Bank of England, Lord Cromer; a policeman and the ultimate Jersey-man, the Bailiff Sir Frank Ereaut; the Rector of Trinity and any number of cheerful sinners. A lovely community, yet as elsewhere in the world concerned observers note that today they just don't seem to make marriages the way they used to . . .

Whenever we give a party I take a few casual shots of the gathering. Like pictures of our garden, this is a wonderful way of watching natural selection and survival over the years, of seeing things thrive and mature – or wither and die. Today when we open the albums to look back across the social years, it seems that most of those blissfully convivial guests . . . are now separated or divorced. We are almost the only couple in the book still together – and we're not married. So if every picture tells a story – what are they all *saying*?

We have not wed for our own good reasons, rightly or wrongly. Allowing for the tolerance and kindness of our friends and neighbours – and society in general – that state has so far presented no problems, other than the trivial matter of what to *call* her? Constant companion, girlfriend, mistress, lover, spouse, my lady . . . each indication seems silly, or arch. Even in these enlightened days it can become a question of 'Hello, I'd like you to meet my . . . er . . .'

The vital and constantly-renewing United States usually leads us in lifestyles, but even that sharp Madison Avenue society still struggles with such an intimate form of address. American Airlines started offering each passenger with spouse a 'Mate Rate', but this was rejected by Government regulators because 'it discriminated against unmarrieds'. Other airlines came up with 'Companion Fare', which brought us right back to our old friend Constant.

Certainly Simone de Beauvoir and Jean-Paul Sartre would introduce each other as Companion, though in English this can sound rather businesslike. For the more flip, Americans offer LIL, for live-in-lover, or housemate. One father I met referred to his daughter's constant companion as 'my sin-in-law'. I don't wish to know that.

At the other end of the scale, the US Census Bureau came up with 'Person of the Opposite Sex sharing living quarters'. As an introduction, it seemed a mite unromantic. The Ford Foundation favours 'Meaningful associate', which also does not trip off the tongue. The George Washington University Hospital uses 'Designated significant other person', so friends inquire tenderly, 'How's your Significant Other?'

With such silliness our only dilemma, it is easy to see how happy life has been. That said, a strange and capricious condition came over me, an affliction as unexpected as it was overwhelming. When you have been together so intimately and for so long, been so content and in tune that most questions are sensed before they need to be voiced . . . it seemed we had moved beyond the basic question. Despite a few warmups in solitude, I found I just could not clear my throat and say: Er, as I *meant* to ask you, about ten years ago . . .

Marriage has become the only unapproachable topic. We had long since passed the point of a tentative, exploratory query. That fluttery will-he-won't-he phase, the impetuous declaration from one knee had been overtaken by a sort of baffled caution. Amid the deeper, calmer waters into which we had passed so serenely, it appeared downright foolhardy to consider rocking the boat and risking my first rejection not on a printed slip. Why try to change something running perfectly?

Most people seem to live life as though it is merely a Trail for the real programme starting at some time in the future. I have always seen it as the Last Complete Performance, without repeats, and I'm enjoying it all tremendously – so far. Yet in any television life, on or off screen, we have grown accustomed to continuing stories and cliffhanging situations. Nothing is ever neat, or cut-and-dried. If it is, that's the end of the story. Fortunately ours seems still to have several episodes to go . . .

So, chained to this railway line as the express approaches,

I ask myself in wonder – what is now about to happen?
Where will the next Mighty Bound take me?

Up music . . . Run credits . . . Fade.

INDEX

BERNARD LEVIN

CONDUCTED TOUR

A delightful journey through twelve music festivals in Europe and Australia, from Adelaide to Wexford via Florence, Bath, Aldeburgh, Hohenems, Glyndebourne, Aix, Salzburg, Bayreuth, Edinburgh and Barcelona.

'The author declares that he has written not a music book, but a travel book. He is wrong. He has written a Levin book ... compulsively readable'

Punch

'Here is exhilarating writing about music ... full of traveller's tales, it has all the beguiling charm that draws the eye to anything he writes'

Sunday Telegraph

Post·A·Book

A Royal Mail service in association with the Book Marketing Council & The Booksellers Association.
Post-A-Book is a Post Office trademark.

ALEXANDER WALKER

PETER SELLERS

What did Peter Sellers do on the last day of his life? Why were some of his marriages so unsuccessful and painful? What really was his relationship with his children? Above all, whence sprang the genius for comedy that made him a great and memorable star in movies like *I'm All Right, Jack*, *Dr Strangelove*, the *Pink Panthers* and *Being There*? Aided by hitherto highly confidential information, and revelations of the utmost candour by Lynne Frederick, Sellers' widow, Alexander Walker has compiled a discerning and compassionate, yet often shocking, study of the British cinema's greatest post-war star and the international screen's finest clown.

CORONET BOOKS

ALSO AVAILABLE FROM CORONET BOOKS

All these books are available at your local bookshop or newsagent, or can be ordered direct from the publisher. Just tick the titles you want and fill in the form below.

Prices and availability subject to change without notice.

CORONET BOOKS, P.O. Box 11, Falmouth, Cornwall.

Please send cheque or postal order, and allow the following for postage and packing:

U.K. – 45p for one book, plus 20p for the second book, and 14p for each additional book ordered up to a £1.63 maximum.

B.F.P.O. and EIRE – 45p for the first book, plus 20p for the second book, and 14p per copy for the next 7 books, 8p per book thereafter.

OTHER OVERSEAS CUSTOMERS – 75p for the first book, plus 21p per copy for each additional book.

Name ....

Address...

....